‘The Soldiers are Dressed in Red’

The Quiberon Expedition of 1795 and the Counter-Revolution in Brittany

Alistair Nichols

Helion & Company

In memory of Norman John Nichols (1931–2020)

Helion & Company Limited
Unit 8 Amherst Business Centre
Budbrooke Road
Warwick
CV34 5WE
England
Tel. 01926 499619
Email: info@helion.co.uk
Website: www.helion.co.uk
Twitter: @helionbooks
Visit our blog at http://blog.helion.co.uk/

Published by Helion & Company 2022
Designed and typeset by Mach 3 Solutions Ltd (www.mach3solutions.co.uk)
Cover designed by Paul Hewitt, Battlefield Design (www.battlefield-design.co.uk)

ISBN 978-1-915070-43-2

British Library Cataloguing-in-Publication Data.
A catalogue record for this book is available from the British Library.

For details of other military history titles published by Helion & Company Limited, contact the above address, or visit our website: http://www.helion.co.uk

We always welcome receiving book proposals from prospective authors.

Contents

Preface

'The expedition of 1795 has perhaps caused more ink to flow than gunpowder was burnt; the letters, the writings, the memoirs of survivors, the … dissertations form a library where the events are often distorted by passions; eras of great suffering have always been eras of great calumnies.'[1]

So wrote Louis-Marie Le Cam (1885–1948), *recteur* of the Île d'Houat, author and First World War infantry officer (Croix de Guerre, palm and three stars) in 1936. Over the years the passions may have become less heated but they still simmer and the calumnies have not been washed away, as Le Cam had wished. Those letters, writings and memoirs are the sources that later writers have relied upon.

If so much has been written before why write more? The simple answer is that little, other than summaries, has been written in English about the 1795 expeditions to Brittany and the Vendée – generally known as the Quiberon Expedition. The chief exception is Maurice Hutt's *Chouannerie and Counter-Revolution: Puisaye, the Princes and the British Government in the 1790s*, a hugely impressive book of two volumes that, although covering the expeditions, is chiefly concerned with the relationships between the different parties mentioned in the title.[2] So this book aims to tell the story of the expeditions for English readers.

Furthermore, very little use has been made of British sources, again with the exception of Hutt, especially primary sources whether published or archival, public such as newspapers or dispatches, or private letters, journals or logs. When such sources have been used by French authors in the past they have unfortunately generally been simply recycled versions from an earlier historian, often with the interpretation being echoed. Research for this book has made use of such British sources alongside many first-hand French accounts to provide a wider perspective and which has also led to some misconceptions being challenged.

For very obvious reasons, the French accounts have centred on the actions and feelings of the French people involved in the expeditions, Bretons and Vendéens, émigrés and chouans, princes and soldiers. In essence, the main

1 Louis-Marie Le Cam, *Quiberon à travers les âges* (Quiberon: Robert, 1936), p.61.

2 Maurice Hutt, *Chouannerie and Counter-Revolution: Puisaye, the Princes and the British Government in the 1790s* (Cambridge: Cambridge University Press, 1983).

involvement of the British has been, at a governmental level, financing and perhaps planning the expedition and, at an operational level, delivery of the émigrés to the shores of France. This has meant that the contribution of the British sailors, marines and soldiers to the operations has been largely ignored. This account seeks to address this while remaining cognisant that it was the French people who not only did most of the fighting but also paid the price in terms of their lives or suffering.

Thus, to answer the question posed above, this book seeks to add to *abbé* Le Cam's library by describing the expeditions to Brittany and the Vendée in 1795 as joint operations: British and French royalists as well as military and naval. Operations that, given the technology of the age, were frequently affected by slow communications, particularly due to the weather, something which is very difficult to fully appreciate in this age of instant messaging, with scheduled ferry crossings from Portsmouth to Spain of less than 24 hours and flights to the region from London of an hour and 25 minutes.

It also aims to provide a comprehensive portrayal of how and why French émigrés, in red coats, stepped ashore in Brittany from British ships in the summer of 1795, as well as the men who had a part, large or small, to play in the events that unfolded. In relation to the distortions and calumnies in the historiography, Le Cam saw 'perfidious Albion' as 'the most attacked party of the era both by the republicans and the royalists' and considered that, with the use of newly discovered documents, it would be 'henceforth cleansed of the accusation of perfidy and cruelty.'[3] The evidence shows that while the British Government was not guilty of these particular accusations, it cannot escape blame for what happened.

Like any work of history, this could not have been completed without help from so many people, I thank them all, particularly my wife Jane and friend Hughes de Bazouges. Much of the writing has been done during a very peculiar time for us all, under the shadow of COVID-19. Although only minor inconveniences compared with what many have endured the closure of archives followed by their tentative reopening has presented some challenges, while also being a reminder of the services they provide. I wish to particularly thank Eamonn O'Keeffe for turning up a published version of the Major William Harness's letters to Elizabeth, his wife; Peter Harrington for his generous help in providing the images from the Berlin Album and Hélène Jacquemard of the Château de Chantilly for going 'above and beyond' in providing me with remote access to material.

3 Le Cam, *Quiberon*, p.61.

Ar Soudarded Zo Gwisket e Ruz

The Soldiers are Dressed in Red

Ar soudarded zo gwisket e ruz
O lin de lin da lan de lin da la la
Ar soudarded zo gwisket e ruz
Ar veleien zo gwisket e du.

The soldiers are dressed in red,
O lin de lin da da la la
The soldiers are dressed in red
The priests are dressed in black.

Traditional Breton folk song

1

Turmoil

The War Begins and a Strategy Emerges

When the French Republic declared war on Britain on 1 February 1793, she had already been at war with Austria since 20 April 1792, and Prussia since 13 June 1792. Jacques-Pierre Brissot had declared in the National Convention that 'Pikes started the Revolution; pikes will achieve it. We must set fire to the four corners of Europe, there is our salvation!'[1]

Britain had initially attempted to avoid entering the war through diplomacy but was committed to a defensive alliance with the United Provinces, also known as the Dutch Republic, which came under growing threat after the French had invaded what is now Belgium and captured Antwerp. When the news of Louis XVI's execution reached London on 24 January, the passports of the French Embassy were withdrawn and the diplomats were given instructions to leave British soil within five days. The French National Convention declared war on the United Provinces, at the same time as Britain, and within days commenced a long-planned invasion that relied on swift action to secure the country before help arrived from abroad. Initially, the French made rapid advances but, by early April 1793, the allied forces, including a British contingent commanded by Prince Frederick Augustus, the Duke of York, had not only driven the French from the United Provinces but also Belgium, forcing them across their own borders. In response, the National Convention harnessed the energy of the whole nation for its defence and pursuit of its war aims by declaring mass conscription, a *levée en masse*, on 24 February 1793. Increased manpower, even if at first ill-trained and undisciplined, allowed French republican generals to use overwhelming numbers to gain victories, despite heavy casualties, such as at the Battle of Wattignies on 15/16 October.[2]

Despite facing a coalition that now included Spain, the Holy Roman Empire (Germany) and Piedmont, in northern Italy, the tide of the war

1 Auguste de Barruel, *Mémoires pour servir à l'Histoire du Jacobinisme* (London: Boussonier, 1798), vol.IV, p.420.

2 Ramsay Weston Phipps, *The Armies of the First French Republic and the Rise of the Marshals of Napoleon I: The Armée du Nord* (London: Oxford University Press, 1926), pp.246–275.

slowly turned in France's favour in 1794. As summer turned to autumn the United Provinces were defended against another French invasion by the British and Dutch armies but neither were up to the task. In January 1795 the Dutch Republic collapsed, to be replaced by the Batavian Republic, a client of republican France. The British forces retreated into Germany, with them were not only foreign and French émigré units raised for British service but also others that had been in the service of the United Provinces. The success of the French Republic's forces in the field went hand in hand with that of their diplomats. Prussia, while maintaining it was a full partner in the coalition, had secretly negotiated a unilateral peace with France finally culminating in the Treaty of Basel on 5 April 1795. While other German states, large and small, were coerced to follow suit, the British troops in northern Germany, separated from those of their only active ally, Austria, came under increasing pressure to leave the Continent. Hanover, despite King George III also being Elector of the state, became inhospitable and then hostile to the troops. Later in the year, a report from the British headquarters stated that 'It has been at length formally notified to this Army, by the Lords in power [in Hanover], that every expeditious measure should be adopted, in order to evacuate this Country, lest the French should take umbrage at British troops being fostered by *any* German Prince!'[3]

The political direction of Britain's war was in the hands of the three leading members of the Government: Prime Minister William Pitt, William Grenville, Secretary of State at the Foreign Office, and Henry Dundas, Secretary of State for the Home Department whose portfolio included War and the Colonies, and then, from 11 July 1794, for War. Loyal to their departments, Grenville advocated the pursuit of the war on the European continent while Dundas favoured a strategy of taking French colonies, one that had, after all, borne fruit in recent conflicts with the Kingdom of France. Dundas was, apparently, the strongest personality of the three and was chiefly responsible for the actual conduct of the war. However, historian John Fortescue wrote, 'Yet so profoundly ignorant was Dundas of war that he was not even conscious of his ignorance.'[4] The triumvirate's policies, in general, lacked clarity and consistency, and they struggled to balance new demands against existing priorities. As a result, they often tried to do too many things, sending too few resources (frequently too late) to any given object, as will be seen at Quiberon.

As the spring of 1795 led into summer, the number of demands that the British Government juggled with only grew, leading to orders and counter-orders. The troops needed to be withdrawn from Germany, given the altered situation there as well as the requirement to use them elsewhere. The fall of the United Provinces, with French dominion over its successor, the Batavian Republic, meant that something had to be done about its colonies, in particular the Cape (South Africa) and Ceylon (Sri Lanka). French control, overt or not, of these strategic positions on the sea route to India would make

3 *The Oxford Journal*, 12 October 1795.

4 John W. Fortescue, *A History of the British Army* (London: Macmillan & Co. 1906), vol.IV, p.72.

access impossible. At the same time there was a pressing need for troops in the West Indies. There was the desire to seize French possessions in the region, not only to acquire their wealth but also to deny France revenue, for which an expedition had been dispatched in November 1793. The advent of the Revolution had opened up the prospect of freedom for the enslaved black people in the French colonies in the Caribbean which led to an uprising in the most productive, Saint-Domingue, now Haïti, in 1791 with a spiral of violence. Two years later, after white French colonists had appealed, unilaterally, for assistance in return for the transfer of the colony to British rule, troops had been sent from Jamaica. This intervention led to an ever-growing commitment, of both British and French émigré troops to the colony.

There was another military commitment a little closer to home, in the Mediterranean, where in August 1793, Admiral Lord Samuel Hood, commanding the British fleet there, was asked by Corsican separatists for help to expel the French from their island. The French hold on the island had been uneasy since its conquest by the King's forces as recently as 1769 and had become far from secure since the Revolution, so the request was not unanticipated.[5] Hood immediately dispatched a squadron to support the Corsicans and this intervention soon required more and more troops not only to defend the island but also to maintain a peace between its various factions.

These overseas commitments not only demanded troops, horses, arms and equipment, but also shipping. Vessels were needed to transport men and horses and to continually supply them with any food, arms, ammunition and equipment that could not be obtained locally. This demand for transports was over and above the existing requirements to maintain and supply not only existing garrisons, such as Gibraltar, but also the Royal Navy at sea. These vessels were civilian shipping hired by a governmental body, the Transport Office, and warships were generally required to escort them to ensure their safety. The availability of transports was a major limiting factor to any military operation. To put it crudely a ship could only be in one place at a time and its movement relied on capricious winds and weather.

A different strategy was required that needed fewer resources: the fall of the French republican regime would be achieved by supporting counter-revolutionary movements within France rather than a foreign invasion of the country itself. This strategy was not entirely new, indeed it had clear parallels with the tactics the French Republic used in its invasion of Belgium and the United Provinces. On 17 April 1794, Henry Dundas stated the Government's position in the House of Commons,

> Great Britain, in common with the other governments of Europe, beheld with a proper anxiety the first progress of the French revolution. This event, when it took place, was more properly a subject for observation, originating in the duty

5 Desmond Gregory, *The Ungovernable Rock A History of the Anglo-Corsican Kingdom and its role in Britain's Mediterranean Strategy during the Revolutionary War (1793–1797)* (London and Toronto: Associated University Presses, 1985), pp.40–42, 51–54.

> of preserving our own constitution and dominions than a matter of positive alarm, from the political innovations which had taken place in the interior of France. ... If it was the duty of the king's ministers to preserve the empire in its existing prosperity; ... Hence they were induced to pause and to observe. They were determined to avoid hostilities, unless the safety of our allies and our internal security rendered it impossible. The period of hesitation in which this political caution could be exercised was indeed but short. The French declaration of war against us terminated it; a war not declared with the common forms of civilized nations ... but with the avowed purpose of carrying their newly-created constitution, and the anarchy and devastation upon which it rested, over all Europe; ... Had not the monstrous system of the French convention threatened, like a torrent, to sweep before it all the kingdoms of Europe? ... Did not the conduct of the convention manifest, that when they should have conquered and plundered our allies, their hordes were to bring their politics and contributions into Britain? Did they not banish all persons respectable for rank, for fortune, for virtue, for religion...[6]

Then he turned to the situation within France, as the British Government saw it, and the new strategy.

> A faction, composed of the most worthless of men, [now] governed that devoted country. The power of this faction was upheld by the most precarious of tenures, the breath of the mob. ... there now appeared manifest symptoms, that numbers in that devoted country, were adverse [*sic*] to it. That many of the French nation detested the anarchy under which they were suffering, required no other proof than the immense emigrations from that country ... the unbounded massacres under which millions had sunk, and the absolute extinction of that security of person and property, of that justice and that religion, which alone can attach rational men to any form of government. From that nature of the case, it must be evident, that multitudes of the French nation wanted only protection and support, to bring them forward to crush that convention, under which these evils had become insupportable. ... large bodies of the French people, hostile to such unparalleled tyranny, must be ready to fly to the arms we proposed putting into their hands, however they may have been hitherto compelled by fear, to conceal their real feelings and wishes. If, then, such a government as that in France, was inconsistent with the safety of other governments, the legitimate object of the war must be, the extinction of this monstrous system. What measure was so likely to produce this end, as making use of the means which were the most closely connected with the object? These means were, to employ great bodies of the unfortunate sufferers, of different ranks, who had been driven from their country, from their families, from their property, and reduced to the last extremity, as principals, as well as auxiliaries, in restoring the peace of Europe. When collected into bodies, such men would erect the standard of exiled religion, oppressed virtue, and expatriated loyalty. For those purposes, they now called upon the British nation to give them arms. Men of this description must have the same

6 William Cobbett (ed.), *The Parliamentary History of England, from the earliest period to the year 1803* (London: Hansard, 1818), vol.XXXI, pp.411–413.

> object that we have. He desired to see a regular government established in France; and the present bill was well calculated for this object. His hope was, that by the proper use of this plan, peace would be restored to this country, and security to Europe. Unless we overthrew the present system of French politics, we neither could hope for peace, nor obtain security.[7]

The strategy relied upon the presence of those who were willing to take up arms to oppose to the Revolution.

The Émigrés

Henry Dundas gave the speech during the debate at the third reading of a bill, which was enacted in on 9 May 1794, '... to enable Subjects of France to enlist as Soldiers in Regiments to serve on the Continent of Europe, and in certain other Places; and to enable His Majesty to grant Commissions to Subjects of France, to serve and receive Pay as Officers in such Regiments, or as Engineers, under certain Restrictions.'[8] The regiments thus authorised were to be formed of French émigrés and used to support internal forces that sought to bring down the current regime in France. These units were to be distinguished by wearing white cockades on their hats, as well as other symbols of the French Bourbon monarchy, in contrast to the black cockade used by the British forces.

The émigrés had left France in opposition to the undermining and then overthrow of the monarchy by the Revolution while also facing persecution and threats. Many of them were army and navy officers as one of the Revolution's first effects, indeed an aim of its more extreme supporters, had been to undermine discipline in the armed forces. This is because they were regarded as one of the three pillars of the monarchy, the others being the nobility and the church. Incidents of indiscipline and mutiny in the army and navy occurred, often with the connivance of the local revolutionary authorities, throughout France. Many of the officers, as nobles, in the face of such threats and attacks from their men and without support, were forced to emigrate. In Nancy, in the northeast of the country, a Swiss officer wrote in his journal for 1790: '... the Régiment du Roi is in continual insurrection ... the soldiers ... imprison their officers, plunder the [pay] chests and commit a thousand disturbances.'[9] In August the garrison erupted in violent mutiny which the central government, as moderates tried to regain control of events, directed the regional commander, François-Claude Marquis de Bouillé, to suppress. His success was to earn him the enmity of the more ardent revolutionaries.

---

7 Cobbett (ed.), *Parliamentary History*, vol.XXXI, pp.413–414.

8 An example of the printed copies of this act is held at The National Archives, Kew (TNA): WO 24/1112.

9 National Archief, The Hague (NA): 2.21.008.01/IN – 19: *Journal de* [Jean-Victor] *Constant Rebecque*, vol.1, entries for 16 June and 20 July. He was serving in the Régiment de Lullin de Châteauvieux before joining the Garde Suisse in Paris.

Meanwhile, King Louis XVI, who had seen his authority indeed his very freedom ebb away, finally fled Paris on 20 June 1791 and headed for the frontier. However, his party was recognised at Varennes-en-Argonne the following day and they were brought back as virtual prisoners. He was now simply a figurehead and a very much diminished one at that. In September 1791, the armed forces were required to swear a new oath that made no reference to the King; for many of the officers this was the last straw. Those that refused to take the oath were threatened with murder and denounced for the new, anti-revolutionary, crime of incivism. Many officers who might have stayed were driven out and over half the officer corps emigrated.[10]

Another result of the King's flight was the dismissal of the four companies of his gardes-du-corps (bodyguards), prestigious units of noblemen which were to be replaced, in time, by the Garde Constitutionnelle du Roi. This new unit was to have 1,200 infantry and 600 cavalry; a third of the men drawn from line regiments and the rest from young men nominated by each département, mainly National Guardsmen.[11] The radical politicians, the Jacobins, reliant on their power base in Paris, vehemently opposed its formation, despite it being conceived in the Constitution of 1790, because its members came from throughout France, but also due to the officers' loyalty to the King. Its commander was the Duc de Brissac who, as well as holding a number of court offices, had formerly been governor of Paris and *Capitaine-Colonel* of the Compagnie des Cent Gardes-Suisses (Company of the Hundred Swiss Guards), otherwise known as the Cent-Suisse (Hundred Swiss), which had guarded the person of King of France since 1481. The cavalry element of the Garde was commanded by Louis-Charles Le Cat Comte d'Hervilly, formerly *colonel* of the Régiment de Rohan infantry. He had served in a staff role during the American War of Independence and had distinguished himself by maintaining his regiment's discipline during disturbances in August 1789 while stationed at Nantes, leading to his appointment to command units forming a 'flying camp' to maintain order in the Morbihan département of Brittany the following year.[12] The Garde began service on 1 January 1792, under oath to serve the 'Nation, Law and King', but its enemies soon managed to have the unit dissolved on 29 May the same year.[13] Brissac was denounced as a counter-revolutionary and imprisoned at Orléans but, recalled to Paris, the convoy in which he was being carried was stopped by a mob at Versailles on 9 September 1792 and he, along with most of the other prisoners, was brutally murdered.[14]

---

10 William Doyle, *The Oxford History of the French Revolution* (Oxford: Oxford University Press, 1989), p.156.

11 Anon., 'Fichier de la garde constitutionnelle de Louis XVI (1791–1792)' Archives nationales 2016, <https://francearchives.fr/findingaid/fe3c62602114da74bf7575d392895499917388fe>, (accessed 21 September 2020).

12 Didier Michel, *Du Héros de Rennes en 1788 à la Contre-Révolution Blondel de Nouainville L'itinéraire d'un noble normand 1753–1793* (Cherbourg: Éditions Isoète, 2012), pp.98–100.

13 Anon., 'Fichier de la garde constitutionnelle de Louis XVI (1791–1792).'

14 For an eye-witness account see François-Louis Janillion, *Versailles et Quiberon* (Paris: Locard et Davi, Delaunay, 1816), pp.20–39.

On the same night as the King had left Paris, the elder of his two brothers, Louis-Stanislas-Xavier Comte de Provence, had escaped, reaching Brussels. He, with the third of the brothers, Charles-Philippe Comte d'Artois, who had left a year before, and their cousin, Louis-Joseph Prince de Condé, became the focal point of royalist opposition to the French Republic. The émigrés assembled around the princes, the King's brothers at Koblenz and Condé at Worms both on the Rhine, and began to form military units to march into France. However, when the allied coalition invaded in the summer of 1792 they were only permitted to take a limited and subsidiary role. The invasion was halted at Valmy on 20 September and a disastrous retreat ensued. The émigré units were dissolved with the exception of the small army formed by the Prince de Condé which had remained with Austrian forces observing the Rhine. One result of the invasion for the émigrés was the passing of the law of 9 October 1792, Article 1 of which stated,

> In execution of the decree that pronounces the sentence of death against the émigrés taken under arms, they will be, within twenty-four hours, … put to death, after it has been declared by a military commission composed of five people and nominated by the headquarters of the army, that they were émigrés and that they had been taken with arms to hand, or that they had served against France.[15]

Taking advantage of the agitation caused by the impending invasion, radical republican politicians enacted a coup d'état in Paris. On 10 August the Tuileries Palace was invaded by a huge crowd in a coordinated attack, leading the Royal family, who could only rely on the Gardes Suisses (Swiss Guards) and some loyal gentleman, such as Hervilly who had remained in the capital ready to defend the King, to take refuge in the National Assembly. Radical representatives dominated the few assemblymen that were present and the King was stripped of his remaining powers and was now, with his family, a prisoner. The Legislative Assembly was replaced on 20 September 1792 by the National Convention and two days later France was a republic. Louis XVI was soon put on trial and then executed on 21 January 1793. His seven-year-old son, Louis-Charles, the uncrowned Louis XVII, remained in the Temple Prison, so his uncle, Provence, assumed the title of Regent.

Insurrection in the West

As has been seen, the passage of the French Revolution was marked by violence, both in Paris and other parts of France. The causes were rarely simple and often, by accident or design, prosaic issues such as food shortages became mixed with those of political ambition and factionalism. The most significant outbreaks, especially in terms of their longevity, occurred in the

---

15 Jean Baptiste Duvergier, *Collection complète des lois, décrets, ordonnances, réglemens, et avis du conseil-d 'état* (Paris: Chez A. Guyot et scribe, 1825), vol.V, p.22. Decree which fixes the mode of execution of the decree which pronounces the death penalty against the émigrés taken with arms in hand.

northwest of France; in Brittany and the Vendée. Initially, these insurrections in conservative regions were not necessarily counter-revolutionary or royalist movements, but in time became so. In 1792 there had been protests, some involving thousands of people, against the persecution of priests who did not submit to republican control of the clergy. These were soon subdued and indeed there was no reaction to the declaration of the republic and the execution of Louis XVI. It was the forced conscription of young men to fight for the new republic that provoked resistance in the Vendéen countryside centred around Cholet. Gendarmes, sent to enforce the levy, were attacked in the region as far as the river Loire in March 1793. Somewhat surprised by their success the rebels grew in numbers, seizing arms and choosing leaders, either from their own numbers or from young noblemen who had returned to their homes, rather than emigrating, after having quit the army or navy. On 14 March the Vendéen rebels took Cholet, defeating a strong garrison. They went on to secure further victories, even interrupting communication between Nantes, the sixth largest city of France, and Paris, but then they dispersed to their homes to work their fields and celebrate Easter. This was to be the pattern of the rebellion, as described by Marie-Louise-Victoire de Donnissan who was married to a Vendéen leader, Louis-Marie de Salgues Marquis de Lescure, and then after his death, another, Louis du Vergier de La Rochejaquelein, brother of the better known, Henri.

> The army was never assembled for more than three or four days. The battle once won or lost, the expedition having succeeded or failed, nothing could retain the peasants, they returned to their homes. The chiefs remained alone with some hundreds of men, deserters and foreigners, who did not have family to go and join; but as soon as we wanted to attempt a new undertaking, the army was soon reformed.[16]

Elsewhere in the region other risings took place, such as at Machecoul, in Bas-Poitou, near the coast where the insurrection took a crueller and more vindictive aspect than elsewhere. It was here that François-Athanase de Charette de La Contrie was to emerge as the leader. A former *lieutenant de vaisseau* in the navy who had been one of the gentlemen who had sought to protect the royal family on 10 August 1792, he was not quite 30 years old, '... perhaps even a little theatrical, in his costume, ... an adroit politician ...' he proved to be an able commander in the field.[17]

The insurrection in the countryside of Brittany arose for similar reasons, along with resentment that any redistribution of land had favoured wealthy town and city dwellers so that those on the bottom rung of rural society had gained nothing, simply seeing a change of master. In addition there was a long-standing tradition in Brittany of protecting the province's privileges that dated from its unification with France in 1532. This had been expressed

---

16 Marie-Louise-Victoire de Donnissan, Marquise de La Rochejaquelein, *Mémoires de Mme la marquise de La Rochejaquelein* (Paris: Baudouin Frères, 1823), p.101.

17 Eugène Veuillot, *Les Guerres de La Vendée et de La Bretagne 1790–1832* (Paris: Ambroise Bray, 1868), p.56.

during violent protests in Rennes in 1788 against the King's efforts to reform provincial *parlements*, the so-called 'noble revolt.'[18] One of those opposing these reforms was a Breton nobleman, Armand-Charles Tuffin Marquis de La Rouërie who as a dissolute young officer in the Gardes Françaises had been banished after a duel. However, he resurrected his military career when he was one of the first Frenchmen to travel to America to help in the fight for independence. There, as Colonel Armand, he proved himself to be not only an intrepid commander but also a talented organiser and leader of men. Frustrated to not receive an equivalent rank in the French army on his return he retired to Brittany where he opposed the curtailing of traditional Breton rights, firstly by the King and then the Assembly. Later he gathered around him young nobles, especially former army officers, in the Association bretonne with the aim to resurrect Breton privileges through the restoration of the monarchy. Having travelled to Germany, on 3 June 1791 he obtained the Duc d'Artois's support for the Association bretonne and on 2 May 1792, the royal princes, together, appointed him their commander in Brittany, '... to give orders in their name ... to [all] military whatever and armed people in this province ... before or during the course of the counter-revolution.'[19] The Association was to be organised, along militarily lines within parishes, with a regular contact among them and also with Britain and the princes at Koblenz. However, before it could become effective La Rouërie was betrayed and, on the run, he fell ill and died on 30 January 1793. Although not directly linked to the Breton insurgents, who became known as chouans, some of their leaders had been members of the Association. For example, Vincent de Tinténiac, a former *lieutenant de vaisseau*, Amateur-Jérôme Le Bras des Forges de Boishardy, a former officer in the Régiment Royal-Marine infantry, and Antoine-Henri d'Amphernet de Pontbellanger, a former *capitaine* in the Régiment Royal-Lorraine cavalry.[20]

In general, the insurgents in Brittany did not assemble in the same numbers as in the Vendée nor, at this stage, did they have leaders who could bring significant numbers into action. The chouannerie was characterised by small-scale raids on republican posts and villages, as *Lieutenant-général* Jean-Baptiste-Camille de Canclaux, a senior noble officer who remained in the army and served the republic in the region, reported,

> The game is not tenable, more than two hundred thousand men rose in Brittany in the second half of March. Their rebellion against the law is born from many causes often independent one from another, but which all relate to two principles: religion and royalty. On the other side of the Loire, the same principles are brought into play by other populations ... but the Vendée shows itself as more menacing: it has already raised disciplined battalions, put generals to flight, and found skilful officers. ... The Vendée has had success, it is in advance; we ought to occupy ourselves with it to the death. Fortunately, in Brittany, things have not

18 Doyle, *French Revolution*, pp.82–84.

19 Christian Bazin, *Le Marquis de La Rouerie: Le colonel Armand: De la guerre américaine à la conjuration bretonne* (Paris: Perrin, 1990), commissions reproduced in full, pp.251–255.

20 Bazin, *Le Marquis de La Rouerie*, pp.168, 178–180.

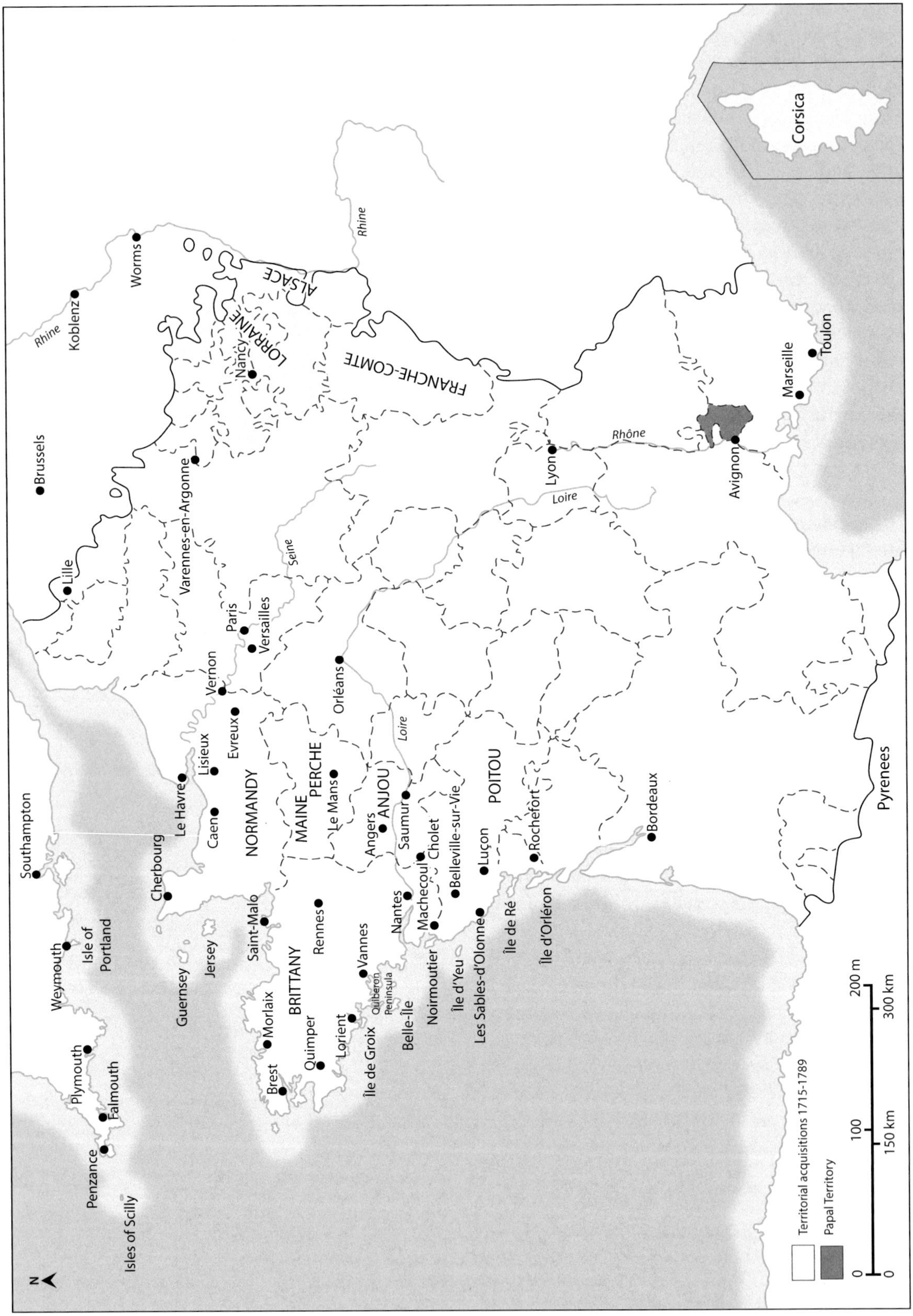

Corsica
Rhine
Worms
Koblenz
Rhine
ALSACE
LORRAINE
Nancy
FRANCHE-COMTE
Brussels
Varennes-en-Argonne
Lille
Paris
Versailles
Seine
Vernon
Evreux
Lisieux
Le Havre
Caen
Cherbourg
Southampton
NORMANDY
MAINE
PERCHE
Le Mans
ANJOU
Angers
Saumur
Orléans
Loire
Lyon
Rhône
Avignon
Marseille
Toulon
Loire
Cholet
Belleville-sur-Vie
Luçon
POITOU
Rochefort
Bordeaux
Pyrenees
Nantes
Machecoul
Noirmoutier
Île d'Yeu
Les Sables-d'Olonne
Île de Ré
Île d'Orléron
Saint-Malo
Rennes
BRITTANY
Vannes
Quiberon Peninsula
Belle-Île
Lorient
Île de Groix
Quimper
Morlaix
Brest
Jersey
Guernsey
Weymouth
Isle of Portland
Plymouth
Falmouth
Penzance
Isles of Scilly
N
Territorial acquisitions 1715-1789
Papal Territory
0
100
200 m
0
150 km
300 km

France 1789.

> turned out so badly … [He advocated taking a conciliatory line in relation to the clergy to drive a wedge between the two elements] … It is necessary to triumph over the insurrection or perish; but, to ensure this triumph, you must make sure to isolate these two provinces, one from the other. Prevent communications by land and sea; smother one by softness, in order to suffocate the other by arms. If you leave them time to combine their attempts, if a man like La Rouërie appeared, there is danger for the republic.[21]

As Canclaux stated, south of the Loire the fighting had intensified as the republicans tried to contain and then crush the Vendéens, sending reinforcements to the region. The Vendéen leaders responded by combining their local 'armies' for an attack on an agreed object or to respond to a threat so the Grande Armée Catholique et Royale assembled at Cholet. This force consisted of about 30,000 men on foot, 1,200 mounted and 24 guns. More men joined as it marched to attack Saumur, which was defended by at least 8,000 men and which fell on 9–10 June 1793.[22] Exploiting the success, Angers, on the north bank of the Loire, was occupied on 19 June and the Vendéens advanced on Nantes, by both banks of the Loire. Capture of this port city would facilitate links with Brittany and abroad, but Canclaux, with about 10,000 men, including a core of at least 1,500 regular infantrymen, successfully defended it when attacked on 29 June, forcing the Vendéens to withdraw.[23]

Federalist Revolts

Meanwhile, between 31 May and 2 June 1793, the Jacobins used their power base in Paris, to take over the National Convention, arresting many of their opponents, the Girondists (or Federalists), and propelling Maximilien Robespierre to power. However, some of the Girondist deputies escaped to gather opposition and many regions of France rose in revolt: principally in the southeast, centred on Lyon, in the Midi, including Marseille and later Toulon; in the southwest, in and around Bordeaux; and in Normandy, particularly around Caen. Nevertheless, these insurrections were largely separate, taking on different complexions, and hardly provided any support to each other.

At Lyon, on 29 May, the Girondists took over the city, imprisoning the Jacobin leaders as well as *représentants en mission* who were deputies from the Convention sent out to départements and armies to enforce its will. Louis-François Perrin de Percy, a royalist and former *lieutenant-colonel* in the Garde Constitutionnelle, was given command of the defence of the city which was besieged from 7 August by troops loyal to the Convention from the Armée des Alpes. In Paris, Robespierre's faction increased their grip on

21 Quoted in Veuillot, *Les Guerres de La Vendée et de La Bretagne*, pp.64–65.
22 Rob Harper, *Fighting the French Revolution: The Great Vendée Rising of 1793* (Barnsley: Pen & Sword, 2019), pp.92, 99–105.
23 Harper, *Fighting the French Revolution*, pp.112–120, 316–317.

power, using the Committee for Public Safety as the vehicle to enact the Reign of Terror, an exercise in the use of extreme violence and fear as public policy. Lyon surrendered on 9 October, after a sustained bombardment, and the Convention ordered a wave of executions and the city to be scarred by the demolition of buildings, it even decreed that it would lose its name and henceforth be known as *Ville-Affranchie* (Liberated City).[24]

Although the Federalist revolt was widely and well supported in Bordeaux, it fell without the need for military confrontation. The ruthlessness of the 27-year-old *représentant en mission* Jean-Lambert Tallien saw to that. He managed to restrict food supplies into the city which caused the ruling council to be replaced by one that submitted to the Convention, allowing him, and other representatives, to enter the city accompanied with troops.[25] Tallien then began his own terror; a programme of political reprisals with around 300 executions. However, his appetite for retribution became somewhat satiated once he took Thérésa Cabarrus, the former wife of an émigré nobleman, as his mistress.

In Normandy several of the escaped Girondin deputies had established themselves at Caen and to further their cause they began formation of an armée départementale. Battalions joined from Brittany and Maine, but in Normandy there was a pervading atmosphere of apathy and few men were recruited. Nevertheless, an advance corps of about 2,500 men, with barely any discipline or organisation, was formed under the command of the army's *adjudant-général*, Joseph-Geneviève de Puisaye. This officer, however, lacked any real military experience. He had held commissions but had hardly served in the line and had purchased his prestigious place in the Cent-Suisse. He, like his father, enhanced his status and wealth by marriage and in 1789 he was chosen to be the only representative of the Perche nobility to the States General. There he showed himself to be broadly sympathetic to the progress of the Revolution, even after Varennes, and sought, unsuccessfully, to take a seat in the National Convention in September 1792. Having gained the rank of the rank of *lieutenant-colonel* in 1790, simply due to his place in the Cent-Suisse, he was appointed to raise the National Guard at Evreux and command one of its battalions. One of his close confidants, Comte Erasme-Gaspard de Contades, described him, after their relationship had descended to mutual loathing,

> He was of a colossal height, gauche and ungainly. His countenance was soft and spiritual, but he was far from having that noble assurance, that air of candour and loyalty, which inspires confidence in those who are destined to serve under his orders. … I was happy with his manners and propriety; few men were really more persuasive than him. … He had too much self-esteem to believe that a good idea could emerge from any other head than his own, and too much insensibility to cede to opinion.[26]

24 Doyle, *French Revolution*, pp.253–254.

25 Tallien described it thus, 'Hunger and fear alone have brought the twenty-eight sections together for even a minute.' Quoted in Doyle, *French Revolution*, p.249.

26 Gérard de Conades, *Coblenz et Quiberon Souvenirs du Comte de Contades* (Paris: Dentu, 1885), pp.104–105.

The raising of the armée départementale in Normandy provided Puisaye with the opportunity to gain a military post to which he aspired and he marched his advance corps from Caen to Evreux. From there, on 12 July 1793, he confidently advanced on Vernon, to prevent food supplies reaching Paris along the river Seine. Halting at Pacy-sur-Eure he issued a summons for Vernon to join the Federalists before spending the night at his home, the nearby Château de Ménilles. The next day, having received no response to his summons, Puisaye marched from Pacy at 4:00 p.m. on to the high ground around the Château de Brécourt. It had been a very hot day and while he retired to the château his men settled down for the night in its grounds, apparently with the help of cider found in the cellars. However, some soldiers, loyal to the Convention, had advanced from Vernon and finding the Federalists at Brécourt fired on them, causing them, for the most part, to panic and flee. As another Federalist officer remarked, '... in the grand début of the military career of Monsieur Joseph Puisaye who, having only ever led in his life the last king of the French from his apartment to chapel to hear mass, dreamt that he could also lead an army to victory.'[27] Puisaye was to insist that he had issued detailed instructions to defend his camp at Brécourt, but if he had these would have only been suitable for trained and disciplined men with an effective chain of command, rather than the force he actually commanded. Furthermore, his claims to have made valiant efforts to rally his men were not supported by any witnesses.[28] The rest of the Federalist army, despite an attempt to make a stand at Lisieux, quickly melted away and Normandy soon submitted to the Convention.[29]

Toulon 1793

In the Midi the Federalist revolt was widespread but attempts by troops of the armée départementale to stop the advance of the Convention's forces were easily brushed aside and Avignon was taken, followed, on 25 August, by Marseille with another wave of bloody reprisals. In response to this advance and the reprisals, royalists seized power in Toulon and invited Hood's British fleet, along with that of the Spanish under Don Juan de Lángara, into the port. The opportunity to secure the French Mediterranean fleet's home port, with its naval arsenal and shipyard, was an opportunity that Hood felt he could not ignore and so he decided to act on his own initiative. On 28 August the allied fleet entered the roadstead and troops landed from the fleet. They were joined by reinforcements, including from allies Piedmont and Naples, until there were 15,370 troops in the port and its environs.[30] On 8 September the city was besieged, an operation in which a young and ambitious artillery

27 La Barberie de Saint Front, an aide-de-camp in the army, quoted in Hutt, *Chouannerie*, p.44.

28 Hutt, *Chouannerie*, p.46.

29 Hutt, *Chouannerie*, pp.44–46.

30 William James, *The Naval History of Great Britain, from the Declaration of War by France in 1793, to the Accession of King George IV* (London: Richard Bentley, 1847), vol.1, p.74.

officer, Napoleon Bonaparte, distinguished himself by his activity and ability, while the Convention's forces crushed resistance elsewhere in the region.

News of Hood's intervention in Toulon reached London on 15 September.[31] The unexpected turn of events presented the British Government with an opportunity but also a dilemma. It was acutely aware that the intervention would be portrayed as one not only by a foreign power but, what is more, one by France's traditional enemy. On 29 October 1793 a formal declaration was published, in the name of King George III, which sought to counter such prejudices while, at the same time, attempting to broaden support for counter-revolutionary movements:

> ... This state of things cannot exist in France; without involving all the surrounding powers in one common danger ... His majesty by no means disputes the right of France to reform its laws. It never would have been his wish to employ the influence of external force with respect to the particular forms of government to be established in an independent country. Neither has he now that wish, except in so far as such interference is become essential to the security and repose of other powers. Under these circumstances he demands from France, and he demands with justice, the termination of a system of anarchy, ... that some legitimate and stable government should be established, founded on the acknowledged principles of universal justice, and capable of maintaining with other powers the accustomed relations of union and peace. His majesty wishes ardently to be enabled to treat for the re-establishment of general tranquillity with such a government, ... as he has already done with respect to those of Toulon. The king promises, on his part, the suspension of hostilities, friendship, and (as far as the course of events will allow, of which the will of man cannot dispose) security and protection to all those who, by declaring for a monarchical government, shall shake off the yoke of a sanguinary anarchy...
>
> It is then, in order to deliver themselves from this unheard-of oppression, to put an end to a system of unparalleled crimes, and to restore at length tranquillity to France, and security to all Europe, that his majesty invites the co-operation of the people of France. It is for these objects that he calls upon them to join the standard of an hereditary monarchy; not for the purposes of deciding, in this moment of disorder, calamity, and public danger, on all the modifications of which this form of government may hereafter be susceptible, but in order to unite themselves once more under the empire of law, of morality, and of religion, and to secure at length to their own country external peace, domestic tranquillity, a real and genuine liberty, a wise, moderate, and beneficent government, and the uninterrupted enjoyment of all the advantages which can contribute to the happiness and prosperity of a great and powerful nation.[32]

Britain, thus, declared its support for the restoration of the French monarchy but avoided prescribing what form it should take, a constitutional monarchy was not precluded, nor was peace with another form of viable government.

---

31 *The London Gazette*, 16 September 1793.

32 Hutt, *Chouannerie*, pp.588–589, where the declaration is reproduced in full in Appendix C (1).

Such a declaration only added to the fears and suspicions of hard-line royalists, in particular those émigrés who surrounded Artois.

Meanwhile, in Toulon, the siege continued but allied numbers were wholly inadequate to defend the city's extensive perimeter. Many of the French navy's officers and crews supported the royalist insurrection and assisted in the city's defence, manning the batteries, while others joined the besieging forces or were released to sail to other ports in five of the naval vessels.[33] French troops were also present in the city, including the first infantry battalion of the armée départementale, that had been formed from various army detachments that had previously been serving on the ships as marines, and full-time, paid, National Guards from the neighbouring département of Bouches-du-Rhône. Men from these units formed the basis of a new unit, the Régiment Royal-Louis. Historian Robert Grouvel wrote of the regiment that it was 'raised in the name and for the service of Louis XVII, approved by Monsieur, Regent of France, … and thus became the first battalion breveted by him with the consent of the coalition powers.'[34] Paid for by the British, the regiment was to be clothed and organised as French army line infantry and it served with particular distinction during the siege. With artillery units and independent chasseur (light infantry) companies, the royalist troops totalled 1,542 men.[35]

Finally, the republican forces overwhelmed the defenders and in the morning of 19 December 1793 HMS *Robust*, the last of the British ships, left Toulon. The night before Spanish and British sailors, with Captain Sir William Sidney Smith, attempted to destroy the arsenal, naval stores and remaining French warships however, under fire and with republican troops approaching, the mission was not completed.[36] As historian Gareth Glover concludes, 'It was a golden opportunity to destroy the French Mediterranean fleet entirely, … but it was botched, the opportunity wasted.'[37] The British took with them 15 French navy ships, with French crews, all the troops and almost 15,000 refugees, including 3,000 on the *Robust* alone, but many Toulonnais died on the beach by republican fire or drowning as they desperately tried to escape.[38] The city now faced the full force of republican terror; the victorious troops were permitted to sack it, and there were numerous scenes of rape and murder. Napoleon later described the next stage of the terror:

> The Representatives established a revolutionary tribunal, according to the laws of the period; but all the guilty had escaped and followed the enemy; all who had resolved to stay, were conscious of their innocence. … a dreadful measure,

33 James, *Naval History*, vol.I, p.70.

34 Vicomte Robert Grouvel, *Les corps de troupes de l'émigration française* (Paris: Les Éditions de La Sabretache, 1957–1964), vol.I, p.118, citing *Mémoire du chevalier de Boisgelin.*

35 James, *Naval History*, vol.I, p.74.

36 James, *Naval History*, vol.I, pp.77–79.

37 Gareth Glover, *The Forgotten War Against Napoleon: Conflict in the Mediterranean 1793–1815* (Barnsley: Pen and Sword Military, 2017), p.11. In endnote 6 (p.12) Glover states Lángara later claimed, when France and Spain had become allies, that he had deliberately hampered the destruction.

38 James, *Naval History*, vol.I, pp.80–81.

> characteristic of the spirit of the period, was resolved to. It was proclaimed that all those persons who had been employed in the arsenal whilst the English were in possession of the town, were to repair to the *Champ de Mars*, and give in their names; and they were led to believe that it was for the purpose of employing them again. Nearly two hundred persons, head workmen, inferior clerks, and other subalterns went accordingly, in full confidence. Their names were registered; it was proved by their own confession that they had retained their places under the English government, and the revolutionary tribunal, in the open field, immediately sentenced them to death. A battalion of Sans-Culottes and Marseillese [*sic*], brought expressly for the purpose, shot them.[39]

Toulon was no longer, it was renamed *Port-de-la-Montagne* (Mountain Port), 800 people were shot without trial and 282 more were condemned to the guillotine while many of the city's buildings were destroyed; only its importance as a naval base shielded it from further reprisals.[40] The Convention had survived through ruthless determination.

39 Somerset de Clair (ed.), *Napoleon's Memoirs* (London: Faber & Faber, 1948), p.24.
40 Doyle, *French Revolution*, p.255.

2

Insurrection

La Virée de Galerne

The Federalist revolts barely touched the Vendée and Brittany, although Nantes declared for the Federalists on 5 July, its support was retracted within 10 days, and Breton units had left Rennes to join the armée départementale at Caen but returned when it collapsed.[1] However the war in the Vendée was about to enter a dramatic new phase.

In the first weeks of August 1793 the Vendéen leaders gathered at the Château de La Boulaye, south of Cholet, to plan an attack on Luçon, in the south of the area. There they were joined by Vincent de Tinténiac, formerly of the Association bretonne, who came as an emissary from the British.

> Until then the insurgents had had no communication with England ... He handed over his despatches; they were sent by M. Dundas and the Governor of Jersey; they contained praise for the bravery and the steadfastness of the insurgents, and showed a strong desire to help them by every sort of means; but knowing no detail on the Vendée, the English posed nine questions, to which they demanded precise answers.[2]

The Vendéens were somewhat surprised how ill-informed the British were, or feigned to be. They were asked if they were royalists or a faction of the republicans, about their strength and resources, and 'Finally what kind of help we would ask for, and what place seemed to us suitable for a landing.'[3] Tinténiac gained the Vendéens' confidence and assured them of the British Government's good faith. Marie-Louise-Victoire de Donnissan prepared the good copy of the response:

> We replied to the English minister quite frankly ... yet we took care to exaggerate a little our strength ... We proposed a landing at Les Sables[-d'Olonne] or Paimbœuf, promising to bring fifty thousand men, at the given date, to the point

1 Harper, *Fighting the French Revolution*, pp.125–126.
2 La Rochejaquelein, *Mémoires*, pp.185–186.
3 La Rochejaquelein, *Mémoires*, p.187.

> that would be chosen; ... [perhaps] the little port of Saint-Gilles[-Croix-de-Vie]. ... but what we demanded especially and with insistence, it is that the landing was commanded by a prince of the House of Bourbon, and composed to a great extent of émigrés; we would affirm that then we could answer for a complete success; that twenty thousand young men would join the disembarked troops, and would consent to leave their own country; that we would cross the Loire, and that all Brittany would revolt.[4]

The Vendéens also wrote a short letter to the French royal princes, assuring them of their loyalty and their strong desire to see one of them at their head. Tinténiac soon left with these messages to travel back to Jersey.

The attack on Luçon on 14 August failed and over the following months the Vendéens faced greater, and more brutal, pressure from the republican forces. The insurrection was weakened when a 'prickly' Charette withdrew from a joint operation on 24 September and took his division back into Bas-Poitou, he would now only operate for and in his own territory.[5] On 16 October Cholet was taken by the republicans and despite fierce fighting the Vendéens could not recapture it. Their main body, the Grande Armée, was forced back onto the Loire, however crossing points had already been secured and over the next couple of days at least 40,000 fighting men and 20,000 non-combatants crossed to the north bank.[6]

On 19 October, Henri du Vergier de La Rochejaquelein, a 21-year-old former *sous-lieutenant*, of the Royal-Pologne and then Garde Constitutionnelle cavalry, and another who had tried to defend the Tuileries on 10 August 1792, somewhat reluctantly accepted command of the Grande Armée. He had only joined the insurrection when the peasants of his area asked him to do so. His second-in-command was Jean-Nicolas Stofflet, a native of Lorraine, who had been an infantry soldier before becoming a gamekeeper on his colonel's estate. He had been a chief since the first outbreak of the insurrection in March and was, 'A natural leader with a forceful, sometimes violent, personality but unquestionably brave.'[7] While the leadership contemplated their next move another messenger arrived from the British Government, with the news that it was ready to provide support to the Vendéens but they needed to secure a port.[8] It was decided to march north.

The first major town that the column reached was Laval where, it was hoped, they would be joined by men from Brittany and Maine. On 23 October about 1,500 men arrived, including a band led by the former smuggler, Jean Cottereau whose nickname Chouan – thought to relate to *chat-huant*, a screech or tawny owl – was the source for the name of the insurrection

4 La Rochejaquelein, *Mémoires*, pp.189–190. The, then, Marquise de Lescure stated that all the others present died during the insurrections leaving her the only witness.
5 Harper, *Fighting the French Revolution*, p.198.
6 Harper, *Fighting the French Revolution*, p.219.
7 Harper, *Fighting the French Revolution*, p.305.
8 Harper, *Fighting the French Revolution*, pp.227–228, identifies the messenger as Le Haye-Sainte-Hilaire, presumably the same as Louis La Haye Saint-Hilaire that Hutt, *Chouannerie*, p.103, states came ashore on 10 August – it is unclear if this was on the same mission.

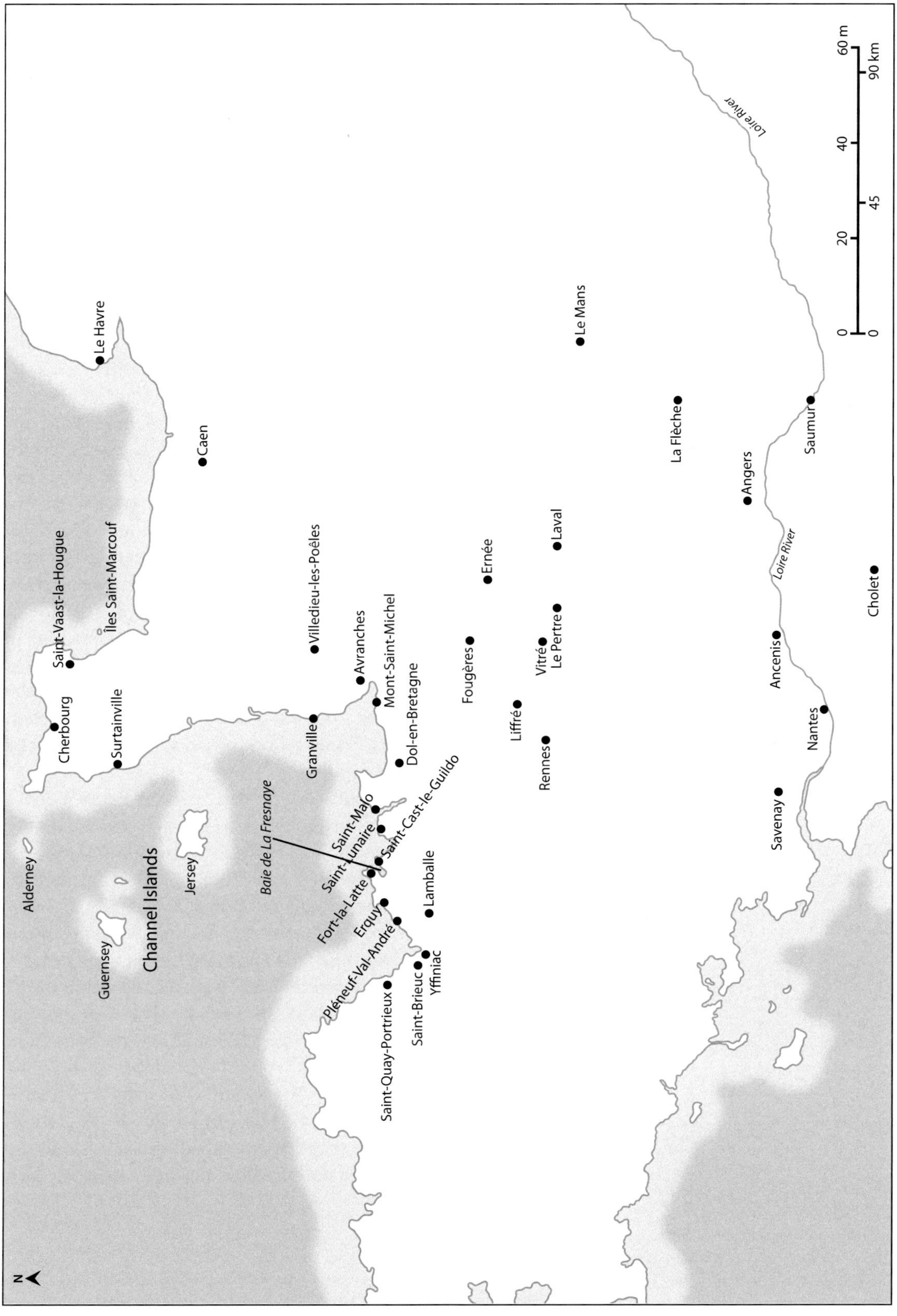

La Virée de Gale‘rne and Côtes du Nord.

throughout Brittany. However, in the end, only about 4,000–5,000 such men from other areas joined the Grande Armée while it was north of the Loire.[9] After defeating the republican vanguard on 26 October the Vendéens marched north, entering Ernée on 2 November and then turned west. They arrived at Fougères the next day, and on 7 November they were at Dol. The republicans had not been idle, the key points on the northern coast of Brittany had been reinforced and on 6 November the main army left Angers to counter the Grande Armée.

At Dol the Vendéens received emissaries from the Channel Islands who brought messages both from the émigré leadership and the British, who again promised support if a port was secured. After some heated debate, the army's morale having decreased as the distance from home grew, it was decided to do so. Saint-Malo was considered to be too well defended, so Granville, across Mont-Saint-Michel Bay, on the west coast of the Cotentin Peninsula, was chosen. On 10 November the émigré messenger left Dol for Jersey with news of the decision. The army reached Avranches on 12 November and, two days later, about half its total strength moved onto Granville, leaving much of the artillery behind. The town refused to surrender so had to be attacked. The Vendéens secured the suburbs that night, 14/15 November, but an attempt to scale the medieval walls in the darkness failed, as did another to outflank them at low tide. Several leaders were casualties, though the losses were comparatively light otherwise, but the Vendéens were disheartened and soon dispersed. Such was the confusion that the men in the vanguard, unaware of the general retreat, found themselves, at 10:00 a.m. on 16 November, alone in front of Granville and had to withdraw in haste. The Grande Armée had lost cohesion. The next day when La Rochejaquelein and Stofflet tried to get the army to march on to Caen, less than 1,000 men obeyed. La Rochejaquelein gave up the advance at Villedieu-les-Poêles and returned to Avranches, but a stubborn Stofflet remained for another day.[10]

In the meantime, the main republican army had reached Rennes on 15 November and then, learning of the Vendéens advance on Granville, sought to trap them against the sea. However, despite their disunity the Vendéens turned on the republican vanguard winning a series of victories, between 20 and 23 November, which forced their pursuers to retreat to Rennes. The way was open for the Vendéens to reach the Loire and they headed for Angers, hoping to cross the river there, but they failed to take the city on 2 and 3 December and the enemy columns closed in. The Vendéens retreated north to La Flèche and then Le Mans, which they captured on 10 December, but when the republicans attacked the city, late on 12 December, the Vendéens were routed after fierce street fighting through the night, and many, particularly their non-combatants, were slaughtered. The survivors fled to Laval, they were no longer an army, they were exhausted, sick and hungry.[11] On 16 December another attempt was made to cross the Loire at Ancenis. La Rochejaquelein and Stofflet along with about 2,000 men managed to reach

9 Harper, *Fighting the French Revolution*, p.229.
10 Harper, *Fighting the French Revolution*, p.252.
11 Harper, *Fighting the French Revolution*, p.283.

the south bank but before they could help any more to cross the republicans dispersed those that remained on the north bank. The latter now headed west pursued by the republicans until they reached Savenay on 22 December where they halted. The following day, outnumbered, they made one last desperate stand. Many were killed but others managed to escape. The royalist Grande Armée was no longer.

In the meantime, Charette had sought to expand his influence into Haut-Poitou where he established himself at Maulévrier, south-east of Cholet. When, on 21 December, La Rochejaquelein and Stofflet arrived, Charette received them coldly, indeed snubbed them, as his new-found ascendancy was lost. The next day they parted company for the final time when Charette returned to Bas-Poitou. The Vendée now faced the terror as republican columns brought fire and sword to subjugate the region in what has, controversially, been called a programme of genocide.[12] While many rebels were driven to submission, the violence and brutality strengthened the resolve of others and the Vendéens continued a guerrilla war. Their leading chiefs, following La Rochejaquelein's death on 28 January 1794, were Charette and Stofflet, both proud men who had no wish to overcome their differences.

British Support

Where had been the promised support from Britain? The straightforward, if obtuse, answer is that the Vendéens had not seized and secured a port. Yet some French writers have blamed the absence of a British fleet, with the promised succour, for the failure to capture Granville. Their argument being that it could have supported the attack and its very presence would have raised the Vendéens' flagging resolve. The presumption being that the Vendéens knew why they were attacking Granville. However, there is evidence that they did not, as their leaders had kept their correspondence with the British secret from the army.[13]

Although the British Government had not given the mission significant priority, any such argument rests on there being swift and sure communication and co-ordination between the British and the Vendéens. The émigré, with the news the latter were heading for Granville from Dol only reached Jersey on 22 November and then had to be passed onto London. Francis Rawdon Hastings, Earl of Moira, commanded a strategic reserve of troops on England's south coast and was to lead the British expedition to France. On 26 November he was informed the Vendéen Grande Armée was on the march for, it was thought, Cherbourg or Saint-Malo and the convoy set sail from

12 This argument was, controversially, presented by Reynald Secher in *Le genocide franco-française: La Vendée-Vengé* (Paris: Presses Universitaires de France, 1986) which was published in English as *A French Genocide: The Vendée* (Notre Dame: University of Notre Dame, 2003).

13 After interviewing an officer and several Vendéens who had escaped to Jersey, the Marquis du Dresnay found that the Grande Armée's leaders had not disclosed that they were, in fact, corresponding with the British; TNA: WO 1/175: 8 January 1794.

Spithead, the anchorage off Portsmouth, four days later.[14] The fleet arrived off Cherbourg at daylight on 2 December and two frigates were sent towards the port, '... carrying the White Pendant ... in hopes the Royalist [*sic*] might have possession of some tenable port, or to receive and answer ... signals ...' but they were fired upon. There was no sign of royalist activity along the coast and the fleet headed for Guernsey.[15]

The issue of misleading and slow communication that prevented concerted action between the Vendéens and the British is graphically illustrated by the series of messages Moira received from France, while he was in the Channel Islands. On 8 December he was informed that the Vendéens had taken Rennes, eight days later that they were retreating to the Loire and, on 27 December, that they had returned home. However, on 30 December he was told they were moving on Caen and then, the next day, that they were making some attempts in the Cotentin Peninsula.[16]

Even if the British had known of the Vendéens' march to the north coast at an earlier stage it would not have been practicable to have the expedition ready, 'on the spot,' in the Channel Islands. To have kept such a large number of vessels in their exposed anchorages in winter would have been too dangerous. The proof of this was that a transport was driven onto rocks while the fleet remained at anchor off Guernsey. When a gale struck on 9–12 December, ships ran afoul of others and one was driven from its anchors out to sea. Finally, the signal was given for the fleet to get under way in the morning of 14 December, '... owing to the uncommon badness of the weather a great deal of damage ensued, which must always be the case, under such circumstances in a fleet of Transports ... the greater part of the ships that got out cut their cables and ran to sea.'[17]

This being said, the generally haphazard management of the war by the British Government meant the expedition would never have been ready to meet the Vendéens at Granville. Moira had initially estimated that he would need 12,000 men, including 200 gunners with 20 cannon, for the mission to the French coast, but he eventually sailed with around 4,700 infantry and perhaps 100 artillerymen.[18] The West Indies expedition which, to add to the confusion and pressure on resources, was being prepared at Portsmouth at the same time, eventually sailed on 26 November, with only half its intended strength and should have already been in that theatre by the date it departed. The draft instructions to Moira were only presented to the King, for his approval, on 20 November and the order for the expedition was only circulated, at Portsmouth, on 24 November.[19] It directed all personnel to

14 Hutt, *Chouannerie*, pp.55, 104–105.

15 R. M. Grazebrook, 'The Campaign in Flanders of 1793-1795: Journal of Lieutenant Charles Stewart, 28th Foot', *Journal of the Society for Army Historical Research*, vol. 29, No. 117 (Spring 1991), p.5.

16 Shown in a series of letters from Moira to the naval commander, Rear Admiral John MacBride, in the Jersey Archive: L/F/08/A/17, 24, 27, 29 and 30.

17 Grazebrook, 'Lieutenant Charles Stewart', p.6.

18 Fortescue, *British Army*, vol.IV, pp.154–155 and TNA: HO 42/27: return of nine battalions dated 19 November 1793.

19 TNA: HO 42/27: instructions 20 November and Grazebrook 'Lieutenant Charles Stewart', p.4.

be embarked by noon next day and showed Moira's force divided into four brigades, each of three infantry battalions:

Major General William Crosbie	3rd	40th	59th
Brigadier General William Lord Cathcart	19th	42nd	63rd
Brigadier General Charles Graham	27th	54th	78th
Brigadier General Peter Hunter	28th	57th	Loyal Emigrants

This was, however, misleading as the only units present were the eight battalions taken from the West Indies expedition, which at least meant they were already at Spithead and embarked on transports. The Loyal Emigrants, a British Army regiment raised from French émigrés in early 1793, were with the Duke of York's army, while the 63rd and 78th Foot were on Jersey so only joined Moira later in December. As for the 40th, its battalion companies had been originally assigned to be part of the reinforcements from Ireland promised for Toulon and, despite being allocated to now join Moira, remained at Cork until January 1794.[20] Finally German subsidy troops, intended to meet Moira at Guernsey, were still in Belgium. Their commanders, suspicious of their intended destination, initially would not countenance embarkation without positive orders from their own rulers. Finally, the Baden contingent offered to join the Gibraltar garrison and the Hesse-Cassel troops were ready to embark, after the Duke of York had provided a written assurance that they were not going to the West Indies.[21] This impasse was, however, largely irrelevant as the transports which were to collect them were prevented from sailing from England by adverse winds and only arrived at Ostend on 24 December.[22]

Moira's force returned to the Solent where he was joined by a Hesse-Cassel contingent, of about 2,500 combatants, on 4 January 1794.[23] Initially the troops were kept onboard their transports which led to high levels of sickness, especially from dysentery, so they were put onshore in the Solent region and retained, either to be deployed in France or to respond to an anticipated enemy attack.

However belated and ill-managed aid to the Vendéens had been, it was clearly intended to not only be substantial but also a coalition, rather than just British, effort. On 29 November 1793, *The Times* reported:

> Besides the 8 or 9000 men which are under the immediate command of the Earl of MOIRA, 6000 Hessians and 2000 Austrian Hussars, are ready to sail from Ostend and follow them… It is believed, that the legions of *La Chatre*, *De Damas*, *Carneville*, and *Béon*, will be sent into Normandy and Brittany …

20 Mary Ellen Condon, *The Administration of the Transport Service during the War against Revolutionary France, 1793–1802* (unpublished thesis, University of London, 1968), p.221.

21 TNA: WO 1/167: 3 and 10 December 1793.

22 TNA: HO 42/27: letter of 25 November mentioning the transports being unable to sail and WO 1/167: 24 December 1793.

23 Paul Demet, *'We Are Accustomed to do Our Duty': German Auxiliaries with the British Army 1793–95* (Warwick: Helion & Company 2018), pp.60–63.

The report added that any expedition would be joined by 1,000 émigrés from England and the Channel Islands as well as 'a great number of those who are in the Prince of Condé's army.'[24]

The Channel Islands provided those fleeing France, particularly from Brittany and Normandy, with an immediate refuge. Many had then gone to join the émigré armies that had formed on the borders of northern France, to return after failure of the 1792 campaign. In April 1793 Louis-Marie-Ambroise-René Marquis du Dresnay, a Breton, *maréchal de camp* and former officer of the Chevau-légers, a prestigious cavalry regiment, had been appointed La Rouërie's replacement as royalist commander in Brittany by the Regent. He was to be 'Commander in chief of the different Corps' in Brittany and:

> to give more vigour and cohesion to the enterprises that he will judge useful, to distribute the means which can be sent to sustain expeditions, to report to him of progress, of needs, of the services of those working with us and maintain a close correspondence with him and the allies who strive for the success of these operations.[25]

On Jersey arrangements were made to form the French gentlemen into a military corps but little progress was made, even after du Dresnay arrived on the island on 12 May.[26] A British officer wrote 'they would want almost everything' in terms of arms, clothing and equipment and, as individuals, many were 'in the utmost distress.' Ominously he also warned of intense rivalry 'between the first Emigrants & what is called the coalition of Brittany' which may have serious consequences.[27] It was only at the end of November 1793 that the men were actually formed into companies, issued with muskets and began to be exercised.[28] The following January there were 600 such men on Jersey when Moira sketched out a structure for the corps, and sufficient progress had been made for it to take part in a military exercise involving the island's garrison repelling a mock invasion on 11 May 1794.[29]

As for the units mentioned in *The Times*, Claude-Louis-Raoul de La Châtre was the colonel of the Loyal Emigrants and his name was sometimes used for the regiment, which the Duke of York was reluctant to release.[30] The others were also composed of French émigrés; the Légions de Damas and Béon in the service of the United Provinces and that of Carneville in Austrian service, all were deployed in the Ardennes region in 1794.[31]

---

24 *The Times*, Friday 29 November 1793.

25 TNA: HO 98/3: copy of instructions dated 14 April 1793.

26 Anon. (ed.), *Mémoires d'Olivier d'Argens et Correspondances des Généraux* (Paris: Baudouin Frères, 1826), pp.41–42.

27 TNA: HO 98/3: letter from Colonel James Henry Craig to Evan Nepean 28 May 1793.

28 Anon. (ed.), *Olivier d'Argens*, p.47.

29 TNA: WO 1/175: memo of 7 January 1794 and Anon. (ed.), *Olivier d'Argens*, p.50. According to the memo the companies were to each have 60 rank and file and three officers. It appears that there were to be two field officers. Du Dresnay considered that in total he could have 1,200 men in two battalions. It is noted that 'Clothing is already prepared 5000 sets' – presumably included in the stores carried with Moira's expeditionary force.

30 TNA: WO 1/167: letter of 3 December 1793.

31 Grouvel, *Les corps de troupes*, vol.II, p.227.

Nevertheless, a return dated 10 December 1793 shows that a small contingent of 1,083 men and 660 horses from unnamed units of the Austrian army was indeed assembled at Antoing, east of Lille, to join the expedition. They were of different arms: hussars with 22 officers and staff, 521 other ranks and 577 horses; infantry with three officers, 190 men and five horses; jäger, two officers, 157 men and eight horses; artillery five officers, 127 men and eight horses as well as 'others' comprising of three officers, 53 men and 62 horses. With them were four 'French howitzers,' twenty 6-pounder cannon, 20 'ammunition casks,' 8,000 French muskets, 800 howitzer shells, 240,000 cartridges, and 30 hundredweight of powder and 30 hundredweight of matches.[32] However, the prospect of the British intervening in northwestern France in 1794, already much reduced by the defeat of the Vendéens, further waned in June when Moira and his troops were sent to Ostend to reinforce the allies in Belgium.

A New Leader of the Chouans?

On 8 January 1794, when Dresnay informed Moira of the destruction of the Vendéen Grande Armée, the only leader he considered active was Charette, although he had '… reason to believe that the little army in the Forest de Pert [*sic*] has not broken up, … I think it hardly considerable … I attach little importance to these assemblies without order or chiefs'.[33] The 'little army' did in fact have a chief, Joseph de Puisaye, the Federalist commander who had been defeated at Brécourt. He, accompanied by some loyal officers, had joined the Breton contingent on its retreat homeward in July 1793 when the Federalist forces in Normandy had dissolved. They first took refuge in the Paimpont forest, west of Rennes, but seeking a role in the chouannerie as a means to bring about the fall of those in power in Paris, Puisaye switched to the forest around Le Pertre, southeast of Vitré, as the insurgency was more active in that region.[34]

He soon began work to establish himself as a leading figure in the royalist cause, gathering some men around him. When the Vendéen Grande Armée reached Laval he attempted to persuade them to march on Rennes and thereby, by their presence, ignite a full-scale insurrection in Brittany. Purporting to be a commanding general, he asserted that there was 'an army of 50,000 men ready to go into action near Rennes,' but the Vendéen leaders were sceptical, replying that 'if this Breton army took the field, it could certainly count on assistance' from the Vendéens.[35] Taking this as an invitation, Puisaye, by his own account, left to join the Grande Armée but missed it at Laval and Fougères, so he decided to turn back. However, the destruction of the Vendéen army inadvertently provided Puisaye with an

32 TNA: WO 1/167: return 10 December 1793 (a hundredweight equates to 50.8 kg).

33 TNA: WO 1/175: letter of 8 January 1794, he had the information about the Vendéens from an officer and several soldiers who had escaped to Jersey.

34 See Hutt, *Chouannerie*, pp.50–51.

35 Hutt, *Chouannerie*, p.51.

opportunity, as about 30 of their officers joined him in the Le Pertre forest after their defeat at Savenay. According to historian Maurice Hutt,

> He looked like a leader: of commanding height and powerfully built, he had an imposing air, a confident manner … Unsuited to be anyone's subordinate, ill-fitted to be anyone's colleague, he was well equipped to command. A gentleman, he was none the less perfectly capable of roughing it, of sharing the hardships of his followers …[36]

In addition, by accident, Puisaye received an official message from the British Government. On 2 December 1793 a royalist messenger arrived on the north coast from Jersey to make contact with the Vendéens to announce that the expedition to Granville was almost ready to depart, but, unable to move inland, he handed the packet of letters on, and it was eventually delivered to Puisaye. The packet contained King George's declaration of 29 October and various letters, including one from Lord Moira in which he described how Provence and Artois looked to the zeal of the royalists and how they in turn could turn for support from King George and the British Cabinet. Puisaye saw the opportunity, the King's declaration chimed with his own political instincts and the support offered would enable him to fulfil his ambitions, with it he could arm the host he wanted to gather around him and the ability to equip them would attract even more followers.

Now aware of the stated intentions of the British and their offers of support, he began to correspond with agents from Jersey while creating a network of links with other leaders in neighbouring territories. In mid-April 1794 Puisaye put this network to the test, moving his base to the south of Rennes to launch an attack on the city, however only 600–800 crudely armed chouans answered his call to arms. Undaunted, he marched his little band around the city, brushing small enemy detachments aside until on 7 May he came up against a sizable enemy force at Liffré, and after some resistance his chouans melted away.

Again, Puisaye received a fillip after a setback. On 9 or 10 May, the royalist agent Tinténiac arrived in search of him. Although they did not meet, Tinténiac stated his intention to visit again on his way back from the Vendée, illustrating to Puisaye that he was now considered a royalist leader worthy of consultation. Furthermore, on 22 May, he received a message from the Marquis du Dresnay, which although it did not mention Dresnay's appointment by the French Regent, convinced Puisaye that he may have some influence on British policy.

Puisaye replied immediately, undoubtedly reflecting on the recent failure, he described the chouans as '… strictly speaking only bands of malcontents and outcasts scattered here and there in the forests … still far from having assumed the character of a major insurrection.'[37] Nevertheless, he considered that a landing of 5,000–6,000 troops, with cannon, bringing with them arms and equipment for 50,000 men, would ignite a general insurrection for

36 Hutt, *Chouannerie*, p.53.

37 TNA: WO 1/391: Puisaye to Dresnay 23 May 1794.

a march on Rennes.[38] Although not a fully-formed plan, Puisaye thought foreign aid could equip and thus maintain a confederation of chouan bands. Furthermore, unaware of Dresnay's post until the latter replied, that to cement his position, Puisaye should receive an official commission to command in Brittany.[39] Despite the dent to his ambitions and a shortage of money, Puisaye was invigorated by the correspondence, constructing a confederation by making links with chouan leaders and bands further afield, and soon he was grandly writing about the 'corps of royalist troops' and 'Armée royale de Bretagne.'[40]

On 13 June Tinténiac brought more messages from the British Government that pledged support but specified that the royalists would have to secure a fortified port and regular lines of communication for a regular supply of men, arms and equipment to be provided. This was clearly something Puisaye, or indeed the chouannerie as a movement, could not do. Nevertheless, a further message provided hope by stating that if the chouans were unable to take a port, through lack of equipment or skilled officers, these could be landed on the coast facing Jersey. As the first phase of a campaign, covering a landing from the sea was a far more practicable objective for the chouans.[41]

On 26 July, at a meeting attended by all Puisaye's leaders as well as three from the neighbouring Morbihan region, a grandiose overall strategy was decided upon. The whole of the Breton peninsula and adjoining regions were to be secured as a base from which the royal princes would lead an army to retake the kingdom. Puisaye was to even inform the British of his plans to take Nantes, as a port for the landing of supplies, in conjunction with Charette who was to attack from the south of the Loire.[42]

However, a succession of setbacks revealed the true state of Puisaye's network. An operation was planned for the last weeks of August, to improve chouan morale and put the republicans onto the back foot. Unfortunately, it was swiftly snuffed out by the republicans before the bands, in their hundreds and not thousands as projected, could even assemble. Harvest time was more important in the rural communities of Brittany.[43] Finally, a demonstration against Vannes by the chouans of Morbihan coinciding with those of Ille-et-Vilaine supporting a landing at Saint-Cast-le-Guildo Bay, west of Saint-Malo, came to nothing when the plans were revealed through the capture of Puisaye's second-in-command.[44]

At around the same time three royalist emissaries came to see Puisaye after their arrival in France on 17 August. One of them was Pierre-Marie-Félicité Dezoteux Baron de Cormatin, an experienced army staff officer and diplomat, who although initially sympathetic to the Revolution had served on Bouillé's staff during the suppression of the Nancy mutiny and

38 Hutt, *Chouannerie*, p.72.
39 Hutt, *Chouannerie*, pp.73–75.
40 Hutt, *Chouannerie*, pp.79, 82.
41 Hutt, *Chouannerie*, pp.81-82.
42 Hutt, *Chouannerie*, p.83.
43 Hutt, *Chouannerie*, pp.86–88.
44 Hutt, *Chouannerie*, p.84.

had emigrated to Britain after 10 August 1792.[45] The three men were tasked to bring Puisaye, Charette and the chouans of Maine into a wider royalist organisation in which Puisaye would be the pre-eminent leader in Brittany. While this flattered Puisaye's self-esteem, what he was not to know was that the plan was designed to prevent him independently developing links with the British and that he was to be quickly replaced by an émigré general.[46]

On 25 and 26 August a military council was called to discuss wide-ranging new plans, as well as organisational reforms, at which the area around Saint-Brieuc was identified as a suitable site for a beach landing of British supplies. Although there was the appearance of confidence, it seems the chouans' leaders wanted to take some initiative over events so it was decided that Puisaye, himself, should go to London on behalf of the Armée catholique et royale to secure the princes' backing and make arrangements for the landing.[47] In his absence, which was expected to be of only three weeks, a permanent council, chaired by Cormatin with the rank of *major-général*, was formed to direct the network. Puisaye soon left for the coast, but republican activity delayed his embarkation and, when he put to sea, it was a perilous crossing. His boat took on water and he was severely sea sick. He arrived on Jersey on 17 September, and he was quickly and secretly sent on to London. His arrival there was at an opportune moment.[48]

Puisaye and Émigré Circles

Puisaye immediately gained the ear of British ministers, arriving as 'a commander … straight from the field' and, what is more, he was different from other counter-revolutionaries they had encountered before, as according to Hutt he 'appreciated the need for the Bourbons to rally opinion behind them by adopting a policy of forgiveness and clemency' so chiming with their own views.[49]

Such a pragmatic view was an anathema to the royal princes and, even more so, to those who surrounded them. These latter, the *purs*, could not countenance anything else than a return to the status quo that existed not only before 1789 but also the earlier reforms of Louis XVI. For them, such changes had undermined the pillars of the French Kingdom and so had heralded the calamities that the monarchy, and its supporters, had suffered since. Furthermore, 'The French nobility thought that a pure royalism, incorruptible fidelity, conduct always without reproach during the first stages of the Revolution, were the only titles which could give [someone] the right to serve

45 Several sources state that he had served as an officer in the Garde Constitutionnelle, however his name does not appear on the personnel list prepared from files in the Archives Nationales. Anon., 'Fichier de la garde constitutionnelle de Louis XVI (1791–1792)' Archives nationales 2016 <https://francearchives.fr/findingaid/fe3c62602114da74bf7575d392895499917388fe>, accessed 21 September 2020.

46 Hutt, *Chouannerie*, pp.90–91.

47 Hutt, *Chouannerie*, pp.92–94.

48 Hutt, *Chouannerie*, pp.95–96.

49 Hutt, *Chouannerie*, p.132.

with them ...' so that those emigrating later, especially after 10 August 1792, who had thus given some level of support to the Constitution, faced suspicion, even hostility.[50] Any man, with Puisaye's record during the Revolution, would not be accepted by the *purs* and any project that he advanced would be treated with mistrust, especially if drawn up with the British, the motives of which the *parti des princes* regarded with, at best, scepticism. This suspicion, in their eyes, was validated by the British Government's reluctance to recognise the Comte de Provence as regent during uncrowned Louis XVII's imprisonment, and unilateral actions, such as at Toulon, Corsica and Haïti. Many in the *parti des princes* considered Spain, a Roman Catholic country with a Bourbon king and an active ally of France as recently as the American War of Independence, as the best source of support. Although, by this time, Artois had become disillusioned by what had been obtained, and could be expected, from that quarter, others still strongly and actively advocated it. One of these was Louis-Alexandre de Launay Comte d'Antraigues, a political adventurer within Provence's entourage, at Verona in Italy, who ran a spy network, the Agence de Paris, supplying information from the French capital. The intelligence provided by Antraigues, and others of a similar mind may not have persuaded Provence and his brother, 'that Spain would do everything he wanted, but it undoubtedly served to keep constantly before his eyes that hostility to and suspicion of England which was the constant refrain of this particular lobby.'[51]

For their part, the British were wary of the *parti des princes*, frustrated by its intransigence, suspicious of the plotting and power-plays within its circles and also regarding it as leaky when it came to secrets. The British Government and *parti des princes* were well-informed of each other's activities and Puisaye found himself caught between them while seeking support from both. He needed the British to provide him the means and the princes' the authority for his projects. The British had wanted Puisaye to keep his brief stay in London a secret, he even adopted the not completely misleading pseudonym of the Marquis de Ménilles. Nevertheless, without telling the British, he contacted the Comte d'Artois, who was already aware of his journey to England; the British, in turn, were soon informed of Puisaye's correspondence but chose not to make an issue of it.

Puisaye's first approach to the prince, on 15 October, came to nothing but finally, on 3 December, Artois eventually gave Puisaye the powers he needed, though short of what he had hoped for, when he gave him the brevet of *lieutenant-général*, to commence at the same time as that given to him by the British, and to make a public address to the chouans, 'The Comte de Puisaye, who so justly deserves your confidence, that of the Regent and mine, will be at this moment my agent ... The only order [I] give [him is] to do everything, to undertake everything, to hasten [the] glorious moment ... [when] I myself will be at the head of this invincible army.'[52]

50 Jean-Antoine de Brons, *Journal d'émigration* (Saint-Quentin-de-Baron: Chez Entre-deux-mers, 2014), p.87. Brons had served as a senior officer in the émigré army organised around the King's brothers.

51 Hutt, *Chouannerie*, p.120.

52 Quoted in Hutt, *Chouannerie*, p.163.

In his bid for authority, Puisaye had made no contact with Dresnay; one reason for friction between them, another being a scheme Puisaye began to provide money for the chouans. The French Republic had introduced the assignat, a bond secured largely against the value of 400 million livres worth of property seized by the state. Very quickly it was adopted as a paper currency and within a year the republic approved the production of 1,200 million of them. The assignat steadily devalued to 63 percent of its face value by January 1792. Nevertheless, the republic continued to print even more so that, when production ceased in February 1796, there were over 34,000,000,000 livres worth still in circulation.[53] Forgery was to have only a small influence on the devaluation, but in their propaganda the republicans sought to use counterfeiting, particularly by émigrés and foreigners, to deflect from the problem of their own making. Several émigrés, including Dresnay, were involved in smuggling forged assignats into France, both for personal gain and as a means to wage economic warfare against the republic.

Puisaye's project was to produce assignats, under the authority of the princes, which, with special marks, could be redeemed when the royal family was restored to the throne. His argument being that the princes had the right to issue currency and, as Brittany was under republican control, it had to be able to be passed like that 'issued by the illegal regime in France.'[54] The British Government provided financial support to establish the workshop but other émigrés objected to their production. One of these was Jean-François de La Marche, Bishop of Saint-Pol-de-Léon, on the grounds that Puisaye had recruited émigré priests for his workshop.[55] However, this understandable objection came from the author of the plan to have Puisaye removed from his command. The Bishop was also closely involved with a number of others involved in smuggling assignats, including Dresnay. Despite the opposition, and the removal of the priests, the workshop remained in operation. Nevertheless, for Puisaye this was one of successive examples of jealous rivals seeking to thwart him. On this occasion he had justification, in many others he did not.

Puisaye's Chouan Network Under Threat

An intervention by the British to promote a successful royalist uprising in western France would crown Puisaye's efforts, but first he had to ensure supplies, both of arms and money, reached the chouans to not only sustain his network in Brittany but also to justify his continued absence. Meanwhile, events in Brittany were threatening to dismantle his network and so undermine his position.

On 28 July 1794, Robespierre was guillotined. His fall from power had been swift, he had only been arrested the previous night. One of the key

53 Doyle, *French Revolution*, p.323. Stephen Clarke, *The French Revolution & What Went Wrong* (London: Arrow Books, 2019), p.373, puts it succinctly 'It was a bubble designed to burst.'

54 Hutt, *Chouannerie*, p.167.

55 Hutt, *Chouannerie*, p.168.

members of the coup that removed him was Tallien, who as *représentant en mission* had suppressed the revolt at Bordeaux. He had attracted the enmity of Robespierre who personally signed the arrest warrant for Thérésa Cabarrus, his mistress. She, facing inevitable execution, chided her lover into action and he began the process in which Robespierre was denounced in the Convention. In the aftermath, the apparatus of the terror was quickly dismantled and, in time, it allowed a different approach to be adopted to counter the royalists in Brittany and the Vendée. This approach was to be directed by *Généraux* Canclaux and Louis-Lazare Hoche.

Canclaux, as a former noble, had been removed from his command on 1 October 1793 but was reinstated to the command of the Armée de l'Ouest in the Vendée after Robespierre's fall. Hoche also owed his appointment to the new politics. He had been a soldier in the Gardes Françaises since he was 16 and when the regiment was dissolved in 1789, he had joined the full-time, paid, element of the Parisian National Guard as a *sergent*. Such units were transferred to the line infantry in 1792 and Hoche was a *capitaine* by the end of the year. The next year he was aide-de-camp to *Lieutenant-général* Alexis-Paul-Michel Tanneguy Le Veneur de Tillières and, when ordered to Paris, he attracted the attention of politicians leading him to be appointed *adjudant-général* and *chef de bataillon* in the Armée du Nord in May 1793. Temporarily imprisoned for his loyalty to Le Veneur, he was released in August and organised the successful defence of Dunkirk. He was promoted to the Armée de la Moselle, in the Rhine Valley and then Alsace, as *général de division*. His performance led to him to further promotion but also attracted the animosity of some politicians who ensured he was arrested in March 1794 and imprisoned, under threat of execution, for treason. The coup brought about Hoche's release and on 1 September he was appointed commander of the Armée des côtes de Cherbourg. This army, responsible for Maine, Lower Normandy and Eastern Brittany, was then, on 10 November, combined with the Armée des côtes de Brest, under his command. The republican forces in the west were now in the hands of two capable but different men, Hoche was aged 26 and Canclaux 54, the latter having held the rank of *maréchal de camp* for a year when, in 1789, Hoche, the son of a stable groom, had been promoted *caporal*.[56]

Hoche arrived at Rennes on 5 September 1794 to find his command disorganised and demoralised; he immediately tried to put things in order. His order of the day on 30 September read, 'Austere discipline, probity, all the republican virtues need to be put into operation … Join with firmness clemency towards the weak … preserving the inhabitant of all types from military harassment, scrupulously respecting property, are the means … to succeed.'[57] Hoche soon deployed mobile columns to disrupt the chouan bands and a political campaign was begun to drive wedges between the chouan chiefs, their followers and the general population. It was recognised that some repressive measures were counter-productive, such as those

56 Ernest Cuneo d'Ornano, *Hoche Sa vie et sa correspondance* (Paris: Librairie militaire J. Dumaine, L. Baudoin et Cie., 1892), pp.3–6 and Etat militaire 1789.

57 Ornano, *Hoche*, p.169.

against non-juror priests who, whatever their attitude to the regime, were forced to remain in hiding, and amnesties were granted for ordinary chouans who renounced violence and returned home.

As Cormatin, and the Comité Central became increasingly concerned about these developments they were hearing little from Puisaye; he had last written to them in September, a message that had taken a month to reach them. They needed some sign of success to sustain their chouannerie movement and also a sign that Puisaye's presence in England was bearing fruit. The delivery of arms and gunpowder would be such a signal.[58]

The organisation that was to be responsible for such a delivery was that which passed agents and intelligence between France and England, via Jersey and Southampton, and was known as the *Correspondance*. In the Channel Islands it was controlled by Royal Navy captain, and Jerseyman, Philippe d'Auvergne. By chance and without any obvious link he had been named as heir by Godefroy de La Tour d'Auvergne Duc de Bouillon, whose duchy was in the Ardennes region of Belgium, so he adopted the title of the Prince de Bouillon. The supply of arms from the Ordnance Department was improved once General Charles, Marquess Cornwallis was appointed Master of the Board in February 1795. However, their onward shipment to France had then been problematic, due to bad weather and republican activity, so only two small shipments had arrived in Brittany by mid-November: a few arms and assignats on 21 October and a little powder and more assignats on 14 November.[59]

On 7 December a consignment of gunpowder was landed and taken to a nearby farm, but it was surrounded by republican troops and the chouans, including Cormatin, barely escaped, leaving the powder behind. As Christmas approached the republican campaign of pardons and pressure which had driven some chouan chiefs to quit and turned others to actively work against the royalist cause, was taking its toll. The committee's lines of communication were disrupted and messages intercepted, several of the leaders, including Cormatin, had become dispirited.

On 20 December the Comité met, although only a few chiefs managed to attend, and a letter was written to Puisaye along with an official message for the British Government. Although diplomatically worded it was clear that they, in the name of the Armée catholique et royale de Bretagne, demanded action by the end of January. They wanted to see Puisaye back at their head in Brittany and a landing, composed of no less than 12,000 men. Their confidence was so undermined that they demanded that 'partial landings' should cease, due to the republican attention this brought to the coast and their supporters in that area. The courier left on 23 December but only managed to get to Jersey on 28 January 1795.

There were concerns that Charette and other Vendéen leaders may have been making peace with the republic, leaving its army to concentrate on Brittany. Chouan leaders were also approached for similar talks and Boishardy, chief in the Lamballe area in north-eastern Brittany since the days

58 Hutt, *Chouannerie*, pp.148–149, 181.
59 Hutt, *Chouannerie*, p.182.

of the Association bretonne, was contacted to this effect by republican *Général de brigade* Jean-Joseph-Amable Humbert. The contrast between the two was marked. Humbert had received no education as a youngster and became a trader, in either rabbit skins or horses. On 1 April 1792 he had joined the 13e bataillon des Vosges, was elected *capitaine* on 11 August and was second in command of the battalion four days later. He later served as *adjutant-général* with the forces sent against the Federalists in Normandy in 1793 before being promoted to the Armée des côtes de Brest on 9 April 1794.[60] Humbert's offer was accepted and Boishardy, accompanied by Cormatin, met with him on 28 December, resulting in a truce on 1 January 1795 and the arrangement that Cormatin would go with Humbert to Nantes to discover for himself the progress of talks between the republicans and Vendéens. The formal peace talks took place at the Château de La Jaunaye and, after Charette and Cormatin had conferred, they both signed a treaty on 17 February. However, Cormatin's agreement was conditional on it being ratified by the Armée catholique et royale de Bretagne and so the truce continued until the Comité convened on 30 March.

The chouan leadership regarded the truce as giving them respite and a chance to press for immediate action from Puisaye and the British. The Conseil du Morbihan, representing the chouans of the region, did not support the truce and sent their own message to Puisaye. He was heartened by the stance taken in Morbihan and considered the truce a mistake. It was clear evidence that the confederation was disintegrating. A unified network was what he had strived for and it needed to be sustained by activity, a truce meant inactivity. Furthermore, it undermined his insistence to the British that they would be landing in Brittany to join a strong and dynamic insurrection. The British Cabinet, however, had already noted the altered stance of the Comité and they were now receiving separate reports of strengthened republican defences along the coast facing the Channel Islands.[61]

Puisaye wanted to undermine the truce by sending messages to Charette and the Comité Central, as well as arranging a significant landing of arms. Messengers were available and the *Correspondance* was being supplied with very large quantities of arms and ammunition. On 15 February Tinténiac arrived in Jersey, he was to land with an advance pathfinder group of several émigrés, and some ammunition, and then join local chouans to support the main landing of arms and ammunition protected by 60 émigrés commanded by a Breton nobleman, Henri Baude de La Vieuville.[62] After the landings Tinténiac was to travel inland to meet the Comité Central and on his return Puisaye would lead a second landing that would not only bring many more arms and munitions but also several thousand troops. Puisaye felt that this needed to take place by 4 April, the equinox. The parties were meant to leave Jersey quickly, after a few days preparation, but Tinténiac only sailed on 27 February, with La Vieuville to follow on 4 March.

---

60 Jacques-Philippe Champagnac, *Quiberon La répression et la vengeance* (Paris: Perrin, 1989), p.262.

61 Hutt, *Chouannerie*, pp.196–197.

62 Hutt, *Chouannerie*, pp.198–200, 203.

When Tinténiac reached the shore near Erquy on the night of 1 to 2 March his party was immediately intercepted by republican troops. Some of them were captured with letters revealing the royalist plans, but others managed to get away, including Tinténiac who made his way to Boishardy's headquarters. He arranged for 1,500 chouans to gather just north of Saint-Quay-Portrieux on 4 March, ready for La Vieuville's landing. The latter left Jersey early the next day but only reached the prearranged landing point in the afternoon of 6 March. It was foggy, the sea was rough, and there were no chouans. As three republican gunboats appeared, La Vieuville turned back. The chouans, only a third of them armed with muskets, had already been dispersed when attacked at daybreak the day before. The first phase of Puisaye's scheme had failed with the émigré volunteers and the chouans blaming each other for the failure.[63]

Tinténiac found the Comité Central disillusioned, despite Puisaye's inflated promises of aid. Their disappointment only worsened when, on 15 March, another attempted landing was abandoned due to republican activity. La Vieuville's third attempt similarly failed on 13 April for the same reason.[64] A variety of views emerged at the meeting on 30 March, with some of the chiefs assuring Tinténiac that they were only agreeing to peace in the face of the prevailing circumstances. Peace talks began at the manoir de La Mabilais and a treaty was signed there on 20 April. The differences of opinion, however, meant only 20 chouan chiefs, led by Cormatin and Boishardy, agreed to the deal and, significantly, all the chiefs from Morbihan refused to sign. Nevertheless, the writing was on the wall. Soon afterwards, Stofflet was forced to make a similar agreement in the Vendée after Canclaux had been able to turn all his attention against him when Charette had become inactive.

In Britain the prospects of a successful intervention appeared to be slipping away, both the Vendéens and chouans seemed to have lost heart and given up. However, Puisaye remained enthusiastic about his project and he was buoyed greatly by Tinténiac's arrival in London on 27 April.[65] The news was positive, Charette was ready to take up arms again as he had only sought peace due to a lack of gunpowder and had not realised how strong the chouans were. Many of the chouans were determined to continue the fight, especially in Morbihan, where new leaders were emerging such as Georges Cadoudal. Based in the Auray region, where he had been born, the son of a comparatively well-off labourer, he had been soundly educated and had initially regarded the Revolution with enthusiasm. However, disillusioned by the laws against the clergy and conscription, he joined the Vendéens, leading a company of Bretons, and after the defeat at Savenay he returned to Morbihan where, aged 24, he quickly established himself as a leading commander.

Despite the peace, violence in Brittany continued as old and new enmities continued and, on the grounds that the chouan leaders were suspected of bad faith, orders were issued for Cormatin's arrest on 25 May and a series of

63 Hutt, *Chouannerie*, p.217.
64 Hutt, *Chouannerie*, p.221.
65 Hutt, *Chouannerie*, p.223.

co-ordinated attacks were made on the chouans.[66] The republicans' strategy had succeeded to pressurise the chouan leadership and then split them with negotiations. The network that Puisaye had constructed was severely damaged.

It was not just republicans who were acting to undermine Puisaye's projects, at the end of April the Agence de Paris made contact with chouans around Rennes. Soon rumours circulated that the British only wanted to promote a civil war in France for their own purposes and were plotting, with Puisaye, to place 'an English prince on the throne of France.'[67] Charette was encouraged to stop contact with duplicitous Britain and correspond directly with Spain. Such whisperings may have gained traction due to demoralisation in the royalist ranks and Puisaye was to blame much on the agency's influence, but it is unclear how effective it really was. It was the republican strategy that was giving them the upper hand and pressure was maintained through attacks such as that in which Boishardy was killed on the night of 16 to 17 June. However, chouannerie's inherent lack of structure meant the movement was not defeated, it was simply being reduced to its original form. Puisaye's model for making it more effective was in jeopardy.

66 Veuillot, *Les Guerres de La Vendée et de La Bretagne*, p.366. Different sources give the date of his arrest as 26 or 27 May, he remained imprisoned until 28 October 1802.

67 Hutt, *Chouannerie*, p.261.

3

Plans

Evolution

The purpose of the émigré and British expedition to Brittany is often misunderstood or misconstrued. Lord Grenville stated it clearly in a letter, dated 8 June 1795, to William Wickham, the British chargé d'affaires in Switzerland. He first explained that reports indicated that chiefs in Brittany and the Vendée were ready to renew their struggle.

> It has therefore been determined to collect a pretty large supply of military stores of various kinds, and to attempt to land this in Brittany, under the escort of about 3000 men being the whole of the Emigré Corps of different descriptions which are now in England ... There is ... great reason to hope that ... these men with the supplies will be landed at the place agreed upon, without even any considerable opposition, and should this be the case they will be immediately followed by about 2000 more troops of a similar description who will have been brought from the Continent with that view.
>
> The nature of such a force landed in a friendly country is evidently such as to admit of great immediate extension, & there seems therefore much reason to hope that if the dispositions should continue the same this may be the signal for a general rising in those Provinces, in which case further measures would be adopted here for supporting them with a more considerable and more regular force.[1]

This intervention was to be part of a broader strategy of concentric attacks on France. Austria, provided with a subsidy, was to cross the Rhine, the émigré Armée de Condé in the lead, and drive through Franche-Comté towards Lyons where another uprising would be fostered. Wickham was charged with supporting and providing money for the royalists at Lyons and the surrounding regions, as well as to the Prince de Condé. These operations were to coincide with invasions by Piedmontese forces into Provence and the

1 TNA: FO 74/9, and reproduced in William Wickham (ed.), *The Correspondence of the Right Honourable William Wickham from the year 1794* (London: Richard Bentley, 1870), vol.I, p.83.

Spanish across the Pyrenean border. Although little was really expected from these last thrusts, three units of French émigrés serving in the Spanish Army – the légion royale des Pyrénées (or Saint-Simon), bataillon de la Reine and bataillon de la Frontière (or Vallespir) – had been gathered at Cádiz in May 1795. An anonymous émigré reported, 'The opinions on our destination do not agree; some detach us to La Vendee, whilst others embark us for St. Domingo. We most earnestly wish to be destined for the former, ... that we shall soon be able to return to our native land.'[2]

Puisaye may have considered himself as the plan's author, but it had evolved with advice and warnings from others, some with different agendas than his, and the final decision rested with the British Cabinet. The Marquis du Dresnay, writing to Moira on 8 January 1794, had provided his '... ideas on the three landing points which seem ... to me to offer in Brittany the most facility and advantage.' His principal recommendation was Quiberon Bay, having many suitable landing places and offering ready access to support from and communication with Charette. Furthermore, he felt the substantial ports of Lorient and Port Louis could be secured with comparative ease. On the other hand, he recognised that considerable naval forces would be required to support such an operation in the bay. The other points he suggested, which he considered only suitable for smaller operations, were on the north coast between Morlaix and Saint-Brieuc; he considered an attempt on Saint-Malo as impracticable.[3]

In the following May Puisaye had sketched out a plan for a landing of 5,000–6,000 troops, with considerable supplies, to sustain a general insurrection and the capture of Rennes. Perhaps with this in mind a few months later the government had asked for the opinions of some leading military officers on such an operation on Brittany's north coast. One was Louis-François Carlet de La Rozière, a respected senior French officer who not only had experience of planning for both the defence of Brittany and an invasion of the Channel Islands and England, but also of command at Saint-Malo. He supported the concept of attacking France as part of a wider concerted strategy but opposed operations on the coasts of the English Channel in winter.[4]

General Cornwallis also provided his opinion and it was particularly valued. At this stage, he had recently returned from India and been considered as a replacement for the Duke of York as commander-in-chief in the Netherlands; as has been mentioned, the following February he was to be appointed Master-General of the Ordnance and so have a seat in Cabinet. Although he supported the strategy of intervention, his experience had taught him to be wary. During the American War of Independence, the last major conflict that involved the British Army, he had commanded a force of regular British Army units sent to Georgia, in December 1778, to inspire loyalists in the southern states to rally to the Crown in such numbers as

2 Report dated Cádiz, 3 June, *The Kentish Weekly Post*, 7 July 1795; also see Grouvel, *Les corps de troupes*, vol.III, pp.313–333.

3 TNA: WO 1/175: letter of 8 January 1794.

4 TNA: WO 1/392: 'Opinion of M De La Roziere, relative to the project of a partial operation on the coasts of France' 15 September 1794.

to gain victory. Loyalist support did not materialise in the expected scale and the British force was too small to secure victory alone. The campaign was a strategic failure and led directly to Cornwallis surrendering to the Franco-American army at Yorktown. As a result, he had two preconditions for sending British troops: the local rising should already be strong and active, and the troops should be in sufficient number, and fully equipped, to operate alone should the necessity arise. Furthermore, having consulted the Admiralty, he discounted any such operation succeeding on the north coast of Brittany in the winter. He was to write, 'I perfectly agree with Lord Moira, in thinking that, if our account of the strength of the Royalists is correct, and not exaggerated, that it would require at least 20,000 good British troops to undertake any solid operations in France, and indeed a much larger body would be required to afford any sanguine hopes of success.'[5]

Despite the advice, Pitt appears to have thought Puisaye's suggestion, which required so few troops, had merit but Dundas was more cautious: 'It will require that this proposition [should] be very distinctly explained and understood before we could venture to send five or six thousand of our troops on such an adventure.'[6] As a result, Puisaye was asked to submit his proposal in writing. He did so on 3 October. He began with a long description of the situation in Brittany, past and present, suggesting that he commanded almost all of the province with 30,000 permanent chouans and another 40,000 men who would turn out for local action, if paid, while half of the 20,000 republicans would desert for food and pay. The only reason that he had had to rely on guerrilla actions was the shortage of arms and ammunition and the inability to feed large numbers. It would have been irresponsible for him to have called for a general insurrection unless success could be guaranteed.[7] He proposed landings on the north coast of Brittany in Saint-Brieuc Bay, which would be supported by 10,000 chouans gathered on the coast and offensives elsewhere, especially in Morbihan where a diversion would come from the sea. '... twenty thousand red coats distributed to the insurgents would show a hundred thousand. Let the actual force [of the expedition] be ten thousand men, not a single drop of blood would be spilled; that it is of six to seven thousand men will be perfectly sufficient.'[8] The force was to have a large staff and extra supporting arms, especially artillery, for the much larger army which would be quickly assembled from local men. Although not explicitly stated in his proposal, Puisaye countered criticism that was to follow in his memoirs by emphasising that he '... requested that the first expedition was solely formed by English troops; and that the émigrés in units [in contrast to those serving individually as officers with the chouans], were

---

5 Charles Ross (ed.), *Correspondence of Charles, First Marquis Cornwallis* (London: John Murray, 1859), vol.II, p.269. Marquess Cornwallis to Henry Dundas, private letter 14 September 1794,

6 TNA: PRO 30/8/157/180: Dundas to Pitt 24 September 1794, ('showed' replaced by should).

7 British Library (BL): Add MS 7982: Puisaye 3 October 1794.

8 BL: Add MS 7982: Puisaye 3 October 1794 and reproduced in Joseph de Puisaye, *Mémoires du Comte de Puisaye qui pourront servir l'histoire du parti royaliste français durant la dernière révolution* (London: Cox, Fils et Baylis, 1803–1808), vol.III, p.60.

kept back for the time …' for when success was secured.[9] Finally he pressed for the expedition to be launched soon because '… the time will never be as favourable'.[10]

The operational section of Puisaye's report was considered too scant for proper consideration, so he had to submit another memorandum which he did on 18 October. This time he went into meticulous detail; specifying the type of units that would form the expedition, of around 10,000 men, and that the landing force would be formed into three divisions of exactly equal numbers. The republicans would be deceived as to the true landing points as émigrés at Jersey, especially priests from Morbihan, would embark on frigates for a diversion in that area, while the three landing forces would come from Jersey, Guernsey, and the open sea.[11] Those from the islands would come on shore at Yffiniac, at the head of Saint-Brieuc Bay, and Pléneuf-Val-André, further to the east while the other would take Saint-Brieuc itself, all supported by gunboats and frigates as well as '… the insurrection of the inhabitants of the coast, and by the spiking of the cannons in the batteries, or their being thrown into the sea.'[12] He continued by assuring those reading his plan that:

> The sea is generally good in these vicinities. It is only before and after the equinoxes that it becomes rougher, which would render the operation more difficult in the spring than in the winter, when the length of the nights again presents a greater advantage. … As soon as everything is ready, and the wind is favourable, the embarkations will be done in such a way that the artillery (destined for the royalists) can be disembarked during the night, on three points, and that the batteries which are to protect [the landing] from the landward side would be ready to play at the break of day; there will be nothing to fear from the forts. … It is certain that embarkation and disembarkation are easy (for small vessels) on all this coast.[13]

If such plans for a landing were, at best ill-conceived and naïve, the assurances about the conditions on the coast were so reckless that when the plan became known to the area's republican authorities, they concluded that the idea either came from someone who had no idea of 'their savage coast' or it was simply a ploy to hide the true landing point.[14]

Puisaye continued by providing a detailed step-by-step schedule for the operation to take Rennes which he regarded as not only simple but also 'the event which is to decide the fate of Brittany.'[15] Having advanced inland from the coast and been joined by chouans, on day four, two columns would march, from their respective starting points, 34 and 26 kilometres on Rennes which would fall so easily that 'there will not even be the need to raise a battery.'[16]

9 Puisaye, *Mémoires*, vol.III, p.73.
10 Puisaye, *Mémoires*, vol.III, p.72.
11 Puisaye, *Mémoires*, vol.III, pp.78–81.
12 Puisaye, *Mémoires*, vol.III, p.82.
13 Puisaye, *Mémoires*, vol.III, pp.83–84.
14 Hutt, *Chouannerie*, p.138.
15 Puisaye, *Mémoires*, vol.III, p.86.
16 Puisaye, *Mémoires*, vol.III, p.87.

The city taken, the Armée royale, equipped from captured supplies, would advance: Saint-Malo would fall without a shot, perhaps Nantes would follow and isolated republican forces would be easily mopped up. The royalist forces, in three equal divisions, would form a cordon along the borders of Brittany before emerging, in spring, from this secure base to achieve the counter-revolution. As Puisaye grandly wrote, 'It is time to convince ourselves that it is only by thinking of and executing great ventures that one can boast of achieving decisive success.'[17]

On reading Puisaye's plan Cornwallis wrote that he could not '… recommend our landing ten thousand men on an open Beach, in order to create an insurrection in France, because I did not conceive that there was a chance of our succeeding.'[18] Moira not only read the plans but also spoke to Puisaye before submitting his conclusions to Dundas.[19] He began by pointing out that he had already stated he would need 20,000 'good quality' men 'upon the expressed condition that we were in the first instance to join an embodied Force of Royalists and to be by them secured in disembarking the Artillery & Stores' while, in fact, this plan envisaged him landing with half that number not to join 'an Army actually existing' but, despite Puisaye's assurance otherwise, 'to give the Royalists encouragement & opportunity to rise.' He considered that the 'scheme does not carry with it any reasonable chance of success' before carefully and incisively criticising every part of the plan. In particular, Moira had serious doubts about how much support the chouans would provide given their previous record; 'They did not assemble to any considerable amount either when the Army of the Vendée approached St Malo with a tide of success which might have tempted the Bretons to join in the enterprise, or when the calamities of that Royalist Army called the most urgently for succour.' Unlike the Vendéens, he recognised that the chouans had not entered the field as organised formations but had waged guerrilla warfare; 'This is the War which Peasants make against the immediate disturbers of their Families: But it does not follow that those Peasants would quit their families to submit themselves to the discipline & restraints of an Army acting from a more distant impulse.' He also could not ignore that Puisaye now claimed much greater numbers than he had previously reported without any 'assignable cause for the augmentation.' He concluded, 'In my best judgement, the enterprise cannot be attempted without knowingly staking the sacrifice of the whole Corps employed.' Then he made some telling observations about the man who had formed the plan:

> M. de Puisaye appears to me a clear & sensible, as well as enterprising man: But he does not seem conversant with those principles of patient progress with which Large Bodies encumbered with Stores & Artillery must be obliged to content themselves. He probably is satisfied of the practicability of all that he recommends, and persuades himself that he can command all the Forces with which he promises to support us. It must not, however, be wholly overlooked

17 Puisaye, *Mémoires*, vol.III, p.96.

18 BL: Add MS 37874: Cornwallis to Windham 30 October 1794.

19 TNA: PRO 30/8/160: Moira to Dundas, 5 December 1794.

> that M. de Puisaye is interested to counsel this effort at all hazards. Without it, his situation is desperate. If it succeeds, it is to give him an opening to great distinction & probably splendid fortune. If it fails, he is not by the disaster into which he has led his Allies in worse circumstances that those which now oppress him.[20]

Moira's report in hand, the British Government decided the more pressing need was to send 'an immediate and effectual reinforcement' to the West Indies.[21] The project of sending troops to western France was not, however, rejected but postponed. Puisaye was of course disappointed and somewhat petulantly demanded that he be returned 'with two thousand Frenchmen … and some cannon on the coast of Brittany and I undertake to subdue the province in six weeks' time.'[22]

In early February the plans submitted by the Comité Central eventually arrived in London. The earliest, from 16 November, broadly followed Puisaye's proposals with three points of attack: a feint on Vannes by a landing of 2,000 troops and another on Saint-Malo which was expected to capitulate on the very appearance of the ships.[23] The principal landing was to be near Saint-Brieuc where the chouans were considered actively supportive. Also, all the troops, except for those arriving off Saint-Malo, were by implication expected to be British. The second plan from the 20 December meeting reflected its mood, it simply demanded that Puisaye returned with 'a first landing, composed absolutely of twelve thousand men' to come ashore at a point between Saint-Brieuc and Saint-Lunaire, just west of Saint-Malo. Arms and munitions would have to come, soon followed by a French prince and 'The French corps in English pay.' It was clear that the leaders were unsure of the level of support the chouans could provide. In the November plan they declared they would take no action until the British appeared when; 'We will join them, we will unite with them; and we will assure their disembarkation.'[24] While by December the first 'twelve thousand men' who arrived were to secure, even by assault, their own landing.[25] It was clear that the troops landing on the Côtes-du-Nord would not be joining a strong and dynamic insurrection, as originally envisaged.

These views and Puisaye's plans to land supplies under La Vieuville and then arrive himself with not only considerably more arms and munitions but also troops, was a significant stage in the evolution of the plans for the intervention in northwest France. Now, (1) the landings were no longer to support an ongoing insurrection but to ignite one; (2) a port did not have to be secured before, or even in the first phase, of the operation; (3) the troops

20 TNA: PRO 30/8/160: Moira to Dundas, 5 December 1794.

21 Arthur Aspinall (ed.), *The Later Correspondence of George III, 1793–1810* (Cambridge: Cambridge University Press, 1962–1970), volume.II, p.282, Henry Dundas to George III, 15 December 1794.

22 BL: Add MS 37857: Puisaye to Windham 18 December 1794.

23 Puisaye, *Mémoires*, vol.IV, pp.206–207.

24 Puisaye, *Mémoires*, vol.IV, p.205.

25 Puisaye, *Mémoires*, vol.IV, pp.194–199, specifically 'Ce débarquement se fera de vive force, …', p.199.

to be used were émigrés, men who had gathered in the Channel Islands and white cockade units raised under the Act of May 1794 (see below for their formation) and (4) the number of troops required was very much reduced.

Puisaye had shifted his position, apparently as he became more anxious that a landing would not take place at all. In February he wrote that all he needed to succeed was some white cockade infantry, the Régiment d'Hervilly and the 'additional company' of the Régiment d'Hector, the half-battalion of Emigrant Artillery (Rotalier's) and 'two thousand English cavalry and I answer that we will hold onto Brittany'.[26] His reference to 'English cavalry' is confusing and cannot be taken literally, as when he claimed in his memoirs that Pitt had promised them to him he wrote, '... four thousand men of the best cavalry in Europe. Those who recall the services of the chasseurs of Béon, Damas, Rohan, Salm, etc, and who know the composition of the English cavalry, and the manner with which it is mounted, know enough that this compliment then had nothing of exaggeration.'[27] Although paid and equipped by Britain, the units he listed were émigré or foreign units. His expectations were reduced still further and his request for cavalry abandoned, when on 26 April, while pressing for urgent action, he declared that 'three thousand Frenchmen organised as cadres, with artillery, some pontoons and 5 to 600 horses will put under arms an army of 100 thousand men.'[28]

A briefing note written at the end of April, apparently in the hand of William Windham, the Secretary at War, provides clarification as to what the expedition was conceived to look like and how it was to be commanded.[29] The troops were to be made up of various elements, or divisions, the first being the white cockade units in England – the Régiment d'Hervilly (1,100 men), those of Dresnay and Hector with Rotalier's artillery (1,000 in all) – and the second 2,000 of the 'French Corps' to be brought from Germany. A third element were 600 men from the Channel Islands, which could only be the cadre corps (see below for their formation and composition). The troops from Germany were to 'be all brought away together' and then, subject to the availability of transports, join, without disembarking, the rest of the force in sailing from Spithead under a naval escort. Immediately the expedition was to divide in two, one half being formed of the Dresnay, Hector and Rotalier regiments, along with half of those from Germany, and the transports for the corps in the Channel Islands (although it was noted these last ships could have sailed ahead). They were 'to go under a strong escort of frigates to those islands and to proceed from thence to a descent at St Cast, St Brieux or whatever other point on this Coast should be thought best.' The Régiment d'Hervilly, with the other 1,000 from Germany, was to proceed to Morbihan. It is not stated what was to be done there, but clearly the troops were to land, as it was additionally noted 'that with this part of the armament it is desirable that there should be a Regiment of Cavalry.' This was likely to be a foreign

26 BL: Add MS 37858: Puisaye to Windham 14 February 1795. See below for details of the units mentioned.
27 Puisaye, *Mémoires*, vol.IV, pp.414–415.
28 BL: Add MS 37858: Puisaye to Windham 26 April.
29 BL: Add MS 37858: unsigned, April.

unit as it continues that the British one that might have been sent was no longer available. The question of who was to command was then dealt with: 'The command of the whole can be given to no one, I conceive, but M. de M. [Puisaye] with a commission from hence in conjunction with one which he has already from the Princes. The separate command to the Morbihan, in which will be one Regiment, may be safely trusted to D'Hervilly.'

However, very soon the British Government decided to switch to the landing being made in Quiberon Bay. There were a number of reasons for this; in the short term the chouans in Morbihan had shown themselves to be more determined and effective, so promising a more successful outcome for any landing, and also reports were being received that Charette and Stofflet were now active again. Indeed Charette, on 30 April, wrote asking for support, 'I would like 2,000 armed Frenchmen to be landed ... in the course of June ... on the St Jean du Mont coast. [Let them bring] powder and saltpetre, but I don't need any arms; a fortnight's warning and I'll be ready.'[30] In the longer term, the Royal Navy and transport service would be better able to supply, support and protect troops and operations in the bay than on the north coast. The ability to do so had been illustrated by the capture of Belle-Île in 1761 and its retention for almost two years, during the Seven Years' War, possession only being relinquished under the terms of the Treaty of Paris.[31]

Puisaye, however, was reluctant to completely abandon the prospect of operations on the Côtes-du-Nord, as envisaged in his original plan, and which was closer to the power base he had striven to construct. So, he proposed that the cadre units in the Channel Islands should operate against the adjacent coast; these were, however, to be demonstrations and not the landings he had previously wanted. Finally, on 12 May, a messenger landed on the north coast of Brittany, sent to tell the chouans of Morbihan that a landing would take place within the month.

The Émigré Units: Cadre Corps

Grenville, in his letter of 8 June 1795, told Wickham that 'the whole of the Emigré Corps of different descriptions which are now in England' would be used as an escort for the military stores to be landed in Brittany.[32] The units were the Loyal Emigrants, three white cockade infantry regiments, and the half-battalion of French Emigrant Artillery commanded by Lieutenant Colonel Pierre-Alexis Petitjean Comte de Rotalier. Other units were to assist in the wider operation including the cadre corps, then in the Channel Islands, that had been raised for a particular purpose and so had organisations to match.

In August 1794 colonels were appointed to form the new white cockade regiments, one of whom was the Marquis du Dresnay and it was intended

30 BL: Add MS 37859: reported by Tinténiac 30 April, cited in Hutt, *Chouannerie*, p.227.

31 Fortescue, *British Army*, Vol.II, pp.530–531 for its capture.

32 TNA: FO 74/9, and reproduced in Wickham (ed.), *The Correspondence*, vol.I, p.83.

that his corps on Jersey would simply be converted to one of them. It was to have the same organisation as the others but 'that the Gentlemen now serving in that Corps are to be formed into distinct Companies and ... should retain their allowance of one Shilling per Diem.'[33] However the émigré gentlemen were not happy to join such a regiment as rank and file and Louis-Jean-David Comte du Trésor de Bactot, who had assisted Dresnay on Jersey, was not unsympathetic when he described them as 'raised in fortune, used to the luxuries of life, accustomed to only serve in the different officer grades ... physically incapable to support the role of soldier, the fatigues and work that comes with it.'[34] They petitioned the island's governor objecting to serving alongside men recruited from prisons (see below) and stating their wish to either remain on Jersey to assist in its defence or land in France. Thus, two *compagnies franches* (free companies) remained on Jersey when several of their number joined Dresnay in England, as officers and NCOs in his new regiment.[35]

In December, as a response, the British Government appointed Alexandre-Louis-Auguste de Rohan-Chabot Prince de Léon, formerly *colonel* attached to the Royal-Piémont cavalry, and Trésor to form two new corps on Jersey. The number of French émigré gentlemen in the Channel Island was growing as the situation in northern Europe worsened for them, especially after the fall of the United Provinces. The corps were, in time, to attract men from different French provinces, although never officially designated to do so. Bretons, who were particularly noted as wishing to remain together, joined Léon, whose family, the Rohan, claimed a lineage stretching back to the first Kings of Brittany, while those from other provinces, notably Normandy, Anjou and Poitou, tended to join Trésor, who was himself Norman.

On 14 February 1795 Puisaye submitted a plan to Windham for the organisation and deployment of these corps as well as another two, to be commanded by two *maréchaux de camp*, Marie-Gabriel-Eléonore Comte d'Oilliamson and Armand-Jean Comte d'Allonville, who were appointed 1 May 1795.[36] Oilliamson, who Puisaye described as his 'particular friend', was descended from a Scottish archer of the guard of King Charles VIII of France, Timothy Williamson, who had settled in Normandy in 1495; he reverted to using the original version of the family name while an émigré.[37] Williamson organised his corps on Guernsey, with a substantial number of men coming from Germany, where Allonville organised his corps, resulting in part of Williamson's and all of Allonville's corps not being available for the forthcoming operations.

33 TNA: WO 6/131: Henry Dundas to Lord Amherst 10 August 1794.

34 TNA: HO 69/23: Memo of 25 August 1794, he continued by acknowledging their commitment to revenge their king and the sacrifices that they had already made to the cause. Du Trésor had formerly been formerly *colonel* commanding the Lorraine dragoons and was appointed *maréchal de camp* in 1792.

35 Anon (ed.), *Olivier d'Argens*, pp.56, 59; TNA: WO 4/155: Windham to du Dresnay 2 December 1794.

36 Grouvel, *Les corps de troupes*, vol.I, p.171.

37 Puisaye, *Mémoires*, vol.V, p.106 and Gérard de Contades, *Notice sur la Commune de Lonlay-le-Tesson* (Paris: Champion, 1881), p.115.

As to be expected from Puisaye, his plan was very precise, detailed and built upon optimism. The corps were each to be a battalion, with a staff and four companies each of 78 émigrés. The companies were to consist of three officers, a *sergent-major*, a *fourrier* (quartermaster), two *sergents*, five *caporaux*, five *appointés* (equivalent to lance-corporals or chosen men), 60 *volontaires* and a *tambour* (drummer).[38] The members of the corps were to provide the officers and senior NCOs to the army which would be formed of the chouans and other peasants who would come to join the émigrés once they had landed in France, hence the name cadre corps. Each corps was to provide the cadre for a brigade, each company that for a regiment of two battalions of five companies each, and an artillery detachment, following the French organisation of 1788.[39]

Table 1: Examples of ranks in the cadre corps and projected brigades.

Rank in Cadre Corps	Rank in projected Brigade
Major commandant	*Maréchal de camp*
Aide-major	*Adjudant général (colonel)*
Capitaine	*Colonel*
Sous-lieutenant	*Major*
Sergent-major	*Capitaine* (artillery)
Fourrier	*Quartier-maître trésorier (capitaine)*
Sergent	*Aide-major (capitaine)*
Caporal & Appointé	*Capitaine* (commanding a company)
Volontaire	*Capitaine en second* to *Sergent*
Tambour	*Tambour major*

Under Puisaye's plan, each of the companies formed in France would each have 119 officers and men, and each brigade 4,812 so, in all, a force of 19,248 would be formed.[40] This presupposed three things: chouans would flock to serve under the émigrés; they would be prepared to serve even outside their region as troops of the line; and émigrés would volunteer.[41]

Who were the volunteers in these corps, expecting to be officers in France? In April 1795 a list was prepared of 220 volunteers in Léon's corps showing their ages and previous service, for all bar 11 of them. They aged from 15 to 63 years old and only 20 had no previous service experience at all, however the largest proportion of those that had, gave their previous military service as having been in the 1792 campaign and so, by implication, none before that. There is nothing to indicate that the profile of the volunteers of the other corps was any different.

38 Puisaye, *Mémoires*, vol.V, p.50.
39 Puisaye, *Mémoires*, vol.V, p.53.
40 Puisaye, *Mémoires*, vol.V, pp.46–58.
41 Hutt, *Chouannerie*, p.214.

Table 2: 'List of Private Gentlemen in the Prince de Leon's Corps, April 1795'[42]

Ages	Army Officer	Naval Officer	Other & Unspecified Service	*Elèves* (pupils)	Loyal Emigrants	1792	No previous service	Total
15–19	0	0	0	1	0	8	9	18
20–24	6	1	2	2	2	25	1	39
25–29	9	1	4	1	0	21	2	38
30–34	7	4	4	0	0	9	3	27
35–39	7	0	12	0	0	9	0	28
40–44	7	1	6	2	0	8	2	26
45–49	1	0	3	0	0	4	0	8
50–54	0	0	2	0	0	10	2	14
55–59	1	0	3	0	0	2	0	6
60–64	3	0	1	0	0	1	1	6
Total	41	7	37	6	2	97	20	210

Those shown in Table 2 as former army officers comprise of 31 from the infantry, eight from the cavalry and two Grenadiers Royaux (picked militia units). Three of the *élèves* had trained for the artillery and the other three for the *marine* (navy). Among those whose service is 'other & unspecified' were three officers of the Gardes Côtes (Coast Guard), two who had served in the Chevau-légers, and another in the Garde du corps du roi, others had been in the civil and judicial service.[43]

Although Léon was appointed on 6 December 1794, the first of his staff 19 days later, and Trésor on 25 December, all other appointments were only made in March 1795, indicating that this was when the corps began to be formed.[44] Soon some pressure, even if only by the implied threat below, was apparently considered necessary to get émigrés in England to join the corps as shown by a report in *The Sun*, a government newspaper:

> The Committee for the French emigrants here, has, we understand, received an intimation from Government, that such of them as are capable of bearing arms, and who will not enlist in the new regiments preparing at Guernsey, shall not receive any further assistance. It is even said, that the alien bill will be applied to those who, young and robust, shall refuse to take arms.[45]

There was, in effect, little time for these units to organise and train before being committed to operations in France in the summer of 1795.

The Émigré Units: Infantry

The infantry destined to sail from England and land in France consisted of the Loyal Emigrants and three white cockade regiments; those of Dresnay,

42 TNA: WO 12/11950.
43 TNA WO 12/11950: 'List of Private Gentlemen in the Prince de Leon's Corps, April 1795.'
44 TNA: WO 12/11950 (Léon); 12/11709 (Trésor) and 12/12034 (Williamson).
45 Reprinted in *The Caledonian Mercury*, 7 May 1795.

Hervilly and Hector. The Loyal Emigrant Regiment was a tried and tested unit. It had been raised in England and joined the British army in Belgium in May 1793. Over time different companies were added to the regiment, including one of veterans. Its men soon gained a distinguished reputation but at a heavy price. As victims of the law of 9 October 1792 if they were taken alive they would be executed, often swiftly and brutally, and no allied officer besieged by the French was to be permitted to include them when negotiating a surrender, they would have to be handed over to republican justice. In March 1794 the regiment had 44 officers and 1,220 other ranks, but suffered heavy losses in the next two months, particularly at the sortie from Menen and the siege of Nieuwpoort.[46] Hard service continued, often at the army's outposts, until the end of the campaign. So, on 9 April 1795, when the Loyal Emigrants embarked for England, there were just 34 officers, 34 sergeants, 15 drummers, 462 rank and file and 13 women.[47] The regiment sailed with the British infantry, considered as such, and so was one of the first units of the army to leave Germany. The convoy left Bremerlehe (now part of Bremerhaven) on 14 April, but it was to be several days before the ships went down river and sailed for England, arriving at Portsmouth on 9 May.[48] This gave it little time to recover or recruit before being committed to the new operations. It had been reduced not only by casualties and the wear and tear of the campaign, but also many of the young gentlemen volunteers had departed to take up more advantageous positions in other units, especially newly raised ones, so at this stage it contained a disproportionate number of veterans.

Although the three other regiments were formed under the same authority they each had very different identities. The white cockade infantry regiments were designated to be organised as the French royal army had been, with two battalions of nine companies – one of grenadiers and eight of fusiliers – each with 89, all ranks, and a regimental staff of 20. As the original intention to include an artillery detachment was soon dropped, the regiments were each to have, at full strength, 1,622 officers and men. The intention had been that all such regiments would be raised on the Continent or the Channel Islands, indeed they were only permitted to be on the British mainland in limited circumstances and they had to wear the black cockade while there. Nevertheless Dresnay, Hervilly and Hector were organised in England.

As has been seen, the Régiment du Dresnay was to have included the émigrés previously organised on Jersey by the colonel but that unit, for the most part, only provided some of the officers and NCOs. In the white cockade regiments, the colonel nominated the officers, so places went to members of his extended family and other members of the Breton nobility and many of the men were to come from the same province.

As with all the regiments, there were plenty of former officers who wished to serve in their previous station as well as suitable young gentlemen who wanted to be officers. The problem was obtaining recruits for the ranks. The

46 Grouvel, *Les corps de troupes*, vol.I, p.12.
47 BL: Add MS 46710: ff.207.
48 Reported in *The Caledonian Mercury*, 14 May 1795.

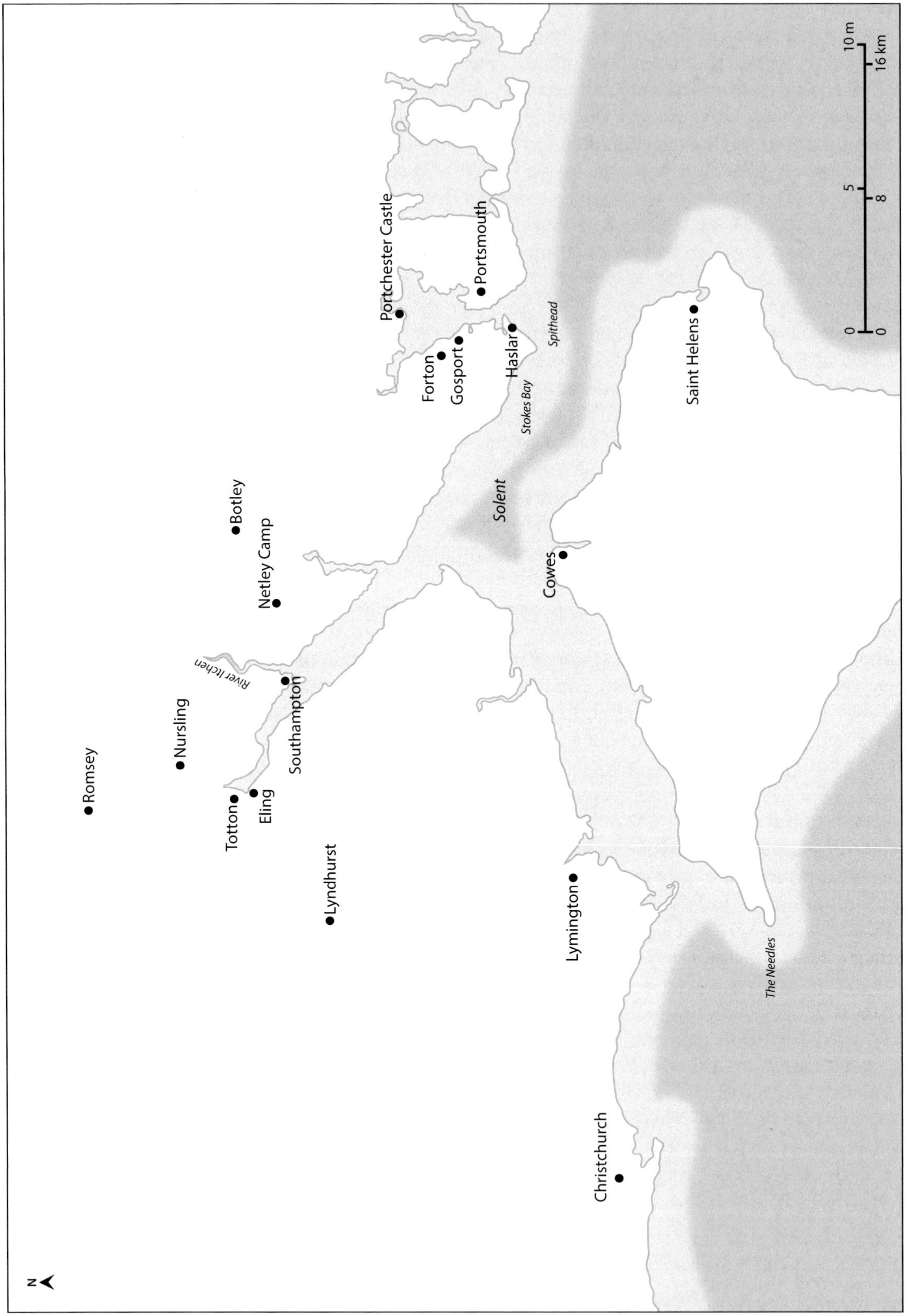

The Solent Region, England.

only Frenchmen readily available were deserters, either from the republican army or after having been taken as prisoners of war. Indeed, in Germany and the Netherlands, where the other such regiments were formed, it was noted that; 'A great many of the French Prisoners who were taken by the Prussians have been sold for a Louis each to the Emigrant Corps'.[49] In England a recruitment office was established in London, but the main source of men were the depots holding prisoners of war.[50]

Anne-René de la Motte de Montmuran, formerly a *lieutenant de vaisseau* in the French navy, *lieutenant* in the Régiment du Dresnay and an English speaker, was sent by his colonel to recruit at Portchester Castle, near Portsmouth. With him were officers from Hervilly and Hector as well as Charmilly, a corps raised for service in Haïti, he described his work in a letter to his sister:

> At the start of the night, all the recruiting officers assemble and enter the courtyard of the prison, then into a guardroom where the goalers bring the prisoners who wish to engage. Then one of the officers of the three first corps says very fine things to try to persuade the men to engage with them; then the officer from M de Charmilly also sells his merchandise by embellishing as much as he could, and he succeeded several times more than us, because the pay of the corps destined for America is much more than ours, ... Every day he takes out a few prisoners. The share is made equally between the three [white cockade] regiments.
>
> You can see that this type of life is not entertaining and is going to become still more tedious beginning from tomorrow. We will spend almost the whole day disguised in the office of one of the commissaries of the prison, who speaks French, and who, under the pretext of asking each prisoner if he received clothes, will pose to them afterwards several questions to learn if they wish to join the royalists; we will pretend to write, and the commissary will ask us in English what we think of the man who he come to question. After our response, he will have him led to a room assigned for such an opinion. We will have the pleasure to review in this manner about six thousand prisoners; but we thought that this was the means to speed up our recruitment.[51]

In a later letter he was able to tell her that he had 'sent to the regiment a certain number of good men and former soldiers' and so felt able to ask to be relieved from this duty.[52]

However, between 24 February and 24 April 1795 Dresnay received only 104 new recruits. The majority came from among prisoners of war; 43 from Portchester, 17 from Plymouth, 10 from Falmouth and nine from

---

49 TNA: WO 1/171: Craig to Nepean 10 November 1794. Dresnay, Hector and Hervilly also recruited in Germany but no recruits appear to have joined the regiment from there before the expedition.

50 In a report on rioting in London, it was stated 'The mob attacked also a recruiting office, destined for the reception of the French emigrants in Bride Lane.' *The Chester Chronicle*, 29 August 1794.

51 Letter of 26 January 1795 reproduced in Charles Robert, *1795 Expédition des Emigres à Quiberon Le Comte d'Artois à l'isle d'Yeu* (Paris: Lamulle & Poisson, 1899), pp.341–342.

52 Letter of 6 March 1795, Robert, *1795 Expédition*, p.342.

Portchester Castle.
(Author's collection)

Chatham. Twenty-three of the others were émigrés from France, several of whom were to be officers or senior NCOs, while two arrived from Spain. In all 53 of these recruits were Bretons and the rest came from other parts of France, except five from Caribbean islands and one from Portugal.[53] The task that Montmuran and his comrades faced at Portchester was not easy, with a Hampshire newspaper noting that 'an unabated spirit of republicanism seems to pervade the whole mass of light-hearted captives.'[54] A letter was later printed in *The Times* in which the writer described encountering some Dresnay recruits when travelling by coach to Southampton in May 1795 in which there,

> ... was also a French Recruiting Officer, who had under his care six or eight recruits going to join their Regiment, then laying at Romsey. These recruits were of such abandoned habits of principles, as to shock every passenger in the coach, and every individual we met, cursing the English nation, blasphemously ridiculing the existence of a Deity, and singing the most noted Republican songs. I could not avoid expressing to the Officer my surprise and indignation at his permitting them to continue such offensive behaviour; but after many efforts, they proved, as the Officer declared they were, incorrigible, and out of reach of subordination. He said he had picked them out of the prisons at Rochester and Chatham; that a great part of the corps to which he belonged was composed of such fellows; and although he admitted, it was not to be expected they could be converted to Royalism, or a faith in religion, yet it was necessary that his Regiment should be completed, which could not be affected without such assistance![55]

As the writer identified himself proudly as 'A True Englishman' the recruits were, perhaps, also having some fun at his expense.

53 TNA: WO 12/11708: 'Statement of the men arrived from 24 February to 24 April 1795.'
54 *The Hampshire Chronicle*, 19 January 1795.
55 *The Times*, 14 August 1795. The regiment was apparently Dresnay.

It should be recognised that recruitment of prisoners of war was common practice in all armies of the period and, indeed, the regulations for the white cockade regiments specified that the soldiers would be recruited from 'peasants, deserters and soldiers from the troops of the line.'[56] The émigré officers recognised that such men needed to be recruited as shown by a memorandum to the British Government advocating the formation of what was to be the Régiment d'Hector; 'To carry out the recruitment of this Corps with ease, it will be necessary to separate in the Prisons the Good from the bad, and above all to prevent as much as Possible, the forms and semblance of revolutionary proceedings which maintain better the spirit of revolt, licence and cruelty.'[57] Several later historians have indicated that the émigré colonels were against such recruitment but their correspondence does not support this view. Indeed, Dresnay expressed frustration when permission to recruit in the prisons was delayed by an oversight and Hervilly complained of what he considered as underhand recruiting practices at Chatham by those acting for 'Charmilly's Regiment.'[58]

Lieutenant Magloire Marquis de Coëtlosquet, of Dresnay, formerly an officer in the Gardes Françaises, was far from unhappy with the men,

> … we are infinitely satisfied with our soldiers; though they are recruited in the prisons. We have managed to set the thing on an excellent footing; discipline without being hard is severe, morale is good. We are committed to take some conscripted Bas-Bretons who were not imbued with bad principles; they are the example of the regiment, they are strongly religious and good royalists.[59]

In June 1795 the Régiment du Dresnay, under the command of its *lieutenant-colonel* René-Claude-Jérôme Comte de Talhouët-Grationnaye, a former infantry officer in the Régiment du Roi, comprised what was in effect a weak battalion. It had an understrength grenadier company with 59 grenadiers, and only 341 fusiliers, but almost all the positions for officers and senior NCOs were filled for two battalions.[60]

It was a similar situation in the Régiment d'Hector. In October 1794, Jean-Charles Comte d'Hector, *lieutenant général des armées navales*, was authorised to raise another white cockade regiment, as its colonel, his letter of service being back-dated to 1 August so it matched that of the other colonels. The officers of the new regiment were 'to be exclusively selected from belonging to the Royal Navy of France, and the Men from among the Sailors now Prisoners of War in this Country and the Crews of the French Ships which were brought away from Toulon who may be willing to engage

56 TNA: WO 24/1112: 'Article 3e, Règlement pour la levée des Corps Français à la solde de l'Angleterre.'

57 TNA: WO 1/392: memorandum of 8 September 1794.

58 TNA: HO 69/23: du Dresnay to Bouillon on 7 and 23 August 1794; HO 50/386: Hervilly, cited in War Office to John King at Chatham, 21 January 1795.

59 E.M.C., *Deux Victimes de Quiberon* (Vannes: La Foyle, 1895), p.13, letter to his aunt, Romsey 5 April 1795.

60 TNA: WO 12/11708: paylist for 25 June to 24 August 1795, the establishment was 72 soldiers per company.

in this Service.'[61] There are indications that it may have originally been intended for an artillery role, one being an early report that it was to be called the 'Corps of Cannoneers of the Marine.'[62] For this reason, and the nature of its cadre, the regiment was also known as 'la Marine royale', although in the forthcoming expedition it was to serve as infantry. Again, there was no shortage of suitable candidates for officers and NCOs, indeed Hector was authorised to add an additional volunteer company composed of former naval officers and *élèves de marine* from 1 November 1794.[63]

The process of recruiting men was extremely slow but *Capitaine* André-Marie Gouzillon Vicomte de Bélizal, in a letter to a friend on 13 March 1795, was able to say that the men were, '... very tranquil, apart from the mania for desertion; 8 men have again been captured yesterday evening'.[64] Bélizal, saw improvements in the men's behaviour by the end of the month, 'If one can count on outward appearances, a great change to their advantage has occurred in three weeks; that came perhaps through the exemplary punishments that have been inflicted. In this time three émigré priests along with our chaplain preach and hold lectures on religion. All the soldiers and officers attend them twice a day.'[65]

On 24 June 1795 the regiment had a full complement of officers, *sergents* and *caporaux* for its 19 companies but only 56 grenadiers, 299 fusiliers and 19 volunteers; 45 of the latter having left between 10 May and 12 June, mostly to take up positions in other units.[66] The regiment was effectively commanded by *Lieutenant-colonel* Claude-René Pâris Comte de Soulanges, a former *Chef d'escadre* (equivalent to rear admiral in the British Royal Navy).

The colonel of the last of the infantry regiments was the Comte d'Hervilly, who, as described above, had formerly commanded the cavalry of the Garde Constitutionnelle du Roi and gone to the defence of the Royal Family on 10 August 1792. After emigrating, he had served amongst a group of officers attached to Lord Moira's force, in '*sa troupe dorée*'.[67] In April 1794 he was already taking steps to recruit men who had arrived at Spithead in three French warships from Toulon – the *Pompée*, *Puissant* and *Arethuse* – as Moira ordered two transports to come 'to receive the Troops serving on Board the three French Ships, together with such of the Seamen & Emigrants as may be inclined to serve under his Lordship's Command.'[68] The men who were 'able & willing to enter into the land service' were three officers, 16 NCOs and 73

61 TNA: WO 6/131: Henry Dundas to Lord Amherst 16 October.

62 *The Kentish Gazette*, 30 September 1794.

63 Grouvel, *Les corps de troupes*, vol.I, p.134. It would seem to be this company that Puisaye wanted to use for a landing he referred to in his letter of 14 February 1795, mentioned above.

64 Vicomte de Gouzillon de Bélizal, 'Journal et Lettres d'un Émigré', *Revue de Bretagne*, vol. XXVII, January–February 1902, p.103, letter to James Frémaux 13 March 1795.

65 Gouzillon de Bélizal, 'Journal et Lettres', pp.105–106, letter to James Frémaux 30 March 1795. His wife was imprisoned until 1796, and prevented from communicating with her husband or children.

66 TNA: WO 12/11741: *contrôle nominatif* 25 April to 24 June 1794.

67 Quote from, Countess of Ilchester and Lord Stavordale (eds), *The Life and Letters of Lady Sarah Lennox 1745–1826* (London: John Murray, 1901), vol.II, pp.97–98, Lady Sarah Lennox to Lady Susan O'Brien, Southampton 10 June 1794.

68 TNA: WO 1/175: letters of Lord Moira, 18 April and Captain Hugh Christian 27 April 1794.

men from the Régiment Royal-Louis; five officers, 10 NCOs and 61 from the National Guard; two officers, 10 NCOs and 87 men of an independent company (Smith's) as well as 28 sailors and a marine 'in a regiment of foot' and four officers, 34 NCOs and 22 men of the marines along with nine NCOs and 22 men of the ship's gunners for the artillery.[69] When the French ships were brought into Portsmouth Harbour, ultimately to be taken into service with the Royal Navy, all the personnel were transferred to transports anchored in nearby Stokes Bay; one for the artillery, two for the Royal-Louis (and, presumably, the other infantry), and three for the sailors who declined to enter British land service.[70]

Days before the parliamentary bill for the raising of the white cockade units had its final reading Moira wrote to Evan Nepean, Dundas's undersecretary:

> If it be determined that d'Hervilly shall have a Corps, it would be eligible that you should privately signify it to him as soon as possible. The advantage is this; that he could immediately nominate three or four Officers ... those officers could immediately take charge of the Men who have entered into the Land Service ... One of those Officers would likewise be employed by him in examining the Prisoners, where there are very many Royalists who have been forced aboard ship & afterwards captured. With the balance of Prisoners so much in our favour it is desirable to employ such Men.[71]

Moira's recommendations were taken up quickly. The soldiers were landed and housed, east of Southampton, at what was to be called Netley Camp.[72] They were formed into four companies under François-Nicolas Junot Comte d'Atilly, formerly *colonel* of the 102e Régiment d'infanterie and then *adjutant général* in the Garde Constitutionnelle, who was later appointed *lieutenant-colonel* of the Régiment d'Hervilly.[73] By 10 June, 600 of 'the Toulonnese people' were enlisted 'into some French Corps here [Southampton].'[74]

Meanwhile the Chevalier de Saint Vincent, another French officer of Moira's staff and soon to be *capitaine* in the regiment, was sent to recruit amongst the prisoners held at Forton, a nearby depot at Gosport.[75] When the nomination of *colonels* for the new units was becoming more politically

---

69 TNA: WO 1/175: 'Return of Officers, Sailors & Seamen on board the French Ships, 27 April 1794.' Another return, in French, names the ship gunners as 'cannoniers bourgeois.'

70 TNA: WO 1/175: return of 15 May 1794.

71 TNA: WO 1/175: letter of 6 May 1794. Evan Nepean, whose name appears in much of the correspondence relating to this campaign, was an outstanding civil servant: Undersecretary at the Home Office 1 April 1782 to 11 July 1794, Undersecretary for War 11 July 1794 to 1 March 1795, and Secretary to the Board of Admiralty 3 March 1795 to 20 November 1804. Member of Parliament from 1796. R.G. Thorne 'Nepean, Evan (1752–1822) *The History of Parliament* <https://www.historyofparliamentonline.org/volume/1790-1820/member/nepean-evan-1752-1822>, accessed 13 October 2021.

72 The camp was not at modern day Netley, on Southampton Water, or the site used later for the Royal Victoria Hospital, but on the higher ground to the east, in the area known as Netley Common around the junction of Botley Road and the A27.

73 BL: Add MS 49088: return 1 June 1794, Netley.

74 Ilchester and Stavordale (eds), *The Life and Letters*, vol.II, pp.97–98, Lady Sarah Lennox to Lady Susan O'Brien, 10 June 1794.

75 TNA: WO 1/175: Moira to Nepean, 18 May 1794.

complicated, Moira explained that he had only given his recommendations when pressed to do so:

> I have named those whose activity I have remarked or whom I have heard mentioned by their Countrymen with general praise ... In the case of M. d'Hervilly whom I counselled you to nominate without further delay, the determination could not be erroneous. Because the universal testimony borne to the merit of that officer & the talents ... recommended him very peculiarly for the distinction ... I have mentioned French Officers to you entirely from their personal qualities. Against that recommendation may be set considerations of interest or local influence ...which can only be learned from the French ...[76]

The recruitment of the Régiment d'Hervilly continued amongst prisoners, like the others and with similar results. Indeed, Saint Vincent did not get 'more than twenty Men from Forton.'[77] However, it had also been decided that the rest of the Royal-Louis should be incorporated into the regiment, despite the protests of British commanders in the Mediterranean where detachments served as marines on British ships and in Corsica. Louis de Boisgelin, *capitaine* of grenadiers and the last commander of the Royal-Louis, observed that his regiment would not have deserved such treatment if it had been badly conducted or failed in its duty,

> ... one would never think that the first French Corps formed by England and which in the posts in which it found itself shared all the fatigues of His Majesty's troops, and suffered considerable losses that accompanied the service ... that this Corps says I, would be disbanded and merged into new Corps, which are not even formed nor trained. One cannot object to us due to our small number [as] we have ... more men than any of the new Corps, when we have more than Fifty men per Company, the ships newly arrived from Corsica provide me a certain means for our completion.[78]

Nevertheless, the merger continued, and Boisgelin was placed as a *capitaine* in the new regiment, which often used the name Royal-Louis. Despite this allusion the Régiment d'Hervilly was the most junior of the white cockade regiments, precedence determined by the seniority of the *colonel* in French service.

Lieutenant André-Louis-Lambert Baron Le Charron had been a junior infantry officer in the Régiment de Lorraine, *adjutant-major* in the Garde Constitutionnelle, and finally officer in the Loyal Emigrants, before joining the Régiment d'Hervilly. He was another who, while realistic, was content, with the state of his unit,

> ... our regiment, composed of officers of all arms, all ages, ranks and grades, with in all thirteen hundred soldiers assembled, for the most part unfortunately in the

76 TNA: WO 1/175: Moira to Nepean 9 June 1794.
77 TNA: WO 1/175: Moira to Nepean 2 June 1794.
78 TNA: WO 1/388: letter, presumably to Dundas, dated 11 December 1794.

> prisons of England, and among them there were many sailors, a type of men very difficult to train to drills and manoeuvres, became, despite these obstacles, and in a few months, by care, activity, justice and the presence of its commander, a model of discipline, subordination and instruction.[79]

After the expedition, Puisaye was to write of the Comte d'Hervilly,

> … the progress that he had made in the formation of his regiment, the assidous care that he gave to its instruction; always on the parade ground exercising his soldiers himself; and having managed to make it a corps which, for turn out, discipline, precision of drill, the cohesion and speed of movements, could march alongside the best troops of Europe …[80]

It was by far the largest unit on the expedition and, by 24 June 1795, was almost complete being only short of two officers, two NCOs, 53 *caporaux*, a drummer, two grenadiers and 184 fusiliers from its establishment of two battalions.[81]

The Émigré Units: Artillery and Engineers

In January 1794 French émigré artillery officers in British pay gathered at Ostend on the Belgian coast ready to join Moira's army when it landed in support of the Vendéens. On 8 April there were 78 of them, commanded by *Colonel* François-Charles de Quiefdeville de Belmesnil.[82] Meanwhile, as has been seen, gunners were being recruited on the south coast of England from the ships arriving from Toulon, under officers already with Moira and some who arrived from Ostend. Together they became the Corps of French Emigrant Artillery. Those with Quiefdeville forming an artillery cadre corps in Germany in June 1795 and those in England a half-battalion commanded by Lieutenant Colonel de Rotalier. The latter was organised at Lyndhurst and then Christchurch, and by June 1795 was close to full strength, with 12 field officers and staff. The four companies had, in total, 24 officers, 28 NCOs, 237 bombardiers and gunners, four drummers, four quarter master commissaries, 20 NCO 'conductors of horse,' 119 drivers, and seven craftsmen.[83] It was decided, apparently at the request of the unit's officers, that it should be equipped with French field pieces, 8- and 4-pounders, of the current Gribeauval system. For this captured pieces were obtained from Bruges by Major George Napier, Moira's deputy quartermaster general.[84]

---

79 André-Louis-Lambert Baron Le Charron, *Expédition de Quiberon, suivie de L'Évasion des Prisons de Vannes* (Paris: Ambroise Dupont et Roret, 1826), pp.127–128.

80 Puisaye, *Mémoires*, vol.VI, pp.10–11.

81 TNA: WO 12/11681: analysis of pay lists.

82 BL: Add MS 40634: pay list and account 21 January to 30 June 1794.

83 TNA: WO 10/281: pay lists.

84 Ilchester and Stavordale (eds), *The Life and Letters*, vol.II, pp.97–98. Lady Sarah Lennox to Lady Susan O'Brien 10 June 1794. Lady Sarah was Napier's wife. The Gribeauval system used the old French *livre*, or pound, which was 1.079 English pounds.

There was also a small Corps of French Engineers. Although several such officers had served with the Duke of York's army as well Moira's force it was only on 1 April 1795 that the corps was formed, commanded by Lieutenant Colonel François-Eugène Lenglé de Moriencourt with a major, five captains, six captain lieutenants and six lieutenants. All were to sail with the expedition except for Captain de Fouigeray who was detached for duty in the East Indies.[85] As with the British service, the artillery and engineers came under the direction of the Master of the Ordnance and Rotalier's half-battalion and the engineers, both organised in England, used British ranks and organisation, in contrast to the white cockade infantry regiments.

85 TNA: WO 54/702: list of corps and Grouvel, *Les corps de troupes*, vol.I, p.180.

4

Sailing

An Attack from the Channel Islands?

For some time newspapers in Britain had carried stories of troops being concentrated in the Channel Islands in preparation for an expedition to the northern coast of France. One, from December 1794, assured its readers it was not only British and émigré troops that were to be involved,

> Government, it is said, received official assurance, … the Empress [of Russia] will immediately furnish twelve sail of the line and twenty frigates, attended by a competent number of transports, on board of which twenty thousand men are to be embarked – their destination Guernsey and Jersey, where barracks are already erected; they are there to be joined by 15,000 English, 5,000 Irish troops, and all the armed Emigrants; the object of this armament is, so early as February or March, to make a powerful diversion on the coast of Normandy.[1]

Throughout the spring of 1795, stories continued that the white cockade regiments were to go to the Channels Islands for this purpose.[2] These were not simply conjecture as, on 25 May 1795, Henry Dundas informed the Duke of York, back in Britain and since 15 February Commander-in-Chief of the Army, that the Régiment du Dresnay and that of Hervilly should 'proceed to Southampton and embark for Guernsey' and Hector was to go to Jersey, transports being provided for this purpose.[3] Indeed, Hervilly's clothing and baggage was sent to Jersey and *Capitaine* de Séran arrived to make arrangements for the regiment's reception on the island.[4]

The Royal Navy gave weight to the stories. By 6 April 1795 a small squadron of three frigates under the command of Captain Sir Richard Strachan, in HMS *Melampus*, arrived at Jersey 'to repress the [republican] Gun & other

1 *The Northampton Mercury*, 6 December 1794.
2 For example, *The Hampshire Chronicle*, 23 March 1795.
3 TNA: WO 6/131: 25 May 1795.
4 TNA: FO 95/605: letter Bouillon to Windham 18 July 1795 and HO 69/13: memorial of the Vicomte de Séran 15 January 1795.

Armed Vessels …' and so assist communications with Brittany.[5] Another similar squadron, under Captain Sir William Sidney Smith in HMS *Diamond*, concentrated on the Normandy coast, from Cherbourg to Le Havre. Smith had received the command of the *Diamond* after his return from Toulon and on 28 March 1795 the ship was joined by a detachment from the Régiment d'Hector, under *Lieutenant* Armand-Nicolas-Charles Carrey d'Asnières and *Sous-lieutenant* François-Marie Le Bihannic de Tromenec, both experienced naval officers, with a *sergent-major*, a *caporal* and 32 *fusiliers* who 'were employed in Cannon and Sailing duties.'[6] These men were the first from a white cockade regiment to take part in active service.

The frigates' task was to harass the enemy and intercept supplies of war materials as well as food, which was reportedly in short supply. Strachan, joined by Smith, intercepted a convoy, on 9 May, which was moving southwards along the west coast of the Cotentin peninsula and that ran under a small battery covering the Plage de Surtainville. Strachan sent the frigates' boats to seize the vessels, which were soon abandoned by their crews, and, despite fire from the battery, two armed-vessels, each with three 18-pounders, and 10 merchantmen were captured.[7] The squadrons then separated and Smith, in company with HMS *Syren* and seven gun-vessels, sailed close into Saint-Malo, observing the ships in the port and raising their colours, 'fired a shot at the fort, which returned three without effect.'[8] A brig of war was chased westwards into the Baie de La Fresnaye, under the guns of Fort-la-Latte. As the pilots refused to take the frigates into the bay they engaged the fort while the ships' boats attacked the brig. Carrey d'Asnières remembered the action went on for two hours, without success as 'the arrival of troops of the line with cannon obliged us to retire.'[9]

Soon special instructions to keep republican attention on the north coast of Brittany, as well as that of Normandy, arrived and on 31 May Strachan passed them on to Smith who wrote with some glee, '… the plot begins to thicken and we shall have some fun ere long.'[10] Then, on 10 June, orders were issued to 'Count Williamson or the Officer Commanding the Emigrant Forces onboard the Ships under the Command of Capt. Sir R. Strachan.' The cadre corps were to embark, with their arms and baggage, on transports sent to Jersey and Guernsey for them and to head for the coast of Brittany or Normandy 'in order to create a Diversion and draw that attention of the Enemy to that Coast …' by making 'such demonstrations as may appear to be best adapted to those ends …' Strachan had discretion as to where they should go but give 'preference, if equally convenient, to the northern part of Bretagne [*sic*] …' It was emphasised that the force was 'in itself inadequate to any Military Operations on shore' but could land if a part of the coast was found to be

5 TNA: FO 95/605: Bouillon to Windham 6 April 1795.

6 TNA: WO 12/11741: pay lists and Archives Nationales, Paris (ANF): MAR/C/7/53: dossier 24, return of service by Carrey d'Asnières 18 January 1817.

7 *The London Gazette*, 12 May 1795 Strachan's report dated 11 May.

8 John Barrow, *The Life and Correspondence of Admiral Sir William Sidney Smith, GCB* (London: Richard Bentley, 1848), vol.I, p.169.

9 ANF: MAR/C/7/53: dossier 24, memorial of 10 July 1824.

10 TNA: HO 69/8: Smith to Bouillon 1 June 1795.

under the control of friendly forces but only on the condition 'they shall have the strongest assurances of finding upon getting on Shore such a cooperation from the interior parts of the provinces as will justify the attempt'. In such a case Strachan was instructed not to leave the coast, unless the squadron was endangered, 'to endeavour to afford the Troops ... every protection and assistance in your power.'[11] However, when Strachan received his instructions at Jersey no transports had arrived so he decided to sail to Guernsey to confer with Williamson. Delayed by the weather he only arrived at Guernsey on 22 June where he found '... the troops under Count Williamson are ready for embarkation but here are no transports, and it will be impossible for His Majesty's Ships to receive & accommodate such a number, with their arms, stores and baggage.'[12] So he undertook to keep his ships available to carry out his orders as soon as transports arrived to carry the émigré troops.

Continuing his own operations, on the morning of 4 July Smith, despite only having the *Diamond*, still with the Hector detachment onboard, and two gun-vessels – the *Fearless* and *Attack* – immediately available attacked a large corvette that had taken refuge, with her convoy, in Saint-Vaast-la-Hougue under the forts on La Hougue point and Île Tatihou. Smith reported that 'at Nine o'Clock began the Action in the Diamond. ... [The] Corvette, continued warping into shoal Water; we followed, engaging her and the Batteries for Three Quarters of an Hour'. Unable to get alongside the corvette and with the tide turning, Smith withdrew. There were three casualties on the *Diamond*, one killed and two wounded, as 'The Enemy fired high, or we should have suffered more materially from their red-hot Shot, the Marks of which were visible in the Rigging. We have shifted our Fore and Main Top-Masts, which, with Two Topsail-Yards, were shot through'.[13] Carrey d'Asnières described the damage as being, 'as if we had been in a combat for two hours against a frigate of equal strength.'[14]

In addition, Smith took possession of the uninhabited Îles Saint-Marcouf, six and a half kilometres off the east coast of the Cotentin Peninsula, and landed some marines who constructed a camp and redoubts.[15] The British were to clearly demonstrate their presence, as well as allude to food shortages in France, as shown by an intercepted republican intelligence report,

> The English are for 6 weeks in possession of the Isles St Marcouf near La Hogue. They construct a fort, disembarked troops and daily exercise there. One sees them very distinctly carry out all their drills. They have planted a mast high above their camp, on which they have ironically a loaf of bread and beneath a large flag.[16]

11 TNA: WO 1/390: orders to Williamson 10 June and Strachan (?) June.
12 TNA: ADM 1/103: Strachan to Nepean 24 June.
13 *The London Gazette*, 7 July 1795, Smith's report dated 5 July.
14 ANF: MAR/C/7/53: dossier 24, 10 July 1824.
15 The date when Smith occupied the islands is unclear but the captain's log of HMS *Diamond* shows he was at anchorage there on 19 July, and on 27 July ordnance and workmen were landed, TNA: ADM 51/1124. NB: throughout dates have been given as that of the calendar rather than that of the ships (which run from noon on day 1 to noon on day 2, with the date being given day 2.).
16 TNA: HO 69/24: the report is undated but describes other events of July 1795.

Although no expedition was launched from the Channel Islands at this stage, as will be seen, the possibility was to arise again, later.

Command of the Expedition

As ships, troops and stores were assembled, the British Government issued their instructions to Puisaye and Captain Sir John Borlase Warren, who was to command the convoy, as well as Hervilly. A myth has arisen that these instructions created a dual command, the source may have been Henri Forneron who wrote, 'Puisaye is selected as general in chief by the English: a hidden influence gave equal powers to the Comte d'Hervilly.'[17] However, an inspection of the instructions clearly shows that this is untrue. What it does show is that the ministers wanted to restrain Puisaye from placing the troops and stores in jeopardy in his anxiety, indeed his desperation, to land, of which he had provided them with ample evidence. That Hervilly, although his abilities had been already recognised, should have been chosen as the officer to, if required, put the brake on Puisaye appears to have simply come about through the evolution of the plan. He had been identified in April as suitable to command the troops intended to feint on Vannes and as the plan had evolved he remained in place.

Hervilly's instruction stated, in sequence:

- '... you are forthwith to embark ... with the regiments ... & so long as you remain on board to continue in command of the same ...'
- '... you are not required to order the landing of the whole, or any part of your Force, unless ... you shall be of the opinion that the attempt is practicable & proper, consistent with the general Interests of the Service, and with a true attention to the Safety of the Troops entrusted to your care.'
- if no landing was made but Puisaye decided he wanted to go ashore, if 'any Part of these Troops, either Officers or Soldiers ... [wanted to go with him] ... you are not to oppose their wishes' as long as Warren considered it practicable.
- 'In case of you landing on any part of the Coasts of France with the said regiments you are from thence forward to be under the command of Count Joseph de Puisaye ... with whose views & plans you will on all occasions endeavour to cooperate ...'
- The only further role that Hervilly was explicitly given responsibility for 'the management of the pecuniary concerns of the regiments which will now be left entirely in your hands ...'[18]

Warren was directed to:

- Go firstly to Quiberon Bay where, 'The situation [is] supposed to be most favourable for effecting the Disembarkation, and for forming the intended junction ...'

---

17 Henri Forneron, *Histoire Générale des Émigrés pendant la Révolution Française* (Paris: Librairie Plon, 1884), vol.II, p.107.

18 TNA: WO 1/390: Hervilly's instructions of 8 June (copy).

- If a safe landing was not practicable there, he should try '... in the Neighbourhood of Bourgneuf or on any other part of the Coast which may be deemed more advisable ...'
- If not, '... it will then become matter for consideration whether the possession of the Isle Dieu [Île d'Yeu] may not be affected, and if ... it should be judged advisable to attempt it ...'
- If a landing on that island was discounted, he was to go to the Channel Islands and await further orders.[19]

As to cooperation with the émigré officers, he was to work with Hervilly. Together they were to decide on whether a landing should be attempted, '... it will be expedient that it should clearly be ascertained how far the circumstances and situation of affairs may favour such an important Undertaking, and to that end you will consult Count d'Hervilly, and in concert with Him endeavour to open some channel for obtaining Information upon that point and govern yourself accordingly.' If a landing took place, he was 'to cooperate with and assist Mr d'Hervilly with the force under your command in that Undertaking.' As for Puisaye, he was 'to consult with Mr de Puisaye and avail yourself of his information and advice.' If no general landing took place, there was nothing 'to prevent you landing Mr de Puisaye, and as many persons as may be willing to follow ...' with as many stores that could practicably landed and taken inland safely.[20]

Puisaye's role, as the '... proper officer to take upon Himself the command of the Troops, and to direct & superintend the Enterprise in the Distribution of the Arms & other Articles ... and many other important arrangements ...' was to begin,

> ... from the time of the Disembarkation of the Forces ... to take them under your command and to employ them according to the existing circumstances, and in concert with such Persons as may join you in acting against the Persons now exercising the Powers of Government in France, in such a manner as may appear to you most conducive to the Establishment of Order and good Government in that Country.

One of his first tasks was clearly articulated:

> The possibility however of your continuing to receive supplies from this Country, at least to any extent, and with the requisite safety and regularity, must chiefly depend on your occupying in force some Place on the Coast to which they might be sent without the risk of falling into the Enemy's Hands. The advantages you may derive from the possession of a Port are indeed so evident, both for communication and cooperation ...[21]

19 TNA: WO 1/390: extract of Warren's instructions of 6 June for Puisaye's information (copy).
20 TNA: WO 1/390: extract of Warren's instructions of 6 June for Puisaye's information (copy).
21 TNA: WO 1/390: Puisaye's instructions of 10 June (copy).

Puisaye's role was clear, and he was 'furnished with a Letter of Service appointing him to take command of the Troops from the time of their Disembarkation on any part of the Coast of France.'[22]

What role was Hervilly to perform once in France? It would have seemed sensible for Puisaye to keep him in command of the regular troops; he was after all the *colonel* of the largest unit, experienced in such a post, and already been in command on board. Puisaye would have enough to do, organising and leading an army in which, as it grew, the significance of the regular troops would decrease. Unfortunately, Puisaye's memoirs would seem to have been written to cloud the issue of Hervilly's appointment. He states that while in London he had had an interview with Windham and Pitt at which he was told that they had selected Hervilly to be his second-in-command. He initially objected, on the grounds that Hervilly was not popular in Brittany because of his previous command there but when they persisted he asked to make the first approach, to help build a working relationship with him, to which they agreed.[23] Then, according to Puisaye, after some hesitation Hervilly accepted his proposals. However, when he described his staff Hervilly was not, unambiguously, second-in command but '… designated Maréchal Général des logis … I assigned the Duc de Levi, and the Vicomte de Chambray, the functions of Aides Maréchaux Généraux des logis.'[24] Thus Hervilly's post equated to that of Quartermaster General and he did not even have the choice of his own assistants. Jacques Vicomte de Chambray, *capitaine* in Williamson's corps who had previously served as a Knight of Malta and then in the French cavalry was the uncle of Puisaye's wife, and Pierre-Marc-Gaston Duc de Lévis, of an elevated rank of the nobility with a distinguished military perdigree, had been *capitaine* of the Gardes du Corps du Comte de Provence (now Regent) when only aged 16.

Comte Erasme-Gaspard de Contades, of a similar background, a cavalry *capitaine* aged 17 and *mestre de camp* (equivalent to colonel) at 24, after travelling to England to find a place on the expected expedition had been introduced to Puisaye by Monseigneur Urbain de Hercé, *Evêque* (Bishop) de Dol, and so had become a close aide. Contades describes the first meeting between Puisaye and Hervilly, 'We went to a tavern where we were to dine. M de Puisaye always walked at a terrible pace; Hervilly, with little legs, had beside him the most ridiculous gait. Here is, I said to myself, two men who will never march in step, and, unfortunately, I was not wrong.'[25] Puisaye later wrote of Hervilly:

---

22 TNA: WO 1/687: Horse Guards to Admiralty, 6 June 1795 also see Maurice Hutt, 'The British Government's Responsibility for the 'Divided Command' of the Expedition to Quiberon, 1795', *The English Historical Review*, Volume 76 No. 300 (July 1961), p.482.

23 Puisaye, *Mémoires*, vol.VI, pp.6–8.

24 Puisaye, *Mémoires*, vol.VI, p.23. Puisaye's account of his receiving his instructions (vol. VI, p.56) and a heated discussion with Hervilly (pp.73–74) appear questionable through inconsistency and doubtful detail.

25 Contades, *Coblenz*, pp.116–117. If the insinuation was being made that Hervilly resented such a height difference, it should be noted that he had appointed Charles Baron de Damas, a man noted for being particularly tall, as *major* of his regiment.

> M le Cat, Comte d'Hervilly, … had conceived, from his infancy, a particular taste for military service, he applied himself, with passion, to the study of his profession, and knew perfectly the theory. Ardent, and full of laudable ambition; when favour alone distributed offices, he had not turned away from cutting a path to honours by his application and his courage … His valour and personal abilities were unquestionable; but too constrained in theory, too exclusively dedicated to the system, and too imbued with the old school ideas, he lacked the first elements of understanding necessary for a man in public life, that of his fellow-men, and that experience without which he is not a General, that of some sort of command, in the face of the enemy.[26]

Many writers have followed Puisaye in their portrayal of Hervilly, an exception is Alfred de Curzon in his short biography of the man. He described him when he commanded Rohan in Brittany, surrounded by authorities that were hostile to the army but still required it to keep order:

> The new colonel was to show himself in the exercise of his functions and in his relations with his officers and men quite different than the historians are more likely to describe him, one does not really know why. Very far from being authoritarian, abrupt, hated by his subordinates, his correspondence with them really clearly shows him to be on the contrary an officer who was correct as to his duty, firm, certainly, but at the same time quite flexible to avoid the 'mishaps', loved by his officers, and true father to his men with whom he busied himself very closely, and with whom Madame d'Hervilly likewise interested herself.[27]

Returning to the issue of command, although it appears unusual to have restrained an army commander from exercising his command until it was ashore, but understandable in the circumstances, the situation was clear. Nevertheless, the myth that the British Government imposed a dual command remains alluring to some. Robert, despite quoting the orders at length, concluded, 'If the English ministers wanted to cast discord amidst the royalist army, they succeeded beyond their desires'.[28] Or as a more recent writer saw it '… the explanation is simple; the very British policy of "Divide and Rule."'[29] If there was discord, it was not because of the orders but the personalities of the two individuals, after seeing their instructions, King George, perceptively remarked, 'I hope the two Counts will not from private vanity forget the main object, the doing their utmost to advance the Service, whilst debating their own consequence.'[30]

The Government had taken steps to prevent issues of precedence complicating matters by instructing both Hector and Dresnay, each of whom outranked Puisaye and Hervilly in the French service, to remain in

26 Puisaye, *Mémoires*, vol.VI, pp.8–11.
27 Alfred de Curzon, *Le Comte d'Hervilly 1755–1795* (unknown: unknown, 1958), pp.6–7.
28 Robert, *1795 Expédition*, p.26.
29 Champagnac, *Quiberon*, p.21.
30 Aspinall, *George III*, vol.II, p.354, the king was sent the instructions in the evening of 13 June and replied the following morning.

England rather than sail with their regiments. There were also questions about their suitability for active service; Hector was almost 73 years old and Dresnay was in poor health, dying less than three years later.[31] Nevertheless, they had grounds for feeling they had been treated shoddily as they had been repeatedly informed that their regiments were not '... going into immediate service.'[32] Even as late as 11 June, Windham assured the colonels:

> Were it true ... that an attempt at landing was to be made immediately, I should still be of opinion that your post was that where I have taken the liberty to place you, in reserve for operations of a higher character, rather than at the head of your Regiments, in any such irregular attempt, as, for some time to come, could alone be looked to. I shall be glad, if even such irregular attempts are as near, as some eager and sanguine spirits are willing to suppose.[33]

It is a measure of the man that, when Hector wrote to Windham a few weeks later, he told him:

> This is not now the time for pretentions, and Your Excellency knows that I assured him I would serve without difficulty under the orders of Monsieur de Puisaye. I would that he knew me well enough to be convinced that I would never put myself in the way, and that I will always sacrifice my self-esteem, for the sake of the cause we serve.[34]

The Expedition Prepares to Sail

After receiving his instruction on 6 June, Warren was kept busy, as he described in a personal letter to Earl Spencer, First Lord of the Admiralty, written on his ship, HMS *Pomone*, at Lymington.

> I have at length arranged everything and got, through all my difficulties ... many of the vessels, said to be ready, were up at the harbour of Portsmouth wanting water and other things, which it was absolutely necessary for them to be supplied with. The flat-boats only arrived yesterday, and six carpenters have been employed ever since in making ready for their reception. The embarkation of troops was finished yesterday about three o'clock, and all Monsieur D'Hector's corps are on board the ships of war, and every ship filled with officers. ... many of my comrades will be eat[en] out of house and home, their furniture destroyed, &c., by their hospitality. I have at least twenty of these people, and am obliged to occupy a cabin below. It has however saved the additional number of transports, notwithstanding which

31 BL: Add MS 37859: Dresnay informed Windham that he was 'in convalescence ... I cannot manage even to join my regiment ...', June 1795.

32 BL: Add MS 37859: Dresnay to Windham, June 1795.

33 BL: Add MS 37859: Windham to both colonels 11 June 1795. Puisaye was to state that Hervilly was also unaware of their destination until at sea (Puisaye, *Mémoires*, vol.VI, p.62).

34 BL: Add MS 37859: Hector to Windham 4 July 1795.

our squadron of vessels amount to thirty-eight in that line, exclusive of the men-of-war.

I have dispatched a cutter to Cawsand Bay [in Plymouth Sound] to order the Standard and Concorde to join me in my passage down Channel, and a lugger to Weymouth for some Frenchmen and a chasse marée at that place, and I fancy your lordship will not be displeased in learning that I am at last off bag and baggage.[35]

The warships anchored at Spithead were joined by the store-ships loaded with an assortment of supplies, equipment and horses:

Food for three months, for an army of six thousand men.
About a hundred riding and draught horses.
17,710 complete infantry uniforms,
4,000 of cavalry [uniforms].
27,000 muskets and bayonets, with cartridge pouches in proportion.
10 field pieces, two 8-pdrs, and eight 4-pdrs, with the necessary tools, caissons and munitions,
600 barrels of powder of 120 pounds each.
Saddles, boots, shoes, sabres, pistols, flints, entrenching tools etc in a considerable proportion.[36]

Meanwhile empty transports went to Southampton to embark the troops who marched to that port:

[Thursday] June 11. The regiment of Hervilly, embarked last Monday, and that of Dresnay, as well as the artillery corps and ordnance last Tuesday. They sailed this morning at 3 o'clock. The corps of engineers will be embarked this evening. The Commissioners and other Civil Officers, … will embark tomorrow.[37]

As the troops embarked, their destination remained a secret, as Louis-Ignace-Jean-Joseph Le Grand du Quellenec, *quartier-maître* of Dresnay, remembered later:

On 10 June in the evening, we received the order to depart and on 11 in the morning, we left Rumsey [sic] to go to Southampton where we embarked the same day, still believing going to Jersey and Guernsey.

The inhabitants of Rumsey testified to us the greatest sadness at our departure, and, wishing to give public testimony of their attachment for us, as well as the good conduct, discipline and subordination of our soldiers, they had printed in one of the public papers the most flattering things on our officers and soldiers of the regiment.

35 Julian S. Corbett (ed.), *Private Papers of George, Second Earl Spencer, First Lord of the Admiralty 1794–1801* (London: Naval Records Society, 1913), vol.I, pp.72–73. The letter is of 12 June 1795, although it is shown as dated 13 June matching that of the ship, TNA: ADM 51/1149: Captain's log HMS *Pomone*.

36 Puisaye, *Mémoires*, vol.VI, pp.59–60.

37 *The Kentish Gazette*, 16 June 1795.

> On 12, the whole convoy composed of more than a hundred transport vessels, and escorted by several vessels and frigates set sail and went to anchor before Lymington.[38]

Some officers, at least in Hervilly, were a little more sceptical about some of their men,

> ... on the eve of the departure from Lyndhurst several captains proposed to M d'Hervilly to leave at the regimental depot the men who they knew as the most dangerous of their comrades. He responded to them that, if it became necessary to punish, it would be better that examples were made of these bad subjects, whenever they made themselves liable to the penalties due by military regulations.[39]

The way the Royal Navy agents allocated officers and men to the transports was problematic. The Régiment d'Hervilly formed up in lines along the quay at Southampton but then, to make things easier for the agents, it changed to columns, so giving

> ... the agents the ability to count us, they, after having found the number of men who could fill each transport vessel, cut the files with their swords, and made us leave on handing in the name of the ship and the number of men that it was to receive. Astonished by this manner of proceeding, the captains made sustained observations through M d'Hervilly; but they were not heard, and we found ourselves on board five officers for two hundred and forty men from three different companies, in the portion from one of them there was not even a sergeant. These agents embarked us like barrels, so many for one such vessel, so many for another, no account made of any consideration, of discipline and subordination; things very essential, above all for our regiment composed in great part of republican prisoners and above all sailors rather than soldiers. They follow, it is said, the same method for their own troops.[40]

On the passage *Sergent-major* Martin Kibre, a veteran of Toulon with the Royal-Louis, discovered that seven or eight men who were unaccompanied by their company's officers or NCOs, were planning to mutiny but, after steps were taken to watch them, nothing came of it.[41]

The ships gathered in Cowes Roads in the Solent for the convoy. Warships moved down from Spithead on 10 June before anchoring off Lymington over the next two days. There the line-of-battle ship, HMS *Robust*, and the frigates, *Pomone*, *Artois* and *Galatea*, embarked the Régiment d'Hector. Bélizal describes this in a series of letters to a friend:

---

38 Claude-Youenn Roussel and Benoît de Bergevin, *Un Survivant de Quiberon Louis-Ignace-Jean-Joseph Le Grand du Quellenec (1753–1830)* (Paris: Guénégaud, 2008), vol.I, p.254.

39 Le Charron, *Expédition de Quiberon*, pp.131–132.

40 Le Charron, *Expédition de Quiberon*, pp.129–130.

41 Le Charron, *Expédition de Quiberon*, pp.130–131.

> It is not transports but English battleships and frigates, that are to come to take us. The English navy having said that it wishes to offer this courtesy to our former royal navy to transport us on warships. It is very decent. … Our soldiers begin to desert again and their bad spirit comes to light. … This evening or tomorrow at the break of day we will embark five companies on each vessel. A total of 18 companies. … we got under way numbering 44 transport vessels, loaded with troops and war supplies. As well as six frigates and three ships. I am on the Robust, which is commanded by the good and aimable Captain Thornborough who does not cease to compliment us with esteem and courtesy.[42]

The *Robust* embarked 28 officers and 150 soldiers from the regiment.[43] Their colonel had previously complained that the muskets they had been issued with had such long butts that his men could not handle them.[44] It appears that the soldiers received new muskets, on or immediately before embarkation, as the warships' gunners were instructed to store the old firearms until they could be transferred to a transport.[45]

At 1:00 p.m. on 12 June Warren gave the signal to sail to the 38 transports that were to leave with him and at 6:00 p.m. they were passing the Needles.[46] Other ships left the following day to join the convoy as it moved down the Channel, including some members of Puisaye's entourage who were picked up by a lugger from Weymouth and brought out to the ships.[47]

On 14 June, off Plymouth Sound, Warren's squadron was joined by HMS *Standard* and *Concorde*, the latter towing a royalist chasse-marée, a class of Breton coastal vessel.[48] They were lugger rigged sloops built for speed, their principal purpose being the transport of sardines, before the age of refrigeration, to market in the cities of western France, such as Nantes and Bordeaux. When in Quiberon Bay, a large flotilla of chasse-marées operated with the squadron in a variety of roles.

There were fewer than 4,000 troops sailing with the convoy, some soldiers had been left at the respective regimental depots and several officers were detached or simply unfit for deployment.

In addition to the troops there were also about 40 priests, including the Bishop of Dol and François de Hercé, his brother and vicar, and about the same number of émigré gentlemen to serve on Puisaye's staff or command the chouans, 'on two transports which had been specially prepared for them.'[49] Along with Chambray, Lévis and Contades was Jacques-Anne-Joseph Le Prestre de Vauban who was, again, from a prestigious background, and had been chamberlain to the Duc d'Orléans, *colonel* of the duke's infantry

42 Gouzillon de Bélizal, 'Journal et Lettres', pp.111–112, respectively letters of 8, 11 (11:00 p.m.) and 20 June.

43 Thomas Wetton, 'Manuscript Journal, Remarks on board HMS Robust', transcribed by Louis Roeder, in *The Trafalgar Chronicle* (West Wickham: The 1805 Club, 1995), p.66.

44 Hutt, *Chouannerie*, p.244.

45 TNA: ADM 80/136: 17 June.

46 TNA: ADM 51/1149 *Pomone* log.

47 Contades, *Coblenz*, p.122.

48 TNA: ADM 51/1111: *Concorde* log.

49 Puisaye, *Mémoires*, vol.VI, p.60.

regiment and had accompanied the Comte d'Artois when he had travelled to Russia to seek the aid of Catherine the Great.

Table 3: The warships under Warren's command 14 June 1795.[50]

Ships	Guns	Captains
Pomone	44	Sir John Borlase Warren
Robust	74	Edward Thornborough
Thunderer	74	Albemarle Bertie
Standard	64	Joseph Ellison
Anson	44	Philip Durham
Artois	38	Sir Edmund Nagle
Arethusa	36	Mark Robinson
Concorde	36	Anthony Hunt
Galatea	32	Richard Keats
As well as five gun-vessels, two luggers and two cutters.		

Table 4: Troops of the First Division.[51]

Unit	Officers	Other ranks
Dresnay	32	455
Hector	108	540
Hervilly	102	1,340
Loyal Emigrant	-	400 (estimate)
Total Infantry	242	2,735
French Emigrant Artillery	30	441
French Engineers	21	-
Total	2,93	3,176

It had been planned that the expedition, on its way to France, would be joined by a second division from Germany, however unfavourable weather and the lack of transports meant that they would have to follow as soon as they were able.

The Second Division

The Second Division, so called despite its numbers hardly warranting such a name, consisted of five understrength light infantry battalions; Salm-Kyrbourg, Rohan, Périgord, Béon and Damas. It was commanded by

50 Corbett (ed.), *Private Papers*, p.67.

51 TNA: ADM 80/136: The report was made up from regimental returns (a note states that none was available for the Loyal Emigrants) apparently while the British ships were still in Quiberon Bay (27 June 1795). A study of the existing regimental pay and muster lists give comparable numbers (324 officers and 3,106 other ranks): Dresnay WO 12/11708; Hector WO 12/11741; Hervilly WO 12/11681; French Emigrant Artillery WO 10/281 and 1/388. There is no pay list for the Loyal Emigrant Regiment available for this period. However, numbers can be estimated from the embarkation return for 8 April 1795 (BL Add MS 46710) adjusted by estimating that there were the same number of corporals as sergeants (WO 12/11732). The list for the Corps of French Engineers shows eighteen officers embarked on the *Middleton* Transport (WO 54/702).

Charles-Eugène-Gabriel de Virot de Sombreuil. Born in 1770 and given a military education, by 1789 he was *capitaine* in the Esterhazy Hussards. The next year he entered Prussian service and then that of Russia before serving with Brunswick's army in its offensive into France in 1792. In February 1793 he was appointed *capitaine* in the Hussards de Salm-Kyrbourg, raised by Maurice-Gustave-Adolphe Prince de Salm-Kyrbourg, former colonel commanding the Esterhazy Hussards, to serve with the Armée de Condé. Sombreuil was retained in Prussian service after the regiment transferred to British service on 22 February 1794 and he arrived to command the regiment in the final stages of the campaign in the Netherlands. There he quickly gained a reputation as a trusted and reliable outpost commander.[52] His family had paid a terrible toll during the Revolution. His father, Charles-François, although in his seventies, was imprisoned and his sister 'Marie-Maurille' was the heroine of the story, whether in fact or myth, she was challenged to drink a '*verre de sang*' – a glass of human blood – to save his life. Although she did so, her father was guillotined in Paris, along with her brother, Stanislas-François-Antoine. On 17 June 1794 their bodies were tossed into a communal grave.[53]

The capitulation under which the Hussards de Salm-Kyrbourg entered British service also contracted the prince to raise a light infantry battalion within three months which was to serve separately from the hussars.[54] The battalion joined the Duke of York's army in October 1794 and soon proved its fighting qualities during the final stages of the campaign. Even as late as February 1795 it was serving, along with Rohan and Damas infantry, in a line of outposts near Almelo and Nordhorn along the German frontier.[55]

Charles-Alexis-Gabriel de Rohan, Duc de Montbazon and Prince de Guéméné, signed two capitulations on 3 March 1794, one to raise a hussar regiment and a light infantry battalion and the other for a single light infantry battalion. Both battalions were apparently recruited quickly, drawing many recruits from the Armée de Condé, and joined the British army in August. They served creditably but, suffering from desertion, they were amalgamated to form a single battalion which gained a reputation for pillaging during the retreat towards Germany. By 23 February 1795 both Salm and Rohan battalions, each commanded by a *lieutenant-colonel*, were to have the same establishments, a *major*, seven staff and six companies, each with a *capitaine*, two *lieutenants*, an *enseigne*, six *sergents*, six *caporaux*, two *tambours* and 124 *soldats*, as well as an artillery detachment of a *lieutenant*, two *sergents*, two *caporaux* and 30 *cannoniers*. The full strength being 905 officers and men.[56]

52 René Bittard des Portes, *Les émigrés à la cocarde noire, en Angleterre, dans les provinces belges, en Hollande et à Quiberon* (Paris: E Paul, 1908), p.87. See also Peter Harrington (ed.), *With the Guards in Flanders; The Diary of Captain Roger Morris 1793–1795* (Warwick: Helion & Company, 2018), p.144 and BL: Add MS 46708: letter from Lieutenant Colonel William Goodday Strutt, 54th Foot, to Lieutenant Colonel Don.

53 Champagnac, *Quiberon*, p.78.

54 TNA: WO 24/1112: capitulation.

55 TNA: WO 1/172: dislocation dated 11 February.

56 TNA: WO 1/172: Estimates for Foreign Corps 23 February.

As the capitulation with Archambaud-Joseph de Talleyrand-Périgord for a battalion-strength light infantry regiment was only agreed on 10 September 1794, it did not serve in the Netherlands campaign but withdrew with the army into Germany. There it continued to recruit, under the effective command of *Lieutenant-colonel* Boson-Jacques Comte de Talleyrand-Périgord who had served as a young aide-de-camp during France's intervention in the American War of Independence. He and Archambaud were the younger brothers of Charles-Maurice, the former bishop who managed to serve successive French regimes as foreign minister and diplomat. The regiment had the same establishment as Rohan and Salm but without an artillery detachment.

The other two so-called regiments, Béon and Damas, were the infantry elements of legions, units comprising infantry and cavalry intended to act together or independently, that had been raised by François-Frédéric de Béon and Etienne-Charles de Damas to serve in the Army of the United Provinces. These legions consisted of French émigré volunteers serving in the cavalry and *chasseur* infantry companies alongside *fusiliers* recruited from any available source. Ordered to retreat with the British to avoid the fate that awaited captured émigrés, they received financial support from Britain and then were provisionally taken into service on 3 February.[57] Under their substantive capitulations, both identical and of 2 April 1795, the infantry establishment was to be of six companies, of a *capitaine*, two *lieutenants*, an *enseigne*, four *sergents*, six *caporaux*, one *tambour* and 100 *soldats*. Although they never reached their establishment, due to their impending departure, they were permitted to have a small staff including a commanding field officer who, even if he was a *lieutenant-colonel*, was to be paid as *major*.[58]

On 1 March, as the British got ready to evacuate the Continent, a detailed review was carried out of the strengths of the eight cavalry and 11 infantry foreign and émigré corps in British pay, who were gathered around Celle, Hanover. The returns for the five regiments that were later to form the Second Division are shown in Table 5.

Table 5: Strength of the Béon, Damas, Périgord, Rohan and Salm infantry, 1 March 1795.[59]

	Senior Officers	Other staff	Company Officers	Other ranks
Béon	–	–	8	226 (including 53 unarmed recruits)
Damas	–	–	7	215
Périgord	3*	3	8	264
Rohan	1 (*Major*)	1	10	464 (including 34 POWs)
Salm	1 (*Lt-colonel*)	6	20	478

* *Colonel, Lieutenant-colonel* and *Major*

57 TNA: WO 24/1112 3 February 1795 and WO 1/172: Harcourt to York 11 February.
58 TNA: WO 24/1112: 2 April 1795.
59 BL: Add MS 37872.

On 22 March Lieutenant General William Harcourt, the senior British officer present in Germany, reported '… notwithstanding the exertions used … Excess and Insubordination still subsist in the Foreign Light Corps' in response to which he appointed Sombreuil 'to restore order in the Depot'.[60] His appointment was timely as soon afterwards Wittgenstein, another unit previously in Dutch service, earlier described by Harcourt as 'composed of Deserters from all Nations' mutinied led by the majority of its officers.[61] Sombreuil acted quickly and decisively to prevent the disorder spreading, the unit was disbanded and the men that remained in the ranks were drafted into Salm. On 4 April he marched some of the infantry regiments to Stade, on the Elbe, the designated point of departure for the foreign and émigré units. With him went Béon, Rohan, Salm and Périgord, there was concern about the rate of desertion from the last and its future existence rested on the state in which it arrived at Stade. Sombreuil's task was not easy due to the 'state of commotion and discontent' that pervaded as crimps swarmed around the column seeking recruits for other armies, as well as other corps in British pay. Nevertheless, it reached Stade on 8 April.[62] The remainder of the infantry, including Damas, arrived at Stade on 14 April. This time there were no desertions and morale was good, as the émigrés expected to be joining the planned expedition to France, now considered imminent.[63]

The transports, which were due to arrive from England's east coast, had not arrived in the Elbe yet.[64] The delay gave time for rest, training and reviews as well as administrative tasks. The units, in general, were '… very Healthy, perfectly quiet & most with no desertion.'[65] On 23 April Béon and Damas were reviewed and the men took the oath of fidelity required by the British service. A Damas volunteer *chasseur*, a French Roman Catholic, being somewhat bemused by the ceremony when 'a Lutheran minister passed through our ranks and made us swear, on a fat book that he told us was the Gospel, the oath'.[66]

It seems that doubts still existed about Périgord as orders were given for Béon, Damas, Rohan, Salm and Löwenstein, another unit previously in Dutch service, each to be 'completed' to a strength of 800 men, excluding officers.[67] Sustained efforts had been made to recruit men throughout the spring, one source being men who had quit the Dutch army during or immediately after the fall of the United Provinces. Périgord is said to have recruited a number of such men who had served in the Bedaulx Regiment as well as bought a number of French prisoners who had been captured by the Prussians.[68] On the other hand, men had also quit the units. Several of the émigré volunteer

60 TNA: WO 1/172: Harcourt to York 22 March.
61 TNA: WO 1/172: Harcourt to York 11 February.
62 BL: Add MS 46704: Nesbitt to Don 3, 6 and 8 April.
63 BL: Add MS 46704: Sombreuil to Harcourt 11 April and Sombreuil to Don 14 April.
64 TNA: WO 1/172: Harcourt to York 5 April.
65 BL: Add MS 46704: Nesbitt to Don 23 April.
66 Bernard de Corbehem, *Dix ans de ma vie ou Histoire de mon émigration* (Paris: A Phian Delaforest, 1827), p.155.
67 BL: Add MS 46711: letter from C. Crawford 6 May.
68 Grouvel, *Les corps de troupes*, vol.I, p.149, and *Saunders's News-Letter*, 20 May.

chasseurs of Béon and Damas and the gentlemen cadets in the other units, had done so to take up other positions that offered better prospects, something that was anticipated in their original engagements.

Finally on 3 June the orders arrived for the five units – Béon, Damas, Périgord, Rohan and Salm – to be embarked immediately. There is no documentary evidence to support the assertion that they were to have been joined by two foreign regiments in British pay, the York Rangers (Ramsay's) and Royal York Fusiliers (Hardy's), before these were diverted for service in the West Indies.[69] A division of nine transports from the Tyne arrived off Cuxhaven on 12 June, after a crossing of eight days, and made their way up the Elbe to Stade where embarkation took about a week.[70]

Table 6: 'Embarkation return of 2nd Division of Foreign Infantry', 20 June 1795, listing the regiments and the transports they were embarked on.[71]

Salm-Kirbourg	
John	9 officers – 1 *capitaine*, 4 *lieutenants*, 2 *enseignes*, 1 *chirurgien* (surgeon), 1 *aide chirurgien*; 169 other ranks – 12 *sergents*, 2 *tambours* (drummers), 155 rank and file; 10 others – 2 domestics, 7 women, 1 child; 7 horses
Rohan	
Leighton	13 officers – 1 *major*, 2 *capitaines*, 5 *lieutenants*, 2 *enseignes*, 1 *adjudant*, 1 *quartier-maître*, 1 *aumônier* (chaplain); 162 other ranks – 15 *sergents*, 13 *tambours*, 134 rank and file; 4 others – 1 domestic, 2 women, 1 child
Aurora	12 officers – 2 *capitaines*, 6 *lieutenants*, 4 *enseignes*; 219 other ranks – 21 *sergents*, 198 rank and file; 5 others – 2 domestics, 3 women; 3 horses
Beckford	3 officers – 1 *aumônier*, 1 *chirurgien*, 1 *aide chirurgien*; 37 other ranks – 1 *sergent*, 36 rank and file; 10 others – 1 domestic, 5 women, 4 children
Périgord	
Disko Bay	12 officers – 1 *lieutenant-colonel*, 1 *major*, 2 *capitaines*, 3 *lieutenants*, 2 *enseignes*, 2 supplementary officers, 1 *aide chirurgien*; 149 other ranks – 8 *sergents*, 4 *tambours*, 137 rank and file; 23 others – 7 domestics, 11 women, 5 children; 3 horses
Damas	
Silver Eel	14 officers – 1 *lieutenant-colonel*, 2 *capitaines*, 4 *lieutenants*, 2 *enseignes*, 3 supplementary officers, 1 *aumônier*, 1 *aide chirurgien*; 174 other ranks – 12 *sergents*, 3 *tambours*, 159 rank and file; 9 others – 6 women, 3 children; 3 horses
Béon	
Aurora of London	18 officers – 1 *lieutenant-colonel*, 1 *major*, 2 *capitaines*, 4 *lieutenants*, 2 *enseignes*, 5 supplementary officers, 1 *quartier-maître*, 1 *aumônier*, 1 *aide chirurgien*; 171 other ranks – 9 *sergents*, 2 *tambours*, 160 rank and file; 3 others – 3 women; 3 horses
Total	
	81 officers; 1081 other ranks; 64 others; 19 horses (including 4 for Sombreuil)

The horses listed were embarked on a separate transport, the *Kingston*.

69 From Bittard des Portes, *Les émigrés à la cocarde noire*, pp.469–470, using Louis-Gabriel de Villeneuve-Laroche-Barnaud, *Mémoires sur l'expédition de Quiberon, précédés d'une notice sur l'émigration de 1791 et sur les trois campagnes de 1792, 1793 et 1794* (Paris: Le Normant, 1814), vol.I, pp.216–218, as his source.

70 TNA: ADM 51/1117: *Venus* log and WO 1/173: Major General David Dundas to Henry Dundas 4, 17 and 28 June.

71 BL: Add MS 46710: The *Disko Bay* is otherwise given as the *Disco Bay*, the first has been used throughout for consistency.

Men had deserted from all five of the units during their embarkation, between 17 and 20 June: Béon – losing 10 from the ranks, Damas – 26, Périgord – 22, Rohan – 91 and Salm – three.[72]

The transports then dropped down the Elbe and, on the afternoon of 22 June, joined the waiting escorts, frigates HMS *Venus* and *Leda* with the ship-sloop *Lark*. The Second Division's commander, Sombreuil, did not sail with it as he travelled separately to receive instructions from the British Government, arriving in London on the night of 1 July.[73] The convoy was already far behind the proposed schedule which would have seen them joining the First Division at sea. Westerly gales only made matters worse, preventing it leaving the east coast of Germany and it was only in the early hours of 29 June that it eventually got underway.[74]

The Voyage of the First Division

Ships sailing from Britain to Quiberon Bay had to pass Brest, the principal French naval base facing the Atlantic, so the Channel Fleet, commanded by Admiral Alexander Hood, Lord Bridport, consisting of 14 line-of-battle ships, five frigates and six sundry other vessels, was to protect the convoy as it passed the port and then to blockade it to prevent interference with the expedition while in the bay.[75] Despite the risk entailed, by now Windham 'was so insistent on the need for Warren not to miss the easterly wind then blowing, that on 10 June he wrote to Spencer that if Lord Bridport, as seemed 'very likely', was not ready to escort Warren's convoy, then that convoy ought to proceed without him.'[76] So, Warren sailed without the protection of the Channel Fleet, however Bridport left Spithead on 15 June and made such headway on the convoy that they were in sight of each other early in the morning of 16 June.

This was fortunate as, unbeknown to them, the French fleet was at sea. On 8 June, off Brittany, a British squadron of five line-of-battle ships, two frigates and a sloop under Vice Admiral the Honourable William Cornwallis, had spotted a convoy of coasters from Bordeaux making their way to Brest, under escort by three line-of-battle ships and six or seven frigates.[77] Cornwallis attempted to intercept the convoy and took eight of the coasters, laden with wine and brandy, but the rest took refuge under the batteries of Belle-Île. As a result, Cornwallis withdrew towards the English Channel with his prizes which he sent to England on 11 June and then turned back towards Belle-Île. In the meantime, *Vice-amiral* Louis-Thomas Villaret-Joyeuse set sail with nine sail of the line, nine frigates and four corvettes from Brest on 12 June to

72 TNA: ADM 1/1913: Halsted, embarkation list 17 June; the high rate of desertion was noted by Corbehem, *Dix ans*, p.170.

73 *The Northampton Mercury*, 4 July 1795.

74 TNA: ADM 1/1913: Halsted to Nepean 4 July, ADM 51/1117 *Venus* log and ADM 51/1167 *Lark* log.

75 James, *Naval History*, vol.I, p.244. Alexander was brother to Samuel, who landed at Toulon.

76 Hutt, *Chouannerie*, p.249 citing Althorp MSS.

77 James, *Naval History*, vol.I, p.237. William was the younger brother of Charles, the general.

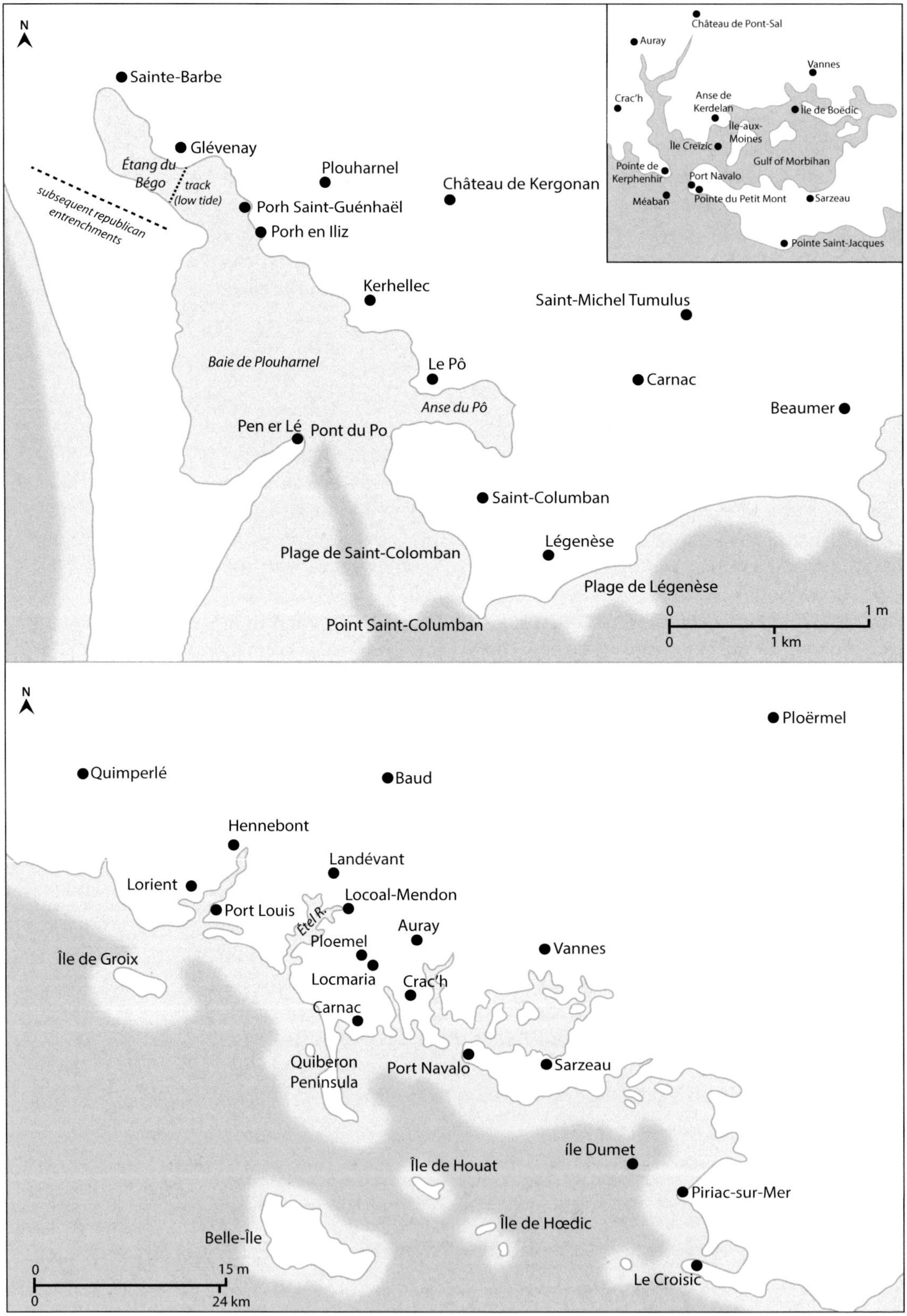

South coast of Brittany.

rescue the convoy, however in the haste, or due to the lack of supplies, several of his ships sailed with provisions for only 15 days. The convoy had however left Belle-Île unmolested and was making its way towards Brest when, on 15 June, it joined Villaret-Joyeuse off the Île de Groix so that when Cornwallis came across them the next day, he was far outnumbered and so drew off. French ships gave chase catching up with the hindmost British ships on the morning of 17 June. When Cornwallis turned to protect them an action began however Villaret-Joyeuse did not press his numerical advantage, apparently concerned that a large allied fleet was fast approaching.[78]

Cornwallis, unaware of the approaching convoy, sailed for Plymouth to warn that a French fleet was at sea while Villaret-Joyeuse prepared to return to port. However, when his fleet was off Penmarc'h, the southerly point on the approach to Brest, it was struck by a gale and it had to seek the safety of the anchorage off Belle-Île. Thus Villaret-Joyeuse, although unaware of it, was perfectly positioned to destroy the expedition at sea. Just as ill-informed, Warren and Bridport, after passing Brest, parted company on 19 June, in a 'violent gale of wind' and the Channel Fleet 'stood out from the coast, in order to keep an offing and be ready to receive the Brest fleet, should the latter quit port … and attempt to molest the expedition.'[79]

Later that day, HMS *Arethusa*, Warren's leading frigate, caught sight of Belle-Île and the French fleet coming away from it so signalled the presence of '16 sail of the line and 10 frigates.'[80] The transports and escorting squadron immediately changed course to avoid this fleet while Warren sent fast-sailing vessels to warn Bridport. Nevertheless, Villaret-Joyeuse made no attempt to chase him, perhaps thinking that it was the Channel Fleet itself that was approaching. Early on 20 June Bridport came in sight of Warren's ships and placed his fleet between the latter and the French fleet, ordering Warren's line-of-battle ships, the *Robust*, *Thunderer* and *Standard*, to join him to give parity with the opposing fleet. It was only in the early hours of 22 June that the two fleets saw each other. Again, Villaret-Joyeuse appeared to wish to avoid an engagement so Bridport signalled for his fleet to give chase. By noon, when the wind dropped, they were about 12 miles apart so only the better handled British ships gained on the French during the rest of the day and the ensuing night.

When, at 3:30 a.m. the following morning, the breeze came up the French fleet was together except for three or four vessels that trailed behind, while the British were scattered in their pursuit, with about three miles between the foremost British ships and the last of the French. At around 6:00 a.m., west of Île de Groix, opposing vessels were close enough to begin exchanging fire and as the fight progressed eight British and seven French line-of-battle ships were engaged. After taking three of the latter the British broke off the action just after 8:30 a.m. and Villaret-Joyeuse took refuge behind the island, expecting a further attack by Bridport. There Villaret-Joyeuse held a council

78 James, *Naval History*, vol.I, pp.239–242. Later French naval officers informed their British counterparts that they were aware of the approach of Bridport's fleet.

79 Corbett (ed.), *Private Papers*, p.77, Warren to Spencer and James, *Naval History*, vol.I, p.244.

80 James, *Naval History*, vol.I, p.244.

of war and as a result he withdrew his ships into Lorient harbour by 8:00 p.m. The threat from the French republican fleet had been neutralised but its presence at Lorient was to remain an ongoing concern which needed to be continually monitored by Bridport. Unbeknown to the British, at least at this stage, many of the crews had to be discharged due to the lack of provisions on the French ships, the men being sent to the republican land forces or deserting to join the chouans.[81]

Bridport immediately sent the captured ships, under escort, to England and Guy-Toussaint-François de Vossey, *sous-aide-major* on the staff of Hector, noted they went, '... taking away as prisoners of war all the sailors belonging to the crews of the three French vessels, without having enlisted a single one into the troops intended for the descent on Quiberon.'[82] Warren once more parted company from Bridport soon being rejoined by the *Robust*, *Thunderer* and *Standard*. They had not taken part in the action so the Hector officers who were on the former had only been spectators from afar.

81 James, *Naval History*, vol.I, pp.245–249, 253.

82 Guy-Toussaint-François de Vossey, 'Récit Fidèle et Impartial de l'Expédition de Quiberon', *Société d'Émulation des Côtes-du-Nord Bulletins et Mémoires*, Tome XXXVI (1898), p.4.

5

Landing

A Beachhead is Established

As the convoy continued towards Quiberon Bay, Captain Joseph Ellison of HMS *Standard*, with the *Arethusa* and two gun-vessels, was sent to blockade Belle-Île. The ships approached the island showing 'French National Colours' and on 25 June anchored at 5:00 p.m. in the roadstead four miles off Palais.[1] The following morning, with the ships now displaying British colours, a lieutenant was sent ashore under a flag of truce bearing a long letter of summons, in English, to the island's commander, Jean-Pierre Boucret. In it, Ellison assured him, 'Do not fear Sir that Bellisle may be subjected to a foreign power it is wished to be surrender'd only to your lawful King, to receive only French troops and be defended chiefly by its inhabitants, my King in his unlimited generosity will furnish them with every means in his power, and secure to them his protection.' Boucret simply replied, in French, 'We have need neither of the protection nor supplies from the King your master, be convinced that we lack nothing, to live freely or die in defending the one and indivisible Republic, under the orders of the Convention, that is my wish; it is that of all the Brave Republican men who I command.'[2] Despite hopes otherwise, this remained the situation throughout the campaign.

HMS *Galatea*, which had had the royalist chasse marée in tow during the voyage, reconnoitred in advance of the convoy. At 6:00 p.m. on 24 June six chests of arms were transferred to the smaller vessel along with three 'Gentlemen' agents from Puisaye, two of whom were Tinténiac and Paul-Alexandre du Bois-Berthelot, a retired naval officer. Both vessels sailed into Quiberon Bay and, after scouting the area for four hours, anchored off the Île d'Houat. The chasse marée with its three passengers then headed towards the shore to prepare the way for a landing.[3]

As the convoy rounded Belle-Île to the south it had to proceed cautiously, as Warren reported:

1 TNA: ADM 51/1149: *Pomone* and ADM 51/1102: *Arethusa* logs.
2 TNA: ADM 1/103: Boucret to Ellison 8 messidor An III.
3 TNA: ADM 51/1153: *Galatea* log.

> … the weather became extremely bad and foggy, that I was under the necessity of conducting it by the lead and Compass; or giving up the object of my orders: I anchored off the Island of Hedic [*sic*] in 19 fathoms water, with the whole Squadron, the weather having just cleared up as to get sight of the Rocks.
>
> The following morning [25 June] I again weighed, and got Pilots onboard, although the fog still continued, and arrived in Quiberon bay where I anchored with the Men of War and Transports … I immediately went onboard a Cutter with General D'Hervilly to reconnoitre the shore as far as it was possible for us to do, at so late an hour. The following day having received information from our Friends, that they were ready to receive us; General Comtes De Puysaye, D'Hervilly, and myself determined to disembark the Army from the Transports …[4]

This account was reiterated in a private letter to Spencer written the same day: '… having that evening reconnoitred the coast, I had a council with Generals de Puisaye and D'Hervilly, and from the information we received, I determined to land the troops the next morning', continuing, 'I am happy to say that from every appearance the business will succeed if properly sustained and protected by Government.'[5] This sequence of events is supported by other contemporary documents, the captains' logs which were internal organisational records, unlike dispatches, that were written with an eye to their publication. The logs also show the complexity of what happened. At noon on 25 June the *Galatea* was already at anchor in the south of Quiberon Bay then she was joined by the *Pomone* at 1:00 p.m., the *Anson* at 4:00 p.m. and the *Concorde* at 7:00 p.m. Then, the following morning and into the early afternoon, the ships shifted further up the bay to facilitate and support the landing; with the *Artois* anchoring off the Pointe du Petit Mont to prevent republican vessels, known to be in the Gulf of Morbihan, interfering with the operation.[6]

On 26 June Tinténiac arrived, with Bois-Berthelot, in a chasse marée, witnessed by Contades. He saw Tinténiac was in '… in full chouan uniform … He was a very brave man, headless, without judgement, but very suitable for this type of mission.'[7] After providing up-to-date information on the situation onshore, they returned to prepare for the landing, which was to take place next morning.

Puisaye, in his memoirs, was to complain about what he considered to be unnecessary delays caused by Hervilly. Criticism that has been echoed by some later historians. In his version Tinténiac and Bois-Berthelot arrived during the night of 25 to 26 June with the news that the chouans were ready to support the landing by acting against the republican positions and so he approached Warren to order the troops to land that morning, 26 June. Hervilly however refused, saying such a

4 TNA: ADM 1/103: Warren to Nepean 29 June.

5 Corbett (ed.), *Private Papers*, pp.77–80. Puisaye had apparently recovered from his sea-sickness, unmentioned in his memoirs, that he made him incapable of any activity during the voyage (Contades, *Coblenz*, pp.124–125).

6 TNA: ADM 51/1153: *Galatea*, ADM 51/1149: *Pomone*, ADM 51/1117: *Anson* and ADM 51/1111: *Concorde* logs.

7 Contades, *Coblenz*, p.129.

decision was his to make, and he would only do so after he had made a reconnaissance himself, which he did in the morning. 'this terrible mania for system … did not leave him an instant. He returned to say that he had seen nothing; and this puerility made us lose twenty-four hours.'[8] Then, in the subsequent conference, Hervilly only withdrew his opposition to the landing after Warren had intervened. Puisaye's version is not only refuted by contemporary and independent evidence but also illustrates his cavalier attitude towards operations.

He gave no heed to detailed planning, despite expecting the landing to be opposed, nor the level of organisation required to transfer troops from transports to the shore in an effective manner. The operation was entrusted to Captains Keats and Durham and instructions were issued for the allocation of boats and crews, provided by both the warships and transports, how they should proceed and the signals to be used. The troops were to land in waves, the Loyal Emigrants were in the first with artillery support immediately behind, followed by the first and then the second battalion of Hervilly. The complexity of the operation is shown in the captain's log of HMS *Robust* entry for the afternoon of 26 June.

> 1/4 past 2 weighed at signal & shifted our birth [*sic*] further to the northward. At 3 came to in 10 [fathoms], hoisted out all the Boats and got Long Boats from the Mary, Penelope & Middleton Transports. At 10 manned them and sent all the Boats on board the different Transports to receive Troops, Arms, Ammunition &c. 1/2 past the Commodore made the Signal for all the boats to Assemble on board the Galatea.[9]

The men of the Loyal Emigrants embarked from four transports into 12 boats, of different capacities, provided by those transports and three others, and crewed by sailors from the seven transports and three Royal Navy vessels (see Appendix I).[10] The *Robust*'s cutter with Surgeon's Mate Thomas Wetton, a lieutenant and a midshipman was busy from 8:00 p.m. bringing troops from the transports.[11]

The troops were to be issued with 30 cartridges, two flints, and food for four days. They were not to take any other equipment than their haversacks and be ready by 11:00 p.m.[12] As Warren reported, they were,

> … in the Boats at Midnight and the whole to put off at 1 o'clock; … I am happy to say, they proceeded in good order, and silence, until we approached the North Point of the Peninsula of Quiberon; when some shots were fired from a Battery, and Signals made from the Shore. On our nearer approach, I could perceive a small body of the Enemy's forces, drawn up upon a Hill, and others upon the

8 Puisaye, *Mémoires*, vol.VI, p.96.

9 TNA: ADM 51/1163: *Robust* log.

10 TNA: ADM 80/136: 'Distribution of troops, boats and sailors to row them for embarkation on 26 and landing on 27 June 1795.'

11 Wetton, 'Journal', p.67.

12 Anon., *De l'expédition de Quiberon. Par un officier François, à bord de la Pomone* (London: Baylis, 1795), pp.6–7.

Plage de Légenèse.
(Author's collection)

> march, and laying down behind a Bank: General D'Hervilly however, by a most able manoeuvre, having made a feint of landing in their front, disembarked the greatest part of the Troops upon the Flank, to which part, I also brought the Pelter Gun Vessel: before it was possible for any firing to take place, they retired with the utmost precipitation and the landing was effected without the loss of a Man on our part.[13]

Conditions were perfect. Puisaye later wrote: 'The sea was calm; the fog that had enveloped us for several days, had been succeeded by superb weather.'[14] An anonymous officer provides another account of the landing,

> … around the break of day on the 27th the coast of Carnac is approached. There were about two hundred Republicans who gave the appearance of wishing to oppose the descent. One thought, one ought even to suppose that this handful of men was only the vanguard of a more considerable corps. …
>
> The boats advance, the Comte d'Hervilly orders the regiment de la Chatre [Loyal Emigrants] which was to the left of the line, to head towards a bay that was to the enemies' right, and wait to disembark until he is ready to land with his regiment on their left, in order to encircle them and cut their retreat. He is the first to land, they follow him with an incredible ardour, the impatient soldiers

13 TNA: ADM 1/103: Warren to Nepean 29 June.

14 Puisaye, *Mémoires*, vol.VI, p.140.

> jump into the sea up to their necks, and the two hundred Republicans seek their salvation in flight ...[15]

The landing was made at 3:00 a.m. on the beaches of Légenèse and Saint-Colomban (often referred to as Saint Clément at the time) near Carnac; they were considered particularly suitable as they were coves, with rocky promontories on either side, and so could be secured against flank attacks, unlike an open beach. The 'Hill' mentioned by Warren was the Saint-Michel Tumulus, a significant feature in the landscape even today, rising above houses and trees. The defenders on the shore were 200–300 men that *Chef de brigade* Balthazar Romand had brought from Auray to support the 130 men at Sainte-Barbe, the nearest republican post.[16] The chouans attacked Romand's soldiers, as described by Jean Rohu who led one of the bands, made up of sailors:

> Général Tinténiac led a column to the village [of Carnac]. And we marched with him towards Saint-Michel where the tricolour flag flew. My sailors, without any hesitation, climbed the mound under the enemy's fire, and we were only outstripped by the général who ran up it with all his strength. On our arrival at the top, the Blues descended rapidly on the opposite side heading towards the village. Immediately the symbols of the Revolution were brought down, Tinténiac undoes his coats, pulls off his shirt, attaches it to the flag halyard, and thus improvises the white flag.[17]

While Tinténiac went to join the émigré troops on the shore he ordered Rohu to pursue the republicans retreating towards Plouharnel. Most of the 'blues' escaped but some were captured near Le Pô. It was reported that the chouans in pursuing the republicans, 'killed 12 of them, and took 7 prisoners, of whom they afterwards shot three, and were going to dispatch the other four in the same manner, when the emigrants prevented it'.[18] Wetton described this or another incident: 'The Chouhans [*sic*] ... brought in a party of republican prisoners and put them to death. One of the head republicans, an Officer, was hung on the ensign staff.'[19] It was a speedy introduction to the bitter conflict that had been taking place in Brittany in which both sides committed atrocities, but rarely admitted them. Several royalist accounts of the expedition, for example, describe the murder of villagers as well as the ransacking of their homes by marauding republican soldiers but do not even try to excuse any atrocities committed by their own side, they simply do not mention them.

---

15 Anon., *De l'expédition*, p.7.

16 Jean Sibenaler, *Quiberon pour le Roi et l'Autel* (Coudray-Macouard: Cheminements Éditions, 2007), p.47, reproducing a letter from Delisle to the National Convention 30 July.

17 Jean Rohu, 'Mémoires autographes de Jean Rohu', *Revue de Bretagne et de Vendée*, Tome II (December 1857), pp.595–613, p.609.

18 'a French Officer on board the Sybille ... June 29', printed in *The Kentish Gazette*, 10 July 1795.

19 Wetton, 'Journal', p.67.

Commemorative stone on the Pointe de Légenèse, translated, it reads, 'At the dawn of 27 June 1795 the regiments of émigrés tread the sand of the Carnac beaches.' (Author's collection)

The Émigrés and Chouans

Chouan commanders, including Georges Cadoudal, arrived during the day and they were joined by crowds of Bretons. The sight was impressive as Warren explained the same day,

> … [I] am busy disembarking all the residue of the stores for the troops. I have already armed between three and four thousand Royalists, and the numbers that come down to join us are inconceivable. I never saw so affecting a scene as the reception of the troops by our friends. Old men and young cried; and men, women and children, brought butter, eggs, milk, bread, wine, and whatever they had both to our people and the troops, and would not receive a farthing in payment.[20]

The landing of arms, ammunition and supplies continued over the next few days. The Régiments du Dresnay and de Hector also came ashore, the distribution of the latter in warships meant that many of the men were off Belle-Île. The 12 officers and 51 men, for instance, who had been on the *Arethusa* being transferred late on 26 June to a chasse marée to be brought round into the bay.[21]

20 Corbett (ed.), *Private Papers*, p.76, Warren to Spencer, private.

21 TNA: ADM 51/1102: *Arethusa* log.

A spirit of optimism abounded, as recounted by an anonymous officer in an 'Emigrant regiment' writing from Carnac on 28 June:

> I have been in France since yesterday. The Chouans received us in the most kind and friendly manner; men, women, and children came to meet us. They call us their brethren, friends: bring us all they have got, and conduct us to their dwellings. They assure us to have in Morbihan 60 or 70,000 men able to bear arms. Although I am led to think that this account is rather exaggerated by enthusiasm, yet it is true that their number is very considerable. We have now 10,000 of them with us, who have sworn an inviolable attachment to GOD and our KING. Every hour bands of Chouans arrive, 500, 800, or 1000 men strong. We have reason to hope a most fortunate change of circumstances. The air resounds far around us with incessant shouts of *Long live the King! Long live the Chouans!*[22]

The next day Warren agreed, writing that the Bretons were '... constantly coming in to Arm themselves, and offer every assistance in their power' and he estimated that, by then, 10–12,000 had been armed and continued to arrive, but there is a note of concern in his additional comment that 'the beach resembles a fair.'[23] Contades, who had some role in the process of arming them, contended that there were attempts to impose some method with weapons and clothes being distributed by the captains of the chouan bands or companies, others were less convinced,

> Without distinction of height, age and sex ... muskets were given without order, without precautions, to all who presented themselves. The weight of the weapons was often beyond the strength of those who received them. The cases of weapons were smashed as they were landed, without examining if they were intended to be distributed. The new arming of the line troops, and even their clothing already is to be found in the hands of the peasants, without it being possible to prevent it. ... The distribution of the weapons continued for several days with the same disorder, more than eighteen thousand muskets of all types had been delivered, without it being known if those who received them were friends or enemies ...[24]

Hervilly thoroughly disapproved of what was happening and protested to Puisaye about it, Contades even accused him of 'losing his head' when doing so.[25]

Hervilly decided that, to maintain discipline, the chouans and line troops should mix as little as possible, but that relations should be respectful. So when he found out Rohu had been subjected to insult by two émigré officers when visiting his headquarters soon after the landing, '... he appeared to me [Rohu] very displeased about what had happened' and taking steps to

22 *The Northampton Mercury*, 11 July 1795.

23 TNA: ADM 1/103: Warren to Nepean 29 June and Corbett (ed.), *Private Papers*, p.79, Warren to Spencer the same day.

24 Anon., *De l'expédition*, pp.8–9.

25 Contades, *Coblenz*, p.137.

discover the men responsible '... he assured me that anything similar would not happen again.'[26]

Immediately after the landing Hervilly had made a reconnaissance as far as Plouharnel, accompanied by a company from the Loyal Emigrants and one from his own regiment. He then returned to place the troops into cantonments in a defensive arc, some chouans on Saint-Michel Tumulus, the Régiment d'Hervilly in Carnac, that of Hector in villages to the right and Dresnay to the left with the Loyal Emigrants a little to the left in advance. The artillery was placed at Saint-Colomban, and Puisaye's headquarters at Légenèse.[27] The latter was irritated by the arrangements considering them superfluous as the enemy were far away, 'too weak, and above all too stupefied,' but Puisaye contradicted his own view when the Bishop of Dol landed and he got him 'to return to his ship until our position was a little more assured'.[28] Meanwhile three bodies, or divisions, of chouans were dispatched to cover the Vannes and Lorient roads and form a perimeter. Vauban, with about 4,000 men, was placed at Locoal-Mendon as a central reserve with Tinténiac on the left and Bois-Berthelot on the right covering the Plouharnel to Auray road at Locmaria.[29] This village, on strategic high ground, had been where hundreds of peasants had gathered in resistance to conscription on 19 March 1793 for a march on Auray.[30]

It was now that the news arrived of the death, on 8 June, of the boy-king Louis XVII, three months after his tenth birthday. He had succumbed to the physical abuse and neglect that he had suffered during his confinement. Puisaye wanted to hold a suitably solemn and inspiring ceremony to mark the event, so he had a tent erected on the beach from which the Bishop of Dol could hold an open-air mass to be attended by all the Bretons present as well as the troops. At the event, the troops were to place white cockades in their hats, removing the black ones they had had in England, and 'the flags with three fleurs-de-lys, that the [British] Government had given these corps, would be presented at the benediction, at the head of the regiments with their bands'. The ceremony was to end with an address by the bishop and the announcement of the accession of Louis XVIII.[31] However, the only regular unit that attended was the Veteran Company of the Loyal Emigrants, with the regiment's band. The Comte d'Hervilly and the other troops attended mass at Carnac. Dresnay's colours, and perhaps those of the other regiments, were only blessed by the bishop on 12 July.[32] Hervilly's snub worsened the already sour relations between him and Puisaye.

Another cause of friction between them was the use of troops alongside the chouans. Puisaye had wanted to attach volunteers from the Loyal

---

26 Rohu, 'Mémoires' (December 1857), p.610.
27 Anon., *De l'expédition*, p.10.
28 Puisaye, *Mémoires*, vol.VI, pp.155, 157–158.
29 Jacques-Anne-Joseph Le Prestre de Vauban, *Quiberon Mémoires pour servir à l'histoire de la guerre de la Vendée* (Paris: Aux armes de France, 1941), p.54.
30 Information notice at the village of Locmaria.
31 Puisaye, *Mémoires*, vol.VI, p.200.
32 Anon (ed.), *Olivier d'Argens*, pp.430–434, Talhouët to Dresnay 13 July 1795.

Emigrants to act as officers to new chouan companies, replacing them in the regiment with experienced Bretons, but Hervilly objected to this.[33] The choice of the Loyal Emigrants may have stemmed from their campaign experience as well as their different status, as a black cockade regiment. Another factor favouring such co-operation was that its commander was Major Louis-François d'Haize, who had been *capitaine de grenadiers* in the Orléans infanterie when the regiment's colonel had been Vauban. However, there was already concern about the lack of trained men and artillery. Warren, writing as early as 29 June; '… the number of regular troops are too small; and the cannon for the artillery, there being no howitzers or 12-pounders, notwithstanding it was mentioned as having been embarked by the Transport Office.'[34] Furthermore, the Loyal Emigrants had already been weakened as, within a few days of their arrival, 150 or so men were sick and unfit for service, still suffering from the effects of their last campaign.[35] The regular troops in British pay needed to be kept as a reserve, indeed Puisaye himself had hinted at such when he informed Windham, '… I will save [them] for the great occasions'.[36]

The aim of the expedition was, after all, to land supplies 'in a friendly country' in the expectation that this would 'be the signal for a general rising in those Provinces.'[37] The local Breton peasantry in their welcome to the landing had illustrated their enthusiasm and devotion to the royalist cause, and many were to continue to do so, but even at this early stage how 'friendly' the country was, in terms of effective control, was open to question. As the witness, on seeing the two hundred republican troops, at the landing point observed, 'It ought to appear astonishing that two hundred men could enforce the law in an area where we were assured that there were so many thousands of Chouans'.[38] The chouans had to not just carry out raids and ambushes but, by making use of their overwhelming numbers, face and defeat regular republican forces in the field for the initial operation, and indeed 'a general uprising' to succeed. The émigré officers of the white cockade regiments, many of whom were Bretons themselves, had their doubts and their relationships with the chouans and Puisaye soon became fragile. These concerns extended to the Loyal Emigrants who were expected, at least by Puisaye, to co-operate closely with the chouans, a member of the unit remembered: 'We expected to find a force at least in the process of organisation, and our disappointment was great at the appearance of these undisciplined crowds. I still recall the troubling impression that we had, foreseeing well that they would only be feeble assistance, if not harmful, if we were before long opposed by some troops.'[39]

33 Puisaye, *Mémoires*, vol.VI, p.183.
34 Corbett (ed.), *Private Papers*, p.79, Warren to Spencer.
35 Puisaye, *Mémoires*, vol.VI, p.139.
36 Puisaye, *Mémoires*, vol.VI, p.188, quoting a letter of 28 June 1795.
37 TNA: FO 74/9: Grenville to Wickham 8 June.
38 Anon., *De l'expédition*, p.7.
39 Chevalier Claude Berthier de Grandry, *Récit sommaire de la déplorable affaire de Quiberon* (Nantes: Vincent Forest, 1861), p.9 – the account was written in 1819.

Even the enthusiastic Warren was worried:

> I cannot dissemble to you that, notwithstanding our friends the Chouans are numerous and zealous, yet like all irregulars, they are uncertain for any distant expedition, and sometimes return, that is to say the married men, in shoals; and if any unforeseen bad luck should ensue, our number of troops are too small to resist the best forces that the Convention will undoubtedly assemble against us.[40]

Jean Guillot, a modern historian of the Morbihan chouannerie, takes a Breton perspective:

> The establishment of companies [of chouans] commanded by nobles just landed from the English ships would not be a success; both parties did not know each other and if the chouans have never had problems with the nobles who were with them from the beginning of hostilities, and who shared their hardships, their joys and their battles ... (... there is no profound anti-nobility movement within the chouannerie, but only a profound aversion for some individuals!), the chouans were irritated by these hundred or so officers, issue for the most part of grand families which had given, perhaps in yesteryears, fighting men to the crown of France, but who in their eyes have not yet proved their worth...[41]

Despite the shortage of troops and the disorganisation of the chouans, Puisaye, whose military competence was quickly doubted by several officers, immediately wanted to stretch the purpose of the landing into a much more ambitious expedition. He was fixed on attempting to enact his original plan of a swift advance on Rennes and into areas where he considered he had more personal support. Many years later, when reflecting on this stage of the expedition in his memoirs, he wrote as if he had been at the head of a large invading army:

> In any case of invasion, if you give your enemy the time to gather themselves, and you have not made use of the first moment of terror in which your unexpected arrival threw him, it only takes a little time to see the inseparable advantages of surprise in this form of attack turn against you. Even more so, if after having made some progress, you stop yourself from following it up, a single backward step is the signal for daring for your adversaries, and of discouragement for your followers.[42]

The Royalists Advance

The landing had caused panic among the republican forces as well as the civil administration. Romand, after the landing and the chouans' attacks, withdrew his men towards Landévant, covering Lorient, before he returned

---

40 Corbett (ed.), *Private Papers*, p 81, Warren to Spencer 3 July.

41 Jean Guillot, *Révolution et Chouannerie en Morbihan* (Gourin: Éditions des Montagnes Noires, 2014), p.189.

42 Puisaye, *Mémoires*, vol.VI, p.208.

to Auray. There, after conferring with the local administrators, both the garrison and the civil officials abandoned the town the next day. This allowed those with royalist sympathies to emerge and the National Guard, about four hundred strong, under its commander the notary Christophe Glain declared for the royalists, to be armed and equipped as the Bataillon, or Régiment, d'Auray.[43] After some hesitation Bois-Berthelot entered Auray on 29 June and Tinténiac took possession of Landévant after it was also abandoned by the republicans, so the royalists controlled an area of approximately 300 square kilometres between the Étel and Auray Rivers.[44] The only republican forces in the immediate vicinity of Carnac were those forming the garrison of Quiberon, under the temporary command of an officer named Delisle.

François-Louis Janillion, now a chasseur in the 19e Demi-brigade d'infanterie légère at Vannes, saw increased chouan activity following the news of the landing and the withdrawal into the city of the advance posts from the Auray road.

> We have already had several men killed at the Auray gate … and the sick and wounded who were in the hospitals were to be evacuated into the interior, which was affected in great haste. The whole town was in the greatest agitation; several soldiers were attacked and killed during the night; the commander of the National Guard had the same fate in the avenue near the port.[45]

Hoche arriving at Vannes, from his headquarters at Rennes, found there were only 500 men fit for service. At first he considered the situation so grave that he ordered the food supplies and munitions to be evacuated to Ploërmel and advised the administration to be ready to follow. He ordered reinforcements from his army in Brittany as well as requesting more from Canclaux in the Vendée and also from Normandy. From 28 June these troops began to march on Ploërmel, which had been designated as the rendezvous.[46]

The arrival of troops in such a manner through the campaign means that it is not possible to identify all the republican units involved in later engagements, primary sources only providing the distribution of troops that were present in the region beforehand, 26 September 1794, and afterwards, 15 January 1796 (see Appendix II).

It had been hoped that intensified chouan activity throughout Brittany, attacking posts and breaking bridges, would fix troops in their own areas and prevent their concentration in Morbihan. However, the activity that did take place was weak and sporadic, leading Hutt to conclude, '… it is clear these eruptions did not fuse into one movement, that what occurred was an intensification of "traditional" Chouannizing and not the birth of a Vendée-type, formed insurrection.'[47]

---

43 Puisaye, *Mémoires*, vol.VI, p.185 and Robert, *Expédition*, pp.38–39.

44 Jean Vidalenc, 'L'affaire de Quiberon', in Anon. (ed.), *Actes du 87e Congrès National des Sociétés Savantes Poitiers 1962* (Paris: Imprimerie Nationale, 1963), p.308.

45 Janillion, *Versailles et Quiberon*, p.43.

46 Robert, *Expédition*, pp.39–40 and Hutt, *Chouannerie*, p.285.

47 Hutt, *Chouannerie*, p.300.

Table 7: Republican troops in, or on the march to, the Morbihan département, 8 July 1795.[48]

Present and under arms in the département, excluding those in Belle-Île	9,200
Column from Côtes-du-Nord going to Ploërmel (*Général* Valletaux)	4,000
Column from Nantes marching via La Roche-Bernard (*Général* Lemoine)	5,000
Column from Rennes (*Général* Drut) marching 29 June, 2 and 6 July:	4,482
1e bataillon, 67e Régiment	495
1e bataillon, 72e Régiment	665
1e and 2e bataillon, 12e Demi-brigade	1,330
1e bataillon, Infanterie Légère de Nantes	468
2e bataillon, 19e Demi-brigade	605
14e Chasseurs à Cheval	38
Marching with them (6 July) were 7 grenadier companies from Normandy	501
Detachment to leave on 9 July to join the Nantes battalion along with 200 *sapeurs*	380
Total	22,682

By 28 June, Hoche had gathered 2,000 men at Vannes and so was able to advance on Auray. Janillion, acting as a skirmisher, was in front of a column of about 500 infantry and a handful of cavalry, chiefly local gendarmerie, which, after some concentrated fighting, drove away an enemy outpost from the Château de Pont-Sal defending the estuary-crossing there. After re-establishing the bridge, the republican vanguard advanced the next day and even entered an apparently undefended Auray before being shot at from the houses and having to retire back to the left bank of the Auray river, after which a limited artillery contest took place over the river.[49] That night Bois-Berthelot evacuated the town and withdrew to his original position at Locmaria. Hoche entered Auray on 30 June. The same day *Général de brigade* Jean-Louis-Gaspard Josnet de Laviolais, with 1,500 men, had attacked Tinténiac's advanced positions that extended out from Landévant towards Hennebont. Vauban arrived with 2,000 men to reinforce Tinténiac but '… he was beaten and put into a complete rout. The royalists fought very badly, although in an excellent position; my [Vauban's] troops followed the movement, fled and I was abandoned, just like the [other émigré] officers, in the midst of the enemy'.[50] Although the perimeter had shrunk at its first test it had not collapsed. Nevertheless, defeat had shaken the morale of the chouans who readily blamed it on the lack of support from the émigré regiments. These last, however, were already committed to a regular operation in which it was considered their organisation and discipline would be required.

Puisaye, in his memoirs, was to point the finger of blame for the defeats towards the regiments of 'paid troops' on the basis that the chouans on the advanced line were already dispirited by the failure of an expected detachment to arrive at Mendon. When he discovered this, late on 28 June, he had contacted Hervilly who assured him that his orders had not been complied with and that 400 men with two cannon would be at Mendon before

48 Champagnac, *Quiberon*, p.40 state of 8 July 1795 referenced as Armée de côtes de Brest B5 28.
49 Janillion, *Versailles et Quiberon*, pp.46–49.
50 Vauban, *Mémoires*, p.57.

the break of day, however they only arrived at 6:00 p.m. on 29 June.[51] The detachment was made up of the Régiment d'Hector reinforced by grenadiers from the Régiment d'Hervilly. *Sous-lieutenant* Jean-Joseph de Geoffroy Baron d'Antrechaus, of Hector, remembered, 'We were received ... as if sent from heaven' by the Bretons but then when they were ordered to return to Carnac that '... desolation and despair seized the unfortunate inhabitants' fearing republican vengeance.[52] Those that have followed Puisaye's line, have seen this withdrawal as a step taken by Hervilly to frustrate the general for personal, political, even subversive, reasons.[53] This, however, ignores the existence of orders, issued by Hervilly on 30 June for the Régiment du Dresnay to immediately march to Mendon to replace the detachment there. The officer commanding Hector was to relay his instructions to his counterpart from Dresnay and then march his detachment back 'to their respective cantonments.'[54] The reason that the detachment withdrew so quickly and was not replaced, as intended, was that the troops were needed for one of Puisaye's 'great occasions.'

Quiberon is Taken

A port had to be captured, and then held, so that aid could be delivered to royalist forces in France in sufficient quantity, especially of heavy equipment and horses, for the expedition to succeed. The Quiberon peninsula offered the opportunity to do so. Warren, for one, considered the position at Carnac untenable, 'in case of a check or being overpowered by superior numbers.' Possession of the peninsula would secure, 'The magazines of provisions, stores, the hospital for the sick, and a place to drill the Chouans ... and a communication with England, to which I look for constant support to enable us to go on.'[55]

In 1795, with fewer buildings and no trees as there are today, the peninsula would have looked, from the beaches at Carnac, like an enormous sperm whale breaching on the western horizon. Effectively it is an island with a low-lying sandy isthmus, confusingly known as the 'Falaise,' stretching from the Palice headland to the mainland.[56] The west side of the island, appropriately

51 Puisaye, *Mémoires*, vol.VI, pp.207–209, 215.

52 Jean-Joseph de Geoffroy Baron d'Antrechaus, *Relation de M. Le Baron d'Antrechaus, capitaine de vaisseau honoraire, député en 1820, échappé aux massacres de Quiberon* (Paris: L G Michaud, 1824), pp.6–7 (his name is sometimes given as Antrechaux but this is not the version used in this book). He wrote, that the village was called 'I think, Landevan[t].' Anon., *De l'expédition*, p.11, recounts the presence of the grenadiers.

53 Hutt, *Chouannerie*, pp.281–283, rejects the suggestion that Hervilly was acting on orders from the Agence de Paris but does not exclude the possibility he had lingering suspicion of the British Government's intentions from previous correspondence from the Princes' circle and also his own experience on Moira's staff in 1794.

54 Order reproduced and displayed at the Musée de Quiberon, Maison du Patrimoine, Quiberon. The orders specified that Dresnay was to concentrate by speedily recalling their detached posts and to then immediately march with its baggage to Mendon.

55 Corbett (ed.), *Private Papers*, p.81, Warren to Spencer 3 July.

56 La falaise translates as the cliff.

named the Côte Sauvage, is exposed to the prevailing weather but the east coast is sheltered and has two small harbours; Port Haliguen to the south and Port d'Orange (Saint Pierre-Quiberon) further north.

At this time the peninsula contained a number of defensive works, the foremost of which was Fort Penthièvre (named Fort Sans Culotte by the republicans), on the Palice headland overlooking the isthmus. Work had begun on it in 1748 in response to a British landing during the War of Austrian Succession (1740–1748), so it was named after the then governor of Brittany, the Duc de Penthièvre. With walls to the front and earthworks elsewhere to form a polygon, it had accommodation for 30 men and a powder magazine. The fort has been significantly reconstructed and enlarged since 1795, with an outer wall dating from 1846, so what is to be seen today is very different.[57] Then it commanded access to the peninsula. The east side of the isthmus, which was then fringed by salt marsh, has been stabilised notably for the construction of the railway and road and it is now significantly narrower as the shoreline, on the west side, has shifted somewhat eastward. A number of shore batteries defended the coast, the largest of which was Fort Neuf on the Pointe de Riberen, to the south of Port Haliguen from which it is separated by a small bay, the Anse du Porigo. Constructed as a battery during the War of the Spanish Succession (1701–1714) and rebuilt as a rudimentary redoubt in 1792, its defences were limited. The ruins that stand on the site now are the remains of the artillery fort constructed in 1883–1886 after its disarmament in 1902.[58]

The first stage of the operation to secure the Quiberon peninsula began on the morning of 30 June. Delisle, the republican commander, in a later letter written to justify his conduct, described what happened:

> Around five thirty in the morning, two frigates, a razeed ship and six gunboats set sail and headed towards our forts established on the East coast. Two frigates and a razee attacked the fort of Bec-Ruberen [Fort Neuf], which is situated almost in the intersection of the South and East coasts and they laid a hellish fire on it. This battery armed with four twenty-eight-pounders and a mortar, replied better and reached the enemy; which obliged them to back away. The battery of Fort Aliguen [*sic*] was attacked as well, the neighbouring houses riddled. It also retaliated, but its fire did not harm the enemy much; its calibre was too small. In turn, or better at the same time, the rest of the batteries were attacked. The enemy, after having reconnoitred them all, moved onto Fort Sans-Culotte around ten thirty in the morning. They ceased fire on the other points. They attacked this last fort with a great deal of vigour, they fired more than 150 cannon shots on it. The fort only replied to make them see that it was on its guard, as its calibre did not permit it to reach the enemy.
>
> The enemy ceased fire totally at midday, taking up position meanwhile still in their points of attack on Fort Sans-Culotte. We only had one man wounded and a cannon dismounted.[59]

57 Dated on the wall and Anon., 'Le Fort de Penthièvre' Le Ministère des Armées 13 December 2013 <http://www.defense.gouv.fr/actualites/memoire-et-culture/le-fort-de-penthievre>, accessed 29 September 2015.

58 Ville de Quiberon, information board at the site.

59 Sibenaler, *Quiberon*, pp.49–50, Delisle letter of 30 July.

Fearing an attack by a landing Delisle ordered all his troops to abandon the shore and go to the fort. 'But our step was seen. The enemy had only attacked us to find out the strength of our batteries and the exertions that we could make to prevent a landing. Having arrived at the fort, we readily recognised this, and we judged that a finer dance was reserved for us.'[60]

Logs show that Fort Neuf was bombarded by HMS *Anson*, *Artois* and four gun-vessels from 7:00 a.m. for two hours. Then some or all of the gun-vessels, but not the frigates, moved to another target.[61] The *Aimwell* gun-vessel which had received a midshipman and 15 men from the *Thunderer* 'to assist working the Guns' before the operation, kept 'constant firing at the Battery pointed out by the Commodore' between 10 and 11:00 a.m. until signalled to stop when it bore away.[62] The *Anson* having been converted, only the year before, from a 64 gun line-of-battle ship into a large frigate of 44 guns by being razed, or having the number of decks reduced, would have been the razee described by Delisle.[63] Puisaye stated, incorrectly, that the *Concorde* was involved and that several shots from Fort Neuf struck the frigates' rigging and three men on the *Anson* and four on the *Artois* were slightly wounded.[64]

The garrison, as described by Puisaye, was 'composed of a battalion of the former Régiment de la Reine [41e Ligne], several companies of National Volunteers, a company of gunners, a company of Negroes, and two engineers.'[65] He estimated it comprised of about 700 men while Delisle, who may have not included all of these units, stated he commanded 450, but later mentioned the presence of some grenadiers of the 141e Demi-brigade. His men were desperately short of food, surviving at the time on the chance discovery of some sacks of biscuit. The indications were that the final attack would take place, by land and sea, the next day and, as Delisle predicted, ships were seen on the move at 5:00 a.m. and Hervilly marched his regiment and Dresnay from Carnac to attack along the isthmus. However, the wind picked up and heavy rain set in which prevented the naval operation, so the attack was postponed.[66]

In the meantime, dispatches were to be sent to London, in the care of Lieutenant White, of HMS *Pomone*, announcing the landing. He, along with 14 French prisoners of war, came out of the bay in a cutter and, at 9:00 a.m. on 1 July, he joined the *Arethusa* off Belle-Île which immediately set sail for

60 Sibenaler, *Quiberon*, pp.49–50, Delisle letter of 30 July.
61 TNA: ADM 51/1153: *Galatea*, ADM 51/1149 *Pomone* and ADM 51/1117 *Anson* logs.
62 TNA: ADM 51/4406: *Aimwell* log.
63 Rif Winfield, *British Warships in the Age of Sail 1793–1817: Design, Construction, Careers and Fates* (Barnsley: Seaforth Publishing, 2005), p.98.
64 Puisaye, *Mémoires*, vol.VI, p.225. The *Concorde* was on patrol near the Cardineaux at the time (TNA: ADM 51/1111: log).
65 Puisaye, *Mémoires*, vol.VI, pp.230–231. Vidalenc, 'L'affaire de Quiberon', identifies the black soldiers as being from the bataillon des Antilles (p.308) and then the compagnie des hussards de Saint-Dominigue (p.312).
66 Sibenaler, *Quiberon*, p.51, Delisle letter of 30 July, and Le Charron, *Expédition de Quiberon*, p.9.

England. The following day HMS *Anson* replaced the *Arethusa*, as the cruiser off the island.[67]

The weather having improved, during the night of 2/3 July the Quiberon garrison heard activity from the ships offshore, and then as the sun rose they saw that the enemy was on the move. At 2:00 a.m. the *Pomone*, *Galatea* and *Artois*, accompanied by gun-vessels, weighed anchor to work towards the peninsula and an hour later 'the Chasse Marées, Flat Boats, Men of War Launches having Troops onboard left the Carnac side and proceeded to Quiberon.'[68] On the Falaise isthmus four columns of Hervilly and Dresnay infantry, each preceded by a French Emigrant Artillery field piece, approached the fort. They were accompanied by about 600 chouans commanded by Contades.[69]

At 4:00 a.m. the ships anchored off the coastal batteries. A soldier in the approaching boats remembered,

> … [we] crossed the bay and advanced in battle lines towards the centre of the peninsula. We were already close enough to it to make out a battery with several pieces pointed towards us, but we saw no movement in it, and we neither heard a single cannon shot, nor even a single musket shot, from the direction of the land attack. We did not know what to think, we were all astonished by this silence. Nevertheless, we always advanced, eyes fixed on the pieces from which we continually expected a discharge, and we landed on the shore, very surprised to find it undefended. Soon, in the meantime, we knew the reason; the fort had capitulated at the first summons …[70]

A Frenchman serving in a gun-vessel reported '… we raised anchor, to go to cover the troops who were going to make a descent on Quiberon … we, all the gunboats and light frigates, anchored all along the shore to fight but there was no need, the republican troops did not fire a single cannon shot at us'.[71]

The royalists went ashore at about 5:30 a.m. on the Plage de Kerbourgnec, south of Port d'Orange. The force consisted of around 2,000 chouans, 250 Loyal Emigrants and a detachment of about 100 from Hector who were joined by 150 marines from the British warships – the detachment from the *Thunderer* was in fact formed of soldiers of the short-lived 118th Foot who served on the ship as marines.[72] There was no opposition on the beach to the

67 TNA: ADM 51/1102: *Arethusa* and ADM 51/1117 *Anson* logs. The *Arethusa* was chosen by Warren so its crew could return to a home port to recover from a high level of sickness, ADM 1/103: Warren to Nepean 29 June.

68 TNA: ADM 51/1149: *Pomone* log.

69 Only Vossey, 'Récit Fidèle', p.4, specifically mentions the presence of Dresnay with Hervilly. Le Grand du Quellenec, on the regiment's staff, simply wrote 'our troops marched to attack the Fort …' in his journal (Roussel & Bergevin, *Un Survivant*, p.261). There is no reason to think that the arrangements made for the original march, which included Dresnay, were not maintained. For the chouans, Le Charron, *Expédition de Quiberon*, p.10 and Contades, *Coblenz*, p.145.

70 Berthier de Grandry, *Récit sommaire*, p.11.

71 TNA: HO 69/30: anonymous report of service 11 June to 23 July 1795.

72 Puisaye, *Mémoires*, vol.VI, p.227, states there were 2,600 chouans and does not mention a Hector detachment whereas Warren (Corbett (ed.), *Private Papers*, p.80) states that there

landing '... despite the presence of a detachment of the former Régiment de la Reine-Infanterie. The officer who commanded it surrendered, indeed, to the summons made to him by M. de Torcy, capitaine in La Châtre's regiment, his former comrade in the Reine-Infanterie, and came to offer his hand to help him disembark'.[73]

As Hervilly's troops had come within range of the cannon of Fort Sans-Culotte and skirmishers had been deployed, a republican officer came out to parley. However, Hervilly sent him back with a summons for the commander to surrender, warning him that if he did not do so within half an hour the fort would be taken by storm and no quarter would be given. In the interval Hervilly exhorted his regiment who replied 'Vive le Roi!'[74] The sound of four cannon discharges, the signal for the landing, seems to have finally disheartened the fort's commander and Hervilly and Lieutenant Colonel Lenglé de Moriencourt, of the engineers, entered the fort to take its capitulation. Captain Durham, of the *Anson*, who had stationed his ship to the west of the peninsula in support of the attack saw that a white flag had been hoisted over the fort at 7:00 a.m.[75] Hervilly assigned the grenadier company of his first battalion, commanded by the Henri-Louis-Augustin Comte de Boissieux, to form the first guard at the fort.[76] It was now that Puisaye and Warren appeared accompanied by detachments of British marines and Hector. Puisaye, by his own account, in which he took a much more important role in securing the fort, was far from pleased that Hervilly had accepted the capitulation instead of him, 'the representative of the King of France'.[77] He exerted his authority by placing the British marines as the first guard of the fort to, as he wrote, 'again confirm ... the alliance which I had contracted for His Most Christian Majesty with His Britannic Majesty'.[78] He also had the Union Flag flown alongside that of the French King, as reported by a more tactful Warren, '... the White Flag and British Colours were hoisted together and of equal height. I directed ours to be hauled down in the evening.'[79]

---

were 1,300 chouans. He again does not include Hector in his list but states a detachment accompanied the British marines to the fort, so it appears he numbered them together when he wrote there were 250 marines present. The presence of the detachment of the 118th Foot comes from the *Thunderer* log, TNA: ADM 51/1103.

73 Vossey, 'Récit Fidèle', p.4. Lieutenant Aimar-Louis de Torcy of the Loyal Emigrants had indeed been *capitaine* in the Reine infanterie, by 1795 the 41e Ligne. The most likely officer to have been this colleague was Louis Vidalain who had been *lieutenant en second* of grenadiers in 1789 and *capitaine* in 1793; the other, but less likely, possibility was Jean François, *sous-lieutenant en second* of chasseurs in 1789 and *quartier-maître trésorier* in 1793. The modest, at best, rate of promotion of these regular officers is in remarkable contrast to that of individuals from more politically acceptable volunteer units.

74 Contades, *Coblenz*, p.147.

75 TNA: ADM 51/1117: *Anson* log. The fact that the *Anson* had left Quiberon Bay in the early hours of 1 July indicates that the date of the attack had been set before then.

76 Boissieux, aged 54, was a very experienced senior officer, *maréchal de camp* since 1788, on whom command at the Tuileries had devolved on 10 August 1792.

77 Puisaye, *Mémoires*, vol.VI, p.229.

78 Puisaye, *Mémoires*, vol.VI, p.230.

79 Corbett (ed.), *Private Papers*, pp.80–81.

Fort Penthièvre from the isthmus (La Falaise) (Author's collection)

Puisaye placed Nicolas-Anne Baudot Comte de Sainneville, *chef de division* in the French navy and *capitaine* in Hector, as governor of the peninsula with six Loyal Emigrant veterans, former officers, as his staff.[80] The fort, now under royalist control, reverted to its original name. Engineers, with 800 chouans, began to construct breastworks on the isthmus in front of the fort.[81] The émigré troops immediately marched back to their positions around Carnac, however having not eaten that day, the heat of the sun and the rum that had been issued took their toll and about 300 men of the Régiment d'Hervilly alone, dropped out of the march. They were left in the charge of some NCOs to recover, and they returned to the regiment later.[82]

The republican troops either agreed to enlist in the white cockade regiments or were treated as prisoners of war. The latter were taken to a church on the peninsula. Delisle stated that on the way two of them were killed by the Bretons, probably because of this they were later transferred to British custody. Indeed, a report circulated among the republicans that, 'The émigrés on entering the fort wanted to run the soldier prisoners through with the sword. But the English took possession of them saying that they would put to sea if they killed anyone.'[83] On 4 and 5 July 102 prisoners were taken on board HMS *Robust* and the *Thunderer* received '100 French prisoners consisting of Men, Women and Children' from Quiberon on 5 July. On 8 July, they were transferred to the *Patty* transport which was designated

80 Sainneville is given in Puisaye's memoirs and some other sources as Senneville.
81 Contades, *Coblenz*, p.150.
82 Le Charron, *Expédition de Quiberon*, p.10.
83 Charles Floquet, *Quiberon presqu'île au cours des siècles* (Maulévrier: Hérault-Éditions, 1984), pp.88–89 quoting a report from an aide-de-camp of Canclaux.

as a prison ship on which detachments of marines were sent to take their turn, every 24 hours, as guards.[84] Later 'in consequence of the great number of French Prisoners which daily arrive,' Warren appointed a navy officer to act as commissary to these prisoners.[85]

Delisle, however, did not join the men on the *Patty* as he was among a party of 10 officers who arrived at Plymouth on the *Stag* cutter on 12 July and were taken to Mill Prison from which Delisle, at least, was released on parole at Tavistock. It was from the Devon town that Delisle wrote his report in which he justified his actions, stating that it was only once he was no longer in a position to resist that it was clear his summons to surrender had not been made in the name of King George but of Louis XVIII of France.[86] It seems that Delisle was only trying to prepare his excuses, given that when Boucret at Belle-Île had been summoned it had been explicitly in the name of Louis, and agreeing to such would have been an acknowledgment of the legitimacy of the French monarch.

Puisaye wrote that 400 men, two-thirds of the 41e Ligne and 100 other troops, immediately volunteered to enlist in the émigré regiments. It seems that the black soldiers were not given the choice to enlist or be taken as prisoners, as he ordered they be 'employed in the works of the fort or in the service of officers who wished to take domestics.'[87] The men from the 41e Ligne were chiefly assigned to Hervilly's regiment where they 'were very well conducted.'[88] Only the existing records of Hervilly and Dresnay are sufficiently detailed to show these enlistments.

Table 8: Recruits (all ranks) enlisted in Hervilly and Dresnay while in France, 1795.[89]

Date	Hervilly	Dresnay
27 June	5	–
28 June	7	–
29 June	3	38
30 June	2	–
1 July	5	31
2 July	3	23
3 July	10	11
4 July	196	5
5 July	–	17
6 July	–	13
7 July	1	–
8 July	1	1
9 July	–	2
14 July	–	4
15 July	–	3
Total	233	148

84 TNA: ADM 51/1163: *Robust* and ADM 51/1103: *Thunderer* logs.
85 TNA: ADM 1/103: Warren to Nepean 18 July.
86 Sibenaler, *Quiberon*, pp.55–57.
87 Puisaye, *Mémoires*, vol.VI, p.233.
88 Contades, *Coblenz*, p149.
89 TNA: WO 12/11681: Hervilly and WO 12/11708: Dresnay.

Rotalier, in his correspondence, indicates that throughout the period he recruited 46 supernumerary gunners and 10 drivers, presumably from Breton royalists – the gunners were probably sailors with experience of crewing guns – and intended to recruit 160 men in all.[90] A later, separate, return shows, with the exception of Dresnay, comparable numbers: Hervilly – 210, Hector – 30, Dresnay – 20, Loyal Emigrants – 25 and the Emigrant Artillery – 120, with the note that, 'These recruits prisoners for the most part with some few others.'[91] It is not clear exactly how these men were incorporated into each unit but it seems that in the Régiment d'Hervilly at least one company was formed of men from the 41e Ligne as well as, on 5 July, a 'company of auxiliary chasseurs' – probably from men that had been in the other republican units.[92]

The Republicans Counter-Attack

By the evening of 3 July the royalists possessed Quiberon peninsula, the white cockade regiments were at and around Carnac, and an outer perimeter held by chouans ran from Landévant, via Locoal-Mandon, to Locmaria. However, no effort had been made to erect defensive works along even the inner perimeter, despite six 9-pounder cannon 'with round, Grape & Case shot' and other requisite equipment having been provided by the *Robust* and *Thunderer* as early as 1 July.[93] On 4 July the republicans, now with a total of 13,000 troops available, pressurised the western section of the outer perimeter around Landévant and, according to a republican report, after a fight of three hours drove back the royalists, who abandoned muskets and supplies in their retreat, and inflicted 300–400 casualties.[94] Meanwhile Hoche, advanced towards Locmaria, one of his soldiers observing, 'This was the first time that we encountered royalists clothed in red; all those against which we had had to fight until this time were dressed in every colour. Meanwhile the greatest part, and notably the chiefs, had more particularly adopted grey.'[95] Hoche's attack succeeded and, with the chouans in retreat on both wings, Vauban's central position was untenable; the outer perimeter collapsed. Again there had been unheeded demands that the paid troops of the regiments should have been detached to support the chouans' line.

On 5 July the dispositions changed with a division of chouans under Vauban taking post at Carnac and the troops, under Hervilly, withdrawing

90 TNA: PRO 30/11/225: He noted that many suitable men would not make a formal, long-term, engagement.

91 TNA: ADM 80/136: 22 July.

92 See Anon., *De l'expédition*, p.23.

93 The *Robust* supplied hers on 1 July (TNA: ADM 51/1163: *Robust* log) although the number provided is illegible in the log; while the *Thunderer* supplied three on 2 July (TNA: ADM 51/1103: *Thunderer* log); also see Wetton, 'Journal', p.68, despite inconsistencies with date and perhaps an error in location in transcription.

94 Patrick Huchet, *Quiberon ou le destin de la France* (Rennes: Éditions Ouest-France, 1995), p.91, report of an aide-de-camp of Canclaux.

95 Janillion, *Versailles et Quiberon*, p.51.

into the peninsula. Although Puisaye in his memoirs denied it, the decision is described as being made at a council of war on 5 July.[96] The regiments retired to Quiberon,

> … to restore some order and discipline among the troops that several days in cantonment had already disrupted a good deal; … to organise and instruct a considerable number of Chouans; to establish order in the provisions & in their distribution, & for the Intendant of the Army … to begin to carry out the functions which were entirely foreign to him, to profit from this moment of rest to learn his role.[97]

The Intendant, Charles-Paul-Jean-Baptiste de Bourgevin Vialart de Saint-Morys, a former counsellor in the Parlement de Paris, a legal body, was responsible for the logistics and supply of the army. He had no experience of his role but had been particularly close to Puisaye in London. The anonymous commentator continued:

> The most exaggerated imagination could not conceive the disorder that did not cease to reign in this part of the army's administration; the distribution which should be made in the evening at the headquarters, in order that the staff of the regiments could deliver the provisions early, were made so late that it was often six o'clock in the evening before the soldiers had had anything to eat.[98]

When the troops arrived in the peninsula at about midday there was no food ready for distribution and in many cases what was to have been their quarters had been taken over by fugitive Breton families. It took some time for this to be sorted out, which became only another source of friction between Hervilly and Puisaye, and their respective officers. As there was no camp equipment with the expedition – it had apparently been sent to Jersey instead – the troops were distributed among the scattered small villages and hamlets of the peninsula.[99]

Quiberon peninsula had a very different aspect to that of today, Chasle de La Touche, who lived there in 1810, wrote in 1838:

> The soil, sandy and hardly fertile, does not produce enough corn to feed a population of 1,800 souls, scattered in twenty or so villages and the small towns of Saint-Pierre and Quiberon; but the potato is carefully cultivated, with the plough. There is little live-stock; the sea is not well-stocked with fish; excellent oysters and other shellfish are to be found in abundance, a precious resource for the inhabitants. It is an error when it is said they were all fishermen; on the contrary, they did not fish at all and do not even possess boats. The majority sail in the

96 Puisaye, *Mémoires*, vol.VI, p.258.
97 Anon., *De l'expédition*, p.18.
98 Anon., *De l'expédition*, pp.18–19.
99 Antrechaus, *Relation*, p.8. Warren had offered to supply sails for shelter as a solution but this was rejected. TNA: FO 95/605: Bouillon to Windham 27 July 1795, in which he said he had camp equipment for 5,000 men and also, in that of 18 July, when he said that he was sending the clothing and baggage for Hervilly on to Quiberon.

> coastal trade, ocean voyages or on the vessels of the state; the rest, a small number, do agricultural work of which the women are almost exclusively left with.
>
> The land, subdivided by dry-stone walls into an infinity of small parcels, presents an appearance all the more sad as it is devoid of trees … There are perhaps fifteen or twenty fig or mulberry trees dispersed in the villages. Day-to-day fuel consists of cow pats, moulded and dried in the sun, and of a type of kelp, or seaweed, that is macerated in fresh water and then dried. Sources of fresh water, although quite numerous, are less abundant in summer. There are in winter three or four small pools which the warmth promptly changes into bogs.
>
> When Quiberon is stripped of its crops, nothing is more arid, one only sees sand, boundary walls and the sea.[100]

The villages houses were tightly clustered together and the troops were '… packed into the cottages of the poor fishermen who lived there.'[101] The units were located as follows: Loyal Emigrants at Saint-Pierre; Hervilly, first battalion at Kerdavid (now part of Saint-Pierre) and the second at Kerhostin; Hector at Port Haliguen; Dresnay at Quiberon and the companies of the Emigrant Artillery at Kerbourgnec, Keridenvel, Kergroix and Portivy with the artillery park also being placed at the last village.

Work continued to improve the defences at the entrance to the peninsula, as Contades put it, 'The engineer officers traced in front of the fort this famous work which was to give us a second Gibraltar.'[102] One of the émigré soldiers described the defences thus,

> A redan was, moreover built in front of its [the fort's] base and occupying almost all the space between the two stretches of sea. Further in front, a curtain was raised, which also stretched from one shore to the other, and the advanced posts were placed at staggered intervals for half a league further on. Finally, the approaches of the entrenched camp supporting the right of the fort, were made more difficult.[103]

The engineers considered that this 'second Gibraltar' would hold out against attack for at least six weeks. This assurance was to give to some royalists a false of security, and perhaps even complacency.

At 4:00 p.m. that day, 5 July, Hoche with 200 cavalry made a reconnaissance of the heathland west of Auray towards Plouharnel, there was no opposition. A republican officer reported that: 'Several villages were searched, among others that of Crach [*sic*] where a prodigious quantity of provisions that the English had landed were found; some remaining peasants asserted that the émigrés intended to re-embark if we pressed them too closely.'[104] Troops were immediately brought up to march the next day.

---

100 Théodore-Gaston-Joseph Chasle de La Touche, *Relation du désastre de Quiberon en 1795, et réfutation des souvenirs historiques de M. Rouget de L'Isle sur ce désastre* (Paris: Delloye, 1838), pp.14–15.

101 Corbehem, *Dix ans*, p.160.

102 Contades, *Coblenz*, p.158.

103 Berthier de Grandry, *Récit sommaire*, p.12.

104 Huchet, *Quiberon*, p.93, report of an ADC of Canclaux.

On 6 July the republicans left Ploemel at 4:00 a.m. in three infantry columns. The cavalry, which was supposed to support them, simply went off to pillage and could not be found for four hours. The republicans were short of food and, after their discoveries the day before, the cavalry appear to have wanted a share of the British largesse. Hoche was to repeatedly complain to the authorities of the crimes committed by his soldiers:

> My soul is torn to see the conduct of the wretched army that I command. All my orders, all possible decrees will not change its spirit; it is necessary to apply the immediate death penalty to the villains who are acquainted with murder, theft and arson. The law leaves no power in my hands ...[105]

The chouan position around Carnac consisted of a forward line from Sainte-Barbe, held by Georges Cadoudal's 3,000 men, through Kergonan, where the bataillon d'Auray was stationed in the château, to the Saint-Michel Tumulus, with Carnac itself behind.[106] Late on 4 July a belated effort to prepare defences commenced. Wetton, who had spent that day with an émigré officer, noted, 'We then received a messenger from the general at Quiberon Fort to inform Chevalier Rottilleau of the enemy's army being within fifteen miles of Carnac with orders to throw up intrenchments on the beach for a retreat ... At four o'clock [p.m.] he lay'd out the ground and set the Chouhan to work'.[107]

The first sign of royalist opposition to the republican advance, on 6 July, was at Carnac itself, but it quickly evaporated.[108] Wetton was still on shore:

> At one o'clock [in the afternoon], Rottilleau discover'd a party of Republicans, about twenty in number, marching down for us then half a mile from us. The Chouhans, which were two hundred and upwards in [number] ran away from the intrenchments to the [chasse-marées], while Rottilleau and myself stop'd to spike two guns, five of the Republicans chased us down to the water's edge where they fir'd upon us wading to a fishing boat ... We landed at Quiberon at three o'clock.[109]

The royalists on the western end of the perimeter faced a different dilemma. Rohu was at Sainte-Barbe, with his chouan company of sailors, and had been ordered to,

> ... maintain the rear-guard and to protect the inhabitants who, from more than thirty parishes, fled before the Blues. The sea was low, and Plouharnel bay was full of women carrying or dragging their children, of carts loaded with all the grain and linen that they had had the time to put in them, men driving their live-stock

105 To a local official quoted in Louis-George de Cadoudal, *Georges Cadoudal et la chouannerie* (Paris: Plon, 1887), p.92.

106 In the nineteenth century the Abbaye Saint-Michel de Kergonan was established on the site of the château.

107 Wetton, 'Journal', p.68. The most likely candidate as Wetton's companion was the Chevalier Alexis-Charles-Félix de Rotalier, captain lieutenant in the Emigrant Artillery and eldest son of the lieutenant colonel.

108 Janillion, *Versailles et Quiberon*, p.52 and Huchet, *Quiberon*, p.93, Canclaux's ADC.

109 Wetton, 'Journal', p.68.

> before them and calling with loud shouts for our help to preserve them from the fury of the enemy, who fired on them and had even already stopped several carts. Many of these people were our relatives, our friends or our acquaintances, and, instead of following the army, we considered ourselves duty bound to defend them and push the Blues back from the bay and hold them there until the sea had risen enough to prevent them from crossing. The bataillon d'Auray, stationed in the château de Kergonan, having been warned too late, was going to be cut off in its retreat and headed at great pace towards the windmill road; but this road previously cut by the sea had become impracticable, time was needed to make up the distance, and the republicans continued to advance M. Glain, notary at Auray, who commanded this battalion, gave me a signal to wait for them and I halted: I rallied my unit when Georges [Cadoudal] came, on behalf of the general, to say to me that it was necessary to follow the army and so not to stop. But, when I had explained to him the dangers that the men and women ran who were in the rear and who had previously rendered us such service, he did not insist and returned to the general. Instantly Tinténiac arrived, at a great gallop, who ordered me to follow. In vain did I speak to him of those who were still in the rear, he would not listen to reason, and displeased returned. It was at this moment, and only then, that I saw my mother, with her clogs in her hand, and who for two hours had followed me in all my movements, without me noticing her, such was my great preoccupation.
>
> Once the bataillon d'Auray disengaged, we continued all day long to skirmish with the Blues, and we only entered the fort at sunset. This day spent without drinking or eating had been so tiring, that I could only follow my company that was bivouacked all night in the Falaise.[110]

The crowds of refugees converged on the peninsula, without any enemy being seen, and chaotic scenes followed as described by Contades who was at Fort Penthièvre:

> … we caught sight of the falaise far off covered with a prodigious crowd, running in the greatest disorder. Some young men arrived first, saying to us that the blues were chasing them. Old people, children, women, officers, chouans, all running pell-mell, struck with a terror that nothing could describe. You would have to have seen this sight to have any idea of it. … The position was critical. The chouans were struck with such a terror that, without seeking the entrance, they had scaled the revetements and crossed the palisades. In one word, they had taken us by assault. … To make matters worse, a voice shouted: "Here come the blues!" This voice was the signal for a general firing [of muskets] and in every direction.[111]

There had only been about 50 men on guard at the fort and Hervilly, arriving at the scene, requested that the Régiment du Dresnay come to support them. However, its commander, *Lieutenant-colonel* de Talhouët, informed him it would be two hours before it could be there as 'his soldiers had gone to

110 Rohu, 'Mémoires' (December 1857), pp.611–612.

111 Contades, *Coblenz*, pp.155–157.

look for provisions.'[112] It was only now that the enemy appeared, about 100 or so skirmishers, who approached the fort but withdrew after two or three cannon shots had been fired, and some more in formation further away on the isthmus.

The influx of refugees in front of the republican advance was a moment of crisis when Puisaye should have shown leadership to all sections of the royalist army. However, according to Contades, he had returned to his headquarters to dine. Although Contades was still part of the general-in-chief's entourage he was becoming disillusioned with him. His observations that 'Puisaye was above all excessively lazy', over fond of his bed and only listened to 'a few veritable adventurers who flattered him on every point' have to considered in this light. Nevertheless, it is clear from all the memoirs, bar his own, that Puisaye was frequently absent or invisible when active leadership was required.[113]

The crowds of Breton refugees were sent further into the peninsula, to join those who had already taken refuge there and some order was restored. However, as night fell, the chouans who had been placed in the outworks and advanced positions, either too tired like Rohu, too dispirited or with families to go to, abandoned them and two companies from Hervilly had to be deployed to replace them.

112 Contades, *Coblenz*, p.156; Puisaye stated that Dresnay was the service regiment that day and should have been at the fort at 5:00 a.m. but arrived at midday (*Mémoires*, vol.VI, p.266).

113 Contades, *Coblenz*, pp.142–143.

6

Quiberon

Trapped Rats

The positions the republicans had taken during the day were marked by their fires the night of 6 to 7 July.[1] What the royalists left behind was remarkable: 'We have taken from them 8,000 muskets, as many suits of scarlet regimentals, a great number of assignats with the effigy of Louis XVIII, and a very large quantity of warlike stores.'[2] The most important position was that of Sainte-Barbe, which in 1795 was key to access between the mainland and Quiberon as Plouharnel Bay extended further north than it does today. An area of tidal mudflats, Étang du Bégo, about a kilometre in length (north to south) and up to 400 metres wide, continued to the foot of the higher ground on which the village stands and is now reclaimed land lying north of the current road, Avenue de l'Océan (D768), and the railway.[3] Republican possession of this point impeded the ability to readily supply royalist forces, the purpose of the expedition. The royalists were to immediately respond with a sortie that night, an anonymous émigré reported how it was to be commanded:

> Undoubtedly this sortie like all the preceding operations, had been concerted between MM. de Puisaye & d'Hervilly; but either through virtue or through taste, the general-in-chief seemed to have left to M. le Comte d'Hervilly the glory & difficulty of command. He followed the columns rather as a volunteer than as a General, without giving a single order, & without anyone believing that he had anything to do with it.[4]

The men marched out of the fort at 10:00 p.m. and along the isthmus. Hervilly placed about 200 chouans, all that were apparently able and willing to join the operation, as skirmishers in front of the regular troops and behind them

1 Anon., *De l'expédition*, p.22.

2 *The Caledonian Mercury*, 25 July 1795, quotation from *Le Batave*, Rennes 10 July.

3 Vidalenc, 'L'affaire de Quiberon', p.313.

4 Anon., *De l'expédition*, pp.23–24. Puisaye, in his later memoirs (vol.VI, pp.276–279), claimed to have taken a leading role with the chouans in advance as well as restoring order in the Régiment d'Hervilly – no other source corroborates this, indeed no other even mentions his presence.

was a detachment from Hector, 200 strong, in five equally-spaced sections across the isthmus, from shore to shore, the intervals between each section adjusting to the available space. They were followed by the two battalions of Hervilly, in separate columns with two field pieces between them, except for the auxiliary chasseur company which was not considered ready. The Dresnay detachment, also 200 strong, was deployed in the rear in a similar manner to Hector.[5]

It was a particularly dark night and the troops marched in silence towards Sainte-Barbe until they suddenly ran into the republican advance position. A sentinel shouted out a challenge and opened fire. The rest of the guard joined in, wounding Antoine-Pierre-Joseph de Chapelle Marquis de Jumilhac, *aide-major* to Hervilly's first battalion, who received musket ball through the body.[6] The republicans rapidly retreated on to their main position, in some confusion, and in the darkness, thinking the royalists had some cavalry 'the advance-guard and the flankers on the right' fired on their own, although apparently with little loss.[7] Then, as the royalist troops continued forward they in turn fell into some confusion when to their officers' surprise some Hervilly soldiers suddenly began to fire their muskets which was followed by a general discharge, either in the air or the general direction of the enemy. As the troops were still in column, several sections became disorganised and it took some time for the officers to re-establish order to enable them advance. As they neared the republican camp they could hear the general alarm and shouts of, 'There are the royalists! Save the cannon'.[8] However, rather than charge the position with bayonets fixed, the royalist troops were halted with their muskets carried 'au bras' as on the march. For their part the republicans, unable to make out the royalists' position in the dark, did not deploy their artillery. However, Hervilly now had the two field pieces brought forward and ordered them to fire towards the camp. Le Charron described the result, 'The enemy … rained lots of balls and shrapnel on us, that the fire of our two field pieces helped them to direct. I had the distress of losing the three men from the right of my section, who were killed by the same shot.'[9]

Hervilly then gave the order for the retreat, which was carried out in good order. The enemy did not pursue as they came under fire from the British gun-vessels stationed off the Carnac beaches, with the fire commencing at 3:00 a.m.[10] The chouans do not appear to have performed well on this occasion, one source stating that they, 'recoiled at the first musket shot & threw themselves into the columns. The general, aided by the officers who surrounded him, could never manage to make them advance, despite the blows with the flat of the sabre that were shared out on them.' Other more sympathetic sources simply make no mention of them at all in the action.[11]

5 Anon., *De l'expédition*, p.23.
6 Puisaye, *Mémoires*, vol.VI, p.279.
7 Floquet, *Quiberon*, p.88.
8 Le Charron, *Expédition de Quiberon*, p.12.
9 Le Charron, *Expédition de Quiberon*, p.12.
10 TNA: ADM 51/1149: *Pomone* log.
11 Anon., *De l'expédition*, p.25. Examples of the sympathetic are Contades, *Coblenz* and Le Charron, *Expédition de Quiberon*.

In the retreat an artillery caisson, damaged by enemy fire, had to be abandoned.[12] There was, moreover, a human cost to the operation. Contades estimated that there had been about 100 men killed or wounded while Puisaye stated that the Régiment d'Hervilly had at least two soldiers killed and two officers and 17 soldiers wounded; 17 chouans were wounded and in Hector one officer, *Sous-lieutenant* Le Fort de Carneville, was killed on the spot – a piece of shell ripping into his stomach – while two officers, one of whom was *Capitaine* de Locmaria, were wounded along with a few men.[13] Lists for Hervilly, the only unit with sufficiently detailed returns, show that five fusiliers were killed and *Lieutenant* de Champflour was mortally wounded, dying on 10 July.[14] Dresnay's casualties were mentioned by Talhouët in a letter to his colonel in which he wrote, more generally, of the regiment's conduct,

> … the spirit is always very good, I even think that the individuals of whom we had suspicions have reverted to the opinion of veritable royalists. It showed the greatest will at the surrender of Fort Penthièvre, and since in the reconnaissance on Sainte-Barbe, where we endured musketry and cannon fire, it had the best bearing. … We only had ten wounded, M. Grenier and nine men. No wound is dangerous.[15]

Casualties are, of course, not just numbers on a return sheet and on 7 July Wetton, 'Assisted in two amputations of the leg. Dress'd five of the wounded and extracted two [musket] balls, one from the breast and another from the arm.'[16]

The performance of such an 'exercice de garnison' (garrison exercise) to simply reconnoitre the enemy's position was naturally going to incur criticism of the commanders, Puisaye and, to a greater extent, Hervilly. That of the latter was not restricted to his normal detractors. The quartermaster of Dresnay, who would not have been present at the sortie itself, later wrote:

> If the Comte d'Hervilly had wanted to profit from the disorder which appeared to reign among them [the republicans], he would have certainly stormed their camp; but he left them the time to prepare and instead of having the charge sounded, he ordered the retreat to be beaten, fearing that his regiment had begun to waver at the first volley from the Republicans.[17]

12 Anon., *De l'expédition*, p.26.

13 Contades, *Coblenz*, p.163 and Puisaye, *Mémoires*, vol.VI, p.279.

14 TNA: WO 12/11681: pay list.

15 Anon., *Correspondance Secrète de Charrette, Stofflet, Puisaye, et Autres* (Paris: Buisson, An VII – 1797/1798), vol.II, p.316, Talhouët to Dresnay 13 July. The wounded officer was *Lieutenant* Vicomte du Giron-Grenier.

16 Wetton, 'Journal', p.68.

17 Roussel & Bergevin, *Un Survivant*, p.263, Le Grand du Quellenc's journal. Contades is the only source to suggest that Dresnay, as well as Hervilly, had fallen into disorder (*Coblenz*, p.160).

On La Falaise facing northwards towards the line of republican entrenchments marked by the Second World War era Tour du Bego. (Author's collection)

Over the next few days the republicans began the construction of what was to become a formidable line of field works stretching across the isthmus about a kilometre south of Sainte-Barbe, thus preventing any use by the royalists of the paths, accessible at low-tide, across the Étang du Bégo. This was no easy task as they only had sand and stubbly turves to work with. Alexandre Moreau de Jonnès was later to claim that he solved this problem by mixing the sand with dung collected from nearby villages.[18] Marked by the remains of Hitler's Atlantic Wall, built on and into them, the lines exist to this day.[19]

Once further artillery had been delivered by sea from Lorient the line consisted of, on the right (west) end, a strong redoubt, named the redoubt of the flag pole, armed with two 16-pounder cannon and two 8-inch mortars. Approximately 150 metres to the left of it was battery Number 1, with two 8-pounders and two 6-inch mortars; in the middle was the 'central redoubt' with two 12-pounders and finally, to the left of the line, was battery Number 2 with two 8-pounders and two 6-inch mortars.[20] In addition, batteries were established on the opposite, eastern, shore of Plouharnel Bay, to support the left side of the line. Contemporary sketch maps show these batteries on the

18 Alexandre Moreau de Jonnès, *Aventures de Guerre au temps de la République et du Consulat* (Paris: Pagnerre, 1858), vol.I, pp.214–215. It must be said that these memoirs, written when he was a very old man, read like a G. A. Henty novel with Moreau de Jonnès ranging through the period and managing to switch units to appear at various pertinent 'scenes of the action.'

19 The Musée de la Chouannerie, de la Vendée et des guerres de l'Ouest is installed in a former hospital bunker which was constructed between 1941 and 1942 within the eastern end of the lines (museum information).

20 Ornano, *Hoche*, p.196.

heights in front of Glévenay, overlooking the modern Avenue de l'Océan, and to the south, on the point between Porhs Saint-Guénhaël and en Iliz.[21]

Janillion described the infantry entrenchments that also formed the line as '... very great and high ... in the manner of the English ... with narrow gaps, to protect the retreat of the skirmishers.'[22] They were armed with 4-pounder field pieces placed at intervals.[23] The line ran at an angle, the eastern end somewhat closer to the Quiberon peninsula and the western end more to the north. This western end rested on the seashore and was marked by a masonry cabin that had been built to '... shelter the coastguards, observation guard corps and transmission of signals.'[24] About a kilometre in front of the line the republicans established a camp, approximately in line with the Pointe de Pô, on the other side of the bay, to support their advanced outposts. A hooked spit now projects into Plouharnel Bay at this point, Pen er Lé, that does not appear on contemporary maps.

The republican troops employed on the field works suffered from a lack of resources. As Janillion states, 'where no house existed, not a single tree, nor a single source of fresh water.' They had to rely on crude measures to desalinate sea water and meagre issues of coarse bread, made from buckwheat mixed with other grains, and salt meat. Nevertheless,

> ... we had daily engagements, and particularly the advance-guard, which went to skirmish up to under the walls of the fort; but these partial combats decided nothing, and it only resulted in the reciprocal loss of some men, and each of the two sides returned afterwards to resume their positions.[25]

While Hoche established his headquarters in the village of Glévenay, *Général de brigade* Louis Lemoine was put in charge of the Sainte-Barbe position, having arrived with his 5,000 troops, including the 5e bataillon des volontaires d'Arras.[26] Lemoine had been a soldier in the Régiment de Brie for eight years before the Revolution, four of them as *caporal*, before being demoted a year before he left in 1791. Later that year he was elected *lieutenant-colonel* in a volunteer battalion, rising through the ranks during a great deal of active service.[27] Reinforcements continued to arrive including, the day after the position was occupied, the 2e bataillon des tirailleur belges, under *Lieutenant-colonel* Pierre-François-Gabriel Ronzier, soon followed by a battalion of Chasseurs Nantais. These last two units were to be the basis for an advance guard under *Général de brigade* Humbert. Cavalry vedettes

21 TNA: MPI 1/199: map (other files contain versions of the same). The way in which these have been drawn, as well as subsequent changes to the local geography makes accurate identification of their positions difficult. Ornano, *Hoche*, p.196 states there were two such batteries, one of two 4-pounders at the point of Ploërmel and another near Saint-Columban point, with two 8-pounders, but this last was constructed later on, see below.

22 Janillion, *Versailles et Quiberon*, p.56.

23 Ornano, *Hoche*, p.196.

24 Huchet, *Quiberon*, p.103.

25 Janillion, *Versailles et Quiberon*, p.56.

26 Champagnac, *Quiberon*, p.46.

27 His record in the Régiment de Brie is in Service historique de la Défense, Vincennes (SHD) GR 14 Yc 35.

were rarely used, the republicans only had about 250 horsemen – who were mainly used as couriers, guides and in other such roles – and the royalists had none. So, in the undulating terrain of the isthmus and without early warnings infantry would run into each other in these 'daily engagements' making them more costly.

Two of the actions were significant enough to be mentioned in participants' memoirs. The first was at daybreak on 10 July when the republican forward camp was attacked by a small force that included the Loyal Emigrants. The republicans abandoned their positions and the royalist 'soldiers returned well pleased, carrying all that they had found in their camp.'[28] The second was on 11 July, apparently in response to information provided by a republican deserter that the fort was to be attacked.[29] The royalists again advanced into the neutral ground, at 3:00 a.m., with 1,500 men of the Régiment d'Hervilly, two cannon and 2,000 chouans who, on this occasion, were reported to have 'behaved with much steadiness and intrepidity.'[30] At first they managed to ambush a republican detachment, advancing into the same ground, which quickly retreated onto its support which included artillery. The royalists now, in turn, withdrew and the Emigrant Artillery provided covering fire, directed by Rotalier. He, however, received a reprimand from Hervilly who considered that the guns should, instead, have followed his columns in retreat. It seems that Rotalier, described by Puisaye as 'a cold man' but 'knowledgeable of his profession,' had difficult relations with most of the other senior officers in the expedition.[31] Cover was also provided by navy boats, which were accompanied by Warren who wrote, 'I attended the march of the army with four launches, each carrying an 18 or 32-pounder, and covered the right wing and annoy[ed] the enemy's tirailleurs much, having killed and wounded about thirty or forty of them, with only one of the latter on our side.'[32] The republicans had engaged the boats with three of their cannon and things were perhaps a little more serious than Warren had reported, Wetton noting that, 'The ROBUST's launch got on ground, the enemy fir'd several shot through her. The GALATIA's launch they sunk and wounded two of her men.'[33]

Such engagements, as Janillion observed, had no material effect on the situation which Hoche summarised in a letter of 7 July when he wrote, '… the anglo-émigrés-chouans are, like rats, trapped in Quiberon, where the army keeps them blockaded. I hope in a few days we will be free of them.'[34]

28 Antrechaus, *Relation*, p.9.

29 Claude-Joseph Rouget de Lisle, 'Historique et Souvenirs de Quiberon' in Anon. (ed.) *Mémoires de Tous. Collection de Souvenirs contemporains* (Paris: Alphonse Levasseur, 1834), vol.II, p.52.

30 Numbers from Puisaye, *Mémoires*, vol.VI, p.302, timing from Wetton, 'Journal', p.68 and quote from Corbett (ed.), *Private Papers*, p.84, Warren to Spencer 12 July.

31 Puisaye, *Mémoires*, vol.VI, p.304.

32 Corbett (ed.), *Private Papers*, p.84, Warren to Spencer, 12 July.

33 Wetton, 'Journal', p.68. There is no indication of this in the *Robust* log (TNA: ADM 51/1163), that of *Galatea* for this period is not in the archives.

34 Huchet, *Quiberon*, p.99, letter to Chérin.

A War of Words

Both the royalists and republicans sought to draw support, and encourage adherents, by issuing appeals and manifestos. Puisaye had brought from England thousands of copies of a proclamation that he issued as, 'Lieutenant-Générale of the Armies of the King, Commander in Chief of the Armée Catholique et Royale de Bretagne, authorised by Monseigneur Comte d'Artois, Lieutenant-Générale of the Kingdom by virtue of the powers confided to him by MONSIEUR, REGENT of France' and which began, 'Frenchmen, It is in the Name of God and the King, it is in the Name of your legitimate Princes, that we bring you Promises of Peace'.[35] It ran a full page and Hutt describes it thus:

> The drafting was skilful, each section having its particular purpose. The first blasted *modérantisme* as a fiction, as no guarantee of social peace in a faction-torn country ... Only a restoration could bring back true peace to France – this was the argument – and here Puisaye preached a doctrine of conciliation and forgiveness which was far removed from that of the declaration which Louis XVIII had issued from Verona only a few days before the landing took place at Quiberon.[36]

Of course, this was to bring accusations from *purs* that it had been 'dictated by Pitt' but it chimed with earlier declarations he had made and tried to put into action since the landing, despite the local chouans wish for revenge.[37]

On learning of the émigré landing, the National Convention had not only issued instructions for the generals in the region to support Hoche but also, on the night of 30 June, had appointed two *représentants en mission* to the west. Jean-Lambert Tallien and Claude Blad were both members of the Committee of Public Safety but the latter, apparently borne down by the burden of responsibility, was very much the junior partner, yielding not only to Tallien but also other forceful personalities. Both came with sweeping powers over civil and military authorities in the départements of the west, so Hoche, who had been under threat of execution only a year before through the malice of another *représentant en mission*, always paid due deference to their opinions.[38]

Tallien and Blad left Paris for Rennes immediately, on 1 July, and so Hoche was there frequently in early July leaving Lemoine in full command of the forces facing Quiberon. Hoche was, however, back at Sainte-Barbe on 12 July and was joined there by the representatives who heard complaints that the army had received no bread for three days. Tallien assured Hoche it would arrive within eight hours, which duly happened. As one historian observed, 'The presence and the authority of the representatives flattened

35 TNA: WO 1/390: copy.
36 Hutt, *Chouannerie*, pp.301–302.
37 Hutt, *Chouannerie*, p.302.
38 Huchet, *Quiberon*, pp.89–90.

the obstacles that had multiplied around the general.'[39] The next day, 13 July, the representatives issued their own proclamation 'in the Name of the French Republic' which begun, 'Citizens, Honoured with the confidence of the National Convention and the Committee of Public Safety, invested with all powers to do good and suppress evil, we bring you promises of peace and fraternity.'[40]

Naval Operations

The warships' crews had been employed bringing supplies and provisions ashore since the landing but this task intensified when, after 7 July, it was decided to bring all the cargoes to stores and magazines established at Port d'Orange, within the defences of Quiberon peninsula. That this was done is generally described as being at Puisaye's request, however it coincides with the schedule within Warren's instructions which envisaged the troops and all the supplies being ashore in 10 days. Then the transports were to leave for England and Warren's squadron was to cruise offshore. It was apparently on his own initiative that Warren chose to remain with the majority of the ships and to continue to support the expedition.[41] In anticipation of the *Thunderer* leaving, on 10 July two of her 32-pounder cannon, complete with carriages, equipment and ammunition, were landed to strengthen the armament of Fort Penthièvre.[42]

The frigates, except for Warren's own ship, the *Pomone*, were occupied in 'the various expeditions that must take place every day.'[43] Their main task was to patrol the waters of Quiberon Bay and beyond, as well as maintaining the blockade of Belle-Île, in particular to intercept and check other vessels. Most were neutral ships bringing trade goods to or from France however, later, French officers attempting to reach Belle-Île were found on two vessels, one American and the other Danish.[44] Several American ships carrying wheat and other foodstuff to Nantes were diverted to the bay, as Warren explained to Earl Spencer in a letter of 10 July:

> I have … purchased the cargoes of several American vessels laden with provisions for the army … until more arrives from England. And it was in good time as the numbers that entered into the Peninsula were near 20,000 of which the army consists of 14,000, of which 10,000 are Chouans as yet undisciplined; the others women and children, who must otherwise have fallen victims to the relentless fury of the Republican Army …[45]

39 Rouget de Lisle, 'Historique et Souvenirs', p.46.
40 Huchet, *Quiberon*, p.116 and Sibenaler, *Quiberon*, pp.65–69.
41 TNA: WO 1/390: summary of Warren's instructions, Puisaye's copy.
42 TNA: ADM 51/1103: *Thunderer* log.
43 Corbett (ed.), *Private Papers*, p.79, Warren to Spencer 29 June.
44 TNA: ADM 51/1102: *Arethusa* log 12 and 16 September.
45 Corbett (ed.), *Private Papers*, p.82, Warren to Spencer 10 July.

Of course, the acquisition of these goods caused consternation among the republicans, particularly in Nantes. However it was not unprecedented as agreement had already been reached between the Unites States and Britain, after an earlier dispute, that the latter would 'purchase the cargoes of vessels detained at the full price which they would obtain delivered in France.'[46] Despite Warren describing the influx of Breton refugees as vindication of his decision, it seems he had taken it very early on in the campaign. His ships began taking American merchant ships from 29 June and they were brought into Quiberon Bay from 4 July.[47]

Another issue of resources caused by the royalist retreat onto the Quiberon peninsula was the lack of fresh water. So on 7 July Warren 'sent a Party of Marines with some light Transports to Houat Island for Water' and they returned the next day having, apparently collected what they wanted.[48] His dispatch of marines with the water party would indicate that Warren considered a show of force may be required to impress the authorities on Houat but when three more transports went with a cutter on 9 July for the same reason they apparently went without marines; it is unclear when exactly the island came under royalist or British control.[49] Indeed it was only on 22 July that Warren informed Spencer that he would 'probably take possession of the Islands' of Houat and Hoëdic and on the 31 July that he had done so.[50] Although it may have been a subtle distinction between control and possession, Warren was again describing actions that he had already set in train as on 20 July he had 'sent a summons to the Magistrates of Hedic [*sic*] Island to surrender it at Discretion; which after some discussion took place.'[51]

During the operations the gun-vessels with Warren's squadron proved to be very useful, especially due to their shallow draughts. Britain had entered the French Revolutionary Wars without any such vessels for anti-invasion service in coastal waters. As a response 12 *Conquest* Class vessels were ordered in 1794 and in the next year were attached to the squadrons in the Channel Islands. They were 75 feet in length and 21 feet in breadth, and, at this time, had a schooner or brigantine rig but could also be propelled by 18 oars. They had a complement of 50 with a lieutenant in command and were armed with ten 18-pounder carronades, two 24-pounder chase guns at the bow and two 4-pounder guns at the stern.[52]

Meanwhile a republican corvette and other armed vessels that were in the Gulf of Morbihan remained a concern, HMS *Concorde* having been stationed off the island of Méaban at the entrance to the bay since 4 July. On 6 July a small force under the command of Captain Bertie of the *Thunderer* was assembled to attack them. It consisted of the four available gun-vessels

46 Corbett (ed.), *Private Papers*, p.82.

47 TNA: ADM 51/1102: *Arethusa* and ADM 51/1149: *Pomone* logs.

48 TNA: ADM 51/1149: *Pomone* log.

49 TNA: ADM 51/1103: *Thunderer* log.

50 Corbett (ed.), *Private Papers*, pp.89, 94. On 22 July, the same day he had written to Spencer, he told the Admiralty, unequivocally, that he was going to take possession of the islands (TNA: ADM 1/103).

51 TNA: ADM 51/1149: *Pomone* log.

52 Winfield, *British Warships in the Age of Sail*, pp.329–330.

– the *Pelter* (with Bertie on board), *Swinger*, *Aimwell* and *Teaser* – as well as boats from the *Thunderer*, *Artois* and *Concorde*.[53] Bertie led this small flotilla through the entrance to the Gulf of Morbihan, between Port-Navalo and Pointe de Kerpenhir near Locmariaquer, at 4:30 p.m. leaving his support – two chasse marées with chouans and three boats from the *Concorde* with 30 marines – to follow if required. He worked his way up the bay between the mainland and the Île-aux-Moines as far as the Anse de Kerdelan in pursuit of a republican cutter and chasse marée and fire was exchanged. The tide, however, changed at about 9:00 p.m. forcing Bertie's vessels to drop down to an anchorage off Île Creïzic.

They weighed anchor at around 2:00 a.m. and moved up the bay again encountering the republican vessels at around 7:45 a.m. to the north of Île-aux-Moines. The cutter was sunk by cannon fire, its 'mast head just above water,' and the corvette retreated further up the bay towards the Île de Boëdic, and was then run aground and set on fire.[54] The British also burnt two large chasse marées and brought away two merchant brigs, one of which was the *Active*, a captured Liverpool privateer. That morning the chouans and marines, joined by Warren, landed at Port-Navalo and started to dismantle a battery there, however they only managed to pitch two 32-pounder cannon into the sea before they had to leave because of the republican attack on Carnac and Quiberon. The gun-vessels got clear of the Gulf of Morbihan by 3:00 p.m. and, with adverse winds to contend with, Warren signalled 'for all [the] Gun Vessels [to] use their Sweeps' so they could get in towards Carnac.[55]

Another mission was to supply gunpowder and arms to Charette in the Vendée, as it was known that he needed such supplies and Warren had received instructions to do so before he left England.[56] Overnight, 7 to 8 July, the *Concorde* sailed out of Quiberon Bay towards Houat where at 7:00 a.m. the following morning she was joined by the *Artois* and the *John and Robert* powder vessel. At noon on 9 July the ships parted company, the *Artois* and *John and Robert* to land the supplies and the *Concorde* to cruise off Île d'Yeu and, intriguingly at 6:00 p.m. on 11 July, she 'landed 4 French Emigrants' on the island. Who they were or the purpose of their mission is not known. However, for reasons that are not stated, the supplies could not be landed and at 4:30 p.m. on 12 July the *Artois* and the sloop re-joined the *Concorde*.[57]

On 10 July Warren had written to Spencer about this shipment of powder as well as the arrival of two officers from Charette who had left their commander '… in arms after having had two skirmishes, but in want of

53 TNA: ADM 1/103: Bertie to Warren 7 July and Warren to Nepean 12 July; ADM 51/1111: *Concorde* log. The *Teaser* is otherwise given as the *Teazer*, the first has been used throughout for consistency.

54 TNA: ADM 1/103: Bertie to Warren 7 July and account by a French sailor in HO 69/30. Bertie identifies the corvette, or 'small frigate,' as *L'Oiseau*, 18 guns, and the cutter as *Le Henri*, 10 or 12 guns.

55 TNA: ADM 51/4406: *Aimwell* log also Puisaye, *Mémoires*, vol.VI, p.268.

56 Corbett (ed.), *Private Papers*, p.76.

57 TNA: ADM 51/1111: *Concorde log* (that for *Artois* is not present) and Hutt, *Chouannerie*, p.313.

officers, arms, powder and arms.'[58] Despite the failure of the supply mission, Warren wrote optimistically about Vendéen activity on 20 July, 'Charette is within six leagues of Nantes, with 22,000 men; Sapineau [*sic*] on his march this way with 15,000'.[59] However such reports were wildly inaccurate, perhaps just wishful thinking by an agent as Charles Sapinaud de La Rairie and fellow Vendéen leaders, including Stofflet, had sent emissaries to initiate negotiations in Paris.[60] Although Charette had repudiated the truce on 26 June and his men had a series of actions with the enemy, he did not act to support the landing. There is no clear reason for this, perhaps it was due to his personal contempt for Puisaye or distrust of the British. Alternatively, he could have indeed been persuaded by the Agence de Paris, which was in contact with him in this period, to not co-operate with them. A crucial influence, if not the deciding factor, is likely to have been that he simply did not have the means, despite hopes and promises, to do anything more, as only about 4,000 Vendéens assembled in response to his call to arms.[61]

Very quickly Warren found that he needed many more small fast-sailing vessels to carry out the variety of roles in Quiberon Bay, including maintaining communication with England, Lord Bridport, and his other vessels, as well as intercepting small coastal vessels, particularly those the republicans used to try to supply and communicate with the garrison on Belle-Île; he continually asked for such vessels. Locally, Warren made increasing use of chasse marées for communication, moving provisions between ships, and even to support his warships, especially the *Standard* off Belle-Île, with chasing down similar vessels and occasionally British sailors were added to their crews. It is undoubtedly these vessels which he referred to when he informed that Admiralty that he had equipped three with swivel guns and other armaments.[62]

Small vessels and boats were also used to attack the republican army, in close fire support to the royalist forces as well as independently. After apparently learning from the experience of 11 July, when boats ran aground in the shallow Plouharnel Bay, ships' carpenters fixed slides in a number of flat boats and mounted carronades in them, which had much less recoil than traditional cannon. These were used to attack the republican positions in front of Sainte-Barbe. In the evening of 15 July 'the [*Pomone's*] Launch & flat boats with a carronade in each went in shore to annoy the Enemy's Camp.'[63] These attacks continued over the next four evenings. Warren commented on 20 July '... yesterday, by firing into their camp, [we] obliged the whole line to be under arms.'[64]

The frigates also carried out similar attacks further afield. On 11 July the *Anson*, to the west of Quiberon, 'stood close on shore and fired several

58 Corbett (ed.), *Private Papers*, p.83. Warren gave a similar message in his letter of 12 July, p.85.
59 Corbett (ed.), *Private Papers*, p.86.
60 Hutt, *Chouannerie*, p.256.
61 Hutt, *Chouannerie*, pp.252–257.
62 TNA: ADM 1/103: Warren to Nepean 4 July; he requested permission to remunerate the Breton crews for this service.
63 TNA: ADM 51/1149: *Pomone* log.
64 Corbett (ed.), *Private Papers*, p.86.

broadsides at a battery situated at the entrance of Ethel [Étel] river – drove the people from the battery and made sail.'[65] Another example was the *Concorde*, on its way back to Quiberon Bay from the Île d'Yeu, that 'exchanged several shots with the Fort on Pillier Island [*sic*]' – the Île du Pilier lying north-west of Noirmoutier.[66]

A Divided Command?

The rift that had developed between Puisaye and Hervilly only widened within the confines of Quiberon. Whenever the seeds had been sewn, there was now clearly a divided command, with two separate armies, or parties, often operating in their own interests and sometimes in competition with each other. Hervilly, it is true, had always concerned himself with the white cockade regiments, which may have been a reasonable position as he was the subordinate officer, but Puisaye, despite being the commander-in-chief, was seemingly solely interested in the chouans who were, to him, his party. In his memoirs he describes a number of things that Hervilly did that he considered had been aimed to undermine him and his party, however it does appear that his complaints were somewhat exaggerated.

An early dispute had arisen over the dispensing of justice, as Puisaye recalled,

> … two soldiers from one of the corps in the pay of England had deserted, with the aim of passing to the enemy. All the avenues were carefully guarded, the indignant peasants arrested them and brought them back to Carnac.
>
> M d'Hervilly tried them at a court martial, which condemned them to death. He had one of them shot and pardoned the other; thus exercising a power which had not been confided to him, and confirming the troops in English pay in the opinion already too generally understood, that my letters of command were only nominal, and that I had no authority over them.[67]

Contades remembered that there were four deserters retaken by the chouans at this time, three from Hervilly and one from Hector: 'The latter was shot, blaspheming until the last moment. One of the three from Royal-Louis suffered the same fate and in the same manner at the head of the regiment. Hervilly pardoned the two others who appeared more Christian and repented.'[68] The records for Hervilly are sufficiently detailed to show that the soldier who was shot was *Fusilier* Jean-Baptiste d'Anguilcourt and what is more he is mentioned in the memoir of Le Charron, one of the regiment's officers. The passage begins after Le Charron, who had remained on board during the landing, joined the regiment onshore. Passing behind the regiment which was formed up, he saw a soldier mocking a group of chouans nearby,

65 TNA: ADM 51/1117: *Anson* log.
66 TNA: ADM 51/1111: *Concorde* log.
67 Puisaye, *Mémoires*, vol.VI, p.223.
68 Contades, *Coblenz*, p.142.

> … feeling the importance of respecting these brave Bretons … I made this bad subject immediately return to his place, reinforcing my rebuke with a blow with the flat of my sword on his shoulder. This man deserted from Carnac that same evening; he was taken and brought back by chouans: he was made a great example of. This was the only man from the regiment d'Hervilly-Royal-Louis who had been shot. He died a true scoundrel. Deserter from the republicans in Holland, this man, after having been a marauder and committed horrors there, had passed to England.[69]

Curiously Le Charron described the soldier as having been 'sent and recommended' by Pitt despite Hervilly pointing out 'the danger of admitting a deserter who was such a bad subject into his regiment composed of so many prisoners' to which Pitt replied 'that one man was as good as another.' However, even after a moment's consideration quite how bizarre it would have been for a prime minister and a colonel to have been engaged in such an exchange about an individual recruit, and of such a character, is clear. The only explanation can be is that Le Charron was being figurative.

Another issue arose after 7 July when supplies and provisions were hastily landed from the transports, following pressure to release these ships from Quiberon Bay. This only added to the strain on the inadequate organisation for the distribution of food already stretched by the sudden influx of refugees along with the soldiers and chouans. The issues this caused for the regiments has already been seen when Dresnay's appearance at Fort Penthièvre had been delayed as the soldiers had had to disperse to find food. The chouans apparently fared worse still, despite attempts to feed all the Bretons, and they, genuinely or not, said that they were unable to work on the defensive outworks through lack of food. Some accused them of taking matters into their own hands, with one of Puisaye's critics writing, '… provisions intended for the army, were distributed, and often even pillaged by the useless Chouans who filled the peninsula.'[70] It should be noted that the seemingly harsh term '*inutile*' or useless, for the Breton refugees was used by both those sympathetic to them as well as their critics.

Although Hervilly may have had some influence, the distribution of the provisions was clearly the remit of Saint-Morys, very much Puisaye's man.[71] Despite, or perhaps because of, this the latter insisted Hervilly hindered the supply of food to the chouans and had an ulterior motive for doing so, '… moreover, everyone knew the reason for the barbaric treatment which the insurgents were being subjected to; that it was obvious that one wanted to take them through hunger, to force them to enlist in the white cockades regiments, and by this means to create an army independent from me.'[72]

69 Le Charron, *Expédition de Quiberon*, pp.135–136.

70 Anon., *De l'expédition*, pp.27–28.

71 Anon. (ed.), *Olivier d'Argens*, p.430, Hervilly to Talhouët 8 July: 'I will be the intendant of the army this evening, and I will make sure I know the reason that prevented delivery of the complete ration to you.'

72 Puisaye, *Mémoires*, vol.VI, p.290. He also noted that only chouans worked on the royalist outworks contrasting this with those of the republicans on which officers and men worked alongside one another.

However recruitment for the regiments was actively, and largely successfully, opposed by the chouan chiefs leading to, on at least one occasion, physical confrontation when a *sergent* from Dresnay was accused of hitting a chouan officer. On investigation, Hervilly stated the NCO could not have distinguished the chouan's rank which Puisaye implicitly conceded as he immediately provided muslin to the chouan officers for sashes and gave orders prohibiting them from 'appearing henceforth without wearing them at the waist.'[73]

A further reason Puisaye considered Hervilly was seeking to create distance between their respective units, or parties, were his actions in relation to émigré officers serving with the chouans. In a letter to his colonel, Dresnay, *Lieutenant-colonel* de Talhouët, explained that Hervilly had ordered that white cockade officers who had, without authority, quit their regiments should cease to receive their British pay, until he had further instructions, and had directed the respective regimental commanders to follow this up. Talhouët informed Hervilly that four Dresnay officers were absent from his regiment and employed with the chouans but that he thought this was authorised by the government. The officers he named were *Capitaines* Vicomte de Pontbellanger, Auguste-Henri de Méhérenec Vicomte de Saint-Pierre and Chevalier de la Marche as well as another officer, Ange-Joseph-Jean Chevalier de Guernisac. Nevertheless, Hervilly persisted so Talhouët sent each a copy of the order and reminded them that they had not served with the regiment. After a long delay Talhouët received a reply from Pontbellanger, on behalf of all four, that having taken the general-in-chief's orders, he was instructed to tell him 'that the British ministers were given notice that these officers would have a particular role in France, and despite that they would not lose their position.' Hervilly expressed his discontent with this reply and told Talhouët that he would take it upon himself to nominate officers to take their places, but events were to overtake any such action.[74] What is curious about Puisaye's complaint about Hervilly, on this point, was that he was told by Pontbellanger in early March that the Marquis du Dresnay, himself, had warned him, la Marche, and Guernisac that they would lose their places if they went to Brittany, with Tinténiac, rather than serve with his regiment.[75] Dresnay seems to have carried out his threat in the case of Guernisac, as he is absent from the regimental list (contrôle) that commenced from 25 June 1795.[76] Pontbellanger, a Norman, was connected to Brittany through his wife, Louise-Exupère-Françoise-Charlotte Bot du Grégo, who had brought extensive land holdings in the province to their marriage. He was not only close to Tinténiac, with whom he had been a member of the Association bretonne, but he was also a trusted confidant of Puisaye.

73 Puisaye, *Mémoires*, vol.VI, p.295.

74 Anon., *Mémoires d'Olivier d'Argens*, pp.430–434, Talhouët to Dresnay 13 July.

75 Anon., 'Antoine-Henri d'Amphernet de Pontbellanger', <http://maison.omahony.free.fr/ascendants/fiche_amphernet_AntoineHenri.html>, accessed 12 May 2021.

76 TNA: WO 12/11708: several sources denote Guernisac as comte, a rank he was to gain in later life.

In this matter Hervilly did not only concern himself with officers from the Régiment du Dresnay, which was notably short of officers doing duty with it during the expedition, but he also sought to make an example by dismissing one of his own officers who Puisaye had just appointed to his staff. The officer, *Capitaine* Philippe Le Cour Marquis de Balleroy, however resigned on 12 July so avoiding that fate, although what is remarkable is that he was Hervilly's brother-in-law.[77] Despite Puisaye's interpretation of Hervilly's actions, they can be seen as the latter's concern to maintain discipline and efficiency in the white cockade regiments which all had former officers serving in the ranks who could readily take the places of the absent officers. This however could not happen while they retained their regimental posts.

Both Puisaye and Hervilly chose to raise their concerns with the British Government. On 8 July Puisaye asked Windham for the brevet of lieutenant general in the British service, explaining, '... it is necessary for me to be able to decide, in the name of His Britannic Majesty, on everything that concerns the troops in your pay; the distance by sea produces delays with regard to decisions which ought to be made on the spot.'[78] Significantly he did not seek, overtly, to remove Hervilly from effective command of the regiments but to have the power to take decisions over his head. Hervilly, on the other hand, while criticised, or even ridiculed, by his detractors for his rigid adherence to orthodox military procedure and system, on 14 July wrote directly to Henry Dundas, in English. His first concern was that he had requested Saint-Morys to supply £600 for the Loyal Emigrants' pay and Puisaye told him that although this would be paid, provisionally, no such further payments would be made as he had not been given money for the troops in British pay. So Hervilly simply asked that 'sums necessary to assure the service' be sent which he would ensure were correctly distributed. Then he went on to explicitly complain about Puisaye,

> ... it is with pain, sir, that I have the honour to inform you that notwithstanding the most positive orders and many severe examples it has not yet been in my power to put a stop to the disorders committed by the very undisciplined troops which have joined us. They are used these past years to make the war as Croats and think themselves entitled to everything they can find, there has been a disorder in all kinds of distribution particularly in the distribution of the arms which have been given indistinctly – which are yet seized with avidity by men the great part of whom make little use of [them]. Count de Puisaye has I suppose given you an acc[oun]t of the strong & repeated Representations I have addressed to him concerning that, but he seems to think he is not to perceive such Disorders (which I have never ceased to complain of and which since the 1st day I have endeavoured to prevent) for fear of discontenting the peasants who are inclined to serve the cause we wish to support but who have their own way for defending it and among whom it is very difficult to establish some order especially when the fear of discontenting them makes us accede to all their demands and tolerate their indiscipline & the pillage which they are inclined to, I will nevertheless never

77 TNA: WO 12/11681: pay list.

78 Puisaye, *Mémoires*, vol.VI, pp.317–318.

> cease all the means that lay in my power to prevent the monstrous consummation which has taken place and would soon absorb the considerable succours Government have had the goodness to grant us.[79]

He continued that because Puisaye had regarded all the clothing brought from England as being there to be distributed to the Bretons, the white cockade regiments, by which he would have meant the infantry, were left in need of everything. Then he listed the requirements to make this good, on the basis that all the men, numbered at 3,848, each needed a complete replacement set of issue clothing and shoes. Also required were, '4,000 muskets to replace those which are unfit for service and which there is not always means or time to repair also to arm the recruits who are daily increasing' were required as well as new pouches, belts and swords for 'the Corporals & Grenadiers of a Better quality than the 1st Delivered.' He concluded by asking that any consignment be clearly marked for the regiments alone.[80]

Much of what the two men were competing about was dealt with in a dispatch from England of 23 July to Puisaye:

> If the regular Regiments are in want of shirts, shoes or any of the articles of clothing, it will be necessary that you should furnish them from the supplies which have been placed at your Disposal for the general service of the Royal and Catholic army, and as they have no military chest, that you should issue their pay to Count d'Hervilly out of any fund you may have in your possession for the use of the army in general.

The instructions about detached officers may have given Puisaye some comfort but there was a sting in the tail for those who gained advancement by being placed with the chouans.

> You are furnished by my former Dispatch with authority to draft officers and men from these [white cockade] corps, to act as officers or non commissioned officers, into other situations, whenever the good of the service shall require it, if placed in a superior situation they cannot however continue to receive the Pay of their present respective Ranks, which must be filled by other Officers.[81]

Despite the clear rivalry there was not only a surprising lack of rancour but even the presence of active co-operation when a light cavalry unit was formed. Projected to be only the first of such formations the captaincy was given to Louis-Gabriel de Marconnay and, in anticipation of more to follow, the position of general of cavalry to Contades. Although a former cavalry officer, Marconnay's appointment was apparently due to his connections. He was a close friend of Tinténiac and also son-in-law to the Baron de Nantiat,

79 TNA: WO 1/390: Hervilly to Dundas 14 July. The letter is in English and the quotation is given as written but with changes to some spelling, re-ordering of words (once) and some punctuation added.

80 TNA: WO 1/390: Hervilly to Dundas 14 July.

81 TNA: WO 1/390: Horse Guards 23 July.

not only a prominent member of the émigrés in England but also an agent for Artois.[82] Men were drawn from both the white cockade regiments and chouans. Contades wrote, 'M d'Hervilly very loyally ceded to us men who he had engaged on the promise to have them passed into the cavalry, when the occasion to do so presented itself.'[83] Clothing and equipping them was not a problem, enough for 4,000 troopers had been supplied from Britain, but there was a shortage of horses. Puisaye placed 25–30 that he had acquired for the regiments' officers at Marconnay's disposal and within the space of a few days, 11 men of the Régiment d'Hervilly – two *caporaux de fusiliers*, six grenadiers and three fusiliers – being transferred on 12 July, he had 'passably equipped hussars' on these horses.[84] A statement for this period shows the unit, with seven officers and 34 other ranks, quartered at Roc'h Priol, between the small town of Quiberon and the southern coast.[85] Puisaye named the unit the Hussards de Warren in recognition of the naval officer's contribution and assistance to the expedition. However, while the British Government gave approval to the raising and naming of the unit, that for 'the Detail of its formation & establishment,' – in brief its size and standing – was going to have to wait.[86]

The March of the Armée Rouge Commences

Soon after the royalists had retreated into the Quiberon peninsula a plan was devised for chouans to make a diversion, or perhaps two, on the mainland. Contades, for one, was somewhat ambivalent about the plan saying it was, 'As much to make a diversion as to be rid of useless mouths.'[87] It seems that chouan leaders, notably Georges Cadoudal, came up with the idea and they, as a body, proposed it to Puisaye on 9 July; he, characteristically, states in his memoirs that he had already fixed upon such an idea.[88] He considered that chouan divisions inserted onto the mainland would be joined by many more Bretons and then they could attack the Sainte-Barbe position from the rear. He went, he says, straight to Hervilly:

> 'We will get out of here,' I said to him, 'if you work with me. I will have Hoche attacked on his rear by twenty thousand men on an appointed day; at the same time we will attack him from the front; and all will be put right. The fate of the

82 Contades, *Coblenz*, p.169. Pierre-Charles-Jacques Martin de Nantiat was on a mission to Charrette in July 1795.

83 Contades, *Coblenz*, p.170.

84 Puisaye, *Mémoires*, vol.VI, p.324, and TNA: WO 12/11681: pay list. Strangely Contades, *Coblenz*, p.170, stated there were 63 mounted men but implied that Hervilly supplied the majority of them.

85 TNA: ADM 80/136: the strength appears to be that before 16 July, Puisaye gives the location as 'Roprior' (*Mémoires*, vol.VI, p.462).

86 TNA: WO 1/390: Horse Guards 23 July.

87 Contades, *Coblenz*, p.164. This is another use of the expression '*bouches inutiles*.' Vauban, *Mémoires*, alludes to similar motivations for the diversions and equally gives them scant consideration (p.67).

88 Cadoudal, *Georges Cadoudal*, pp.85–86 and Puisaye, *Mémoires*, vol.VI, p.295.

> expedition is again in your hands.' To this proposition, … [Hervilly] ceded to his military inclinations; he consented to all.[89]

The plan to land a force of around 3,500 men in four chouan divisions, including one led by Cadoudal, along with a detachment from the Loyal Emigrants, near Sarzeau on the Rhuys peninsula was adopted. Overall command was given to Tinténiac, who brought with him nine or 10 émigré officers to act as his staff, among whom was Pontbellanger as his second-in-command. The chouans were supplied with red coats, hence they were called the Armée rouge, although several of their leaders, including Cadoudal retained their own dress. Another landing was to be made by party of 3,000 or so chouans led by two chouan leaders, Jean Jan – otherwise known as Jean-Jean – and the Comte de Lantivy. According to Puisaye he instructed both groups to march inland, gathering men as they went, and rendezvous at Baud on 14 July. From there they were to march to within a league of Saint Barbe by the following evening so they could attack the rear of that position at daybreak on 16 July.[90]

Tinténiac's men embarked at Port Haliguen on a convoy of 26 chasse marées, commanded by Lieutenant Matthew Smith of the *Teaser* gun-vessel, and set sail at 2:00 p.m. on 9 July.[91] At 8:00 a.m. the following morning the *Teaser* anchored off the Plage Suscinio, near the château of that name, and fired some shots at the enemy, 300 republicans, who rather than defend the beach, retreated to the nearby town of Sarzeau where there were already a further 500 troops, with four cannon.[92] This allowed the chouans to land unopposed and advance on Sarzeau which was taken with little resistance, with two republicans being killed.[93] Meanwhile, the crew of the *Teaser* dismantled 'a Battery of two Guns,' presumably on the point at the west end of the beach, Beg Lann, dismounting the cannon and breaking their carriages and then, at 7:00 a.m. the following morning, 11 July, the *Teaser* ran close to the shore and 'fired several 24 pound shots to annoy the Enemy in the Wood.' The convoy left the shore at 4:00 p.m. for Quiberon Bay.[94]

When the chasse marées returned, they not only brought news of the success, but also something of a defiant gesture and perhaps even a snub to the émigrés:

---

89 Puisaye, *Mémoires*, vol.VI, p.296. He cleverly places Hervilly in an equal, but somehow more responsible position in this passage.

90 Puisaye, *Mémoires*, vol.VI, p.297.

91 TNA: ADM 51/4042: *Teaser* log; Wetton, 'Journal', p.68 gives the time as 4:00 p.m. See also Eugène de La Gournerie, *Les Débris de Quiberon: Souvenirs du Désastre de 1795* (Nantes: Catholique Libaros, 1875), p.78.

92 TNA: ADM 51/4042: *Teaser* log. Rohu, 'Mémoires', (December 1857) p.613 and Puisaye, *Mémoires*, vol.VI, p.305. Smith gave the location as being between Pointe de Penvins and Pointe de Saint-Jacques where as Puisaye's description of the landing point is contradictory, that it was at Saint-Jacques, facing the Château de Suscinio despite Saint-Jacques being about seven kilometres to the west of Plage Suscinio.

93 Rohu 'Mémoires', (December 1857), p.613 and Jules Le Falher, *Le Siège de Josselin Juillet 1795: Épisode de l'histoire de l'Armée rouge d'après des documents inédits* (Vannes: Lafolye frères, 1909), p.5.

94 TNA: ADM 51/4042: *Teaser* log.

> The Chouans, as if to avenge themselves for the diet that they were made eat in the peninsula, sent us cattle and casks of wine, of which they had set a certain number apart, to testify their recognition of the brave Commodore and the officers of his squadron.[95]

Tinténiac marched his men east of Vannes, without meeting any opposition, to the Château de Callac, half way between Vannes and Ploërmel, where the chouans '... passed a night [11/12 July] and a day, during which several men of the Loyal Emigrant regiment were placed in each company, some in the rank of officers, others as sergeant instructors'.[96] Although Puisaye described the detachment as a company, leading some later historians to put the number of man at about a hundred, it must have been smaller as such a number would have amounted to a quarter of all the regiment's personnel on the expedition.[97] Furthermore it was not led by a senior officer, its commander was Gabriel-François-Charles de Coquet who, although a former *lieutenant* of the Régiment d'Agenois infanterie, was ensign in the Loyal Emigrants, being promoted lieutenant on 22 July 1795, although Puisaye gave him the rank of *capitaine* in the royalist army.[98] Tinténiac had also begun to attract other Bretons to join him so that by the time he left the Château de Callac he is thought to already have had a total of between 4,000–5,000 men with him.[99]

A reason that the republicans did not initially react to the march of the Armée rouge was misinformation. On 13 July the administration of the département was told, 'The small garrison of Sarzeau withdrew in good order onto Port-Navalo; but troops coming out from Vannes changed the face of events; and the Chouans, apart from a few who penetrated inland, were force to re-embark.'[100]

At nightfall on 12 July the chouans marched south to arrive at first light at Elven and Rohu's company charged into the village at the run: 'A sleepy official, who encountered us on the main road, was taken in hand, and did not have the time to give a warning to the garrison; so that the soldiers surprised from their sleep, came out of the houses with only their shirts on; consequently they were beaten and dispersed, without us losing any of our own.'[101]

The Armée rouge did not remain at Elven but continued its march westwards through Plaudren to halt at L'Hermitage for the night of 13 to 14 July.[102] It was on schedule to fulfil its part of the plan described by Puisaye.

---

95 Puisaye, *Mémoires*, vol.VI, pp.305–306. Late on 11 July the *Thunderer* received three bullocks 'for the use of the Ship's Company' (TNA: ADM 51/1103).

96 Rohu, 'Mémoires', (December 1857), p.613. Rohu declined to have such men.

97 Puisaye, *Mémoires*, vol.VI, pp.296, 301. For an example of later historians see Huchet, *Quiberon*, p.109.

98 TNA: WO 12/11732: paylists and rolls.

99 Vidalenc, 'L'affaire de Quiberon', p.315.

100 Le Falher, *Siège de Josselin*, p.5, departmental record.

101 Rohu, 'Mémoires', (December 1857), p.613; Le Falher states about 50 republicans were killed (Le Falher, *Siège de Josselin*, p.6).

102 Le Falher, *Siège de Josselin*, p.6, identifies it as La Chapelle de Notre-Dame de Burgo, west of Plaudren, celebrated for an action in 1800.

It seems that not a great deal was expected from the chouans with Jean Jan and Lantivy. Contades wrote, '… as for Jean-Jean, I always thought … that on landing, he and his soldiers would hide their arms and their red coats, to return home, promising themselves to never enrol in an army in which one died of hunger.'[103] Nevertheless they embarked, apparently on the chasse marées that had returned after landing Tinténiac's force and sailed at 8:00 p.m. on 12 July, again under the command of Smith of the *Teaser*, going eastwards along the coast.[104] Puisaye's wish was to put these chouans ashore on the eastern side of the bay, behind Tinténiac, and so by them having a long march home – to Pontivy and the west of the Morbihan département – have a more disruptive effect on republican forces. By late in the morning the following day, 13 July, the convoy was cruising along the coast near Piriac-sur-Mer seeking, unsuccessfully, a suitable location for a landing. At 2:00 p.m. the same day the *Teaser* and the accompanying vessels tacked to the northwest, passing the Île Dumet on the shore of which troops were seen to be encamped, and headed back towards the Rhuys peninsula on the north of Quiberon Bay, where the gun-vessel annoyed 'the Enemy with 24 pounders.' Although no landing took place, the cruise had stirred up the republican forces, with the lighting of 'fires along the Enemy's Coast.'[105]

André-Charles Marquis de La Jaille, Puisaye's aide, makes no mention of this cruise when he reported on the events during this period, stating that 'On 13 [July] at eleven o'clock in the evening 3,000 men left on chasse marées under the escort of two gun sloops. These men commanded by M Jean Jean … are to land … in the vicinity of the Quimperlé river and to march on Quimper'.[106] Puisaye was to develop this by suggesting that a detachment was to march on Quimper to free 1,500 British prisoners held there, however this unrealistic proposal seems to have been simply inserted to please the British Government.[107] Whatever the motivation it was now decided to try to land the chouans to the west of Lorient.

The *Teaser* escorted the chasse marées to the west of the Quiberon Peninsula and at 6:00 p.m. on 14 July they were joined by the *Borer*, soon passing the Île de Groix. Smith's log noted that on 15 July the *Teaser*,

> … approached the Shore at 5 PM to cover a Landing … began to land the Troops in a small sandy Bay between two Forts, at 11 finished Landing and firing AM [on 16 July] at 4 weighed anchor with the Borer & Chasse Marées and made sail for Quiberon Bay.[108]

---

103 Contades, *Coblenz*, p.165.

104 TNA: ADM 51/4042: *Teaser* log. Smith states he sailed with 'three flat boats and 24 Chasse Marées under our Command' but does not provide any further details but, at noon on 13 July, he was directly north of Houat.

105 TNA: ADM 51/1103: *Thunderer* log.

106 TNA: WO 1/390: La Jaille's report of 18 July.

107 Puisaye, *Mémoires*, vol.VI, gives various locations where these chouans were to land depending on the mission he was describing saying it was to be near Quimperlé (p.306) and at the mouth of the Étel River (p.321).

108 TNA: ADM 51/4042: *Teaser* log.

The bay in which they landed was the Anse de Rospico, in the commune of Névez, southwest of Pont-Aven. This is confirmed by the mayor of Pont-Aven when he reported his administration's activity at the first warning of an attempted landing on the Névez coast:

> At the instant we went there with those of our citizens we had been able to arm. The citizens of Névez gathered at the sound of the tocsin had already gone to the Fort de Raguenez where the enemy had appeared in the first place to want make their landing. But repulsed by the artillery of this small fort they abandoned their first plan and landed at half past seven in the small anse de Kervuen situated between the village of Keranglas and Kerascoet, at an equal distance from the batteries of Riec and Raguenez and out of range from both; twenty-six chasse-marées were employed in this landing which was made under the protection of a corvette and a schooner.[109]

Given when and where they landed, the chouans with Jean Jan and Lantivy were never able to take part in any attack to the rear of the Sainte-Barbe position.

The Reinforcements

As previously stated, the convoy bringing the Second Division had sailed from the Elbe estuary on 29 June, later than had been planned. It made steady progress in the North Sea, reaching the Downs, off the Kent coast, late on 3 July and anchoring at Spithead at 7:00 p.m. on 5 July.[110] When, the next day, Captain Lawrence Halsted reported his arrival to the Admiralty, he requested that his ship, *Venus*, have three or four days alongside so his crew could be paid, for the first time since April. However, when he received his instructions, at 9:00 p.m. on 7 July, he was told that as his current service was of 'so pressing a nature' that he was only to take on the water and provisions that he needed and to 'proceed … without a moment's delay.'[111]

Urgency was required as the Government, that morning, had received news of the successful landing in Quiberon Bay; Lieutenant White having landed, from the *Arethusa*, with the dispatches at Portland at 11:00 a.m. on 6 July.[112]

On 8 July, Halsted reported that the naval ships and transports would have left that morning but for him being told the ships bringing ordnance stores, which were to join the convoy, would 'not be ready before tomorrow evening'

109 Huchet, *Quiberon*, p.112. Some names are now given in a slightly different form and Kervuen does not seem to be used any more. The first battery mentioned appears to be now marked by the remains of Fort de Bélon on Pointe de Penquernéo, in the commune of Riec-sur-Bélon. Historians have previously identified the landing place as elsewhere because they have not used Smith's log.

110 TNA: ADM 51/1117: *Venus* log.

111 TNA: ADM 1/1913: Halsted to Nepean on 4 and 6 July; ADM 1/1011 Admiral Parker to Nepean 7 July.

112 TNA: ADM 51/1102: *Arethusa* log.

when he would immediately put to the sea.[113] There were, however, further delays but these were not, in fact, significant as the winds had turned southerly and light, so ships leaving Spithead were making very little progress.[114] In the meantime Sombreuil arrived at Portsmouth and immediately went on board the transport *Silver Eel* where he dined with the Damas officers; one of whom, Ensign Claude-Augustin de Tercier, recalled the meal:

> The conversation only turned on the affairs of the times and on our hopes. He [Sombreuil] was on the brink of marrying in London Mlle de la Blache ... when he received a letter from the English minister that announced to him that the expeditionary fleet that had left Hanover had just anchored at Spithead, from where it was directly to set sail again for the coast of Brittany and the Vendée, and that he did not have a minute to lose, if he wished to join it at Portsmouth. On this advice, the brave Comte de Sombreuil, forgetting everything for honour and glory, did not hesitate a single moment. He took the mail coach immediately, and to be more certain of arriving in time, he paid a guinea to each driver. He found on arrival at Portsmouth the flotilla which was at anchor, and embarked. He said to us: 'I would have paid two thousand guineas for the good fortune to have remained twenty-four hours longer in London for the celebration of my marriage; but,' he added sadly, 'I must sacrifice all for honour and the cause of the King who we are going to defend.'[115]

Sombreuil had other misgivings as is shown by a letter he wrote to Windham, dated 8 July, from his berth in the *John* transport. In it he wrote that he had had only one interview with the minister and his urgent departure had prevented him from clarifying 'several points of importance' which he then outlined:

> I have the honour to observe to you, Sir, that I am going with troops, of whose destination I know nothing but by public report, neither am I acquainted with their means of subsistence, nor, in the smallest degree, with the rules by which I am to regulate my conduct. What will be necessary, with regard to ammunition, with which I am not, to my knowledge, provided, and with regard to the support of those with whom I am to act, the means by which I am to carry on my correspondence with you, in a distant situation; and from whom I am, in all cases, to receive orders. These are the points on which I request you to give me such instructions as will serve as a basis for my conduct.[116]

The Admiralty wanted the convoy to be off as soon as possible and so ordered Halsted to leave an ordnance vessel that was not ready behind. On the evening of 10 July he informed them that all such vessels were ready 'except

113 TNA: ADM 1/1913: Halsted to Nepean on 8 July.

114 TNA: ADM 1/1011: Parker to Nepean on unrelated matter.

115 Charles de La Chanonie (ed.), *Mémoires politiques et militaires du général Tercier (1770–1816)* (Paris: Plon, 1891), p.105.

116 *The Times*, 19 April 1796, as read in the House of Commons by Richard Brinsley Sheridan of the opposition in a debate seeking to censure the Government for its conduct of the expedition.

the Grenville, which will not be ready before tomorrow evening,' and so he would sail at first light. The convoy accompanied by six ordnance vessels set sail at 3:30 a.m. the next morning.[117] Halsted maintained the urgency during the convoy's voyage, regularly instructing the masters of transports to take on more sail and for the Royal Navy vessels to take them in tow where necessary.[118]

In response to the news of the landing, the Government had immediately replied to Puisaye, on 7 July, informing him that the Second Division would leave without delay, along with a large supply of 'Artillery & Ordnance stores' and three months' provisions for 3,000 men. He was also informed of other items he had asked for, but which could not be collected in time to go with this convoy, including dollars 'to the amount of £50,000 Sterling' as well as 150 troop and 350 draft horses. These were to be sent with the next convoy, which would be 'very soon followed by a Corps of about 800 French Hussars in readiness to embark at Stade' where they awaited transports.[119]

When news reached London on Sunday 12 July of the capture of the Quiberon peninsula, the British Government not only, again, reacted immediately but also decided to step-up its support by committing British troops. That day the Duke of Yok was asked to issue orders for a contingent to be sent to Quiberon as he was informed:

> In the present situation of affairs in that quarter, the preservation of this peninsula, considered either as a military post, or as a safe channel of communication with the Fleet and this Country, is an object of the utmost importance … therefore … not a moment should be lost in taking advantage of such means as can be furnished immediately from England.[120]

In pursuit of these aims at least 3,000 men, from the regiments under Moira's command on the south coast of England, should embark on transports and warships, it being believed that many of these regiments already had their baggage on board. The regiments in the highest state of readiness and 'in the best condition for Foreign Service' should be selected. A major general, present with Moira's corps, was to sail, as commander, of these troops.[121]

Reinforcements had been demanded since the landing and so another source of these was looked to. Transports had finally arrived in the Channel Islands, arriving off Guernsey on 8 July, to embark the cadre corps for the diversions on the French coast.[122] Strachan was initially unaware that all the cadre corps, from both islands, were to embark, nevertheless on 12 July he was able to report that Léon would embark at Jersey that day and that he intended then to go to Guernsey, where he would superintend the embarkation of Williamson, before rendezvousing at Jersey and then proceeding to the

117 TNA: ADM 1/1913: Halsted to Nepean 10 and 11 July, the *Grenville* remained behind.
118 TNA: ADM 51/1167: *Lark* log.
119 TNA: WO 1/390: Horse Guards to Puisaye 7 July.
120 TNA: WO 1/390: Horse Guards to Puisaye 7 July.
121 TNA: WO 1/390: Horse Guards to Puisaye 7 July.
122 TNA: ADM 51/1133: *Fly* log.

French coast. However, he received new instructions that very day ordering him, instead, to convoy Léon's corps to Cawsand Bay as soon as the troops had embarked and the transports were ready to sail.[123] The urgency was to ensure that this corps, at least, would be ready to join the convoy carrying British troops to Quiberon, and on 17 July Strachan reported its arrival off Plymouth.[124]

The change in plan for the cadre corps was apparently in response to Puisaye's letter of 8 July to Windham in which he wrote, 'I am anxious that our cadres have not arrived. If they were here, they would be complete. … They are indispensable to me.'[125] It was as early as 14 July that the Government was able to inform Puisaye of the steps that had been taken. He was told that Major General Charles Graham would be coming with 3,000 British troops, that the convoy would also bring horses, clothing, provisions and military stores that missed the last convoy, with the Second Division, and also that the escorting warships would bring the promised dollars.[126] This dispatch ended by telling him that, 'Orders are given for sending the Corps of Emigrant Gentlemen under the Prince de Leon & M.M. du Tresor and Williamson to Quiberon with all possible expedition.'[127]

Graham received his initial orders to depart on 12 July, these clearly stated that his principal mission was 'the security of the Peninsula of Quiberon against any efforts of the Enemy, and the means of rendering this Position the most useful possible either as a military Post, or as a channel of communication with the Fleet and with this Country.' To do so he was to garrison 'the Forts and Posts which constitutes its defences, against any attack on the landside.' His instructions emphasised that Puisaye had taken the peninsula in the name of Louis XVIII and to prevent any 'misunderstanding' the British flag would only ever be flown alongside that of the French Royalty, 'even though the Post should be occupied by British Troops only, in which case it will be proper that the two Colours should be hoisted together and precisely upon the same footing.'[128]

The regiments that were selected to sail were the 12th, 14th, 27th, 28th, 57th and 80th Foot which were hastily embarked at Gosport and Southampton. Strangely the 80th Foot, that had been guarding prisoners of war at the Forton depot, just outside Gosport, was marched to Southampton to embark there, as Thomas Baldwin St George, a subaltern in the regiment noted in his diary, 'On Monday July 13th marched from Forton having received order to go to Romsey, halted at Botley that night (14 miles) where we received orders to proceed the next morning to Southampton to embark

123 TNA: ADM 1/103: Strachan to Nepean 12 July.
124 TNA: ADM 1/103: Strachan to Nepean 17 July.
125 Puisaye, *Mémoires*, vol.VI, p.318
126 Charles Graham was promoted major general on 26 May 1796 (Army List 1796).
127 TNA: WO 1/390: Horse Guards to Puisaye 14 July. Some sources wrongly identify Graham as Thomas, the future Lord Lynedoch, who was only promoted colonel on 22 July 1795 and was serving with his regiment, the 90th Foot.
128 BL: Add MS 7975: Portland to Graham 12 July.

on a secret expedition.'[129] On 16 July Graham left Southampton with the 12th and 80th Foot, along with 175 draft horses, and the 14th sailed the next day, while more commissariat and artillery horses were still to embark.[130] The convoy of transports gathered at Cowes Roads to sail under the command of Captain Mark Robinson of HMS *Arethusa* on which *Lieutenant* Carrey d'Asnières's detachment from Hector now was, having transferred from the *Diamond* on 15 July.[131] Graham had also been instructed to ensure that he took with him any members of the units already at Quiberon, who were at Southampton and ready to embark.[132] Officers and men from the depots of Hervilly and Dresnay were embarked on the transports. There were 39 of Hervilly: an *aide-chirurgien*, a *capitaine*, two *lieutenants*, six *sous-lieutenants*, seven *sergents*, seven *caporaux*, a *tambour* and 14 *soldats*, four grenadiers and 10 fusiliers.[133] There were 78 in Dresnay's contingent, including the Marquis du Dresnay himself, along with six staff officers, four *capitaines*, 13 *lieutenants*, 13 *sous-lieutenants*, two *sergent-majors*, a *fourrier*, eight *sergents*, five *caporaux* and 26 fusiliers; the number of staff and company officers illustrating how short the regiment was of such ranks when it landed in Brittany.[134] There are no records to show how many of Hector embarked however a newspaper report indicates there were recruits suitable for it or Dresnay with the convoy:

> Among the ships companies of the three Republican men of war taken by Lord Bridport ... are a number of Chouans, who had been forced to go on board during the Peace between the Royalists and the Convention. They immediately demanded leave to enlist in the regiments of Emigrants on board the Convoy, which has been granted to all such as were able to prove that they are Royalists, and were pressed for the sea-service of the Republic.[135]

On 20 July Major William Harness, 80th Foot, wrote to his wife from the *Convention* transport in Cowes Roads; it was her birthday,

> The wind is fair, and the signal is just made for sailing. ... The weather is beautiful and all bears the fairest looks. Everybody in the Fleet are busy. The Bands are playing on all sides, and in every countenance is happiness and content. ... I shall drink your health. We have a very sober set on board.[136]

129 H.C.B. Cook, 'The St George Diary: A Junior Regimental Officer in the Low Countries, 1794–95' *Journal of the Society for Army Historical Research*, vol. 47, No. 192 (Winter 1969), p.245. St George was promoted lieutenant on 15 July 1795.

130 TNA: WO 1/176: Doyle to Duke of Portland 17 July.

131 TNA: ADM 51/1102: *Arethusa* log.

132 BL: Add MS 7975: Portland to Graham 13 July.

133 TNA: WO 12/11741: muster roll.

134 TNA: WO 12/11708: the muster roll states that all embarked on 15 July. No such entries are in Hector's equivalent roll (WO 12/11741).

135 *The Hull Advertiser*, 18 July 1795.

136 Caroline M. Duncan-Jones (ed.), *Trusty and Well Beloved: The letters home of William Harness, an officer of George III* (London: SPCK, 1957), pp.79–80.

The regiments were considered those 'in the best condition for Foreign Service' however they were under strength so, while off Cowes, 'the Regiments received drafts from the 85th Regiment.'[137] The 85th provided 347 men, so most of its privates, to the six regiments in drafts of 55 to 62 men, those transferred to the 80th being paid from the 17 July.[138] The regiments were also under equipped, as Moira described on 19 July, 'This unfavourable wind still detains Graham in Cowes Road. I hope the delay has allowed him to receive the supply of firelocks wanted to complete his Regiments as to arms; for the number deficient was serious.'[139] Discontent among the troops was rife, as indicated by two separate reports in *Saunders's News-Letter*, an opposition leaning publication:

> Southampton, July 16. A disturbance of a very serious nature took place this morning: the 14th regiment refused to embark until the arrears due to them for upwards of two years were paid them. The soldiers and officers were resolutely determined not to yield. ... at last the soldiers were paid in part, but this step not pacifying them, the whole regiment resorted to the several ale-houses and got completely drunk: in this situation many were dragged into the boats, and others were allured by Gen. Doyle's accompanying them on board the transports, promising them beer, and also in due time a redress of their grievances.
>
> Cowes, dated July 17, ... A disagreeable circumstance has just happened: the soldiers of the 85th regiment, who have been some time in barracks here, have refused to be drafted for service, and have even resisted with violence the attempts of several of the officers to enforce obedience. General Graeme [*sic*] is, in consequence, about to land to try his authority; though the men mutinously swear to yield to no power that endeavours to break them as a regiment.[140]

The convoy, with 42 transports, raised anchor at noon on 20 July and slowly worked its way out of the Solent but a contrary, south-westerly, wind had been blowing steadily for several days and the convoy made slow progress, taking shelter in Portland Roads between 22 and 25 July before finally dropping anchor in Cawsand Bay from 5:00 p.m. on 26 July.[141] The delays, however, meant that the cadre corps that had been left behind in the Channel Islands were able to join Léon in Cawsand Bay. Trésor embarked at Jersey on 17 July and Williamson embarked at Guernsey two days later; they both arrived in Plymouth Sound on 21 July.[142]

137 Cook, 'St George Diary', p.246.
138 TNA: WO 12/8812 and WO 12/8455: pay lists.
139 TNA: WO 1/176: Moira to Huskisson, Southampton, 19 July.
140 *Saunders's News-Letter*, 24 July 1795.
141 TNA: ADM 51/1102: *Arethusa* log and *The Times*, Thursday 30 July 1795.
142 TNA: WO 12/12034 and HO 69/14: returns, and report in *The Times*, Monday 27 July 1795.

Table 9. Embarkation returns: Léon, Trésor and Williamson, 12, 17 and 19 July 1795 respectively.[143]

	Léon	Trésor	Williamson	Totals
Staff	7	6	6	19
Company officers	7	7	7	21
Sergents	16	10	16	42
Caporaux & Appointés	40	19	20	79
Volontaires	163	132	159	454
Tambours	4	2	-	6
Soldats	4	-	-	4
Aumôniers	5	-	-	5
Servants	26	-	-	26
Women	-	-	4	4
Total	272	176	212	660
Already in France	38	14	37	89

There were some differences in organisation: Williamson had no *appointés* (only *caporaux*) unlike the other two and Léon is shown with five *aumôniers* (chaplains), in addition to the one in the staff in common with the other corps, as well as four *soldats*, presumably remaining from Dresnay's earlier unit. Those already in France were 37 *volontaires* and a soldier from Léon; two *sergents*, one *caporal* and 11 *volontaires* from Trésor and two *capitaines*, the *chirurgien-major* and 34 *volontaires* from Williamson.

While the convoy with Graham's troops was slowly making its way along the Channel, the Government received dispatches from Puisaye, dated 8 July, as well as a round-up of events between 5 and 11 July. In response, on 21 July, he was informed the reinforcements were delayed by contrary winds but that the cadre corps were at Cawsand Bay, '... and will avail themselves of the first fair wind to proceed to Quiberon, together with the six British Regiments embarked under the command of Major General Graham, forming a force of between three and four thousand men.' The rest of the British troops, which it was hoped would be no less than 5,000 infantry with a detachment of cavalry, would follow with Moira who was appointed to the 'chief command of the Forces to be employed in this Expedition.'[144]

143 TNA: HO 69/13 (Léon), HO 69/15 (du Trésor) and HO 69/14 (Williamson).

144 TNA: WO 1/390: Horse Guards to Puisaye 21 July.

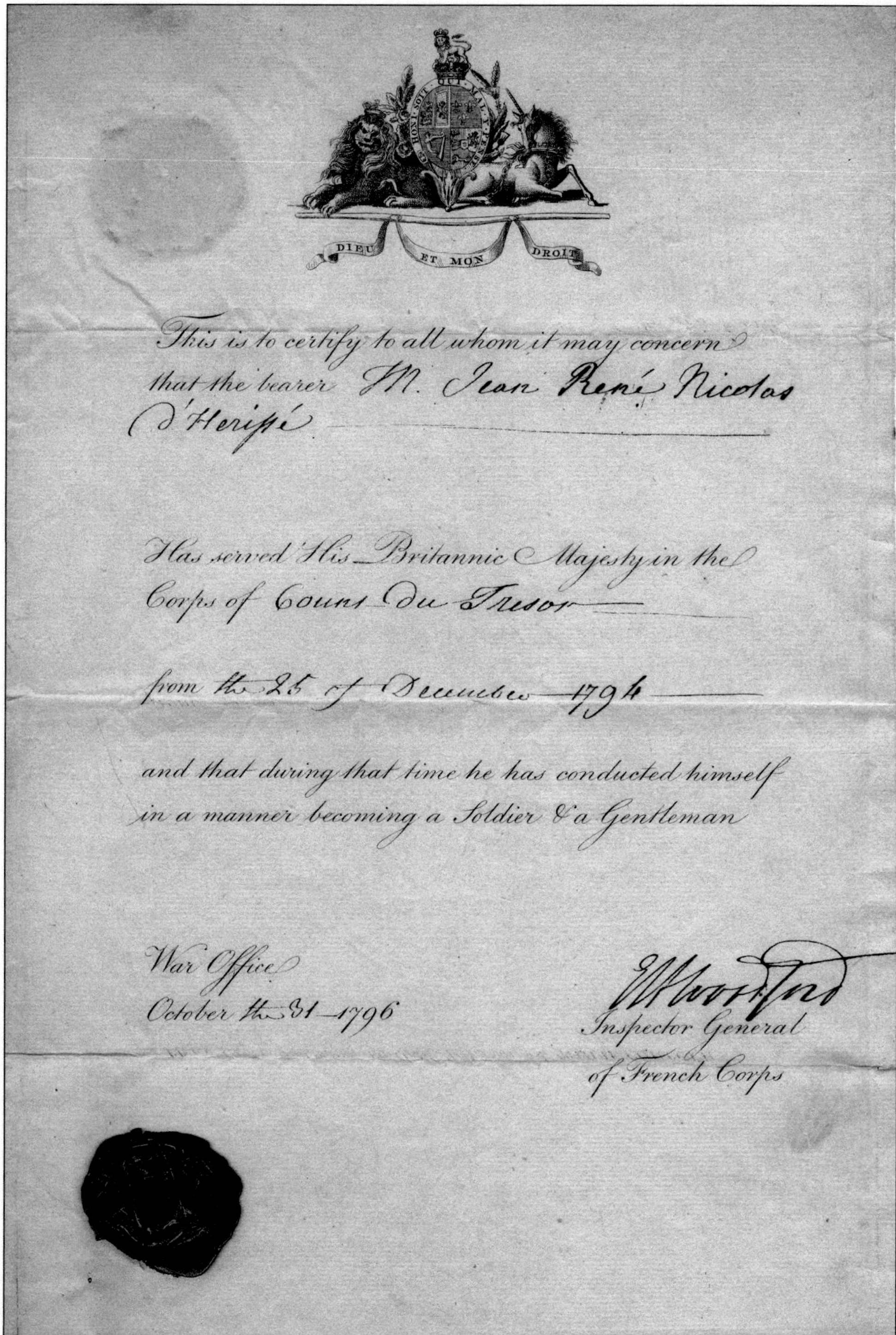

DIEU ET MON DROIT

This is to certify to all whom it may concern
that the bearer M. Jean René Nicolas
d'Herissé

Has served His Britannic Majesty in the
Corps of Count du Tresor

from the 25 of December 1794

and that during that time he has conducted himself
in a manner becoming a Soldier & a Gentleman

War Office
October the 31 1796

Inspector General
of French Corps

Certificate issued to Jean-René-Nicolas d'Hérissé, a Norman gentleman, who embarked with Trésor's corps on 17 July 1795 as *caporal* in the first company. (Collection of La Sabretache)

7

Attack

Sainte-Barbe Assaulted

'Nothing remarkable happened, on the 12, 13, and 14 of July. These days were employed on the works of the fortifications, preparations for the attack which was to take place on 16, and several administration regulations.'[1] This was how Puisaye described what was somewhat of a lull for the troops and chouans on Quiberon peninsula.

The Second Division was about to arrive; on the evening of 14 July Halsted briefly conferred with Lord Bridport and continued with the convoy to begin working into Quiberon Bay in the afternoon of the next day. It joined the transports already at anchor in the bay between 9 and 11:00 p.m. on 15 July.[2] Ensign Louis-Gabriel de Villeneuve-Laroche-Barnaud, who had formerly served in the Dutch army before joining Périgord, remembered, 'There is no need to say what emotion seized us … the shout of *vive le Roi*, repeated three times, rose up, at the same instant, from all vessels of the convoy, as if the brave brothers in arms to whom we had come to join could hear us and respond to us.'[3]

Despite the convoy's imminent arrival being known the day before, the plan to attack the Sainte-Barbe position, which consisted of coinciding attacks, could not be delayed to allow the Second Division to disembark. As Puisaye wrote:

> On 15 July, the plan for the attack of the camp of Ste. Barbe was definitively decided between Sir John Warren, Comte d'Hervilly, and me. This plan was simple. It consisted … of making a general sortie, from Fort Penthièvre, and attacking Hoche from the front, while Tinténiac and Jean Jean would attack him by the rear.[4]

1 Puisaye, *Mémoires*, vol.VI, p.322.
2 TNA: ADM 51/1117: *Venus* log; ADM 51/1167: *Lark* log and WO 1/390: La Jaille to Dundas 18 July.
3 Villeneuve-Laroche-Barnaud, *Mémoires*, vol.I, p.234.
4 Puisaye, *Mémoires*, vol.VI, pp.324–325.

Puisaye makes it clear that the plan and the timing for the attack was, at least, a joint decision, and not Hervilly's alone as some subsequent commentators, following Vauban, have implied. Indeed Warren commented, '... the attack made by our troops on the 16th ... which the generals resolved to undertake before the reinforcements disembarked.'[5] At this time Puisaye was very much in command, his aide, La Jaille, noting his cancellation of a sortie scheduled for 15 July.[6]

On arriving in the bay, Sombreuil immediately conferred with Warren and then, accompanied by *Lieutenant-colonel* de Talleyrand-Périgord, his second-in-command, and *Capitaine* Pierre-René-Marie Comte de Vaugiraud, of Hector and liaison officer to Warren, landed to see Puisaye; finding him in bed at his headquarters at the manoir de Kerdavid. Puisaye recalled that Sombreuil brought him a letter from Windham which, '... put an end to the false pretensions of M d'Hervilly, in declaring that the paid troops had been put entirely under my command, and in announcing the brevet of Lieutenant General in the service of His Britannic Majesty.'[7] According to Puisaye when he shared the news with Hervilly, who was to retain command of the First Division, he appeared satisfied, only regretting that the issue had not been clarified earlier. Puisaye continued, 'From that moment, I had only praise for M d'Hervilly.'[8] Contades, however, stated that Hervilly greeted Sombreuil's arrival and the letter's contents with bad grace, a version which some later writers have embellished.[9]

In addition to the main attacks on the Sainte-Barbe positions, Vauban was to make a diversion by landing near Carnac with 2,000 chouans, supported by about 150 to 200 British marines, '... to surprise a post that the Republicans had placed at St. Clément [*sic*]. If he succeeded in this enterprise; he was to seize a battery, newly raised on the shore between Plouharnel and the post, ...That done, he was to exploit his advantages, and advance on the left of the Ste. Barbe camp.'[10] He was to signal with a rocket, or flare, on his successfully landing and proceeding inland and once more should he be forced to re-embark.

The new battery had been built near Kerhellec, about 680 metres from the limit the British gun-vessels could go into Plouharnel Bay at low water, and was intended to hinder their access. How far he continued with the diversion, moving through the three stages was left for Vauban to decide. An important factor being the quality of the men he had with him. The best of the chouans had either gone with Tinténiac or been retained by Puisaye for the sortie, so he 'only had, properly speaking, newly armed peasants.'[11] Indeed it is clear that his arrival at the left of the Sainte-Barbe position, to coincide with the attack on its front, was not really expected. This supposition is supported by

5 Vauban, *Mémoires*, p.104, and Corbett (ed.), *Private Papers*, p.88, Warren to Spencer 22 July.
6 TNA: WO 1/390: La Jaille's letter of 18 July.
7 Puisaye, *Mémoires*, vol.VI, p.328.
8 Puisaye, *Mémoires*, vol.VI, p.329.
9 Contades, *Coblenz*, pp.172–173, an example of such a later writer is Bittard des Portes *Les émigrés à la cocarde noire*, pp.476–478.
10 Puisaye, *Mémoires*, vol.VI, p.325.
11 Puisaye, *Mémoires*, vol.VI, p.326.

considering the time it would have taken him to reach the position. The simple distance between the beach and the approach to the Sainte-Barbe position is comparable with that from Fort Penthièvre, just over six kilometres, so may have taken about an hour and 20 minutes.[12] However, going via the batteries the distance would have been almost nine and a half kilometres, so about two hours, discounting any engagement he may have on landing at Saint-Columban and the battery near Kerhellec. So, there would be a delay even if both Vauban's party and the troops on the isthmus began from their starting points at the same time, which as will be seen, was never expected to be the case.

Unfortunately, Vauban's account of the diversion is too full of falsehoods and invective against Hervillly to be relied upon. He states that his instructions were that his chouans were to be embarked at 10:00 p.m. at Port d'Orange; the arrangements for the boats to arrive an hour earlier being entrusted to one of Hervilly's staff. After conferring with Warren on the *Pomone*, he returned to the port at 9:30 p.m. to find the chouans there but no boats, the staff officer, the Marquis de Balleroy, having forgotten his charge. Enough boats arrived, one by one, to enable him to embark 800 men at 11:30 p.m.; so he returned to see Hervilly complaining that he could not succeed in these circumstances, but the latter told him to, 'Leave, leave with what you can, but leave immediately, I hold you responsible for it.'[13] Having left the port, he rendezvoused off shore with the gunboats and those carrying the marines at midnight and then headed for the shore in a cutter with Warren.

Vauban explains that the delays meant it was getting light when he arrived before the beach at Carnac so any chance of surprise was gone:

> I found the coast lined by superior forces; the republicans, who I estimated at fifteen to eighteen hundred men, had cannon.
>
> I tried to disembark and landed, but, by the dispositions of the enemy, I was immediately obliged to re-embark; I had several killed and wounded; and Admiral [*sic*] Warren, who had disembarked with me, was the first to recognise that there was nothing more to do. The royalists also felt it and they had reason, but they re-embarked in a rush and behaved very badly; they all soaked their muskets in the sea so as not to be obliged to serve with them: never was ill will more manifest. We pulled away from the coast.[14]

He makes no mention of firing any signal rocket whatsoever.

Vauban's account falls down from the start because, as has been seen, Balleroy was not a member of Hervilly's staff but Puisaye's. Furthermore logs of the warships not only show that the boats were to be provided by the Royal Navy but also give no hint of a delay. The log of the *Pomone* notes that at 11:00 p.m. the marines were sent with a party of chouans 'to make a false attack.'[15] For the *Robust* it was noted that at 10:00 p.m. the marines were

12 Carnac Plage and Glévenay, direct, being 6.4 km and Fort Penthièvre to the front of the position is 6.1 km.

13 Vauban, *Mémoires*, p.69.

14 Vauban, *Mémoires*, pp.69–70.

15 TNA: ADM 51/1149: *Pomone* log.

embarked in the cutter and all the boats, manned and armed, were sent to the *Pomone* and that at midnight, 'they proceeded with a Number of Flat Boats to the Beach and landed the Troops to the Eastward of Carnac.'[16]

Warren's own account to the Admiralty, written only two days later, stated that he,

> ... would land a Body of eleven hundred Chouans on the Carnac side of the Bay to make a false attack; ... I directed that Marines of the Squadron to be landed at the former place in order to support the Chouans, which having [been] effected with very little opposition as the Enemy retired with some loss; I was informed by the Officer Commanding those Troops that it was too late to advance further ...[17]

Puisaye's aide-de-camp, La Jaille, wrote a report on 18 July as well, presumably after having had a briefing from Vauban. He explained that Warren left his ships with the chouans and marines at midnight and they landed at 2:30 a.m. on 16 July,

> ... the descent was effected without a great resistance; the agreed signal was made at half past three ... Général Vauban coming to the height that dominates the site of his landing observed two columns of about 800 men which sought to take him on the flank: he was fearful of being attacked at the same time at the front by the enemies distributed in great numbers in the villages between St Clement [*sic*] and Ste Barbe. He judged it prudent to re-embark, but, he neglected to make this known by a signal.[18]

Thus, he explains why no one saw another signal rocket to the east, there had not been one, but despite La Jaille's apparently reliable assertion, Puisaye contradicted it in his memoirs writing, 'I assured myself, after the affair, that this second flare had been fired, but the sun just having appeared; there was not a cloud in the sky, it was not seen.'[19] While Vauban had made this reconnaissance, the marines and most of the chouans had remained 'camped on the edge of the shore' under the cover of the gunboats before re-embarking.[20] The republican account of the morning's events put little weight on the diversion: 'In order to make a diversion, the enemy had wished to disembark some troops level with Beaumer. They effected their landing; but the presence of chef de brigade Romans, at the head of some mobile columns, made them promptly take to their launches.'[21]

16 TNA: ADM 51/1130: *Robust* log. The force included the whole detachment of the 118th Foot from the *Thunderer* (ADM 51/1103: log).

17 TNA: ADM 1/103: Warren to Nepean 18 July.

18 TNA: WO 1/390: La Jaille's letter of 18 July 1795.

19 Puisaye, *Mémoires*, vol.VI, pp.331–332.

20 TNA: HO 69/30: anonymous account by a sailor.

21 Huchet, *Quiberon*, p.123, giving the reference Archives départementales de Morbihan, K 3855. This, supported by the *Robust*'s log, places the landing to the east of that of 27 June, at the eastern end of Carnac-Plage or even, perhaps, round the Pointe Churchill, at Plage de Beaumer or du Men-Du.

Vauban's landing was, at best, meant to be a diversion while success would need both the attack on the front of the Sainte-Barbe position, led by Hervilly with around 2,500 regular troops and about 1,600 chouans, to coincide with that on the rear by Tinténiac and Jean Jan, with the Armée rouge and the chouans that had joined him since his landing. The entrenched camp was held by a sizable force. One republican account stated there were 8,000 men in the main position.[22] Even if Hervilly managed to capture it, he did not have enough men to resist a counter-attack on the position. Only by crushing the republicans between the two attacks could a convincing enough victory be gained to clear them from the position and so secure access to Morbihan, and Brittany, beyond. This was what was required for the expedition to succeed in its aim.

Unfortunately, there was to be no surprise involved in the attack as the republican report explained:

> Two deserters from the enemy camp arrived at our forward-posts in the afternoon of 27 messidor [15 July], and informed Général Lemoine, commanding the camp of Sainte-Barbe, that the enemy was making ready to attack today 28, very early in the morning. This advice having been repeated by two other deserters, Général Lemoine immediately made the dispositions set out in case of attack, and waited for the enemy …[23]

Hoche was absent at Rennes with Blad and Tallien. Who the deserters were, chouans or paid soldiers, is not stated and although some historians have assumed they were from the Régiment d'Hervilly, this is the one unit they could not have come from.[24] This is because its lists are not only complete but in enough detail to show when men deserted and, after the attempts to desert immediately after the landing, only four men had deserted since, all before the attack was planned.[25]

The troops and chouans moved off from the outworks in front of Fort Penthièvre at 1:00 a.m.[26] The Loyal Emigrants, deployed as skirmishers, were in advance followed by three columns of, from left to right, Hervilly, Dresnay and Hector; the artillery, two 8-pounders and six 4-pounders, initially marched between the columns. The chouans provided a reserve, the Duc de Lévis with about 600 was on the right behind Hector and another 1,000 or so, under Saint-Pierre, behind the centre. Hervilly marched with

22 G. Thomas de Closmadeuc, *Quiberon 1795 Émigrés et Chouans Commissions Militaires: Interrogatoires et Jugements* (Paris: Société d'éditions littéraires, 1899), p.42, Pacqueteau, a volunteer in the Légion Nantaise, to his father 4 thermidor.

23 Huchet, *Quiberon*, p.123.

24 Bittard des Portes, *Les émigrés à la cocarde noire*, p.524, made this assumption and others have followed.

25 TNA: WO 12/11681: pay list; 11 July a *caporal de fusiliers* and a *fusilier* and 12 July a *tambour de fusiliers* and a *grenadier*, all recruited before arriving in France. These desertions were probably made during sorties.

26 Times given by participants range from midnight to 'two hours before daybreak' (Puisaye, *Mémoires*, vol.VI, p.330). 1:00 a.m. is given as it is compatible with the fighting being heard to commence at 2:30 a.m. (TNA: ADM 51/1111: *Concorde* log).

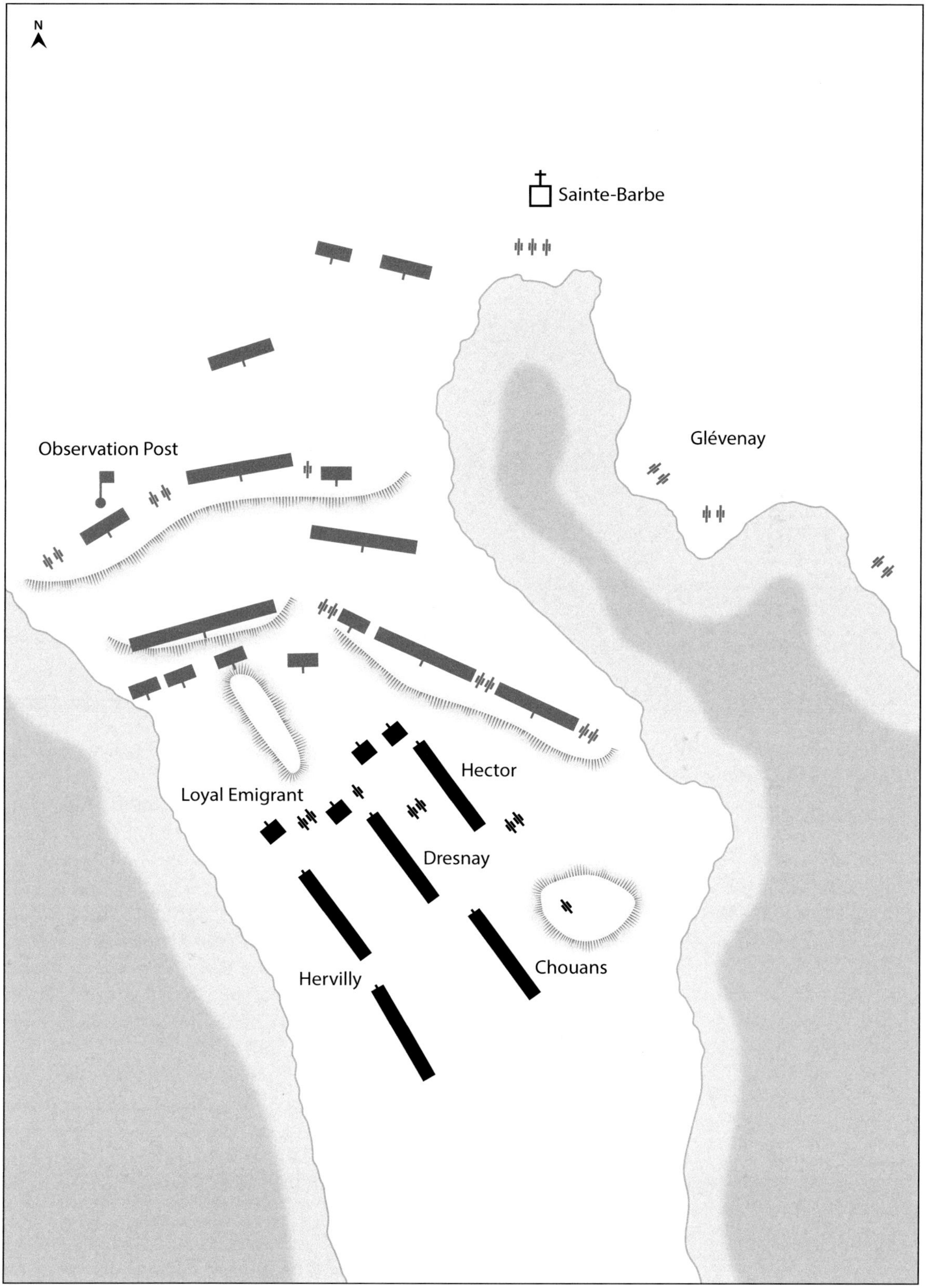

Attack on the Sainte-Barbe lines, 16 July 1795.

The entrenchment line, the person standing at the base of the current slope is just over six feet (1.85 m) tall. (Author's collection)

his regiment while Puisaye, with Sombreuil by his side, was with Saint-Pierre's chouans.[27]

The troops advanced in silence and halted in a dip, about halfway along the isthmus, where their commanders waited for the signal from Vauban that he had landed and was advancing. This signal was seen and Puisaye had Hervilly wait 15 minutes in case a second should be seen, but it was not.[28] Dawn was just beginning to break, the columns continued their advance, and they soon encountered the republican outposts who immediately opened fire in a display of resistance but, in compliance with their orders, steadily withdrew. All sources indicate that Hervilly had not shared any of his plans or issued any orders to his unit commanders before the action began and, indeed, had no designated second-in-command.

By now Rotalier, commanding the artillery, had provided two 4-pounders to each of the three infantry columns and intended to deploy his two 8-pounders to counter the batteries on the far side of Plouharnel Bay and also the left (east) of the republican line from which he feared the most threat, it being further forward than the right. However as soon as the

27 Puisaye, *Mémoires*, vol.VI, p.330 gives him as the Chevalier de Saint-Pierre but all other indications are that he was the Vicomte, an officer of Dresnay.

28 Puisaye, *Mémoires*, vol.VI, p.331.

republican skirmishers were encountered Hervilly ordered Rotalier to bring all his guns forward and the 8-pounders were to support his left column. Thus, the artillery found itself, '… having been obliged to march without respite in advance, under fire from the skirmishers, and finally under that of musketry from the enemy line, without having had, so to speak, the leisure to fire two shots in our turn'.[29]

According to Puisaye it was at this stage that he and Hervilly felt that the republicans were reacting to another attack.

> We were confirmed in this mistake by a movement that we remarked, very distinctly, on the left of the enemy camp. M d'Hervilly, who had taken himself to the front, returned to say that he had observed a lot of disorder, and that a fusillade was heard in the distance.
>
> I advanced, and was myself witness to what he had reported to me. 'It is Tinténiac," I exclaimed; "advance, and let's charge.'[30]

The royalists took the advance camps where 'a large quantity of provisions and booty plundered from the wretched inhabitants of the country' was found.[31] They pressed on towards the first of the field works in front of the main Sainte-Barbe position, despite the fire of the muskets and field-pieces of the republican skirmishers commanded by Humbert. The main body of the republican troops were under orders not to fire or show themselves, as Janillion explains:

> Nothing indeed was finer nor more imposing than the sortie of these superb regiments, all dressed anew, in coats of scarlet, deploying themselves in three columns; they advanced at port arms, beating the general, up to pistol range of our entrenchments. All the army that Lazare Hoche commanded was crouched behind these same entrenchments, with orders to not rise up, nor to make any movement than at the command of the general …[32]

The spaces between the columns of émigré troops had widened as they had approached the republican position, matching the widening of the isthmus. The connection between the columns was also hindered by a spine of higher ground running along the isthmus on the approach to the republican entrenchments.[33] *Lieutenant* Le Charron, of Hervilly, later remembered:

---

29 TNA: PRO 30/11/225: Rotalier to Cornwallis 18 July; the fact that as an artillery officer he was writing directly to the Master of the Ordnance, rather than the War Office, perhaps permitted him to write so critically of Hervilly's performance.

30 Puisaye, *Mémoires*, vol.VI, p.332.

31 *Saunders's News-Letter*, 15 August 1795 'extract of a Letter from an Officer of the Emigrants who was on the spot.'

32 Janillion, *Versailles et Quiberon*, p.60.

33 Such a spine is to be seen today just to the east of the La Guèrite beach car park which may be the same. It is of sufficient height to mask the 'buildings' of the surf school, made of shipping containers, from being seen until entering the car park.

> When we had arrived well within cannon range, M de Saint-Cran [Saint-Cren], aide-major of the second battalion of Royal-Louis, gave the order for the drummers to beat the charge, and the unit marched gaily in the sand, thinking to seize the enemy camp by storm. The other columns were likewise in movement, but the very heavy fire from the republicans appeared to present a violent obstacle on the right, the regiment was made to halt, and I saw M de Saint-Cran, who had approached M d'Hervilly, fall dead from his horse.[34]

The Régiment d'Hector's advance on the right had stalled and so Hervilly now decided to concentrate on two points of attack. He issued orders for Hector to move to the centre and take the front of the central, Dresnay, column. It was now that the columns were as close as 20 paces away from the republican line that the battery at the extreme left of the field-works, of 12 and 8-pounders began firing, striking the royalists' flank.[35] Sources describe this battery as being unmasked, one specifying that 'a small Republican corps which had remained stationed on a height to the right, and before the entrenchments, retreated, and in an instant unmasked a battery of six guns and two howitzers.'[36] However La Jaille's report suggests that the royalist command, at least, was aware that additional batteries had been constructed, 'in the form of lunettes' but did not know they had been armed with artillery.[37] *Sous-lieutenant* Jean-Baptiste-Louis de Jarrige de La Morélie, of Hector, described the results in a letter he wrote only a month later,

> … we were ordered to continue our march, and to proceed behind a small mound, where the regiment was under cover from the grape shot. We remained in this position for about five minutes, when we heard the charge sounded, and M d'Hervilly gave us the order to advance at the same pace.
>
> We thus emerged between two small hillocks and had the order to join the Dresnay column; for this object, we were obliged to run 20 to 25 minutes at the charge, parallel to the carmagnole [republican] entrenchments, at the distance of half musket range. Our troops were formed in platoons and at port arms. You can judge that, in such a position and in terrain as smooth as ice, 12 to 15 artillery pieces loaded with grape were to cause great devastation in our ranks …[38]

His sense of time was clearly affected by what he saw and experienced, another Hector officer, recalled many years later, 'in three minutes half of our little army was on the deck.'[39] The chouans under Lévis had already

34 Le Charron, *Expédition de Quiberon*, pp.14–15.

35 The weight of the guns is as given by the republican report (Huchet, *Quiberon*, p.123), those on the royalist side described them as 24-pounders e.g. Warren in his letter of 18 July (TNA: ADM 1/103).

36 *Saunders's News-Letter*, 15 August 1795 'Officer of the Emigrants.' The Musée de la Chouannerie, de la Vendée et des guerres de l'Ouest displays quantities of grapeshot that were discovered on the field of battle, 200 metres from the museum.

37 TNA: WO 1/390: La Jaille 18 July.

38 Louis Guibert, *Les Émigrés Limousin à Quiberon* (Limoges: Ducourtieux, 1886), pp.11–12, letter to one of his brothers from Southampton 15 August.

39 Antrechaus, *Relation*, p.9.

hesitated but encouraged by him and Contades they started to follow the men of Hector, but then:

> The column of the Duc de Lévis fell into such a rout that at a good gallop of his horse, he could not follow it. Several chouans rallied behind the first dip, but the greater number only stopped at the fort. … The intrepidity of the Marine [Hector] made a furious contrast to the feebleness of the chouans.[40]

The disintegration of the right and centre was soon complete, as related by Jarrige de La Morélie, of Hector:

> Our column having joined that of Dresnay, the carmagnols, to the number of 10 to 12 thousand men, drawn up in battle line the length of their entrenchments, began a fire by file so rolling that all the troops were put to the most complete rout, and retreated in the greatest disorder, the greatest part throwing away their muskets and pouches to run the better, without the officers being able to rally them.[41]

The Régiment d'Hervilly, covered from the enfilading fire, remained in formation but its losses were mounting, Le Charron described their situation:

> Amidst the terrible noise which echoed in the air darkened by the smoke from the guns, an officer from Dresnay came to ask me for a place in my platoon. 'And your regiment, Monsieur?' I said to him in surprise. 'It is no more,' he answered. I went up the elevation that dominated the terrain on which we were posted, and, to my great astonishment, I could see no more than a general jumble among the remains of the two regiments d'Hector and Dudresnay, of which more than half were stretched out on the field of battle. Rejoining my unit, I asked the officer, to whom I went to speak, to place himself on the left of my platoon with the guard of the flag.
>
> This reverse induced M d'Hervilly to order the retreat; and at the moment that we executed it, we had the grief to see pass near us the mortally wounded general, pale, without strength, and held up on his horse by two grenadiers.[42]

Hervilly was, indeed, severely wounded and expected to die very soon; a biscayen, a small cannon ball or piece of grape about the size of a small egg, had ripped into his stomach.

The artillery had lost guns from the beginning of the final advance when the limber of one of the 4-pounders, in the centre, broke and it had to be left where it was. As Rotalier brought the 8-pounders forward, in compliance with Hervilly's orders, they came under fire and their horses were killed so they also had to be left where they were. Two 4-pounders were with the right column, so Rotalier only had three guns, of the same calibre, remaining to bring forward as instructed. Soon one of these could not be moved as the

40 Contades, *Coblenz*, p.180.
41 Guibert, *Les Émigrés Limousin*, p.12.
42 Le Charron, *Expédition de Quiberon*, pp.15–16.

horse team was killed when a shell exploded among them and another had to be sent to the rear of the Hervilly column, with its caisson, after it had expended its ammunition. When the retreat was ordered Rotalier brought away the last 4-pounder that remained with him and also recovered one of the 8-pounders by using spare horses, the other cannon being damaged. The only other gun which was not left to the enemy was the 4-pounder with a broken limber; hooks and chains were used to haul it away.[43]

As soon as the republicans saw their opponents turn they emerged from their field-works. Their official report described the royalists as, '… shaken, they were charged by the cavalry, having three battalions in pursuit, and two others on their left flank; their retreat then degenerated into a rout'.[44] There were in fact only about 300 light cavalry, led by *Adjudant-général* Charles-Alexandre-Antoine Vernot-Dejeu, who attacked with great ferocity, indeed Contades described them as being drunk.[45] As the disorder became more general, neither Puisaye nor Sombreuil made any real impression on events. Of the regiments, Hervilly was, 'the only one that still presented a shadow of regularity'.[46] As Contades commented:

> It remained to this regiment, its chiefs and above all a man more capable than anyone to command. M de Boissieux, who, at this critical moment, displayed his talent and courage … he put his company in battle line and protected the retreat. [The company, initially composed, was somewhat shaken when their captain was shot in the arm but he inspired them to remain firm.] … M de Boissieux, always the last, protected the retreat of the army which was in absolute flight. The Loyal Emigrant and a quantity of officers rallied to it.[47]

As for casualties, one of the Loyal Emigrants who had been in front of the Hector column wrote, 'dispersed as skirmishers, already almost at the foot of the entrenchments, [we] only sustained very few of them. All this volley of iron passed over their heads'.[48] This witness was on the edge of the republican works when they emerged and seeing the other émigré troops already in flight he ran fast to join them:

> Nevertheless the pursuit was close, the grape shot and shells reached us for a long time. We lost many still in this rout … If the enemy had only had a squadron of cavalry, it was all over for us, no one would have returned to the fort; but fortunately they only had forty or so chasseurs, who, skirting our left at a fast trot,

43 TNA: PRO 30/11/225: Rotalier to Cornwallis 18 July.

44 Huchet, *Quiberon*, p.123 report.

45 The number of cavalry is given in Ornano, *Hoche*, p.202 and Contades, *Coblenz*, p.184. Lambert, Henri, *Pour Dieu et Le Roi ou l'inutile sacrifice Quiberon, juin–juillet 1795* (Lons-le-Saunier: Éditions Marque-Maillard, 1987), pp.148–149, provides a detailed biography of Vernot-Dejeu who had been a *capitaine* in the 23e Cavalerie until appointed on 22 February 1795 *adjudant-général chef de bataillon* on Hoche's request, a staff appointment ('général' having its original meaning denoting a post that was not regimental rather than a senior rank).

46 Anon., *Pomone*, p.33.

47 Contades, *Coblenz*, pp.182–184.

48 Berthier de Grandry, *Récit sommaire*, p.13.

> fell on the two rows of our dispersed mass, and sabred us several times without anyone thinking of making the least resistance.[49]

It took one of his comrades, Charles-Jacques-François de Corday, a *grenadier volontaire*, who shouted that they should not let themselves be overrun by a handful of such men, to rouse others to put up a resistance.[50] The cavalry were successful elsewhere in capturing the 4-pounder that had been withdrawn after its ammunition had been expended, however Vernot-Dejeu, was killed at their head, apparently shot by a republican NCO as 'his grey frock-coat, [was] similar to those worn by the royalist officers over their jackets'.[51]

The republican pursuit continued, but they were coming under increasing fire from the Royal Navy boats on their left. After Vauban had retreated to the boats Warren had acted decisively,

> … hearing an extreme heavy fire from the Army on the left, I immediately gave orders for the Boats with the Troops to push over to that side, where I soon learned that the Army … [was] obliged to retreat.
>
> The Enemy following them, I ordered the Marines to line the Works, and immediately proceeded with five of the Launches, each carrying an 18 pounder, with my own Boat as near as possible to the Shore, when the Enemy pressing forward, I commenced a very warm fire upon their left Flank, by which they lost great numbers of Men, and were obliged to retire.[52]

Once under the protection of Fort Penthièvre, 'M d'Atilly, lieutenant-colonel, commanding the regiment [d'Hervilly], put us in line of battle, facing the enemy. The flags were riddled by balls'.[53] Then a 32-pounder fired from the fort showed the republicans that they were now in range and they gave up the pursuit.

The royalists, émigré troops and chouans, reached the safety of the fort and the outworks, and Contades described the scene, 'The interior of the fort was horrifying; it was full of the wounded and the dying. The remainder of the troops had dismay painted on their faces.'[54] It is probably due to this dismay that the marines and soldiers from the British fleet remained and only returned to the warships on 17 July.[55]

Out to sea, in the bay, sailors and the newly-arrived émigrés of the Second Division were witnesses, from afar, of the events. On the *Thunderer* it was noted, 'AM at 3 heard very heavy vollies of Musquetry on the Peninsula & soon after Great Guns, it proved to be the Royalist and Republican Armies

49 Berthier de Grandry, *Récit sommaire*, p.14.

50 Corday's sister, Charlotte, famously assassinated Jean-Paul Marat, the radical republican journalist and politician, in his bath on 13 July 1793.

51 Janillion, *Versailles et Quiberon*, pp.61–62.

52 TNA: ADM 1/103: Warren to Nepean 18 July. Vauban stated he placed his chouans in the outworks apparently ignoring that he had already described them soaking their muskets in the sea to avoid further service (Vauban, *Quiberon Mémoires*, p.72).

53 Le Charron, *Expédition de Quiberon*, p.17.

54 Contades, *Coblenz*, p.185.

55 TNA: ADM 51/1130: *Robust* log.

in Action, the Gun Boats were employed harassing the Enemy, at 6 the firing ceased & the Royalists were obliged to retreat.'[56] The émigrés could not be so dispassionate, as Villeneuve-Laroche-Barnaud remembered:

> On 16, at four o'clock in the morning, woken by the desire to be the first to again take up the telescope, I go up on the deck of my vessel. Hardly had I got there, when I hear several cannon reports, the noise of which seems to me to come from the far end of the roadstead: I immediately bore my regard on that end, and I see the fire of several other shots, fired with a great precipitation. Several minutes afterwards, a new discharge of artillery, and soon a rolling fire of musketry becomes mixed with it. No more doubt then that this is the beginning of a very lively engagement, which approaches the environs of *Fort Penthièvre* ... I hasten to call my comrades, still asleep: they run onto the deck; all eyes are fixed with disquiet towards the theatre of combat. The fire continues without interruption and we are forced to remain peaceful spectators of this engagement, while the royalists have perhaps need of our help![57]

On land the most pressing need was to tend the wounded and so at about 9:00 a.m. the surgeons of the Second Division were ordered ashore, with their equipment, the rest of the division staying where they were.[58] The parish church at Quiberon was used as a hospital and along with the priests and the women of the units, nursing was provided by seven nursing sisters, *religieuse hospitalières*, from Auray.[59]

It was now that the human cost could be counted. Wetton, who presumably worked among the wounded states, 'The loss of the Royalists were six hundred and sixteen kill'd and wounded, of which ninety five officers.'[60] There were several tales of the valour of the wounded and dying, an example being François Commandeur de la Laurencie, *capitaine de grenadiers* of Hector, who had 'both thighs taken away by a ball, with one hand gave his purse to his grenadiers and, with the other, in breathing his last, showed them the path of duty and honour.'[61] The republicans retained control of the scene of most of the fighting:

> The enemy left on the field of battle three hundred and fifty dead; among them are many officers ... five pieces of cannon, the caissons, muskets, munitions, many officers swords, and twenty or so draught-horses. We have had twenty-three men killed ... and seventy-one wounded including many officers of recognised merit.[62]

56 TNA: ADM 51/1103: *Thunderer* log.

57 Villeneuve-Laroche-Barnaud, *Mémoires*, vol.I, pp.235–236.

58 Villeneuve-Laroche-Barnaud, *Mémoires*, vol.I, pp.236–237.

59 Eugène Le Garrec, *Les Héroïnes de Quiberon (1795)* (Vannes: Imprimerie Galles, 1936), pp.3–13.

60 Wetton, 'Journal', p.69. He does not specify where he was or what he did but his note of events indicates he was serving at the fort. A later report (TNA: ADM 80/136: undated) estimated that '730 were killed & wounded' in the action.

61 Contades, *Coblenz*, p.181. La Laurencie was a former *chef de division des armées navales*, his title of commandeur related to his position in the Knights of St John of Malta.

62 Huchet, *Quiberon*, p.123 report.

Plate 1 (top left)
Régiment d'Hervilly. (Courtesy of Anne S.K. Brown Military Collection, Brown University Library)

Plate 2 (top right)
Loyal Emigrant Regiment. (Courtesy of Anne S.K. Brown Military Collection, Brown University Library)

Plate 3 (right)
Officer, Volontaires Nationaux. (Courtesy of Anne S.K. Brown Military Collection, Brown University Library)

Plate 4 (left)
Fusilier, Volontaires Nationaux. (Courtesy of Anne S.K. Brown Military Collection, Brown University Library)

Plate 5 (below)
Fusilier, Infanterie de la Ligne. (Courtesy of Anne S.K. Brown Military Collection, Brown University Library)

Plate 6 (right)
Grenadier, Infanterie de la Ligne.
(Courtesy of Anne S.K. Brown Military
Collection, Brown University Library)

Plate 7 (below)
Chasseur, Régiment de Béon. (Courtesy of
Anne S.K. Brown Military Collection, Brown
University Library)

Aftermath of the attack of the Sainte-Barbe lines. (Giorgio Albertini © Helion & Company 2022)

Plate 8 (top left)
Régiment de Périgord. (Courtesy of Anne S.K. Brown Military Collection, Brown University Library)

Plate 9 (top right)
Régiment de Rohan. (Courtesy of Anne S.K. Brown Military Collection, Brown University Library)

Plate 10 (left)
Régiment de Salm. (Courtesy of Anne S.K. Brown Military Collection, Brown University Library)

Plate 11 (right)
Régiment des Uhlans Britanniques.
(Courtesy of Anne S.K. Brown Military Collection, Brown University Library)

Plate 12 (below)
Régiment des Hussards de Choiseul.
(Courtesy of Anne S.K. Brown Military Collection, Brown University Library)

Plate 13 (right)
Fusilier, Régiment de Damas. The distinctive black cockade of Britain had replaced the orange cockade of the United Provinces by the time of the unit's departure from Germany. (Courtesy of Anne S.K. Brown Military Collection, Brown University Library)

Plate 14 (below)
Chasseur, Régiment de Damas. (Courtesy of Anne S.K. Brown Military Collection, Brown University Library)

Significantly there is no mention of any prisoners being taken, the wounded who were left on the field of battle were immediately killed by the republican soldiers. A *capitaine* of artillery remarked in a report, '... I cannot tell you the number of their dead but the ground is covered with them in three places in which there were several wounded that our soldiers finished off'.[63] The same soldiers stripped the dead and, to Hoche's dismay, his friend, Vernot-Dejeu, shared the same fate.[64]

The number provided by Wetton appears correct but specific numbers of casualties for each unit, let alone the chouans, is hard to quantify as many of the records are inadequate for this purpose. Only officer casualties are known for the Loyal Emigrants and, as has been mentioned, they were comparatively light: only a captain and two lieutenants, including Torcy, were wounded.[65] Le Charron recalled that Hervilly 'lost ninety men, officers and soldiers.'[66] He must have included the wounded and the muster rolls show that two officers and nine men were killed, two officers died later of their wounds and eight officers, including Hervilly, and 14 men were so seriously wounded they were evacuated to England.[67]

Despite being in the thick of the action, the artillery suffered comparatively light casualties: a driver killed, and two officers, a sergeant driver, 10 gunners and five drivers wounded. Rotalier put this down to him having 'been obliged to lead them so close, the shots of the enemy passed for the most part over our heads.'[68] The sergeant had presumably been protecting his gun from the republican cavalry, as he was gravely wounded from three sabre blows to the head.

In contrast Dresnay is listed as having lost, killed, its *lieutenant-colonel*, *major* and four other officers, five NCOs, eight *caporaux*, seven grenadiers and 71 fusiliers (including 11 who died of their wounds).[69] The unit's *quartier-maître*, after listing the killed, noted that, 'Lots of officers and soldiers were wounded, so that, between killed and wounded one could reckon that half the regiment was put out of action.'[70] The situation in Hector was comparable, Jarrige de La Morélie writing,

> ... also, of the 440 men of our regiment, the rest being detached in different posts, we had 228 killed or wounded, and of the 72 officers, 55 were taken out of action, of which 18 killed and the rest wounded. I was in the number of the latter: I received in the left leg a ball which passed through one side and out the other, plus a spent biscayen which gave me a bad contusion to the kidneys.[71]

---

63 Robert, *Expédition*, p.67 report of *Capitaine* Trutat to *Chef de Brigade* Guiote, 28 messidor An III.

64 Robert, *Expédition*, pp.67–69.

65 TNA: WO 12/11734: muster roll.

66 Le Charron, *Expédition de Quiberon*, p.17.

67 TNA: WO 12/11681: muster roll.

68 TNA: PRO 30/11/225: Rotalier to Cornwallis 18 July.

69 TNA: WO 12/11708: muster roll.

70 Roussel & Bergevin, *Un Survivant*, p.266.

71 Guibert, *Les Émigrés Limousin*, p.12.

The wounded included the Comte de Soulanges, the regiment's *lieutenant-colonel*. Fourteen officers were killed and five died of the wounds, including *Capitaine* Alexandre-Mathurin-Auguste Chevalier de Kerouartz, brother-in-law to both Soulanges and Hector, who died in England after Jarrige de La Morélie had written his letter. Of the 17 *élèves de marine* who were present, serving as volunteers, three were killed and 12 were wounded in the action.[72]

The effect on the émigré regiments was shattering and all respect for their commanders was lost. Puisaye, after visiting Hervilly, returned to his quarters, apparently distancing himself from responsibility. Contades remarking of Puisaye, 'Until then, he was hardly liked; from then, he was detested.'[73] Others, particularly from the Régiments d'Hector and du Dresnay, placed the blame on Hervilly, as the tactical commander in the field, an anonymous officer stating that they complained, ' ... that they had been led to the slaughter, without being allowed to fire a musket shot, & blaming for their misfortune the General who until then had had their confidence.'[74] Jarrige de La Morélie reflected that the casualties of his regiment were, '... the unfortunate victims of the ambition, or better to say of the ignorance of he who commanded.'[75]

Hervilly had certainly performed badly. He had made a number of errors in the attack: the lack of briefing and orders for the unit commanders; his deployment of the artillery over the head of Rotalier; and crucially the handling of the right and subsequently centre columns. The Hector column was placed so that it neither attacked the far left of the republican position nor was in support of the Dresnay column. When he attempted to rectify this fault, he only exposed the already under-strength unit to devastating fire. If he had intended the Hervilly column to be the main attacking force, which seems to have been his aim in concentrating the artillery in its support, the other columns were not deployed to fulfil this aim. Together with Puisaye, he should have made contingencies for his being unable to continue in command, especially in identifying a successor.

Some have stated that Hervilly had carried out the sortie in a fit of temper or indeed of pique, afraid that he may be replaced by Sombreuil. This firstly presupposes that he was willing to sacrifice the émigré regiments, even his own, for his personal feelings when he had spent so much effort in maintaining them. He had certainly displayed a quick temper during the expedition, but it is far-fetched to think he would have maintained such an emotion and motivation throughout the planning process in which both Puisaye and Warren were involved.

Puisaye, by his own recollections and others' recognition, was commander-in-chief. As has been seen, he depicted himself as overseeing not only the planning of the operation but also its execution, he could have prevented the sortie if he had wished but he did not.

72 TNA: WO 12/11741: muster rolls.

73 Contades, *Coblenz*, p.136.

74 Anon., *De l'expédition de Quiberon*, p.34.

75 Guibert, *Les Émigrés Limousin*, p.13.

Where was Tinténiac and the Armée Rouge?

In his account of the events of 16 July Puisaye wrote:

> M de Tinteniac had not appeared, and we were betrayed! Such were my conjectures; they had only come too true. There was no more than to think of making a good retreat; I sent the order for it to M d'Hervilly. At the moment that he gave it, he was struck by a biscayen ...[76]
>
> If M de Tinteniac had fulfilled the part of the plan the execution of which was confided to him, this fatal day would have ended otherwise. I had only ordered the attack in the entire conviction that he was there. His valour, his activity, and his so renowned rigour, did not allow it to be doubted.[77]

He clearly blamed the defeat on Tinténiac and the chouan forces he had gathered around the Armée rouge failing to deliver the attack on the rear of the Sainte-Barbe position. He would have known that, regardless of other doubts, Jean Jan's party could not have assisted, having only left the Quiberon peninsula during the night of 13 to 14 July. After landing late into the evening of 15 July, the chouans advanced through Névez towards Pont-Aven. Composite local republican forces, including gardes territoreaux and nationaux, attempted to defend the town but were outnumbered and overwhelmed by the chouans who briefly held it until they were, in turn, driven out. There was no attempt to march on Quimper. Many of the chouans dispersed to their homes, while the more determined continued in their separate bands. That from Baud marched some distance along the high road to Quimperlé before taking to the countryside to skirt the town and make its way to Pont-Scorff, north of Lorient, before turning inland towards its home territory. There the men returned to chouannerie, their own form of resistance against the republicans, and took no further part in the story of the expedition.[78]

As Puisaye remarked more was always expected from the diversion led by Tinténiac, not just because of the quality of the men he had with him, but also his own courage and proven personal loyalty to Puisaye and the counter-revolutionary cause in general. As has been described, according to Rohu, he was in position west of Plaudren, on the night of 13 to 14 July, on schedule for the plan and apparently waiting to rendezvous with some of Jean Jan's group, should they appear. However, in the early hours of 16 July, when Hervilly was leading the attack on the front of the Sainte-Barbe position, Tinténiac was leading his men towards Josselin, about 70 kilometres away, to the north-east.

The authorities in the town were first alerted that chouans dressed in red were converging on the town from at least two directions at 11:00 a.m. The assault began, two and a half hours later, when two of the gates were attacked. The chouans soon succeeded in entering the town and the

76 Puisaye, *Mémoires*, vol.VI, p.334.
77 Puisaye, *Mémoires*, vol.VI, p.340.
78 Huchet, *Quiberon*, pp.112–114.

garrison of 300–400 men, formed by about 235 soldiers of the 3e Bataillon 12e Demi-brigade and 2e Bataillon 17e Demi-brigade with local forces, had to withdraw to the shelter of the château.[79] The chouans dispersed to burn public buildings and pillage the homes of known *bleus* as without artillery they were unable to attack the château. Relieving republican columns marched from Loudéac, to the northwest, and Ploërmel, to the east and although chouans, Rohu amongst them, succeeded in halting the advance of the Ploërmel column those in the town afraid they would be trapped between the columns fled. Rohu wrote, 'While we were thus at grips with the enemy, our army having come out of Josselin in disorder, assembled pell-mell on a plain behind us ...'[80]

Tinténiac then marched his men north, through the Forêt de Lanouée to Mohon before continuing to La Trinité-Porhoët where he encountered *Général de brigade* Jean-Pierre-Clément de Champeaux with a flying column. After a combat of about two hours, the republicans were beaten and fled, however they soon rallied, while Tinténiac continued north towards the Château de Coëtlogon, arriving there on 17 July.[81]

The Lull Before the Storm

The Chevalier de Vossey, who was in Hector's regimental staff, remembered:

> 16 July 1795, the army lost its distinguished commander, the Comte d'Hervilly, mortally wounded, and all the corps that formed it were disorganised by the loss of the courageous commanders and officers who had won the confidence of their soldiers and had excited in their hearts sentiments of honour and devotion with which they themselves were imbued.[82]

As well as the physical casualties, morale collapsed in the regiments. There had been some cracks already showing before the defeat, since they had been shut up on the peninsula. Contades observed, 'The soldiers, who (I have no doubt) would have been good with rapid and brilliant success, became worse every day. It was proved to me daily, but the ill was without remedy.'[83] *Sous-lieutenant* d'Antrechaus of Hector agreed, 'Shut up in the peninsula, the soldiers whom we had recruited among the prisoners ... believed they had simply changed prisons and became disheartened.'[84] The results of 16 July, thus, were devastating and immediately effected the Second Division, as described by Joseph-Chéraude de Montbron, of Rohan's artillery detachment:

79 Le Falher, *Siège de Josselin*, p.8.

80 Jean Rohu, 'Mémoires autographes de Jean Rohu', *Revue de Bretagne et de Vendée*, Tome III (January 1858), pp.28–42, p.28.

81 Chasle de La Touche, *Relation*, p.64 states the opposing forces were similar in numbers, so at least 3,000 but Rouget de Lisle, 'Historique et Souvenirs', pp.61–62 gives the republican strength as 1,500.

82 Vossey, 'Récit Fidèle', p.8.

83 Contades, *Coblenz*, pp.168–169.

84 Antrechaus, *Relation*, p.9.

> [The First Division] remained plunged in consternation and discouragement, … The news produced the same effect on the spirit of our soldiers: as their hopes had been exalted, their despondency could not be lessened; they were beaten from this day. … I saw again my homeland as a son seeing his father again after a unjust condemnation: the resentment does not stifle at all the disposition in his heart, but at least it imposes silence on him. We had brought hope; we only found terror and desolation.[85]

The men of the Second Division began landing at Port d'Orange on 17 July, their disembarkation continued at a leisurely pace until 19 July. Sombreuil had asked that his men have two days rest after being cooped up in the ships for so long. The division is shown as having a strength of 1,131 all ranks: Béon, 18 officers and 165 other ranks; Damas, 13 and 175; Périgord, 13 and 161; Rohan, 26 and 377; and Salm, 10 and 173.[86] Neither Puisaye nor any other senior officer of his entourage came to welcome them. Tercier of Damas recalled however, 'The good Bretons greeted us with joy; they embraced us and thanked us for coming to aid their land and their religion.'[87] The units were distributed among different settlements in the south of the peninsula: Rohan at Kernavest, under the hill on which the windmills stood; Damas and Béon in and around Saint-Julien, where Sombreuil was also quartered; and Salm and Périgord around Quiberon.[88]

Several men of the Second Division met relatives and friends serving in the white cockade corps, one was Louis-Marie de La Villegourio, a cadet in Rohan:

> I went to spend the day of 20 July at the quarters of the Marine [Hector], to see my eldest brother, *lieutenant de vaisseau* and officer in this corps; he had left me at Utrecht the previous winter, named by the Comte d'Hector to make part of his regiment … I dined with him and many officers of this corps. I only returned to Rohan's quarters at seven or eight o'clock in the evening …[89]

The only military duty that the men had in their quarters was an inspection of their arms; there was no general issue of ammunition, despite Sombreuil's 'repeated requests.'[90] Cartridges were now only issued when it was absolutely necessary to do so, a result of the earlier profligacy in the distribution of arms and ammunition, as Rotalier was to explain,

---

85 Joseph de Montbron, *Récit de l'Evasion d'un Officier pris à Quiberon* (Paris: Adrien Egron, 1815), pp.5–6.

86 TNA: ADM 80/136, presumably these are the numbers on landing although the date is given as before 16 July.

87 TNA: ADM 80/136; Villeneuve-Laroche-Barnaud, *Mémoires*, vol.II, p.100), Louise-Françoise de Houssay de Bennes, *A narrative of the sufferings of Louise Françoise de Houssay, de Bennes, who served in the army as a volunteer, from 1792 to July 21, 1795, when she was made a prisoner at Quiberon* (London: Author, 1796), p.35, La Chanonie (ed.), *Tercier*, p.106 and Montbron, *Récit*, p.5.

88 Puisaye, *Mémoires*, vol.VI, p.462.

89 Louis-Marie de La Villegourio, *Cinq Lettres sur la catastrophe Quiberon* (Paris: Delaforest, 1826), p.27, his brother, Joseph-François-Toussaint-Charles, was *sous-lieutenant* in Hector.

90 Anon. (ed.), *Olivier d'Argens*, pp.435–437, Sombreuil to Warren, via Hoche, 22 July.

> … the few that remained of 400 thousand which had been landed and almost entirely distributed, either to the troops, or to the chouans, having been deposited in the fort, to be there under cover, and more to support the needs of the troops, who always assembled there for all the expeditions and enterprises.[91]

Only troops doing duty at the fort received them at this time. The field guns that had been brought back after 16 July had also remained at the fort, so that they were ready for any sortie while sparing the remaining artillery horses.[92]

Puisaye now had full control of military matters. On 17 July he issued congratulations to the regiments for their conduct the day before and distributed promises of the award of the Croix de Saint-Louis. One recipient of such a nomination was Corday, as a comrade observed, 'less, without doubt, for this action [killing a republican trooper with his bayonet] than for the exclamation which had preceded it, and which saved the life of a great many of our men.'[93] Puisaye also sought to reinforce his control with new appointments, for instance he appointed Contades *Major Général de l'Infanterie*, but he was only to take over Hervilly's role as *Maréchal des Logis*, as Sombreuil was to retain provisional command of the troops in British pay as he was 'the only colonel in the service of His Britannic Majesty.'[94] However Puisaye was planning to change Sombreuil's role as he had received a letter from Rohan Prince de Guéméné, brought by an officer of his regiment, in which the latter expressed his regret that he had not come in command of the Second Division in response to which Puisaye considered moving Sombreuil to command of the cavalry and the prince to that of the infantry.[95] Such grandiose appointments were ridiculous given the condition and situation his force was now in. One new arrival remembered:

> I was … at the headquarters, and I found at the court of M. de P[uisaye] what is found too often amongst courtiers; a great pretension, founded on little differences. Imaginary ranks were solicited there; rewards wrangled for were yet unmerited; and on the very edges of the abyss opening under our feet, ambition leapt towards fortune.[96]

A malaise descended on the troops, as Warren, certainly no enemy of Puisaye, later reported:

> I must proceed to state to you that in consequence of the attack made by our troops on the 16th … in which Comte D'Hervilly received his wound, there has been little regulation or arrangement among the troops; and I am sorry to add, it did not appear that the General-in-Chief enjoyed the confidence of the military men in the army … The exertions, however, made by the artillery and

91 TNA: PRO 30/11/225: Rotalier to Cornwallis 29 July.
92 TNA: PRO 30/11/225: Rotalier to Cornwallis 29 July.
93 Berthier de Grandry, *Récit sommaire*, p.14.
94 Puisaye, *Mémoires*, vol.VI, pp.430–431.
95 Puisaye, *Mémoires*, vol.VI, pp.438–439.
96 Montbron, *Récit*, pp.6–7.

> others in putting things in a state of defence were slack beyond measure; and, notwithstanding every exertion and assistance on our part, it was impossible to get things forward, or to have them take necessary precautions.[97]

The new arrivals were unimpressed, Sombreuil could not hide his disillusionment with what he found, a very different situation from what he had been led to expect.[98] A junior officer of Dresnay, *Sous-lieutenant* Louis-Joseph Harscouët de Saint-George, remembered:

> From the 16th to the 21st, he [Puisaye] occupied himself exclusively drafting discourses full of fine promises for us, then proclamations to the patriots. As to precautions in case of attack … none. As to general orders, assembly points identified in advance … nothing, nothing! If duty was still done in the battalions, it was by habit and as mechanically.[99]

A volunteer serving in the Damas chasseur company recalled,

> … military duty was neglected, or to put it better totally forgotten. Sombreuil's division alone maintained that warlike attitude and strict discipline by which it was so highly distinguished in Germany … The hero who commanded it had too much experience and too perfect a knowledge of his calling, to not perceive to what extent the lack of organisation in this ill-formed gathering of men, strangers to one another became harmful to the common cause …[100]

Whatever his deficiencies, Hervilly's activity and conscientious application to military duty was sorely missed.

The Royal Navy, as Warren mentioned, continued to contribute to the defence of the peninsula, in particular the armament of Fort Penthièvre. On 17 July 'an Officer and a Party of Men' were sent ashore from the *Thunderer* to transport a 24-pounder cannon and a 13-inch mortar, and bombs, from Fort Neuf to Fort Penthièvre.[101] According to Puisaye, it was considered that they were not required at the former point, 'while the English squadron remained in the roadstead;' and the sailors finished the task in two hours.[102] It is noteworthy that Puisaye, in his narrative, placed this episode at an earlier period, stating that Hervilly had declined to carry out the task, as evidence of the latter's lack of co-operation.

The emphasis on Fort Penthièvre was not without criticism, even if this may have been with the help of hindsight, Contades observing:

> The advanced work was almost complete; the fort bristled with cannons, but one only thought of this single point of defence. It taken, there was no other

97 Corbett (ed.), *Private Papers*, p.88, Warren to Spencer 22 July.
98 Contades, *Coblenz*, p.189.
99 Floquet, *Quiberon*, pp.94–95.
100 Corbehem, *Dix ans*, p.162.
101 TNA: ADM 51/1103: *Thunderer* log.
102 Puisaye, *Mémoires*, vol.VI, pp.288–289.

> expedient, not a battery in the interior of the peninsula under the protection of which one could rally. The fort was really impregnable in daytime; only at night, one would fear a surprise. The only means to protect ourselves from this danger was to establish, well in advance of the posts, good troops and continual patrols.[103]
>
> The English navy … lavished cannons of all calibre on us, judging a fortress in terms of a vessel, strong because of its ordnance, without considering that at night artillery is almost useless …[104]

The peninsula's defences, from the landward side, had been substantially increased from the previous simple palisades that had extended from Fort Penthièvre, there now was an entrenched camp which, in turn, had an incomplete advanced work armed with a cannon. Furthermore, extensive entrenchments had been established in front of Kerhostin, on the eastern shore.[105]

Additional firepower was provided by two naval guns which were now placed on the Île Téviec, off the western shore of the Falaise.[106] On the afternoon of 18 July the *Thunderer* was preparing to leave for England, so on Warren's orders had distributed provisions to other vessels, her launch to the *Leda*, a cutter each to the *Galatea* and *Pomone* 'and the Jolly Boat to General Puisaye,' in addition the *Swinger* gun-vessel took on board two of *Thunderer*'s 32-pounders with ammunition and equipment.[107] The deployment to Téviec was an attempt to replicate the cover provided by the launches and other boats carrying guns in Plouharnel Bay. On the morning of 17 July, the *Teaser* and *Borer*, which had returned from landing Jean Jan's chouans the previous evening, left Quiberon Bay with the *Swinger* and sailed to the other side of the peninsula. There in the morning of 19 July while the *Teaser* bombarded the enemy positions, the *Swinger* and *Borer* landed the cannon and 30 French Emigrant gunners, under First Lieutenant de Flavigny, to serve them. Then from 2:30 p.m. the *Teaser* and *Borer* 'began to fire on our Enemy's Camps and Entrenchments with Grape & Canister at 8 ceased firing, the Enemy retreated;' the gun-vessels anchored close to the shore before sailing for the bay at 4:00 a.m. the next morning.[108]

The garrison of the fort was still entrusted to the Régiment d'Hervilly, however, despite its losses on 16 July being less severe than the other regiments, its low morale gave rise to increased desertion. Nevertheless, this has been grossly exaggerated in some accounts, the earliest claiming that around 150 men deserted between 16 and 20 July.[109] Puisaye claimed that, on 20 July, by chance, he learnt, '… that thirty soldiers of the Régiment

103 Contades, *Coblenz*, pp.165–166.
104 Contades, *Coblenz*, p.168.
105 Rouget de L'Isle, 'Historique et Souvenirs', p.49.
106 Puisaye, *Mémoires*, vol.VI, p.456.
107 TNA: ADM 51/1103: *Thunderer* log.
108 TNA: ADM 51/4042: *Teaser* log (there are no equivalent logs for the *Swinger* or *Borer*) and Villeneuve-Laroche-Barnaud, *Mémoires*, vol.II, p.102. After 16 July Hoche had had a battery constructed to protect the right flank from the fire of gun-vessels off the west coast.
109 Anon., *Pomone*, p.35.

d'Hervilly, … had passed to Hoche's camp with arms and equipment. This news dismayed me; neither duty report, nor situation state that the Comte de Contades had received made mention of this.'[110] As to the numbers, Puisaye's recollection is supported by the regimental records that show the following desertions for the period, 16 to 20 July:

17 July	*Sergent* Nicolas Littée and four *fusiliers*
18 July	*Sergent* Antoine Mauvage and 15 *fusiliers*
19 July	*Sergent* Nicolas Le Gras and seven *fusiliers*
20 July	*Caporal* Jean-Baptiste Evrard and nine *fusiliers*

All the men were from fusilier companies, apparently numbers 7 and 8. All three *sergents* had enlisted, as *fusiliers*, on 4 July: Le Gras and Littée being promoted *sergent* on 11 July and Mauvage the following day.[111] Of the others, only seven, all *fusiliers*, had been recruited at Quiberon on 4 July, the rest having come from England; Evrard had been promoted from *fusilier* on 3 July.[112] The records of Hector and Dresnay are too vague to ascertain if any men deserted from these regiments.

It appears that this desertion, which undermined the security of the peninsula's key defensive position, was not only motivated by poor morale, as an émigré officer recounted:

> Since the 16th up to 21st, … During this interval the patriots had in the peninsula agents who with cash and assignats corrupted or completed the corruption of the soldiers of the Royal Louis, perhaps a few of those of Dresnay. On 20th a soldier of Hervilly was got for ten thousand assignats.[113]

Rather than replace the Régiment d'Hervilly, in its quarters and post, by the Second Division as Sombreuil proposed, Puisaye chose to settle for a risky compromise; the division was to send a detachment to join the guard for each tour of duty, so the dangers Sombreuil hoped to mitigate remained while his own command was weakened by these detachments.[114] Puisaye does not mention this suggestion, or indeed the compromise, but

110 Puisaye, *Mémoires*, vol.VI, p.452.

111 Only Littée and Mauvage can be identified as being from the 41e Régiment that had been the republican garrison at Fort Penthièvre. Le Gras may, of course, have been a nickname. Littée was born near Argueil in Normandy in 1767, engaged in 1784 and was *sergent major* from 1792 and Mauvage was born at Mussey-sur-Marne in Champagne in 1766, engaged in 1785 and was *sergent* from 1794 – SHD: GR 14 Yc 59: registre matricule 41e régiment d'infanterie de La Reine.

112 TNA: WO 12/11681: pay list. The *fusiliers* recruited on 4 July deserted on the following days: two on 17th, three on 18th, one on 19th and one on 20th – none of them can be identified as being from the 41e Régiment.

113 Roussel & Bergevin, *Un Survivant*, p.267 'Relation inéite du debarquement de Quiberon' archives des Affaires étrangères fonds Bourbon vol.634, ff73 – the officer appears to have been in Dresnay. Puisaye suggests that this particular report of bribery may have been speculation (Puisaye, *Mémoires*, vol.VI, pp.452–453).

114 Villeneuve-Laroche-Barnaud, *Mémoires*, vol.II, p.109 and Corbehem, *Dix ans*, pp.162–163.

states, perhaps to deflect criticism of his decision, that he had had some vessels purchased to be broken up for materials to construct barracks for the Second Division on the esplanade of Fort Penthièvre.[115] This is just one example of Puisaye portraying himself, in his memoirs, as being fully engaged and conscientious in command, making effective decisions, after Hervilly's incapacity.

The compromise was in fact quickly adopted and Ensign de Tercier served in what was probably the first detachment of Sombreuil's troops:

> On 19 July, I mounted guard at Fort Penthièvre with four hundred men drawn from different corps. I distributed my posts in the manner that I thought the most suitable for the security of the army. I ordered the greatest watchfulness and a great attention in this duty. … Throughout the night, I had patrols carried out one after the other. I kept half of my unit awake. I did not allow myself any rest, constantly having an ear open to the sounds and eyes fixed on the seashore for fear of a surprise. All was quiet, that night. After the sun rose, I was able to take a few moments sleep on the platform of a battery. … I stood down from the guard of the fort the next day, 20 July, at midday.[116]

Men from different units did duty together, so at one post a Damas corporal commanded two men of his own regiment and two from Périgord. This is mentioned in an anecdote which illustrated how the social dislocation of the revolution had also affected the royalist forces fighting against it. One of the Périgord soldiers was a volunteer, the Comte de Choiseul-Praslin, and the Damas corporal had been a *marmiton* (cook's boy) in his family's household before the revolution.[117]

An event, which on another occasion may have been seen as innocuous, indeed perhaps even sensible, also effected the morale of the royalist troops. After dinner on 19 July Puisaye and his entourage rode onto the Falaise to inspect the royalist forward positions and recce those of the republicans. A party of republican troops approached and Contades decided to take the opportunity to confer with them, something he had apparently considered doing for some time. He tied his handkerchief on his sabre tip and rode forward. As a result, he, accompanied by Marconnay, started talking with Humbert, who had a cavalry *capitaine* with him. The conversation began with Humbert asking why the émigrés had come to bring war to their homeland and he soon suggested that they should contact Tallien in person, as if some form of reconciliation could be met. He assured Contades that the officers and men left wounded on the field on 16 July had been well cared for, expressing his regret of the loss of Talhouët and the naval officers of Hector in particular. Vauban then arrived, sent by

115 Puisaye, *Mémoires*, vol.VI, pp.432–433 and 452.

116 La Chanonie (ed.), *Tercier*, pp.107–108.

117 Corbehem, *Dix ans*, pp.163–164; the noble mentioned appears to have been César-René Comte de Choiseul-Praslin (1779–1846), the third son of Renaud-César-Louis de Choiseul Duc de Praslin (1735–1791).

Puisaye to cut the meeting short.[118] Although nothing came immediately from the parley, Sombreuil when told of the conversation by Contades remarked that the republicans had changed and expressed a wish to speak to them as well.[119] As the rumours of what had been said ran through the ranks of the white cockade regiments, their loyalty was further eroded, as one officer observed, 'This conversation, false or true, spread and did an incalculable ill. From then our soldiers no longer feared only finding death in the enemy ranks'.[120]

No active military operation took place between 16 and 20 July. Puisaye's suggestion that he led a sortie into the isthmus on 18 July is not supported by any other account. He claimed this was done as a show of defiance and in case Tinténiac should appear at the rear of the Sainte-Barbe position, Puisaye having been led to believe this might happen by a message from the Conseil du Morbihan.[121]

On 18 July the latest dispatches from England arrived, announcing the reinforcements that were on their way, including that of Léon's corps, the other cadre corps were not mentioned so Puisaye was left to presume that they were still on board Strachan's squadron or, if not, in the Channel Islands.[122] In addition he was told of the dispatch of British reinforcements and his reply to Windham illustrates his hopes of what their appearance may bring, but also his frustration with the troops he had with him:

> I will not conceal that *a reinforcement of English troops, be it only of two thousand men, would produce the best result, as much among the Republicans, as among us. ... it is my duty to tell you that the intervention of your troops is necessary, This view is also political as military; and I would now prefer two thousand Englishmen, to six thousand Frenchmen.*[123]

At 5:00 a.m. on 19 July the *Thunderer* left for Portsmouth, as well as carrying the official dispatches and letters, Captain Bertie had undertaken to represent Puisaye's views to members of the Government in London. His ship anchored in Spithead in the morning of 22 July and Bertie had delivered his messages by the end of the day.[124] Preparations were being made for more ships to sail for England and on the afternoon of 20 July, Warren issued orders for the *Venus* and *Lark* to prepare to convoy the light transports home, their cargoes having been unloaded.[125]

---

118 Contades, *Coblenz*, pp.191–200; various sources provide different accounts of the meetings, occasionally with different participants.

119 Contades, *Coblenz*, pp.199–200.

120 Antrechaus, *Relation*, p.11.

121 Puisaye, *Mémoires*, vol.VI, pp.431, 435–436; further Puisaye contradicts this by stating that the parley with Humbert happened on 18 July (p.447).

122 Puisaye, *Mémoires*, vol.VI, p.440.

123 Puisaye, *Mémoires*, vol.VI, pp.440–441. Italics as original.

124 TNA: ADM 51/1103: *Thunderer* log and WO 1/390: Horse Guards to Puisaye 23 July.

125 TNA: ADM 51/1103: *Thunderer* and ADM 51/1149 *Pomone* logs; that day, 20 July, Warren informed the Admiralty that he had 'sent [the transports] back under Convoy of the Venus, Anson and Lark' (ADM 1/103).

The republicans continued to strengthen both their position and numbers.

Table 10: State showing republican troops in and around the Sainte-Barbe position, 20 July. [126]

Brigades		Men	Men
Humbert	2e Bn des tirailleurs belges	358	
	1er Bn chasseurs Nantais	310 }	918
	4e Bn de l'Orne	250	
Valletaux			2,647
Lemoine			2,220
Meunier			1,311
Romand			1,819
Drut			1,782
Evrard			1,487
Déborde (artillery)	64 artillery pieces		280
		Total	12,464

The arrival of the deserters from the royalist forces on Quiberon provided important intelligence, *Sergents* Litté and Mauvage were interviewed by Hoche and described the route they had taken from the peninsula. They had dropped from the parapet of Fort Penthièvre, scrambled down the west face of the cliff onto the shore and then evaded the attention of the patrols by walking through the sea. They recommended the route to seize the fort and offered to guide such an attack.

Another informant from the peninsula, who is given particular prominence by republican leaning commentaries, is a man known as David Goujon or simply David. Moreau de Jonnès describes him as arriving at the redoubt in which he was stationed and that he was a gunner who recognised the writer from the Siege of Toulon.[127] Rouget de L'Isle states he had a conversation with this deserter at the headquarters on 18 July in which he described himself as a sailor from Dieppe who had been captured at sea and that he had only succumbed to enlist in Hervilly after deprivations as a prisoner and after having been flogged, having tried to escape.[128] These last details may well have been added to satisfy French readers imbued in the later, Napoleonic, propaganda about prisoners in British custody and were thus repeated in later histories. However, the nearest name to that given in any of the existing records of regiments in British pay – that is all bar the Loyal Emigrants – is a *fusilier* who deserted from Hervilly named Jean-Philippe David. However he deserted on 19 July, so could not have spoken to Rouget de L'Isle the day before. This is identification is supported by the fact that when the three deserters were subsequently rewarded by the National Convention for their services, Litté and Mauvage were made infantry *capitaines* whereas 'Jean-

126 Robert, *Éxpedition*, p.55, citing Etat des troupes campée devant Quiberon 2 thermidor in the Archives de Guerre, gives the strength as 12,284; the numbers of troops are reproduced by Bittard des Portes, *Les émigrés à la cocarde noire*, p.527.

127 Moreau de Jonnès, *Aventure de Guerres*, p.216.

128 Rouget de L'Isle, 'Historique et Souvenirs', pp.68–70.

Philippe David' was appointed a *sous-lieutenant* of cavalry.[129] Thus it is very unlikely he was ever either a sailor or gunner. Whatever the truth of his origins, David brought the most up-to-date information of the situation and attitude of the men of his regiment.

The tide of events had turned against the émigré incursion and as Hoche planned the seizure of the Quiberon peninsula, and thus to inflict a severe blow to the royalist cause in Brittany, even the weather came to his aid.

129 *Gazette Nationale ou Le Moniteur Universel*, 15 Thermidor an III (2 August 1795), reporting the 8 Thermidor an III session of the National Convention in which Tallien's recommendation of these appointments was ratified.

8

Defeat

Fort Penthièvre Attacked

Monday 20 July began with light, variable, winds but as the afternoon drew on a north-westerly became the prevailing wind and the clouds in the darkening the sky heralded a stormy night of gales and rain. An émigré officer later wrote:

> To comprehend fully what is about to be said on the events ... it will be necessary to have an idea of the ground. At the bottom of the Isthmus, or of the steep shore which connects the peninsula with the main land, is situated Fort Penthievre constructed on the rocks at the left bank. An intrenchment occupied the whole of the defile or narrow pass; and this intrenchment was covered by an advanced work not yet finished, insomuch that the fort commanded the whole. On the right side of the peninsula, where it widens, was a battery, which commanded the entire scope of the low marshes on that side.[1]

In some of the accounts the entrenched camp is also called the lower fort, Fort Penthièvre itself being called the upper fort. The incomplete outwork, in the form of a redan, was closed at its eastern side from 'the low marshes' by a dry-stone wall, which was to have been seven feet high, along the high-water line. In addition, the battery on this same side was tiered, the lower platform at the front being armed with two guns.

The commander of Fort Penthièvre was the engineer Captain Antoine de Folmont and the guard was provided by detachments from Rohan and Périgord and Captain Pierre de Boucheron de Russey's company (4th) of the Emigrant Artillery. They were joined, at 9:00 p.m., by four companies of the first battalion of the Régiment d'Hervilly, commanded by *Capitaine* Edme-Charles-François Marquis de Grave, former *colonel* of the Chasseurs de la Guyenne, so there were 300 to 400 men present.[2] The entrenched camp

1 *Saunders's News-Letter*, 15 August 1795, 'extract of a Letter from an Officer of the Emigrants who was on the spot.'

2 Anon., *De l'expédition*, p.40; Villeneuve-Laroche-Barnaud, *Mémoires*, vol.II, p.115; and Contades, *Coblenz*, p.200.

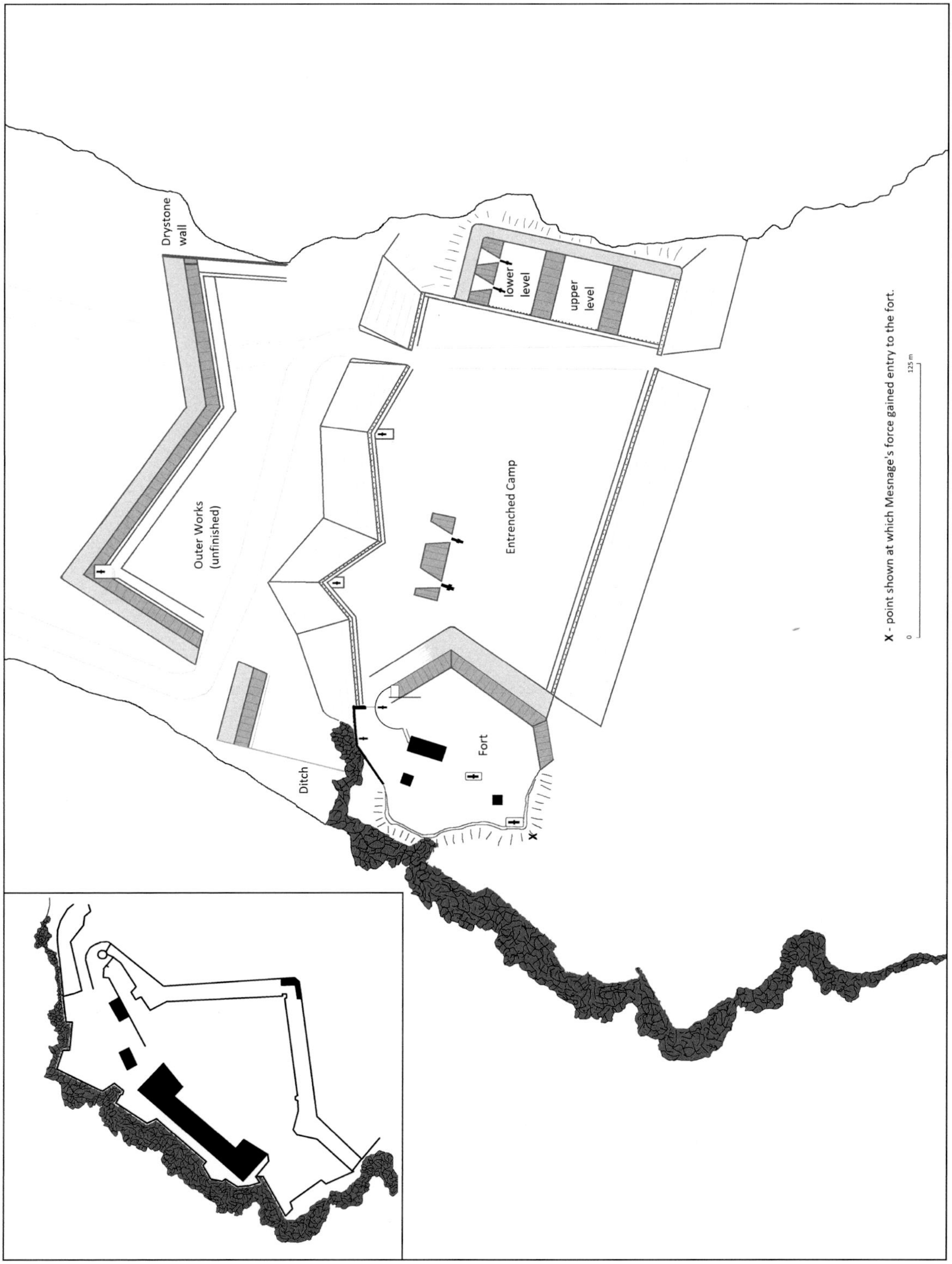

Fort Penthièvre on 21 July 1795 (from a plan in BL: Add MS 37875) and today, inset.

and advanced work were defended by the Loyal Emigrants, with additional gunners, and 600 chouans who were also to provide the advanced patrols. A vedette of the Warren Hussars was posted in advance of these defences. One Hervilly company, commanded by *Lieutenant* Louis-Castor-Henri de Chambon Comte d'Arbouville, the fifth company of the second battalion, was posted immediately in front of the fort, while the rest of the battalion was quartered at Kerhostin, as the nearest support for the defences.[3] The Second Division remained quartered at the southern end of the peninsula with many of the chouans' families and Breton refugees between them and the fort.

A 'statement of the Forces on Quiberon' gives the following numbers, of officers and men, who were present: Hector – 546, Dresnay – 404, Hervilly – 1,600, Loyal Emigrant – 284, Artillery – 566 and the Second Division – 1,174. In addition, there were 5,365 'peasants, including women, children and men ... of whom one-half may have been capable of carrying arms' giving at most about 7,255 potential combatants.[4] Puisaye estimated that there were 5,000–6,000 refugee Bretons as well as about 1,500 chouans under their appointed commanders, including Vauban and Lévis.[5]

Hoche dictated his plan at Vannes, preparing it with care, clearly assigning specific roles for his subordinate commanders; a marked contrast to Puisaye and Hervilly a few days before. The attack was originally scheduled for 19 July, to make the most of the low tide, which exposed the flanks of the royalist defences on the Falaise, being at a propitious time of night:

> The peninsula of Quiberon will be attacked today 1er Thermidor [19 July] at eleven o'clock in the evening.
>
> Général Humbert at the head of five hundred élite men of his vanguard, and led by a guide who I will send to him, will proceed towards the village of Kerostin [*sic*], going along the foreshore exposed by the low tide, leaving Fort Penthièvre [*sic*] to the right, and the fleet to the left. He will march in two files with the least noise and the least interval possible. Having arrived near the village, he will turn right sharply, and will make his troops run up to the fort which he will seize on getting through the palisade; he will slaughter everyone in the fort, less the fusiliers who come over to join his troops, the officers, infantry sergeants and gunners will have no quarter.
>
> Général de brigade Botta will follow Humbert with the rest of the vanguard, and in the same order. He will seize the village of Kerostin; he will shoot all armed individuals who come out of the houses. The soldiers without arms who come over to join him will be welcomed; the officers and NCOs will be shot on the spot.
>
> On arriving in the peninsula, these two generals will have their units shout: *Lay down your arms! To us patriots!*

3 Le Charron, *Expédition de Quiberon*, p.24.

4 Corbett (ed.), *Private Papers*, pp.90–91. Lists printed in *The Staffordshire Advertiser*, 8 August, and *The Chester Courant*, 11 August, give the same numbers for Dresnay, Loyal Emigrants and the Second Division but 448 for Hector, 1,400 for Hervilly and 500 for the artillery as well as 3,298 'Chouans, or peasants, in array' giving a total of 7,508.

5 Puisaye, *Mémoires*, vol.VI, p.512.

Adjudant-général Menage [*sic*] will aid Général Humbert's attack, by himself attacking the enemy's main guard posts. He will overcome them, pass over their bodies, and will march straight to the fort. After having cleared the palisade, he will follow with the ditch on his left up to the crag. Citizen Menage will not have a musket fired; he will have all of the enemies he encounters run through with the bayonet. The troops who are to make this attack will be Général Valletaux's élite.

Général Valletaux will support Menage's attack with the rest of his brigade. He will deploy so as to rush at the fort, by getting as close as possible, so as to avoid its fire.

Humbert will set off by his left at midnight precisely. Menage will march on the right a quarter of an hour later. The two columns will follow the tide, even should they march a bit in the spume.

Général Lemoine will bring his brigade to the position of the advance guard; he will leave a battalion there with two pieces of 4, and march in battle line level with the tail of Général Valletaux's column which he will support.

The camp will be guarded by the two battalions of the reserve, and the 3rd of the 12e demi-brigade. Général Drut will command these troops. This same officer will give the order to the commander of the 24-pounder battery to fire red-hot shot on the vessels that try to interfere with us.

The cavalry will hold themselves in battle line behind the battalion left with the 4-pounders in the position of the advance guard.

The soldiers will be without packs, and all the officers on foot; eau-de-vie will distributed at eight o'clock in the evening.

Orders will only be given to the troops at 9 o'clock; dispositions will be made in silence; it will be forbidden to hawk, cough, or smoke.

The pioneers, loaded with sandbags filled in advance, and fascines, will march at the tail of Menage's column; they will fill ditches or hollow ways which form an undue obstacle to the march. Twenty-four of the strongest and most able will be bearers of axes and iron bars, with which they will break down the barriers.

Général Valletaux will have his column followed by a company of gunners who will be placed in the enemy batteries; which will be used by ourselves as soon as possible.

The fort in our sway, all the troops will pursue the enemy, but in an orderly manner. They will form up at Kerostin, near the mill, and march afterwards on Portivy and S. Pierre. Général Lemoine will leave two battalions at the fort, and will take position at Portivy …

Général Lemoine is instructed to give the generals their particular and relative orders. He should assemble them at the headquarters where I will be at seven o'clock in the evening.[6]

Originally scheduled for 19 July the attack was, however, postponed 24 hours. The reason for this is not specified and so it has been suggested that the night was moonlit may have been the reason.[7] However it is more likely that David, or another deserter, had brought additional intelligence which

---

6 Alexandre Rousselin (de Corbeau Saint-Albin), *Vie de Lazare Hoche* (Paris: Buisson, 1798), vol.II, pp.191–195.

7 Moreau de Jonnès, *Aventure de Guerres*, p.218.

not only resulted in the postponement but also that *Adjutant-général* Jacques Mesnage's force was assigned a more significant role.[8]

The republican soldier, Janillion, recalled the evening before the attack:

> Around ten o'clock in the evening, 2 thermidor an 3 [20 July 1795], a senior officer of the general in chief's staff, presented himself at our post, ... At this time the rain fell in torrents.
>
> After having questioned us on ... the course of our duty ... he said to us: 'Shortly you will see a flame raised from the centre of the entrenchments occupied by the bulk of the army, this will be the signal for you to advance, taking care to keep close to the sea, which will lead you to the fort. You will answer, he added, *armée catholique et royale*, when the first posts shout to you, and you will continue to advance without responding, if they fire. ...' ... The appointed signal was given a little before midnight, and we marched forward.[9]

Confident that they had the royalists' password the 3,000 republicans advanced in their allotted columns. When he reported the action to the National Convention, in suitably dramatic terms, Tallien described the difficulties the columns encountered,

> ... the troops marched at eleven o'clock in the evening ... a terrible thunderstorm then broke upon these parts, rain fell in great floods, a cold and sudden wind blew in the eyes of the soldiers, and robbed them of the ability to see their way. Wandering on this vast sea of sand without any land mark that could guide their march, our columns collide, break and mingle ... It required, to deal with [the chaos] all the activity, all the sang-froid of the general ...[10]

What happened that night, as experienced by the combatants, was inevitably confused and so the sequence of events can be compressed and muddled in their memoirs. Le Charron, with Hervilly's second battalion, was based at Kerhostin, and saw what happened on the eastern side of the isthmus and entrance to the peninsula:

> On 20 July, at the evening roll-call, the companies of the second battalion of Hervilly, being assembled in front of Kérostin [*sic*], ... M. d'Atilly ... [gave the order] for us to gather on the same ground, should the enemy come to attack Fort Penthièvre and the entrenched camp, during the night. Three gun discharges and a lantern hoisted on the pole of the white standard were the alarm signals.
>
> After the roll-call, our companies returned ... to Kérostin ... [he lay down fully dressed and fell asleep] ... On the 21st, awoken by a cannon report a bit before two o'clock, ... I opened the door, and I called the sergent-major in the road. The vigilant Kibre answered me: 'I am assembling the company.' And, in an instant, we

8 Jacques Mesnage's early career, being a *sergent* in the Gardes Françaises, matched that of Hoche during the early years of the Revolution.

9 Janillion, *Versailles et Quiberon*, pp.62–65.

10 Anon., *Rapport fait à la Convention Nationale, par Tallien, dans la séance du 9 thermidor, An 3, sur la défaite des Émigrés à Quiberon* (Besançon: Chez Métoyer, 1795), pp.4–5.

> are leading them onto the ground indicated in the previous evening. M. d'Atilly had already got there. He sent us to line a small dry-stone wall at the base of the redoubt on the right of the entrenched camp, which, at high tide, closed the gap between this redoubt and the sea. Soon getting to our post, it was still night; I tried to see the enemy, and I saw nothing, when a soldier, with better sight than me, said to me to look a little to the right, and instantly he cried: '… they are in the water up to their knees.' Then I made out a large black column, which soon stopped and recoiled, having received a volley from the Loyal Emigrant battery, the three shots of which, after having whistled over our heads, killed seventeen *blues*. This column, the left of the three that Général Hoche had had march on us, retreated, and we very distinctly heard the republicans cry: 'Treason! We have been sent to the slaughter.' Alas! But that it was the same on our left![11]

Janillion's unit, apparently part of Valletaux's élite, made its first contact with the royalists' outposts:

> Arrived at the first posts which were very close to the fort, they shouted to us *Qui vive!* [equivalent to who goes there] we replied, as we had been ordered: *armée catholique at royale*. But the royalists not recognising the response, opened fire on us. They did not know at all from which side we had come, it could only be the enemy. Immediately these posts drew back, and went into the fort shouting: *To arms!* One or two of our men opened fire, despite the contrary order that had been given to us.
>
> We arrived on the right at the foot of the fort. … Grenadier companies had been detached from the main army force which came to join us, and which, like us, waited at the foot of the fort for the signal to assault.
>
> The night was very black, and the rain fell as torrents. The sea was heavy and very agitated, the groaning of the waves was horrible. Finally the charge was sounded, the order for the assault was given, and Général Humbert commanded the vanguard. The royalists forewarned, rained the fire of their artillery on us, and when a ball by chance struck one of the stones of the rock, on which stood Fort Penthièvre, the shards that flew from it inflicted many casualties and caused us much more harm than the ball itself. From our side we barely replied to the violent fire directed against us, realising that our arms could hardly work in such heavy rain, and that our position meant the besieged were entirely sheltered from our musketry. During this interval the rest of the army took position behind us, at about a quarter of a league from the fort …
>
> Hardly had we taken some steps upwards than assailed by a lively fusillade, each, as if by common accord, went back without knowing the reason at all, but only because he realised the man next to him had gone back; we thus regained our position at the base of the rock, where we risked nothing, the cannon balls being unable to reach us, no more than the musketry.
>
> Animated by our chiefs, after a moment of the most gloomy silence … we climbed up anew. Arrived at about two-thirds of the distance from the fort, the royalists' fusillade redoubled: artillery, grape-shot rained on us, and shredded

11 Le Charron, *Expédition de Quiberon*, pp.20–22.

> us completely. Then each sought his safety in flight, and ignored the voice of his commanders. We tumbled on going back down again, and the cries that we uttered; mixed with those of our wounded, brought fear to the breast even of the army, that had been brought up towards the fort. It suffered more than us from the artillery, and this tumult and our second descent were taken by them as an enemy sortie. Nothing then could restrain it, generals, representatives, all shared in this disorder, and [it retreated] ... For us, we had remained at the foot of the fort, as vanguard, as well as the grenadier companies that had been drawn from the army for the assault. A voice made itself heard, and I think that it was that of Général Humbert, [who rallied these men] ...
>
> Cries of war were heard, we climbed up once again. I believe that the same terror that had seized our army, took possession of those charged with guarding the fort, ... for the abandonment of the ramparts and the opening of its principal entrance was not the result of storming ... I do not count meanwhile the gunners called Toulonnais, who for the most part were cut down on their pieces.
>
> Scarcely had we entered the fort as victors; we replaced the white flag, that the royalists had hoisted there, by the tricolour flag. ... It was only at daylight, that on seeing our flag waving on the ramparts, that the commanding general and the representatives learnt to their shame of our victory.[12]

Tallien did, however, go some way to admitting just how close the attack was to defeat in his speech of 27 July but ascribed a new cause for it:

> At the break of day we found ourselves in the presence of Fort Penthièvre; our centre was seen the first, and began the attack. Meanwhile, the lateral columns advanced in silence towards the points that were allotted to them; soon they were spotted by the English gun boats that ringed the shore, and in the waters in which our soldiers had to cross up to the waist. These intrepid soldiers had no other means of defence that their courage; the complete success of this affair had been confided to their bayonets, ... Blasted to the front by the batteries of the fort, on the flanks by the English gun boats and frigates, the troops were daunted for an instant and made a retrograde movement; the next instant they were rallied; but it was too late; the enterprise appeared lost, and the greater part among them sadly again took the path to their lines. Suddenly a muffled muttering was to be heard: *a column of ours got in, said the soldiers*. I raise my eyes towards the fort, and I no longer see fluttering the standard of the rebels, the tricolour flag had replaced it.[13]

The involvement of British naval vessels, of any size, is an invention. The weather had forced the gun-vessels to remain safely off shore with the squadron and there is no evidence from the ships' logs, unlike all the other occasions, that any of their boats were in action. The weather was simply too bad, as Warren wrote soon afterwards, 'the Night being remarkably dark with a hard gale of wind at NW: rendered it impossible for the Gun Vessels to work up close in shore'.[14] This was not the only falsehood, or exaggeration,

12 Janillion, *Versailles et Quiberon*, pp.65–70.
13 Anon., *Rapport*, p.5.
14 TNA: ADM 1/103: Warren to Nepean 22 July.

that Tallien was to introduce to his account and, which some, subsequently, have accepted as an accurate depiction of events.

Pacqueteau, a 20-year-old student and standard bearer in the Légion Nantaise, was so full of republican zeal in his letter to his parents describing the attack that he gave no hint that the army in which he served could take a backward step:

> We approach the fort. The enemy, warned by the imprudence of some skirmishers who had gone before us, are put on alert and almost have time to put themselves on their guard. The precipitation with which we advance does not give them the time necessary to make all their dispositions.
>
> The first sentinels are slaughtered; the outposts also. O cruel fate, they were our brothers, our family, but they are traitors; let us renounce them to their unhappy fate. The enemy's fire knocks down beside me two fourriers, detailed to guard the flag. Another discharge brings down almost all the front rank of a company which precedes me. Soon again I see fall at my side this young man, particular friend to me … More persuaded than ever that my death was certain, I still advance, resolved to at least make a trial of the strength of my arm against the enemy, before he can get me. At the same moment of this reflection, I receive a spent biscayen in the left calf, which makes me suffer some pain, but that does not make me abandon my aim. Finally, despite a murderous fire, and from which I fortunately emerge, we already arrived at Fort Penthièvre. We mount to the assault. Any who find themselves in our way is slaughtered and killed. The enemy gunners, it is necessary to say to their glory, were killed on their pieces. We are masters of the fort; and my flag succeeds the white, which had fluttered impudently for several day before us.[15]

The 'same terror' had taken 'possession' of the defenders of the fort because Mesnage's daring mission with 250 or so grenadiers had succeeded. Rather than attack the main defences, as in the original plan, he led his column along the seashore, guided by at least one of the deserters. Some émigré sources state that many of his men had put on the coats and hats of royalist troops killed on 16 July to evade or trick the defenders' advance patrols. A patrol of the Loyal Emigrants was apparently overwhelmed and all killed by means of this ruse.[16] The column reached the base of the cliff before scrambling up a steep, narrow and slippery path that led to the western side of the fort; about a dozen of Mesnage's men slipped and fell, perhaps two of them being killed.[17] The path led to a low wall, which had been left in disrepair, presumably as it faced away from the Falaise, and had thus been used by the deserters to slip away from the fort. As the grenadiers scaled the wall, defenders rushed out from where they had been sheltering from the stormy night, but were cut down on the spot. If any organised resistance was offered it was when Folmont tried to repel the invaders with the Rohan

15 G. Thomas de Closmadeuc, *Quiberon 1795 Émigrés et Chouans Commissions Militaires: Interrogatoires et Jugements* (Paris: Société d'éditions littéraires, 1899), p.55

16 For example, Le Charron, *Expédition de Quiberon*, p.23.

17 Chasle de La Touche, *Relation*, p.85, account of an officer of the Gironde.

and Périgord detachments but they were overwhelmed. Only a handful of men from these two units survived, escaping to the lower defences, which, as has been described, continued to resist. The speed of the attack, from an unexpected quarter, meant that the lantern, to signal to the fleet, was not raised and First Lieutenant Louis d'Origny d'Agny was only able to fire two of the signal guns before he was overpowered as he went to the third, nearest where the republicans had got into the fort.[18]

Despite the suggestion by some commentators that soldiers of Hervilly in the fort, apparently in conjunction with their former comrade who guided Mesnage's column, helped the republican grenadiers gain entry to the fort, it seems rather that it was once they had gained entry that some of 'the soldiers of Royal-Louis raised their muskets' butts in the air, and even tendered their hands to the patriots who began to arrive by means of the glacis of the lower fort.'[19] Some went further in assisting the republicans: 'As to the royalists, at the point where I was, that did not make the least resistance. ... The others, surprised in their guardroom, were slain as much by our soldiers as by theirs, who aided us to escalade.'[20]

The news of the capture of the upper fort, especially when its guns were turned on the other defences, drained the confidence of the remaining defenders and infected the Hervilly soldiers with a spirit of defection. The émigré officers and loyal soldiers now had to face the republicans with the knowledge that they could not rely on their erstwhile subordinates and comrades. The survivors from the fort and the other defences, sought safety. The chouans, as a fighting force, were finished; the priority for the men now was the safety of their families as they rushed to join them and seek refuge in the boats to be found at the peninsula's tiny ports.

Le Charron, the only émigré from Hervilly who was present at this stage to record his memoirs, described the situation in his regiment,

> ... our soldiers who up until then had conducted themselves well ... abandoned us. Forced by their dispersal to retreat individually [he went back with his *capitaine*] towards Port d'Orange, we saw the ground covered with muskets; the idea arose to rally the soldiers who ran from all sides, and we thus found ourselves at the head of a hundred or so men, when our sergent-major Kibre joined us with the flag of the second battalion. He had been to collect it from M. d'Atilly's quarters who was dying from a gunshot, received at the moment he had led us into the entrenched camp after the surprise of the fort.[21]

It is significant that he simply describes the regiment's soldiers scattering rather than turning on their officers as do several sources, who either were not present or are of a later date. Some describe Atilly as being killed by his own soldiers after he had led the second battalion from Kerhostin.[22] Le Charron's

---

18 TNA: PRO 30/11/225: Rotalier to Cornwallis 29 July.
19 TNA: PRO 30/11/225: Rotalier to Cornwallis 29 July.
20 Chasle de La Touche, *Relation*, p.85, account.
21 Le Charron, *Expédition de Quiberon*, pp.25–26.
22 Bittard des Portes, *Les émigrés à la cocarde noire*, p.548, but citing Le Charron as his source.

account does not support this, nor does that of Janillion, from the republican side.[23] Nevertheless some gunners who tried to reach a small battery on the shore, to continue the resistance, were prevented from entering it, at the point of the bayonet, by some Hervilly soldiers who were posted there.[24]

The sudden change in fortune meant that Hoche could soon turn to securing the peninsula.

The Peninsula is Taken

The staff at Puisaye's headquarters were first woken by the sound of the signal guns. It is hard to be exact about their individual reactions and roles as the accounts of Contades, Vauban and Puisaye seek to portray their own actions in the best light and, in doing so, contradict the others. It does seem that Contades was the first to react, he states that he was woken at about 1:30 a.m. by the sound of a cannon discharge, but was not too concerned as it was not unusual to have some alert before daybreak; it was followed by a second, but not a third. However, looking through his window he saw the fire of musketry and, as Puisaye grumbled about being woken by him, he left to ride to the fort. There he found, 'The drummers beat the general alert; I encountered a patrol of the Warren Hussars, that had passed the night on the Falaise and told me that the enemy was at the palisades. I entered into the [lower] fort, where I found the greatest confusion.'[25] Soon the troops came under fire from the upper fort: 'There was then a horrible disorder, everyone wanting to get out at the same time. I rallied the troops and put them in battle order at the foot of the glacis. … the fort was taken, but, badly fortified from the peninsula side, it could be retaken with good troops.'[26]

Puisaye portrays himself as active in the emergency, 20 minutes after Contades had left he mounted and set off towards the fort, ordering his two aides to follow. On the way he saw a gunner, one of Rotalier's men, who was grievously wounded being taken to the hospital at Saint-Pierre by two comrades:

> I was going to question his guides, when a Warren hussar, rushing out of breath, came to inform me that the fort was in the possession of the Republicans since about two o'clock; … this man could not tell me more. I turned to the Marquis de Jaille, and said to him: 'Well, if the fort is taken, we must retake it.' I ordered the hussar to go in all haste to M. de Sombreuil's quarters, and to give him the verbal order to have his division take up arms, as well as the Marine Royale [Hector] and Dudresnay, and to come to join me without losing a minute.[27]

23 The same can be said of the colourful account by Moreau de Jonnès (*Aventure de Guerres*, pp.218–222) who claimed to be part of Mesnage's column, although he may not, actually, have been a witness himself.

24 TNA: PRO 30/11/225: Rotalier to Cornwallis 29 July.

25 Contades, *Coblenz*, p.202.

26 Contades, *Coblenz*, p.203.

27 Puisaye, *Mémoires*, vol.VI, p.473.

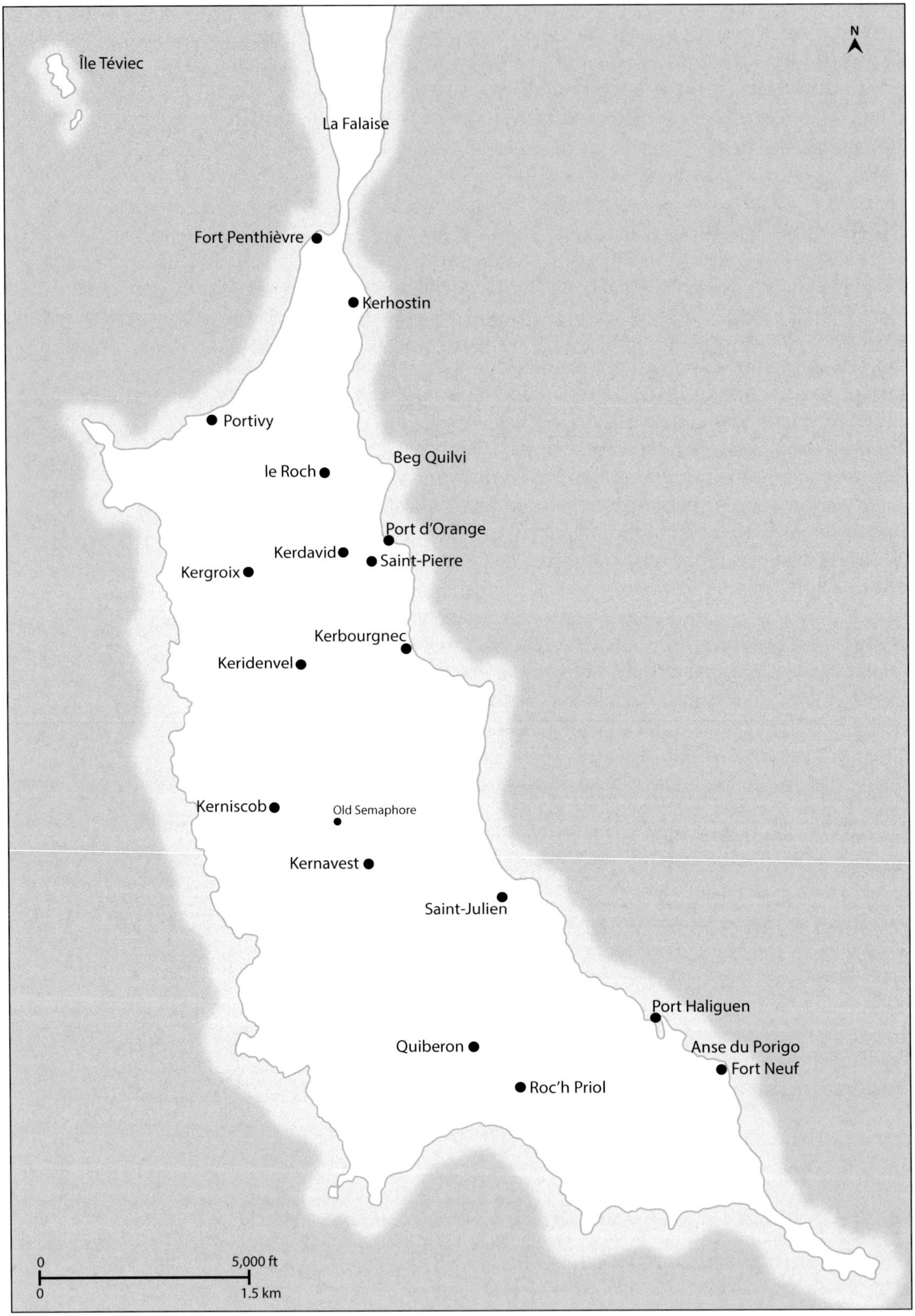

Quiberon Peninsula.

Vauban states he arrived at the fort a little after Contades, who by this time was telling the men in the other defences that they had done all they could do, and they should rally on the troops that remained in the south of the peninsula.[28]

Meanwhile many of the men of the Second Division had awoken at about 2:00 a.m. to the sound of gun fire and some at first thought it was the sound of thunder. Any doubt was dispelled by the arrival of the hussar and the call to arms was sounded. The men, who slept 'as usual, fully dressed' were ready quickly.[29] Sombreuil immediately set the units of his division in motion to march northwards under *Lieutenant-colonel* de Talleyrand-Périgord while he went to Puisaye for further orders. When they met Puisaye, in his own words, ordered Sombreuil 'to take a position at some distance, on a height where a windmill is situated.'[30] Then as the latter explained, only a day later, with unrestrained bitterness, 'M. de Puisaye, having given me the order to take a position, and to wait for him there, had the extreme prudence to very quickly take a boat, abandoning to chance the fate of the numerous victims who he sacrificed'.[31] Puisaye makes lengthy efforts, in his memoirs, to counter the accusation, however Chambray, Puisaye's relative and a loyal member of his entourage, clarifies the matter: 'I was at Fort Penthièvre at three o'clock in the morning. I saw Monsieur de Contades, who breaking through with his horse numbers of men and fugitives, confirmed to me that the fort had been taken. I returned to Monsieur de Puisaye's quarters. He had gone to board the vessel of the English admiral'.[32]

The lack of leadership and direction simply added to the confusion, particularly as the republicans had reformed for their push into the peninsula along both the west coast, initially onto Portivy, and the east, to Saint-Pierre. The portion of the Loyal Emigrants who had remained at Saint-Pierre that night was the next to approach the fort, led by Major d'Haize, who as he prepared to push on was stopped by a senior officer, apparently Vauban, who told him the fort was taken. Haize was determined to try to take it back, but he was ordered to retreat to an advantageous position. He first marched the unit to Portivy to get some cartridges from the artillery park there but none were to be found as they were stored at the fort, 'so that the least resistance by us became impossible, if it was not by the bayonet.'[33] Haize continued to retreat southwards further into the peninsula.

The scene Puisaye left behind at Saint-Pierre and Port d'Orange, in particular, was turning to chaos. Indeed, most of the wounded officers only escaped due to the dedication of their own men, soldiers, chouans or servants, who got them off in boats. Those caring for the semi-conscious Hervilly – his

28 Vauban, *Mémoires*, pp.80–81.

29 Corbehem, *Dix ans*, p165.

30 Puisaye, *Mémoires*, vol.VI, p.517.

31 Anon. (ed.), *Olivier d'Argens*, pp.435–437, Sombreuil to Hoche for Warren.

32 Archives départementales de l'Eure (ADE): I J 240: *Mémoires de Jacques de Chambray* (1812).

33 Berthier de Grandry, *Récit sommaire*, p.19, he states that it was Puisaye who had stopped Haize advancing on the fort, so adding to his suspicions of the former's treachery, but Vauban, himself describes halting Haize, Vauban, *Mémoires*, p.80.

servants, the brothers Tiéphanie, and *Sous-lieutenant* Joseph de Raymond de Nougarède, his aide-de-camp and son-in-law – took some time to get him away.[34] Engineer Lieutenant Jacques Cazotte was woken up before the break of day by a fellow officer with the news that Fort Penthièvre had been surprised, which he at first did not believe. '"Look," continues Néhou, "the fugitives; wounded go by headlong: the fire that was to be heard in the fort has ceased." Soon there could be no doubt on the event. Everyone is in a clamour, in fear around us, and cannon shots began to be directed against our village.'[35] Wetton was caught up in the confusion:

> St. Peter at half past three a.m. I was awoke by a rumour in the street of the Republicans having storm'd and taken the fort by surprise. I immediately jumped out of bed with the loss of my shirt & cap and inform'd Mr Gramair [who shared the quarter]; he in a state of insanity ran down stairs in his shirt, I never saw him afterwards.[36]

The first senior officer who appears to have taken a decisive role in trying to establish a rallying point to defend the peninsula was Rotalier. He had arrived at Kerhostin just as day was breaking where he met one of his staff who told him the fort was lost and he soon saw the troops, including a large number of casualties, retreating in some confusion. Presently, the remaining artillery horses arrived, harnessed ready to haul away the field guns that had been stored at the fort, so he sent them back to the artillery park at Portivy to bring two 4-pounders, which were kept equipped and ready for service, to le Roch (or Roc or Roc'h-en-Aud). This village, tightly clustered around a prehistoric dolmen, is on the first piece of higher ground to the south of the fort.

Rotalier was joined by his other companies, from the villages in which they had been quartered, 'Having had neither the opportunity, nor the means to employ them, they were put in line, although without arms, but to present a more imposing front to the enemy'.[37] Several Hervilly companies, led by *Major* Baron de Damas, arrived, as well as the Loyal Emigrants, without cartridges. Rotalier got them to defend Le Roch assuring them of support from his two cannon. These duly arrived and he placed them at the left, and just outside the village. He then sent his gunners away to try to embark and join the British ships, retaining only the men required to serve his two guns.

The units of the Second Division arrived at le Roch around 5:00 a.m. and they deployed in battle lines just outside the village.[38] The Régiment du Dresnay also came up and was placed on the left, covering the lane from Portivy. It was now that Sombreuil arrived at le Roch and immediately addressed his division's officers, informing them of Puisaye's departure and that as the

---

34 Curzon, *Comte d'Hervilly*, p.24; he was first taken onboard HMS *Lark* (see below) before being transferred to the *Anson*.

35 Jacques Scévole Cazotte, *Témoignage d'un royaliste* (Paris: Adrien Le Clere et cie., 1839), pp.238–239.

36 Wetton, 'Journal', p.69.

37 TNA: PRO 30/11/225: Rotalier to Cornwallis 29 July.

38 Villeneuve-Laroche-Barnaud, *Mémoires*, vol.II, p 125.

most senior officer with a British commission he was to take command of all the troops. Recognising the quality of the men he was addressing, he made no secret of their desperate situation and the briefing concluded with a unanimous shout of 'Vive le Roi! Vive la France!'[39] To secure the position's right flank Sombreuil sent the Rohan regiment to occupy Port d'Orange, and the adjacent coastal battery on Beg Quilvi. Possession of the port would mean that embarkation could still take place from there; Rohan was also charged with rallying the chouans to its defence. However, the regiment's tasks were impossible as the battery was found to be without defences and its one or two guns were without ammunition or equipment to serve them.[40] Furthermore,

> … the armed chouans who were in the cantonments neighbouring the fort, arrived in crowds and in the most deplorable state; they were all heads of families, aged for the most part, and to whom muskets had been given when their children had passed into Morbihan, under the orders of général de Tinteniac [*sic*] … Terror had turned their heads; few, on arriving with us, had kept their arms; they fled without knowing where. It was in vain that we sought to rally them; they considered themselves lost and only thought of finding as soon as possible a place to embark. In vain would we keep them, they defied our threats and would have preferred to perish at our hands, to the horror of falling into those of the enemy, who they told us, advanced rapidly.[41]

Meanwhile, through fine rain, republican forces were seen to advance from the fort towards le Roch, preceded by skirmishers:

> At this sight … all the [Béon and Damas] volunteers were ordered to quickly get into skirmishing order. This order was executed instantly. … despite our numerical weakness and the multitude of our enemies, we succeeded, by our valour and well-aimed fire, to make their skirmishers fall back onto the main body.[42]

Unidentified troops were also seen moving around Portivy towards the artillery park, to the west of le Roch. It was not known who they were so the Dresnay contingent was sent with orders to cover the park, if they were enemies, or to reinforce them if they proved to be friends. Finding that they were part of a republican column, most of the Dresnay soldiers promptly raised the butts of their muskets in the air, as a sign they would not fight, and deserted to the republicans. The few loyal soldiers amongst them could do nothing but hastily retreat to le Roch, unhindered by their former comrades and the republicans. This republican column advancing along the west coast threatened to turn Sombreuil's position and cut the line of his

39 Villeneuve-Laroche-Barnaud, *Mémoires*, vol.II, p 127.

40 Louis-Marie de La Villegourio, *Ma Sortie de Quiberon* (Saint-Brieuc: Prud'homme, 1815), p.12 describes finding a 24-pound cannon in a poor state 'without a carriage, and without ammunition, nor objects needed for its service.' Montbron states he was in a battery with two guns but no powder, Montbron, *Récit*, p.9.

41 La Villegourio, *Ma Sortie*, p.13.

42 Corbehem, *Dix ans*, p 170.

retreat south along the peninsula. At the same time Sombreuil received the report from Rohan's commander, *Major* Toussaint Léonard de La Villéon, that Port d'Orange could not be defended so he gave the order to retreat. The shortage of infantry ammunition was critical. The Béon and Damas chasseurs had almost expended the few cartridges they had had, while the Périgord Regiment, which only had six cartridges per man, was ordered by their commander to share them with the Salm soldiers who had none.[43] The men slowly retreated to a position on the heights above Kerniscob, marked by two windmills and a semaphore station.[44]

The situation on the east coast was chaotic with so many people trying to find any means to escape to the British ships offshore. The chasse marées had left Port d'Orange with the wounded and then anyone who could find a space. Men, women and children, fleeing in front of the advancing republicans sought any means to get away; most could not swim. Wetton got to the beach about 5:00 a.m.:

> We were disappointed there. All the boats had left that part. I very fortunately saw three Chassmarees about a mile lower down the peninsular. A party of Republicans were then marching out of the fort.
>
> By the time we got to the place they were all full. I therefore took off my hat and coat and swam to a boat astern of them; cut her adrift and row'd her ashore. Before I had got everything in, I perceiv'd some Republicans running down towards us. I therefore pull'd away, with the loss of my hat and coat ...[45]

The Duc de Lévis, who had been wounded on 16 July, had been brought down to Port d'Orange with difficulty by two chouans, but,

> The last embarkations had just left; many overloaded boats had sunk, and already the sea had thrown these bodies up: a dismayed multitude covered the jetty. A single English rowing boat was within hailing distance; but it maintained a distance, for fear of being submerged by the great number of those who would rush to it.

Reassured by those around Lévis, the boat approached and he was put onboard, along with a colour of the Régiment d'Hervilly. 'No one tried to follow me: heroic resignation so ill rewarded. We were still very near the shore when two cannon brought onto the height which dominated the port fired with grapeshot. In a few minutes the jetty was swept: all perished.'[46]

The small body of loyal soldiers with Le Charron, had sought to embark at Port d'Orange, but deciding that this was not possible, they made their way along the coast, gathering soldiers on their way, before coming to a halt at a small bay. There they formed up to await rescue by one of the launches

43 Villeneuve-Laroche-Barnaud, *Mémoires*, vol.II, p 129.
44 The semaphore stood on the site of what is now the Tour de Locmaria.
45 Wetton, 'Journal', p.69.
46 Le Normant Fils, *Le Conservateur* (Paris: Le Normant Fils, 1819), vol.IV, pp.346–347, letter of the Duc de Lévis, Paris, 6 August 1819.

from the British warships, again the danger was that the boats would be swamped by those seeking rescue. Le Charron gave orders that, if necessary, the soldiers should fire,

> … on the crowd of fugitives who broke through our ranks to throw themselves into the launches that we waited for with great impatience. We finally saw a dinghy heading towards us, taking the middle of the bay to avoid the flood of chouans, men and women, who covered the sloping and slippery banks on the right and left of our position. These unfortunate people going blindly towards that which they considered a means of safety, immediately rushed into the sea, and sixty or eighty drowned.[47]

The dinghy did not venture forward, and anyway could not take more than seven or eight men. By wading out as far as he could *Sous-lieutenant* Auguste de Tassy, one of the original Royal-Louis from Toulon, who was notably well-built, managed to place the battalion's colour, as well as that of the Loyal Emigrants which was handed to him, in the dinghy.

While the main body of the troops with Sombreuil withdrew in the centre of the peninsula, the Rohan Regiment did so along the east coast and so encountered the Régiment d'Hector making its way towards the fort. Their somewhat tardy arrival may well have been a result the losses they had suffered on 16 July, affecting their organisation and morale. They had received the same message as the other units and so the general assembly was sounded, however, as one of the regiment's officers explained, 'The drummer not being able to make himself heard, it was not easy to wake our soldiers.' He estimated that they met Rohan at 7:30 a.m.[48]

Meanwhile, Sombreuil's retreat was covered by a skirmish line formed by the volunteer chasseurs of Damas and Béon who were continually pressed by the republican column:

> We executed our retreat always in skirmishing and protecting the corps which was before us. The enemy that we had repulsed, then returned on us in still even greater number than before and with an ardour difficult to contain; they were so close to us, that arrived at the gardens of the houses which we came to occupy, and which were enclosed by small stone walls about two feet in height, I only had time to leap without thought over one of these walls, to not be taken or killed. One of my comrades who was at my side having had the misfortune to take a false step fell against the wall and was instantly massacred with bayonet thrusts.[49]

The dry-stone walls offered scanty protection from the republicans' artillery,

47 Le Charron, *Expédition de Quiberon*, p.28; there were similarities in his account to that of Lévis but Le Charron was convinced that they were two different episodes, meaning the colours of both Hervilly's battalions were saved (p.124).

48 Antrechaus, *Relation*, p.12.

49 Corbehem, *Dix ans*, p.171.

Drystone walls at Kervihan on Quiberon Peninsula. (Author's collection)

> ... these walls, which seemed to offer a form of entrenchment, soon became deadly: the stones, that the enemy's artillery tore out, fell on our soldiers, and caused them dangerous wounds; the Comte de Rouvenac, former officer of the Gardes Françaises, captain of the Béon Regiment and commanding the forward posts, was killed by one of these fragments.[50]

The walled enclosures bordering the route made the passage of the Emigrant Artillery's two guns particularly difficult. Finally, they had to be abandoned at Saint-Julien, after one of the horses in the team drawing the leading cannon had fallen and rolled on its back 'in a narrow, enclosed and winding lane'. Although surrounded by men fleeing the advancing republicans, all appeals to help to free the animal from the harness and get the guns moving fell on deaf ears.[51]

In the retreat some of the men slipped away to try to escape by sea, but as the majority arrived on the heights Sombreuil began to form a defensive line:

> His right, resting on the sea, was composed of the Rohan Regiment; the la Marine corps [Hector] formed the centre, with the debris of Damas, Béon and Loyal Emigrant; the left was entrusted to the remains of the corps of Hervilly and Dresnay; a windmill formed its extremity, and where this mill was placed,

50 Villeneuve-Laroche-Barnaud, *Mémoires*, vol.II, p.129.
51 TNA: PRO 30/11/225: Rotalier to Cornwallis 29 July.

> presented the double advantage of observing the enemy's movements with success, and of bringing our forces to the most endangered spot.[52]

Ten troopers of the Warren Hussars were deployed in front of the position as skirmishers. The heights appeared to be a strong position offering some protection for those embarking on boats on the east coast, particularly at Port Haliguen, but it was it was too far south to be used as a springboard for retaking control of the peninsula if, of course, this was now at all feasible.[53]

The attack on Fort Penthièvre had been spotted from the warships in the bay between 3:00 and 3:30 a.m.. It was at the latter time that 'a heavy fire of musquetry & some cannon' was seen from HMS *Lark* and Commander William Ogilvie went to Warren for orders. An hour later he returned with a pilot, set sail, cut the cables and got under way but, due to the adverse wind it was only at 6:30 a.m. that the Lark got close into shore off the Anse du Porigo, alongside Fort Neuf,

> within Pilot Shot of the Enemy's advancing Column my broadside then Bearing I commenced a heavy fire of Cannon & Musquetry, the French Royalists as they came on board being all employed by my orders at small arms, the Enemy keeping up a heavy fire of musquetry on us which damaged our sails, rigging & boats ...[54]

At 4:45 a.m. HMS *Robust* 'sent the launch manned & armed to the beach [as per] signal, ½ past 5 Perceived the republicans had stormed & taken the fort, sent all our Boats on shore to take the people off'.[55] At 6:00 a.m., presumably after Warren had received more information about what was happening on land, the frigates and gun-vessels in the bay weighed anchor to run closer inshore.

It seems that at this stage that the first suggestions were made that an agreement could be made to stop the fighting. Antoine de Pécholier, *aide-major* of Hervilly, apparently made the initial contact with the republicans before returning to Contades to report that the indications were positive but that the first condition was that no one embarked. Contades considered this too high a price but reluctantly agreed to go to the republicans to talk over the matter. However, when he reached Petit Rohu the republican troops tried to take him prisoner, but he escaped.[56]

In the meantime, with the republicans advancing along the west coast and outflanking his new position, Sombreuil decided to make a stand at Fort Neuf, sending Salm and Périgord in advance to occupy it before the republican columns on the flanks reached it. He apparently considered that by making a formidable front there he may be able to negotiate a capitulation which would prevent further bloodshed. Neither Contades nor Rotalier had any faith in the republicans' words, and both decided to try to reach the boats

52 La Villegourio, *Ma Sortie*, pp.15–16.
53 TNA: PRO 30/11/225: Rotalier to Cornwallis 29 July.
54 TNA: ADM 51/1167: *Lark* log.
55 TNA: ADM 51/1130: *Robust* log.
56 Contades, *Coblenz*, pp.207–208.

offshore. Although the weather had improved, the sea remained rough from the earlier storm. Rotalier's horse obediently swam out to a launch with him before returning, riderless, to the shore while Contades, whose horse was not so well behaved, was almost drowned and had to be pulled from the sea.[57]

Many of the men with Sombreuil had not seen the shore that morning and the sight was shocking,

> … we could see different tableaux, each of which would have excited compassion in the hardest heart. On the rocks weeping women were to be made out, mixing their tears with those of their children, who all were in the most deplorable state; old men trembling and seeking refuge from the victorious enemy; men almost naked and ready to throw themselves into the sea, which was horribly rough, and covered with corpses that it hurled furiously against the jagged points of the rocks. On this stormy sea long-boats were seen wandering here and there to go to bring some help to the wretches who struggled against the violence of the waves; debris of several ship's boats scattered on all sides, and to which were attached other unfortunates, who, escaped from the enemy's sword, had come, in seeking their safety, to find a death even more cruel; along the coast, packs, haversacks, weapons, and other military effects which had been abandoned, the wretches we had seen, the corpses, floated at the mercy of the sea, that seemed, with our enemies, conspirators to our ruin; finally, in the middle of the bay, a strong squadron, with a hundred transport vessels battered by the tempest, rendered this spectacle as terrible as it was imposing. A secret horror seized our souls, but it was soon replaced to the feeling of our duty.[58]

It seems that few, if any, of the chasse marées were involved in rescuing people from the shore, after leaving with the first embarkation from Port d'Orange. All witnesses describe the boats as being from the warships. One was commanded by Vossey, who had been sent with five Hector grenadiers to Vaugiraud on the *Pomone* the previous evening and been unable to return due to the storm. That morning he commanded the *Pomone*'s launch, manned by British sailors and the Hector grenadiers.[59] Cazotte may well have been rescued by Vossey's boat, he and his fellow engineer lieutenant, the Chevalier Mouton de Néhou, arrived at the bay:

> The spectacle was frightful. The crowd pressed into the water up to the waist, up to the shoulders, before the boats: as soon as the first man was taken in, those around threw themselves on him: the surge like a wave drove the boat out to sea, and the greater part of those who believed themselves to have found safety were seen to disappear. The noise of the cannon, the cries of grief of the women, of the children; the headlong rushing in all directions of men in despair, that is what we found …[60]

---

57 TNA: PRO 30/11/225: Rotalier to Cornwallis 29 July, and Contades, *Coblenz*, pp.209–213.

58 Villeneuve-Laroche-Barnaud, *Mémoires*, vol.II, pp.131–132. The rocks of the Pointe Riberen on which Fort Neuf stands are thick with rock crystal and so particularly abrasive.

59 Vossey, 'Récit Fidèle', pp.8–11.

60 Cazotte, *Témoignage*, pp.240–241.

Anse du Porigo looking towards the Pointe Riberen on which Fort Neuf stands. (Author's collection)

They were joined on the shore by their major, Antoine-Jean-Louis Du Portal. Cazotte was the only one of the three who could swim so the other two persuaded him to save himself. Taking his leave from them, he worked round to the point of the bay and then swam out towards a boat which was returning to the squadron. It changed course, picked him up and brought him to the *Pomone*.

Fort Neuf, as has been described, was a coastal battery which offered little defence on the landward side. However, the men lined the low walls; the remains of the First Division, mostly officers with some still loyal soldiers, formed the front rank with the Second Division ranged behind them. In all there were between 500 and 1,000 of them within the small fort, but this show of defiance was hollow as each man, at best, probably had only one or two cartridges left.[61] Fortunately, the naval vessels could now provide them with fire support – the *Lark* having been joined in the bay by the *Pelter* gun-vessel, while the frigates, *Pomone*, *Venus* and *Anson*, along with the gun-vessel *Teaser* were further off Fort Neuf.[62]

Ogilvie of the *Lark* noted, 'At ½ past 9 found our fire, with a little assistance from one Gun Boat which Anchored a little without us, and the Ships in the Bay whose round shot reached, had compelled the Enemy to retreat.'[63] The

61 La Villegourio, *Ma Sortie*, p.19; Corbehem, *Dix ans*, p.173 and Villeneuve-Laroche-Barnaud, *Mémoires*, vol.II, p.138.

62 TNA: ADM 1/103: Warren to Nepean 22 July.

63 TNA: ADM 51/1167: *Lark* log.

émigrés sought to aid their defence by their own efforts as well. A party of officers and volunteers from Rohan recovered one of the small cannon from Saint Julien and the *Lark* temporarily ceased fire to allow them to pass as they manhandled it into the fort. However, the effort was all in vain as the fort contained neither the expected ammunition nor artillery equipment for the field piece. The fire from the ships prevented the republicans from approaching the flanks of the fort, forcing them only to form up in battle lines at the front, at about a musket shot's distance.[64] From the *Lark*, it was seen that 'at ¾ past 9 a large Column of the Enemy advanced with two field pieces behind a hill to the left.'[65] Some pro-republican accounts, following Tallien's speech to the Convention, state that the naval fire was indiscriminate, striking royalist and republican, however those émigrés who were present either make no mention of it or deny the accusation. La Villegourio unambiguously stated, 'No, … no, the English did not fire on us …' and Berthier de Grandry called the accusation an 'odious calumny' remarking, 'If it is true that some of their shots had fallen in our ranks, it is because the republican columns were to be found extremely close to them and that, the correctness of the fire being very uncertain, on a very heavy and rough sea, it was almost impossible that several of these projectiles did not come to stray among us.'[66]

The Surrender

What exactly happened next is confused and particularly contentious but what can be said with certainty is a lot happened in a very short time. The two sides faced each other and the republican soldiers called to their opponents with such shouts as '*Surrender, brave émigrés; no harm will be done to you: we are all Frenchmen!*'[67] Some individuals paid heed,

> … their cries of peace, which they always repeated, produced a really dangerous effect on the soldiers of the First Division, who were the closest to the first outer wall. A great number among them threw their arms over the wall, crossed it and ran to the enemy who, at this first success, redoubled their shouts, to invite us to lay down our arms.[68]

Perhaps about 50 surrendered, or deserted, in this fashion and from them the republicans learnt of the defenders' lack of ammunition and weakness. Nevertheless, some émigrés considered making a desperate sortie under the cover of the ships' guns, when as one of them wrote 'we would rush into their

64 Corbehem, *Dix ans*, p.173.

65 TNA: ADM 51/1167, *Lark* log.

66 Louis-Marie de La Villegourio, *Cinq Lettres sur la catastrophe Quiberon* (Paris: Delaforest, 1826), p.46 and Berthier de Grandry, *Récit sommaire*, pp.21–22. See also, La Chanonie (ed.), *Tercier*, p.115, contradicting Tallien's speech.

67 Villeneuve-Laroche-Barnaud, *Mémoires*, vol.II, p.136. Italics as original.

68 Villeneuve-Laroche-Barnaud, *Mémoires*, vol.II, p.137.

ranks sword in hand, where at least, if victory did not second our courage, we would find a glorious death.'[69]

It was now, according to the émigrés' memoirs, that Sombreuil negotiated a capitulation with either Hoche or Humbert, or both of them together. A great deal has been written since about whether a capitulation was, or was not, ever agreed, and it still remains a contentious issue. Its importance being whether what followed was, in modern parlance, a war crime or the tragic but legitimate punishment of criminals. There are, to this day, two distinct camps of opinion, one following the royalist version and the other a republican view. There is no common ground between them. Sombreuil and Hoche each provided very different versions and their status, each unblemished heroes to their respective parties, prevents any compromise.

The royalist version is that the republican commanders agreed that the émigrés would be treated as prisoners of war, with the exception of Sombreuil himself, and that the men at Fort Neuf had an immediate opportunity to embark. The émigrés not only accepted but as will be seen, rigidly adhered to it as a matter of honour thus, the reasoning being, if there had been no capitulation why did they behave as they did. The republican version begins by denying that there ever was a capitulation and that any promises that their soldiers made during the conflict were made without authority simply to end the fighting. Historians, with this view, have argued that a capitulation is made through negotiations resulting in a written agreement, so one could not be made in such circumstances – seemingly a verbal agreement is not enough.

A more convincing argument is that an agreed capitulation, verbal or written, was never in Hoche's gift, the contemporary law excluded the possibility. The penalty for émigrés under arms who were captured was, since 1792, summary death and this would have been known to all the relevant parties. Hoche, who had narrowly escaped execution recently after attracting the ire of politicians, was hardly likely to jeopardise himself again for such a reason. Particularly given, from his perspective, the royalists' bad faith over the agreements made only a few months ago at La Jaunaye and La Mabilais. He was to flatly deny talk of any agreement, 'I was at the head of the seven hundred grenadiers, who took M. de Sombreuil and his division: no soldier shouted that the émigrés would be treated as prisoners of war; which I would have contradicted on the spot.'[70]

Sombreuil's state of mind may also have been a factor in him giving the order for the émigrés to lay down their arms. He was clearly dismayed by the situation he had found at Quiberon. Disheartened and then abandoned by his commander-in-chief it is not inconceivable that Sombreuil had simply become overwhelmed by the situation he found himself in. Undoubtedly personally courageous, he may have clutched at wishful thinking to prevent the men for whom he was now responsible being slaughtered at Fort Neuf.

---

69 La Villegourio, *Ma Sortie*, p.20.

70 Rousselin, *Lazare Hoche*, p.204. The integrity of his word is somewhat undermined by the fact that he went on, in a somewhat flamboyant fashion, to say that there was no shortage of cartridges amongst the émigrés despite all the evidence to the contrary.

Whatever the truth, the royalists and, apparently, many republicans who were present, believed a capitulation had been made when Sombreuil finally gave the order for his troops to lay down their arms and surrender. As the order was passed along Louise-Françoise-Claudine de Bennes, a woman serving in Damas as the Chevalier de Haussay, recalled, 'our major exclaimed to me, "Chevalier, throw down your musket"'.[71] Many received the command with disgust, some throwing their arms into the sea, others breaking them against the rocks.[72]

Republican soldiers immediately entered Fort Neuf and mingled with the royalists, many of whom considered they had a period of grace to embark, '... many of the soldiers raising in the air, some their hats, others their handkerchiefs, made signs to the English to come and fetch us; some who knew how to swim threw themselves into the sea to get closer to them'.[73] Two more senior officers attempted to swim out with their horses; Talleyrand-Périgord managed to gain the safety of a boat but Major de Damas and his horse, 'were engulfed in front of [Vossey's] eyes and disappeared with many other victims tossed by a frightful sea'.[74]

Several of those who clambered down to the water's edge were non-swimmers who were persuaded not to throw themselves into the sea by republican soldiers. The three brothers Villeneuve-Laroche-Barnaud, were such. The eldest, Jean-Louis-Alexis, was serving as a supernumerary *lieutenant* in Damas. François was *lieutenant* in Rohan, and Louis-Gabriel held the same rank in Périgord. They had had a reunion at Fort Neuf, Louis-Gabriel recalled that after laying down their arms, 'We went to the base of the fort, at the edge of the sea and on a rock ... the Republican grenadiers had accompanied us there. The fire of the corvette still continuing, we all made signs to it with white handkerchiefs.'[75]

It was now that Hoche demanded that the naval gunfire cease. *Sous-lieutenant* Jean-Hughes Duroy de Chaumereix, Hector, described what happened in his memoirs, published that same year, 1795: 'Some persons who spoke English went to the shore and desired the sloops [launches] not to approach, as the troops had capitulated. The Lark still continued her fire, until M. Gery [*sic*], an officer of the marine, swam to the cutter and desired the firing to cease. Faithful to the terms of the capitulation he returned among us'.[76] The *Lark* complied and the actions of Joseph-François-Anne Gesril de Papeu, *sous-lieutenant* in Hector, are frequently cited not only as being heroic but also as evidence of a capitulation. Why else would Hoche have been able to demand the fire to cease and why would Gesril de Papeu have returned if there had not been one?

---

71 Bennes, *A narrative*, p.35.

72 Corbehem, *Dix ans*, p.176 and La Chanonie (ed.), *Tercier*, pp.116–117.

73 Corbehem, *Dix ans*, p.174.

74 Vossey, 'Récit Fidèle', p.9 and Antrechaus, *Relation*, p.13.

75 Villeneuve-Laroche-Barnaud, *Mémoires*, vol.II, p.146.

76 Jean-Hughes Duroy de Chaumereix, *Narrative of M. De Chaumereix, who escaped from the Massacres of Aurai and Vannes, after the Expedition of Quiberon* (London: T. Baylis, 1795), p.8. The text was in English having clearly been translated from French so the 'sloops' in the first sentence would have been written as 'chaloupes' – which actually means launch or long-boat rather than the larger vessels indicated by sloop.

Monument on the Plage du Porigo, translated it reads, 'Here on 21 July 1795 the émigrés surrendered to Général Hoche.' (Author's collection)

This was not the only example of courage displayed on the shore that morning, some recalled the Christian resignation shown by the Bishop of Dol and his brother and vicar, the *abbé* de Hercé to their fate.[77] Others the conduct of the Marquis de Sainneville who Vossey saw in the sea, up to his waist, trying to save others. The *sous-aide-major* tried to persuade him to join him in the launch but 'Sainneville answered him with calmness and courage: "Busy yourself in taking those who run the greatest dangers; I was named governor of the peninsula, I will embark myself the last."'[78]

Unfortunately, the story of Gesril de Papeu is somewhat contradicted by Ogilvie, commanding the *Lark*, who gave a different account of why he stopped firing:

> ... at 10 the Royalists ... hung out a white Flag & waved to me which I understood meant ceasing firing, which I did & sent a boat on shore to know if they had capitulated, the boat immediately returned with a man who had been taken in close to the rocks, who informed me that Count Sombreuil had surrendered on Condition that all the troops in the British pay should be allowed to embark immediately for England.[79]

It may well have been the boat from the *Lark* that the Villeneuve-Laroche-Barnaud brothers saw:

> We then made out a long-boat under a flag of truce, which cut straight towards us; but soon, on slowing its course, it arrived at cannon range, and suddenly it went about and returned to the squadron. It is difficult to describe the sentiments that stirred in us; a half hour elapsed without us perceiving in the squadron any sign that they were coming to snatch us from a shore that was witness of our calamities.[80]

Warren, further off shore, ceased fire when he received the message from Talleyrand-Périgord: 'I only discontinued the fire from receiving a messenger from Comte Sombreuil, who commanded them (and who has been the only active man since D'Hervilly's misfortune in being wounded), that he had made terms with the enemy, and that the two regiments [Béon and Damas] were to be embarked.'[81]

Those who thought that they were to be permitted to escape were naturally bitterly disappointed that no boats appeared for them to embark although

---

77 Contades, *Coblenz*, p.273.

78 Vossey, 'Récit Fidèle', p.10.

79 TNA: ADM 51/1167: *Lark* log. If Gesril de Papeu was the man 'who had been taken in close to the rocks' that is the only mention of him.

80 Villeneuve-Laroche-Barnaud, *Mémoires*, vol.II, pp.146–147.

81 Corbett (ed.), *Private Papers*, pp.87–88, Warren to Spencer 22 July. The source of the messages is given in the 'Biographical Memoir of Rear Admiral Sir John Borlase Warren, Bart. K.B'. in *The Naval Chronicle*, vol.III, January to July 1800, p.348: 'It seemed to be the general wish that the brave Sombreuil might be saved: terms were accordingly offered, which allowed himself and his gallant followers to embark, on the fire ceasing from the frigates: for this purpose, several messengers went on board *La Pomone*, with the Officer who was second in command under Sombreuil, and at their request the firing ceased.'

it appears that some men did get away despite republican guns raking the shore with grapeshot.[82] One reason that no further British boats approached the shore could be that the royalist and republicans were clearly seen to be mixing together and so the former could be assumed to have already been taken prisoner. Certainly, the *Lark* soon left its station off the shore, weighing anchor and sailing at 10:30 a.m.[83]

Although he was rescued Chambray, writing during Napoleon's regime, was bitter about the British response:

> The English could have put 60 long-boats to sea, and they had only sent 6. …The six English long-boats were overladen with Royalists, and there were more than 800 who drowned trying to reach the boats, although there was no more room. … There I found Brisson, my friend, treasurer of our army, who had 5,000 louis in five small chests. Captain Keats, major of the English fleet, commanded this frigate. He speedily embarked in his launch, to come to collect the chests, but he did not want those who bore them. I said that he would not have them if he did not take us at the same time. He decided to do so. … Captain Keats deposited us on an English corvette, named the Lark. She was anchored near the land and laid a terrible fire on the enemy column …[84]

Despite all impressions, and Chambray's invective, many were rescued from the shore and brought out to the British fleet. However, when, on 22 July, Warren wrote of his satisfaction with the efforts of the Royal Navy officers and crews he recognised one of Chambray's criticisms, with barely concealed anger.

> I have been able to save about One thousand Troops, with all the Generals and Staff, greater part of the Corps of Artillery, and nine of the Engineers, with One thousand four hundred Chouans, and several Regimental Colours; and should have been able to have embarked a greater number if the Masters of the Transports had paid the least attention to my Signals for their Flat Boats which I repeated with Guns four times without seeing any one having arrived.[85]

The rescued were taken onboard various ships, HMS *Robust*, for instance, received 380 including 112 wounded.[86]

At Fort Neuf the republican soldiers surrounded and mixed with their disarmed opponents who were soon secured as prisoners. How they were treated varied greatly. Some, like the Villeneuve-Laroche-Barnaud brothers, were well-treated by the republicans, offered a degree of protection and even

82 Montbron, *Récit*, p.17.

83 TNA: ADM 51/1167: *Lark* log.

84 ADE: I J 240: *Mémoires de Jacques de Chambray*. By contrast Montbron was frustrated that peasants were rescued by British while he was not, despite shouting that he would give 50 louis as a reward (Montbron, *Récit*, p.17).

85 TNA: ADM 1/103: Warren to Nepean 22 July; the transports were privately owned vessels under charter to the Transport Board (Roger Knight, *Britain Against Napoleon: The Organization of Victory 1793–1815* (London: Allen Lane, 2013), pp.176–196).

86 Wetton, 'Journal', p.69 and TNA: ADM 51/1130: *Robust* log.

advised that their lives were in jeopardy. Others were stripped of their money and any belongings of value, Bennes remarking, 'The Republicans carried away everything I possessed, both goods and money.'[87] Tallien arrived and his later speech, although requiring circumspection, sheds light on the sequence of how events had unfolded:

> Two battalions remain as the guard of the fort, the rest of the army presses on into the peninsula, in the footsteps of the general and the representatives of the people. In a blink of an eye it has traversed this peninsula … The enemy flushed out everywhere, surrenders or flees in confusion. Some of them rallied on a height, and gave the appearance of resisting. A petty combat takes place between them and our skirmishers; but the sight of two columns that were going to envelop them, extinguishes this fleeting rush of courage; they flee and hasten to join their companions in shame and felony.
>
> Chased like a vile flock, they all gather on the rock, beside the sea, at the foot of the peninsula. It is this rock that comes to break their foolish pride, parricidal hopes, extravagant audacity. In vain do they seek to delay the blow that is to strike them; in vain do they send several emissaries to us to obtain some conditions.
>
> What relations could exist between us and these rebels? What was in common between us, only vengeance and death? … the English squadron, numbering 154 sail, tries in vain to impose on our troops by a terrible and unceasing fire. Shots, grape rain on our columns; but nothing can stop the republicans. Seven hundred grenadiers swoop with impetuosity on the rock, bayonet to the fore. The vanquished give cries of despair; they demand to surrender. The general sends the order to lay down their arms, and to make the English cease fire. 'Eh!' they cry, 'do you not see that they fire on us as on you?' Meanwhile the general perceives that they exploit the moment of respite that he was kind enough to give them, to make several embarkations. In an instant, two cannons are drawn to the edge of the sea, and twenty or so rounds of grape prevent the boats from returning. This moment was the fatal occasion for so many crimes and treasons to be punished … What a spectacle for France, for Europe, for the entire world, as these so proud émigrés, humbly placing their arms into the hands of our volunteers, thanking them with tears of shame and remorse … [and] following the victors in vomiting imprecations against the perfidious foreigner, whose disastrous assistance rendered them at the same time the most culpable and unhappy of men! …[88]

The prisoners, under Tallien's gaze, were quickly formed up to be marched away in batches to Fort Penthièvre, with republican soldiers on either side. When they arrived there in the early afternoon they found a large number of women, children and old men gathered, along with soldiers who had been captured in their cantonments or elsewhere in the peninsula. All the prisoners were tired and hungry, the soldiers had not eaten anything that day, but nothing was given to them to eat or drink.[89] The republican soldiers who escorted them were no better off, although some of their comrades were

87 Bennes, *A narrative*, p.35.

88 Anon., *Rapport*, pp.6–8.

89 La Chanonie (ed.), *Tercier*, p.119 and Corbehem, *Dix ans*, p.179.

already sampling from the vast amount of stores, food, drink and munitions, that had been found at the fort and Port d'Orange. Le Charron, now a prisoner, remembered, 'Reaching level with Port d'Orange that we left on the right, we saw the bleus giving themselves up to pillage there, and firing in their drunkenness musket shots at random. Balls whistled passed my ears, and without the fear they desired, I had the thought that a musket shot would deliver me from this dreadful situation.'[90]

The severely wounded, along with the women, children and old men remained on the peninsula while the émigrés and chouans were soon on the move. At about 4:00 p.m. republican officers formed the prisoners in a column and they were marched to the Sainte-Barbe camp.

90 Le Charron, *Expédition de Quiberon*, pp.34–35.

9

Retribution

Auray

From the Sainte-Barbe camp the prisoners were then marched to Auray, but beforehand, '… Général Humbert had communicated to us from the head to the tail of the column … that we could count on the respect due to prisoners, if we would give our word of honour to not try to escape enroute. Exhausted as we were, having no knowledge of the countryside, death in the soul, we promised to follow.'[1] It appears that the prisoners were formed into three columns, Sombreuil in the foremost with the senior officers and priests, and escorted by four battalions. An émigré officer recalled the march:

> While we sadly made our way towards Auray, the weather changed suddenly. A considerable rain arrived unexpectedly. We were soaked. Our escorts were themselves fatigued to such an extent, that they had difficulty to drag themselves along and follow us; the soldiers were starving and exhausted. There was no more order nor supervision, and still less when the night came. The roads were so bad that we sank knee-deep into the mud. Everything was pell-mell, soldiers and prisoners; some slipped or fell on their neighbours. It would have been very easy for us to take advantage in such favourable circumstances to escape. But all bound by the word of honour that had been asked of us, and that we gave on leaving, we would have thought ourselves dishonoured to break it …[2]

Many of the chouans, and apparently some of the soldiers, slipped away during the march but the émigrés remained, indeed there was at least one example of a man who had dropped out of the march who continued into Auray on his own in the morning.[3] Several of the republican soldiers urged the émigrés to take the opportunity to escape rather than be executed. Moreau de Jonnès, for one, regarded their refusal to do so as hubris, 'There was those who rejected the advice and the means that were offered to them

1 Le Charron, *Expédition de Quiberon*, p.37.
2 La Chanonie (ed.), *Tercier*, p.121.
3 He was identified as the Chevalier Robert de Boisfossé by Jean-Baptiste-Joseph de Jacquier de Noyelle, both Damas chasseurs, cited in La Gournerie, *Les Débris*, pp.4–5.

to escape, either through a false point of honour, or through mad hopes, or perhaps through unjust defiance of our advice.'[4] The columns arrived at Auray during the night and most of the prisoners, still without food or water, were immediately locked into the town's churches. Others were left to sleep in the streets.[5]

Hoche, in his report to the Committee for Public Safety describing the victory, is of course laudatory and neither mentions a retreat nor a capitulation:

> Yesterday, 3 thermidor, two o'clock in the morning, Fort Penthièvre [and] the entrenched camp of the Quiberon peninsula, were attacked by three thousand men from the Sainte-Barbe camp, which after an hour of combat, were seized by storm, under the fire of the English gun-boats. The attacks were led by Généraux Humbert, Valletaux, Botte (this excellent officer had his foot taken off by a biscayen) and Adjudant-général Menage [*sic*]. He, with less than three hundred men, braved the fire of the fort, that of the gun-boats, and the waves of the sea which grew and were very bad at this time, climbed the rocks of the West point, and helped the attack from the front of Général Valletaux. Soon our troops were in pursuit of the enemy, and the presence of two thousand men in the peninsula made the Régiments d'Hervilly and Hector put down their arms. Damas, Béon, Rohan, Saluce [Salm], and Périgord, forming the Comte Charles de Sombreuil's division, Loyal Emigrant, and the chouans made the appearance of wishing to defend themselves, in withdrawing from the coast by the port, where they should re-embark. The heads of the columns were directed on these rebels; and seven hundred grenadiers, holding them in check, forced them to copy their comrades, which they did, having no other hope than to throw themselves into the sea, or to be run through at the point of the bayonet.
>
> Already the embarkations had taken several chiefs onboard; twenty or so cannon shots of grape prevented them from returning; and there, on a rock, in the presence of the English squadron, that fired on us, was taken the staff, at the head of which was Sombreuil, the unit commanders, artillery and engineer officers.
>
> Our troops were on their feet since ten o'clock in the evening, through the most horrible weather: they only made a halt at this time (six o'clock in the morning). All the prisoners, of whom none were insulted, were led to the fort, and from there transferred to Auray. The chouan women and their unfortunate children were set at liberty.
>
> I still cannot rightly say what was found on Quiberon: they talk to me of seventy thousand muskets, fifteen thousand pairs of shoes, of immense stores of food, munitions, pieces of equipment and clothing.[6]

As early as 11:00 a.m. Warren 'sent an officer with a flag of truce on shore' to try to negotiate an exchange of prisoners as he held 192 republicans, but Hoche rejected this out of hand.[7] Warren's squadron then shifted further offshore,

---

4 Moreau de Jonnès, *Aventure de Guerres*, p.227.
5 Montbron, *Récit*, p.23.
6 Rousselin, *Lazare Hoche*, pp.197–199, Hoche to the Committee of Public Safety 22 July.
7 TNA: ADM 51/1149: *Pomone*, log; ADM 80/136, report and Huchet, *Quiberon*, p.150.

presumably to be safe from artillery fire from the shore. That afternoon the *Borer* and *Swinger*, off the west coast, came under fire from Fort Penthièvre while they recovered the gunners from the Île Téviec.[8] It appears that in this action at least two of the *Borer*'s crew were wounded.[9]

Meanwhile the republican troops who remained on Quiberon continued to enjoy their spoils. Moreau de Jonnès painted a loyal and homely picture,

> … in the evening, very late, … I had returned to Fort Penthièvre. It was full of troops who celebrated the victory by drinking excellent English beer and Port wine … It was with great difficulty … that I could find room at Fort Penthièvre to pass the night. The majority of the army was there in a triumphal orgy. Republican frugality had not been able to resist the temptation of an evening of feasting, and the citadel was changed into an immense hostelry where, in a hundred improvised booths, between two cannons, were cooked in all manners an innumerable quantity of Cork hams and sides of salted beef, the best from Ireland. The table-companions, ranged in a circle around a barrel of strong beer, drew from it in turns while waiting for their succulent meal, and did their best to sing, in a thousand different keys, the hymns of the Republic.[10]

Puisaye, ever optimistic, appears to have suggested that an attack with 400–500 men would succeed as 'The republican soldiers, and the most part of their officers, drunk with rum, were cast here and there, some sleeping profoundly, the others continuing to drink, and unable to make the least resistance.'[11] Nothing came of it, the royalists were in no state to do so, even though Warren reported, on 22 July, that '… all the Republicans here [are] drunk with rum' and, a week later, that 50 men had died as a result of this excess.[12]

Later that day, 21 July, at 6:00 p.m. Warren again tried to negotiate the freedom of the imprisoned émigrés, sending Captain Keats, with Lieutenant Cotton, of HMS *Pomone*, to Lemoine, who Hoche had placed in command of Quiberon. Keats was a good choice for such a mission not only was he Warren's effective second-in-command he was a fluent French speaker having lived in France for four years until 1789. Vauban explains,

> … Warren sent one of the captains of the vessels of his squadron as a bearer of a flag of truce to ask and solicit the exchange of prisoners or to offer such ransom and condition that it would please the enemy to propose; this ship's captain had orders to accept any condition that would be made. M Comte de Sombreuil and the officers of la marine [Hector] were particularly designated; he represented that

8 TNA: ADM 51/1130: *Robust* log, see also Puisaye, *Mémoires*, vol.VI, p.456.

9 There is no record of the *Borer* being in any other action. She, in company with the *Swinger*, re-joined the squadron late on 25 July and the following morning the *Venus* received two wounded men from her 'for passage to Haslar Hospital' (TNA: ADM 51/1130: *Robust* and ADM 51/1117: *Venus* logs). That Haslar was specified at this stage indicates that the wounded men were British naval personnel.

10 Moreau de Jonnès, *Aventure de Guerres*, pp.228–229.

11 Puisaye, *Mémoires*, vol.VI, pp.554–555.

12 Corbett (ed.), *Private Papers*, pp.88, 93, Warren to Spencer 22 and 29 July.

> being English officers, the laws of war should shelter them from any ill treatment; that they were only, and should be regarded as, prisoners of war …[13]

Keats also mentioned that should harm come to the émigrés that retaliations could result to prisoners held by royalists; Charette apparently holding 2,000. Keats returned at 8:00 p.m. and Warren reported that, 'The flag of truce I sent to the Republican General cannot obtain any exchange of prisoners, all of whom I fear are in prison, and exposed to insult.'[14] Contades was more explicit, 'they were very ill received, and they laughed in their faces'.[15] Lemoine mentioned Keats mission in a report to Hoche:

> My dear general, yesterday two officers from the English fleet asked to speak to me. The post as a result sent to seek me and, during this time, they had landed. I was on horseback then and as a result I took myself to the place, with Généraux Valletaux and Drut, more to make them re-embark than to hear them. Doubtless what I said to them did not satisfy them; as a result they left for their boat.
>
> Following the orders that I am going to give, I hope that these gentlemen will not place another foot on the island [*sic*] to come under a flag of truce. I send you today more prisoners that I have had gathered in the island by patrols.
>
> The war commissaries are to make an inventory of the stores. These magazines are immense and I doubt that with 4,000 vehicles all the merchandise could be transported in a month …[16]

One man who was captured by the patrols sweeping up solitary royalist soldiers was Jean-Baptiste Catoire, a soldier in Périgord, who, given his previous record, had apparently slipped away from his unit before Sombreuil's capture,

> … not having been able to embark, I took the resolution to go to some spot where I could be in safety; but unfortunately I was encountered by one of their patrols that took from me everything that I possessed, leaving me for all though a poor torn shirt that they gave me, having taken from me that which I had on my body which was new: but what made me the most displeased was to see torn up before my eyes, my extract of baptism, as well as all my Certificates that I had from all the Regiments in which I had served …[17]

Catoire managed to escape that night, as his guards enjoyed more captured liquor, and was hidden by locals for over two months.

As for the stores, Hoche saw them for himself a few days later:

---

13 Vauban, *Mémoires*, p.102, he states the mission happened on 22 July.

14 Corbett (ed.), *Private Papers*, p.90, postscript in his own hand Warren to Spencer 22 July; TNA: ADM 51/1118: *Pomone* log for the timings.

15 Contades, *Coblenz*, p.216.

16 Closmadeuc, *Quiberon 1795*, pp.61–62.

17 TNA: HO 69/31: undated memorandum. Catoire had a flexible attitude towards service, having been trained for the clergy, he had joined the Régiment Royal de Vaisseaux infanterie but deserted in 1792; in 1793 he joined Damas but deserted in 1795 during the retreat into Germany before joining Périgord.

> I can assure you, citizens, that the stores brought by the English to our shores are without price. What will impede us the most, is the lack of transport … Quiberon offers the eye the spectacle of the port of Amsterdam. It is covered with bales, barrels, cases full of arms, flour, dried vegetables, wines, strong and other liquors, sugar, coffee, saddles, bridles, and items of equipment and clothing, horse shoes, etc. It will seem surprising that an infantry battalion has seized buildings packed with rice, vegetables and sugar; this deed is meanwhile real.[18]

However, the republicans did not take everything. In Britain, over a month later, it was reported that 'The Ordnance Board have lately passed a vote of Thanks to their Store-keeper who went out with the last [Second Division] Expedition to Quiberon Bay; by whose address the gun-powder intended for the Emigrants, was prevented from falling into the hands of the Enemy.'[19] This report also shows that Wetton was not the only Briton at Saint-Pierre on 21 July.

Ironically, at noon, soon after the action had ended on 21 July, a cutter, the *Sprightly*, brought dispatches to the squadron from England.[20] They included the notice, dated 14 July, that in response to the capture of the Quiberon peninsula Graham was on his way with 3,000 British troops and that the cadre corps would also be sent. At a personal level, Warren had the satisfaction of receiving his commission as commodore and that of his protégé, Thomas Eyles, as captain of the *Pomone*.[21]

Warren had sent a brief note to Lord Bridport on 21 July informing him of the loss of Quiberon and, the following day, he wrote a more detailed letter to the Admiralty. In it he summarised the events and his actions, as well as the customary recognition of various officers' service, and he concluded:

> I intend to take possession of the Islands of Hedic [*sic*] and Houat until joined by the Army under Earl Moira, who are I am informed on their Passage, or receive orders to the contrary.
>
> I shall soon be in want of Provisions and water for the Army and Ships, I therefore request their Lordships will please to order our Victuallers with those Articles without a moments loss of time. …

Then he added an understated postscript, 'I shall be glad to receive their Lordships orders as early as possible.'[22]

The letter was entrusted to Captain Durham of HMS *Anson* which set sail at 10:00 a.m. on 23 July, with 128 republican prisoners.[23]

From 21 July there were four concurrent series of events which progressed. These were those surrounding the Armée rouge, the fate of the royalist prisoners, activities in England, and what happened to the royalists

18 Rousselin, *Lazare Hoche*, pp.199–200, Hoche to the Committee of Public Safety 24 July.
19 *The Oxford Journal*, 29 August 1795.
20 TNA: ADM 51/1149: *Pomone* log.
21 TNA: ADM 51/1118: *Pomone* log. Eyles wrote, 'Sir J. B. Warren read his Commission as Commodore, read my Commission to the Crew.'
22 TNA: ADM 1/103: Warren to Nepean 22 July.
23 TNA: ADM 51/1117: *Anson* log.

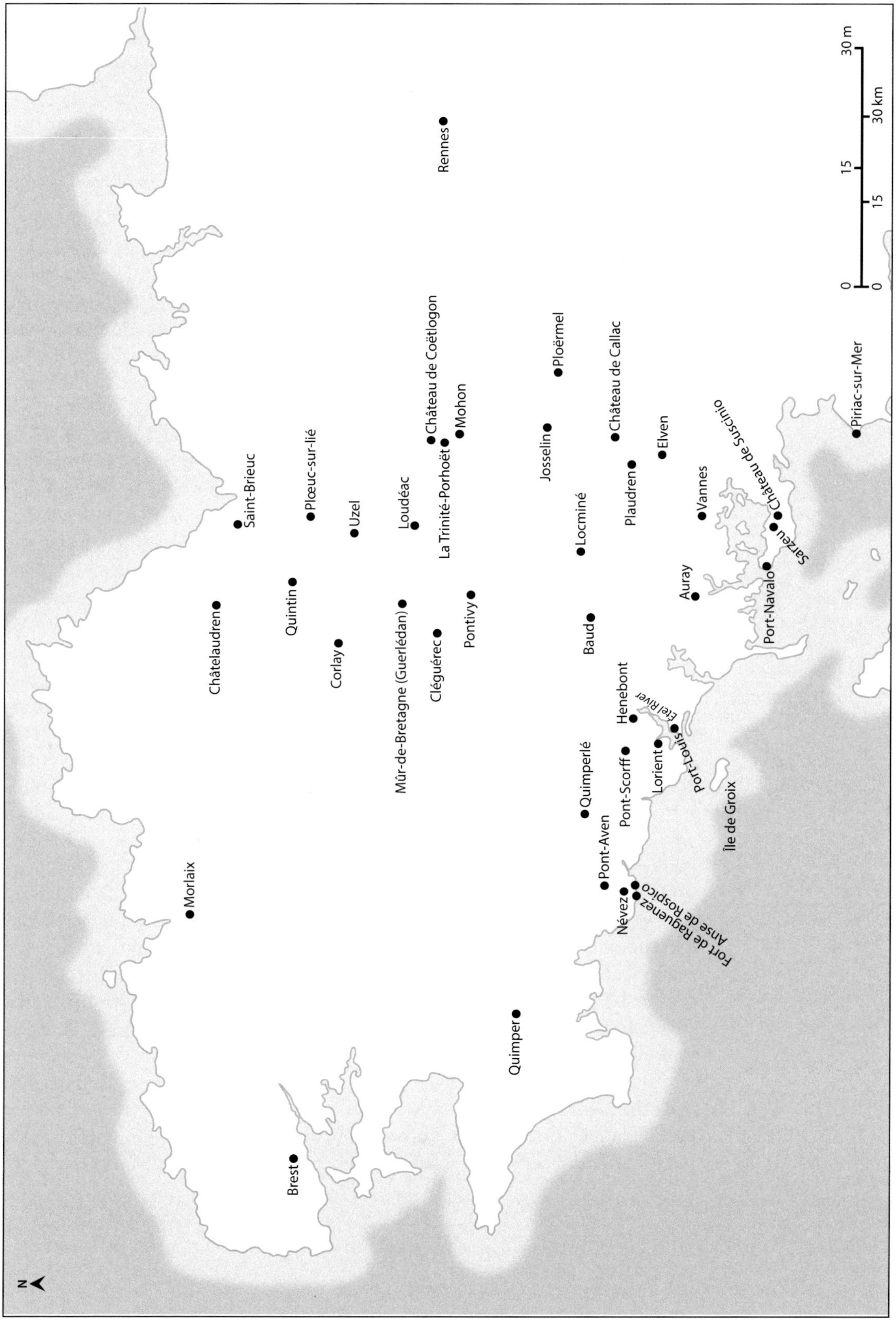

The route of the Armée rouge.

who were on the ships in Quiberon Bay. For the sake of clarity, the stories of the first two series will be concluded before those of the others are followed to the conclusion of the expedition.

The Fate of the Armée Rouge

On 17 July Tinténiac had arrived with his chouan force, of about 3,000–4,000 men, at the Château de Coëtlogon, about 70 kilometres west of Rennes, to camp in the castle's grounds. At the château were a number of Breton ladies, including Guernisac's wife and sister, and in the afternoon of 18 July Tinténiac, accompanied by all the émigrés who formed his staff, dined with them. Georges Cadoudal and the other chouan chiefs remained outside with their men. Rohu was among them, and he remembered that there was a sudden warning that 1,300 republicans were attacking.[24] After some initial confusion, Georges repelled the outnumbered republicans, who had apparently expected to surprise a much smaller force of chouans. Hearing the conflict outside, the dinner guests rushed outside swords in hand and Tinténiac, 'Forgetting the duties of a general, impetuously rushed on the blues already in full retreat.'[25] A sole republican grenadier was ducking between the trees in the avenue in an effort to get away but when Tinténiac closed on him he turned and shot him at point blank range; soon both Tinténiac and the grenadier were dead.

When it came to choosing a new leader, the chouans wanted Georges but the émigrés held sway in the council so Antoine-Henri d'Amphernet de Pontbellanger, Puisaye's trusted confidant who had been Tinténiac's second-in-command, now took over. He continued the march northwards, in two columns separated by approximately 24 hours, bypassing Loudéac to the east, and reached Plœuc-sur-Lié on 20 July, where a republican detachment was dispersed. The Armée rouge continued through the Forêt de Lorge and Pontbellanger and his staff occupied the Château de Lorge on 21 July, before appearing before the small walled town of Quintin the next day.[26] Its population had republican sympathies but the town was only defended by two National Guard companies, plus some gendarmes and volunteers. When the chouans pressed the attack, although there was a strong château, the republican troops fled the town and once secured, Pontbellanger required the town's patriots to pay, 'A contribution of a hundred thousand livres in silver, cloth and other belongings … but it was far from being discharged in total.'[27]

The chouans remained at Quintin for two days. Morale was steadily declining among them, some more joined but many left for home. Pontbellanger then led the chouans northwards again, leaving 500 to 600 at Quintin, and arrived at Châtelaudren on 23 July. It was abandoned by its

24 Rohu, *Mémoires* (January 1858), p.29.

25 Cadoudal, *Georges Cadoudal*, p.101.

26 Anon.(ed.), *Olivier d'Argens*, p.494, certificate.

27 Cadoudal, *Georges Cadoudal*, p.107.

defenders and Pontbellanger made another requisition, acquiring 50,000 livres from Quintin and Châtelaudren together.[28] However the republican forces were closing in. Champeaux was already outside Quintin, and now the news broke of the defeat at Quiberon. The Armée's leadership seems to have disintegrated, essentially falling into two camps.

Rohu, in Georges's camp, remembered, 'At the news of this catastrophe, our general, … found himself completely at a loss, and, not knowing what path to take, he had us return to Quintin, where six thousand Republicans arrived at almost the same time as us'.[29] The republicans, as the night set in, took up positions to attack in the morning. However, the chouans did not wait for them and slipped away from the town towards Corlay, southwest of Quintin, but not before Pontbellanger had distributed money amongst them. Rohu, who commanded the rear-guard, remembered that at about midnight one of his patrols reported the approach of some riders who were challenged and the reply came, 'It is me, my children, it is your general, fear nothing; the enemy makes no move. – It was in fact M. de Pontbellanger, our general who, without stopping, crossed the route behind us and disappeared with his staff, abandoning us in the presence of the enemy'.[30]

Thus Georges, and his supporters, accused Pontbellanger of having been indecisive and then fleeing with the army's funds. The latter, on the other hand, was to say that the Morbihan chiefs refused to push onto Saint-Brieuc, demanded to return home, then retreated to Quintin, seized the funds and distributed the money amongst themselves. Conduct which left him no option but to quit his command.[31] On the morning of 26 July, at Corlay, Georges announced to the chouans the disappearance of Pontbellanger and the other émigrés and he took command. The situation was critical, republican troops were close in at the rear and Hoche was approaching from the south, having left Sainte-Barbe with 12 battalions on 24 July.[32] On 27 July, Hoche was at Uzel, 20 kilometres east of Corlay, where he detached four battalions under Mesnage to intercept the chouans. After reassuring his men, Georges began the march back to the Morbihan. One of their first actions was to discard their red coats, 'which would make them too noticeable, when it was on the contrary necessary to hide their tracks'.[33] Having instructed his men to return home should they be near the route, Georges led the chouans south via Mûr-de-Bretagne (Guerlédan) and Cléguérec and so avoided the attentions of his pursuers. He finally disbanded the Armée rouge around Locminé after a march of three days.

The crucial question is why the Armée rouge marched north, rather than attack the rear of the Sainte-Barbe position on 16 July. Puisaye explains this in his memoirs by saying that Tinténiac received a number of messages, emanating from the Agence de Paris, which, as they were issued in the name

28 Hutt, *Chouannerie*, p.361.
29 Rohu, *Mémoires* (January 1858), pp.30–31.
30 Rohu, *Mémoires* (January 1858), p.31.
31 Hutt, *Chouannerie*, p.361.
32 Rousselin, *Vie de Lazare Hoche*, vol.II, p.196.
33 Cadoudal, *Georges Cadoudal*, p.109.

of Louis XVIII, persuaded him and the émigrés around him to obey them rather than Puisaye's original instructions.[34] The agency's instructions were to turn north and go to the Château de Coëtlogon where he was to receive further directions which had been entrusted to the ladies there. He places no blame on Tinténiac, a chivalric hero of the royalist cause, stating that he always considered he could return to Baud in time. According to his narrative, the agency had been able to carry out this subterfuge by, among other things, being supplied by the *abbé* Boutouillic, member of and administrator for the Morbihan Council, with information and the active participation of both Pontbellanger and La Vieuville, who had been active in trying to land arms from Jersey earlier in the summer. Conveniently, by 1807 when Puisaye wrote his memoirs, neither Pontbellanger nor La Vieuville could defend themselves as they were already dead – killed serving with chouans, respectively on 24 February and 28 March 1796. As Georges's biographer, and nephew, put it, 'For his justification before history, he has proposed an infernal intrigue, entwined by his enemies of the comité de Paris, of which the abbé Boutouillic, mesdames de Guernisac and la Vieuville, were to have been the agents. History should only be written on actual documents, and this is entirely like a novel invented for the needs of the cause.'[35]

Despite this observation, Puisaye's explanation for the chain of events has largely been accepted, indeed Maurice Hutt suggests that Rohu's account that the Armée rouge continued westward after Elven should not be relied on as by the time he wrote his memoirs Puisaye's version was so well established.[36] Subsequent writers have developed and expanded the tale.[37] For instance the identities of the ladies at the Château de Coëtlogon vary according to the source and the tenor of the narrative. Most agree that Guernisac's wife and sister were present, and others include Boishardy's widow and sister, while some state that Pontbellanger's wife – the 'terribly beautiful' Louis du Bot du Grego – was there as well. Her presence, with the added suggestion that she was Hoche's lover, allowing speculation that the republican attack on Château de Coëtlogon was no accident but a chance to assassinate Tinténiac, in the same way she later facilitated the attempted capture of Charette in January 1796.[38]

Hutt in his 1973 article conclusively argues that the plan for the Armée rouge to attack the rear of the Sainte-Barbe position on 16 July, coinciding with that from the front, was invented by Puisaye. Used in his memoirs to show he was fully in command on 16 July as well as to explain the rationale for the attack, apparently doctoring the papers he relied on to support his version.[39] Hutt's evidence principally rests on accounts written by participants at the time, and certainly before 1807, including Puisaye himself, which show

34 The main part of his account is in Puisaye, *Mémoires*, vol.VI, pp.337–429.

35 Cadoudal, *Georges Cadoudal*, p.110.

36 Maurice Hutt, 'Quiberon : l'attaque du 16 juillet 1795', *Annales historiques de la Révolution française*, No. 211 (1973), p.33, (footnote 29).

37 An example being Adolphe Lanne, *La Mystère de Quiberon 1794–1795* (Paris: Dujarrie et cie, 1904).

38 Champagnac, *Quiberon*, pp.239–240.

39 Hutt, '16 juillet 1795', p.38.

that the expeditions under Tinténiac and Jean Jan were principally to regain the initiative and to tie up republican forces by stirring the inland areas up against them. Any concerted attack on Sainte-Barbe would only occur when significant reinforcements had reached Quiberon. Puisaye's suggestion that the Agence de Paris had interfered with the plan excused Tinténiac and, more importantly, added to the evil it had done to the royalist cause and to him, its loyal agent.

If this matter is settled two questions, however, remain. Why did the Armée rouge march to the Côtes-du-Nord and specifically towards Saint-Brieuc? Why did the frontal assault of 16 July go ahead if there was to be no attack from the rear?

Tinténiac was to have encouraged the chouans inland to rise up, to harass the republicans and so pressurise Hoche's forces that restricted the royalists to Quiberon, before an attack on Sainte-Barbe was to be contemplated. Warren seems to have believed that to be the case: 'Tinteniac, one of our people, is upon the skirts of our enemies, that blockaded by land, with 8000 Chouans.'[40] Puisaye, in his construct, explained that he was, instead, marching away to the north due to the machinations of the Agence de Paris which simply wished to thwart him. However, this scenario does not explain why the Agence would want the Armée rouge to march towards the Côtes-du-Nord through what Puisaye regarded as his home territory. The network wanted Charette to be the agent of royalist victory, and not Puisaye, so why contrive that this diversion marched north, rather than east where it could aid the Vendéens? The approach of the Armée rouge towards Nantes, for instance, would have at the very least drawn forces away from the south of the Loire and may even have aided an attack on the city.

There is only one person who had the motivation and opportunity to arrange for the Armée rouge to march on Saint-Brieuc. Georges is said, by the *abbé* Guillevic, to have stated that the Armée was sent from Quiberon with orders to invigorate the chouannerie and,

> … to go quickly to the Côtes-du-Nord, to bring together and revive the scattered and almost extinguished remains of Boishardy's brave army; in Saint-Brieuc Bay to instigate and protect the landing of munitions, arms and émigrés from Jersey and Guernsey that had been promised, as soon as we present ourselves there to receive them; from there, always gathering in strength like a storm, all the armed men who would be part of it and those who had had the order to hold themselves ready for its march, this army was to turn back to the Morbihan with all the speed of lightning, the impetuosity of the thunderbolt, and to swoop down, with twenty thousand combatants, when it is agreed, on Hoche's rear who, in concert with the Quiberon army, will be crushed in his camp, or wiped out in his retreat. … [After Tinténiac's death] M. de Pontbellanger, who he had named his deputy, then takes command and makes his soldiers continue their march on Saint Brieuc …[41]

40 Corbett (ed.), *Private Papers*, p.86, Warren to Spencer 20 July.

41 Hutt, '16 juillet 1795', pp.28–29, quoting an account in notes assembled by Guillevic to refute Puisaye's version, Georges was executed in 1804.

This plan had all the hallmarks of those Puisaye had harboured for some time and advocated to the British Government, even the language used could have been copied from one of his projects. Although Hutt considers the above account may not be completely reliable, substantial corroboration is provided by, of all men, Pontbellanger. On 7 September 1795 he wrote a memorial to justify his actions:

> After the death of M. le Chr. De Tinténiac ... I had the provisional command of the troops ... The next day I marched on Lorges [*sic*] and from there on Quintin. M. le Venuer [de la Roche] and many canton chiefs of the Côtes-du-Nord had joined the army and testified the greatest desire to unite their troops to those that I had the honour to command. But [their] troops ... lacked arms, for the most part, and the munitions that remained with me were insufficient for the operations which an army that promised to grow in such a significant way would allow me to undertake. In such circumstances, I thought that it was indispensable to obtain from England great assistance in cannons, arms, munitions, clothing and particularly in generals and other officers of all arms. To achieve this, it was necessary to send a confidential officer to Jersey ... [Thus] Monsieur d'Allègre embarked ... The site of the landing [i.e. of the munitions etc.] was indicated and fixed for the period of 10 days. The interval that was to elapse enabling me to take advantage of the intelligence that I had gathered in the town of St. Brieuc, orders were given to attack this town the next day ...[42]

It should be recalled that until 21 July Puisaye thought the cadre corps were still in the Channel Islands and that their last orders were to act against the Côtes-du-Nord in co-operation with Strachan. Indeed, Puisaye may have been in contact with Bouillon, on Jersey, in relation to his plans. As, on 15 July, just as Tinténiac started his march northwards, Bouillon was pressing for an expedition to Saint-Brieuc, as he informed Windham:

> I am without loss of time going to General Gordon to confer with him upon what with our present means can best be done to effect the purpose of a useful diversion that may secure the gallant efforts, and draw the attention from our brave friends in the Morbihan; on the first view of our limited means, however, I have no expedient likely to operate that useful intention better than embarking the Comte du Tresor's Corps, and calling in the aid of that of Williamson from Guernsey, and making a show with such of the Small Armed Vessels as I can muster off some part of the Coast near St Brieux [*sic*] ...[43]

Bouillon specifically excluded any action around Saint-Malo until the whole Clos Poulet peninsula could be secured. It was the latter operation that La Vieuville consistently advocated, despite Puisaye accusing him, as part of the Agence de Paris conspiracy, of engineering the Armée rouge's march north to

42 Hutt, '16 juillet 1795', pp.44–45, from BL: Add MS 37861: ff.68–71 and TNA: HO 69/31/41.

43 TNA: FO 95/605: Bouillon to Windham 15 July (copy also in WO 1/921). Major General Andrew Gordon was appointed 'Commandant of the Forces in Jersey during the Absence of the Governor of the said Island.' (*The London Gazette*, 23 May 1795).

enhance his position. Bouillon knew Léon's corps had already embarked on 12 July but he was not to know that the orders for the other two cadre corps to embark would arrive the day after he had written his letter. Puisaye seems to have been confident of success, as he wrote a hurried note on 19 July to Bouillon, his mood somewhat jarring with that of the rest of the royalists on Quiberon by that date. After asking for news he continued, '… I am finally, my Prince, on the way to Paris; the journey will surely be long, but we will arrive'.[44]

The answer to the second question, why the frontal assault of 16 July went ahead although there was to be no attack from the rear, is closely related. Hutt writes: 'In all probability it was d'Hervilly who insisted on this lunacy: but Puisaye was supposed to be in command of operations on the peninsula and cannot, therefore, be exempted from his share of responsibility for the launching of an ill-conceived, ill-executed and therefore self-mutilating attack.'[45]

If Hervilly had indeed decided on the attack and declined to give enough time for Sombreuil's men to land when there was to be no attack from the rear, it would have been lunacy but there is no evidence that he was indeed mad. Those critical of him may point to him being conservative, perhaps even pompous, and having a propensity to lose his head under pressure, not an uncommon feature of those who are very active people in less trying circumstances. They also accuse him of being particularly protective of the regiment, and the white cockade regiments in general, that he commanded. None of these traits would cause him to hurl the troops into a 'self-mutilating attack' on the entrenched position of Sainte-Barbe on 16 July. Even if his ambition may have been challenged by the presence of Sombreuil, as some have suggested, would he really have done so in a fit of pique? And a fit that lasted through the planning stage to the moment of action? He had declined to press ahead with an attack on previous occasions but clearly, however bad his leadership in the field, he was convinced there was a sufficiently important reason to do so on 16 July.

The conviction that an attack on the rear of the position was to take place would be such a reason. There is indeed some supporting evidence that officers in the regiments expected such an action to take place. An unnamed officer, most likely from the Régiment d'Hervilly, wrote on 18 July '… In the night between the 15th and 16th instant we attacked 5000 men strong, the enemy's entrenched camp near St. Barbe … Very unfortunately it so happened, that General Vauban; who had landed near Carnac, could not come up in time to take the enemy in flank, whilst General Tintiniac [*sic*] harassed them from another side.'[46] Finally Puisaye himself says, as shown in Chapter 7, that he had convinced Hervilly that it was so and the separation of their commands meant that the subterfuge could be maintained.

44 TNA: HO 69/22: Puisaye to Bouillon 19 July.

45 Hutt, *Chouannerie*, p.307.

46 *The Kentish Gazette*, 28 July 1795, introduced as 'we present the following extract from a private letter:' the regimental identification is based on only two officers being named as wounded on 16 July, both from Hervilly.

It should be recognised that, before 16 July, Puisaye had come to have little regard for the émigré officers in the regiments, of whom he wrote,

> … if valour in war is an indispensable quality, it is the least meritorious because it is the most common … the man who only knows how to confront death, is always a bad officer, and rarely a good soldier. Gentlemen who had exercised higher command in France, and who their zeal for the King's cause had come to believe in England that they would be suitable to serve it in the subaltern rank, would show themselves less disposed to submit to privations and to endure fatigue, than eager to brave dangers. Many … came … to assail me with the same representations. They had, they said to me, only accepted employment in the corps in English pay, to make conventional war, and not to chouaner; they needed riding horses, and troop horses; they needed, in fact, everything that we lacked.[47]

If Hervilly followed form, he would not commit the regiments to an assault but simply make a show of defiance. Quiberon would, as the engineers had assured him, be secure for six weeks, by which time strong reinforcements would arrive and a full, co-ordinated, attack be made. On 16 July the main priority was the Armée rouge, it, rather than the troops in Quiberon, was delivering Puisaye's ambition for a vigorous drive northwards and then, with the support from the Channel Islands, the thrust southwards again. The republican force that had been collected at Sainte-Barbe could not be allowed to interfere with the march of the Armée rouge at this critical time and so had to be kept occupied where they were. The sortie on 16 July would do this and there could be no delay, even for the two or three days for Sombreuil's men to disembark and be ready.

It is unclear what became of the men of the Loyal Emigrant detachment, broken up to serve among the chouans. Some certainly remained in the north, Coquet staying with some chouans near Saint-Malo before returning to his regiment in January 1796. Others may have returned to Morbihan, the evidence, which is admittedly tenuous, being that on 8 September 1796 when Bouillon reported the arrival of Bois-Berthelot, now Cadoudal's aide, he added that his 'companions are of the wrecks of the gallant regiment … of Loyal Emigrants.'[48] Unfortunately, when Coquet joined the regiment he found he found that rumours among his comrades had him involved in some way with the theft of money from the funds of the Armée rouge, so he wrote, in March 1796, to the Conseil de Morbihan and Georges asking them to restore his good name.[49] If any reply was received, it did not succeed so he transferred, as ensign, to the Royal Foreigners (La Tour's) on 27 April 1796 which was serving in the West Indies. There he soon joined the 57th Foot as it was short of officers and he was promoted lieutenant in this regiment on 7 April 1797. By 1799 he had passed into half pay, in the 82nd Foot, to live in

47 Puisaye, *Mémoires*, vol.VI, pp.205–206.

48 TNA: WO 1/921: Bouillon to Dundas 8 September 1796.

49 Anon.(ed.), *Olivier d'Argens*, pp.492–495.

Grenada until 1818 after which he returned to France where he died in 1831, still in receipt of his half pay as a lieutenant in the British Army.[50]

The Republican's Triumph and their Prisoners

On the morning of 23 July Hoche presented a return of the prisoners taken at Quiberon. There were 6,262 in all, in the following categories: 'émigré officers' – 278, 'émigré soldiers' – 260, 'Toulonais [*sic*]' – 492, 'prisoners, enrolled by force in England' – 1,632 and 'chouans' – 3,600. In addition, it was reported that 150 royalists had been 'killed in action' and 100 'drowned' while it was specified that none of the prisoners were British.[51] That same day Blad ordered, in the name of the *représentants en mission*, that the Military Commission that had been decreed on 21 July would,

> pronounce on the classes of the below individuals, being:
> All the former nobles, without distinction, émigrés or non-émigrés, taken in the peninsula.
> All the former bishops, priests and monks.
> All the inhabitants of Toulon, emigrated during the recapture of this port from the English.
> All the farm workers dressed in the uniform of the chouans … [52]

The first priority for the republican authorities was to separate the different categories and house them apart. So, on the morning of 22 July the émigré officers had been led away to the former church of Saint-Esprit which had been transformed into a prison. The chasseurs of Damas and Béon, entitled to the French rank of *lieutenant*, were to be included in this category as well as volunteers in the Loyal Emigrants and Hector. Sombreuil was lodged separately at one of the town's inns, along with republican officers. On the same day, the 22nd, Sombreuil composed his letters to Hoche, one of which was to be forwarded on to Warren. In it he demanded that 'the conduct of the knavish coward', Puisaye, should be investigated, accusing him of being negligent about the defence of the peninsular and having abandoned his men and command.[53] The letter to Warren was duly sent on, undermining, as it did, a key leader of the counter revolution in Brittany.

Meanwhile, other churches, chapels and convents in Auray were pressed into service to house other categories of prisoners.[54] An immediate problem was feeding the influx of captives. This was a responsibility of the army commissaries, but there was already a shortage of food and supplying the army was a higher priority for them. The situation was alleviated for the

50 TNA: WO 25/753/151 and Army Lists.
51 Closmadeuc, *Quiberon 1795*, pp.75, 161.
52 Closmadeuc, *Quiberon 1795*, p.76.
53 Both letters are reproduced in Anon.(ed.), *Olivier d'Argens*, pp.435–438.
54 La Villegourio, *Ma Sortie*, p.25; Villeneuve-Laroche-Barnaud, *Mémoires*, vol.II, p.161; Closmadeuc, *Quiberon 1795*, pp.103, 161.

émigrés who were permitted visits from sympathetic local women, often noble ladies, some of whom had family members amongst the prisoners, as well as townsfolk. They brought in food and other comforts for the detainees as well as news and information which, for some, enabled them to escape when the opportunity came.

Those that were to be condemned and executed soon gained the status of martyrs for the royalist cause. This is particularly so in the case of the émigrés and much has been written by and about their experiences and appearances before the military commissions. Memoirs, published after the Restoration, of those who escaped dealt with these events in great detail and, in time, gave rise to some myth-making which later historians added to or disputed.[55] The fate of the other categories of prisoners, although more numerous, has attracted less coverage.

The émigrés, including about 50 priests, had taken part in an armed incursion and fell afoul of the law of 15 November 1794, the most recent of the laws against them, that decreed: 'Item IV, Section 1, Article 1 – The émigrés are banished in perpetuity from French territory, and their property is acquired by the Republic. Article 2 – Violation of their banishment will be punished by death.'[56] They were to be treated in the same manner as was decreed by the earlier law of 9 October 1791.[57] Nevertheless the commissions had to consider the cases of four other categories of prisoners:

i) Soldiers and sailors from the French forces who had deserted to join the royalists, regiments or chouans, who, if found guilty, should be shot.
ii) Chouans, either those who had voluntarily joined to fight the republicans or those who had been forced to join the royalists, of these latter some were to be punished with short terms of detention of between two to four months while others were acquitted and set free. Among them were young men who had escaped conscription and they were to be enlisted in the republican forces.
iii) Foreigners in the émigré units who were to be treated as prisoners of war and detained until the end of the war or until exchanged, unless they enrolled in the French Republic's army.
iv) The large number of French soldiers and sailors who had been captured and enlisted in the émigré units, about 3,000 or so. To be acquitted they had to persuade the commission that they had done so unwillingly to avoid ill treatment and with the aim to desert as soon as the opportunity availed itself. Such stories, particularly of ill treatment, found ready and sympathetic audiences not only in the commissions but among republicans more widely, the 500 or so Toulonnais were, however, to find their task more difficult.[58]

55 Examples of the latter being La Gournerie, *Les Débris*, and Le Garrec, *Les Vrais Martyrs de Quiberon (1795)* (Vannes: Lafolye & J. de Lamarzelle, 1935) from the royalist camp and Closmadeuc, *Quiberon 1795* from that of the republicans; a more recent example of the latter is Champagnac, *Quiberon La répression et la vengeance*.

56 Duvergier, *Collection complète des lois*, vol.VII, p.404, in Decree concerning the émigrés (pp.366–408).

57 Duvergier, *Collection complète des lois*, vol.VII, p.405, Item V Section I Articles 7 and 8.

58 Closmadeuc, *Quiberon 1795*, pp.162–163.

The military commissions consisted of five members; a president who was normally a *chef de bataillon* (by whose name the particular commission was known), four assessors or judges of varying ranks from several units, and a secretary who could be a civilian but was often a soldier, a quartermaster, or a *fourrier*. For example the first commission to sit at Auray on 27 July was presided by *Chef de bataillon* Raymond Barbaron (1er Bataillon de la Gironde) who sat with *Capitaine* Ducarpe (of the same battalion), *Lieutenant* Moisey (1er Bataillon, 8e Régiment d'infanterie), *Sergent-major* Bouvet and *Caporal* Cunit (both of the 1er Bataillon des 83 départements), and a M. Hamon was secretary.[59] The same day another sat at the manoir de Kerdavid, Puisaye's quarters while on Quiberon, presided by *Chef de bataillon* Emmanuel-Joseph Dinne, of the 2e tirailleurs.[60]

That afternoon, 27 July, the Barbaron Committee condemned 16 prisoners to death. They were Sombreuil, *Lieutenant* René-Vincent-Marie de La Landelle of Hervilly, François Petitguyot, an elderly émigré and former army officer, and 13 clergy including the Bishop of Dol, and his brother, François, his *grand vicaire*. They were sent that evening to Vannes where they were briefly held in the tower of the Porte-Prison before being taken the next day, 28 July, to the Parc de La Garenne, just outside the city's walls. At 11:30 a.m. they were shot. Why, of all the émigré officers, La Landelle was chosen to be condemned within this first group is not stated, however it is unlikely to have been chance that he was from a local family and had been born in Vannes.[61]

There had been some delay in establishing the commissions, they were not popular assignments in the republican army and different commissions changed as personnel left or arrived in the area. Indeed, very quickly it was reported that the regular units did not want to take part in either the judgements or the executions. Warren, on 11 September, reported that '… all the Line are enraged at the treatment of our prisoners after their capitulation at Quiberon, and refused to shoot them. Only one detachment of Belgians and the villains who betrayed us at Fort Penthièvre were found equal to the task.'[62] Many of the subsequent memoirs followed a similar theme but Closmadeuc, with evidence, carefully rejects the suggestion that Belgians did the work the French refused to do, nevertheless it remains a common accusation of writers with royalist sympathies to this day.[63]

The commissions appear to have been diligent about their roles, so that on 28 July the Barbaron Committee, which had begun to sit in judgement of other prisoners, asked for clarification from Blad:

> Citizen representative, almost all the émigré prisoners, who we come from interrogating, assert their faith in a capitulation; they answer that they only

59 Closmadeuc, *Quiberon 1795*, p.165.

60 Closmadeuc gives his first name as Arthur. The manoir is perhaps the oldest dwelling on Quiberon Anon., 'Manoir de Kerdavid. Plus ancienne demeure de la presqu'île de Quiberon', *Le Télégramme*, 6 April 2018.

61 Biographical details from La Gournerie, *Les Débris*, pp.149, 166–167.

62 Corbett (ed.), *Private Papers*, pp.104–105, Warren to Spencer.

63 Closmadeuc, *Quiberon 1795*, pp.193–195, see Guillot, *Révolution et Chouannerie*, p.214, for a modern example, particularly against one of the commission presidents, *Capitaine* François Bouillon, of the 2e bataillon de titraileurs belges.

> surrendered because several officers and soldiers of the army of the Republic assured them that they would have their lives spared, if they laid down their arms; that relying on this verbal promise, they had surrendered to spare the blood of both parties. They were so convinced that one of them swam to go to announce this capitulation to the corvette or frigate, the fire of which troubled our troops; that it ceased at the same moment and that this officer returned to land.
>
> We do not know if this capitulation exists; if it does, our course of action is set. We invite you as a result, to let us know the truth, and to lay out the conduct that we should take in the painful function that we pursue …[64]

In the meantime, they did not condemn any further prisoners. Indeed, when Blad denied the existence of a capitulation, the commission still hesitated so Blad dismissed it and replaced it with another. Commissions were to sit at Auray, Quiberon, Vannes, Port-Louis and Hennebont, concurrently or successively, with those at the last two locations only hearing the cases of chouans.

Hoche would not oversee the process as he had quickly left to see to the pressing need to defend the Côtes-du-Nord. Some have suggested that this was a convenient excuse to avoid being 'witness to the executions that he had too much reason to foresee'.[65] The task fell to Lemoine and Blad; Tallien having left Vannes early in the morning of 22 July accompanied by his aide, Rouget de Lisle, to personally announce the victory in the National Convention. His speech was, if there was ever any doubt, to seal the fate of the captured émigrés. It took place on an auspicious occasion, the first anniversary of Robespierre's fall, in which Tallien had had a notable role. According to Rouget de Lisle, on the way to Paris, Tallien planned to demand that the émigrés be given an amnesty and banished. However, arriving in the capital Tallien was told by Thérésa Cabarrus, now his wife, that his enemies had raised a chorus of denunciations and rumours, saying that he had betrayed the republic which, according to this story, made him change his mind.[66]

The 27 July 1795, the anniversary, was a day of ceremony and music in the National Convention and when Tallien appeared those present, aware of the news, erupted in applause. He began:

> Representatives of the people … The committee of public safety ordered us to vanquish the enemies of the republic who had dared to sully its territory. It is obeyed. The republican army vanquished that of the counter-revolution. … the vile gathering, of Pitt's stipends, these execrable authors of all the disasters and of all the heinous crimes against which France struggles for five years. … dared to set foot again on their native land … their native land devoured them. … Providence reserved for them a punishment of which the vigour and opprobrium should be proportionate to their crimes, and they did not wait long to suffer. … It

64 Closmadeuc, *Quiberon 1795*, pp.179–180, reproduces the letter in full.

65 Rouget de Lisle, 'Historique et Souvenirs', p.111, followed by Robert, *Expédition*, pp.103–104.

66 Rouget de Lisle, 'Historique et Souvenirs', pp.121–123.

> would have been to compromise the dignity of our arms not to attack the lair of these brigands … to allow them the possibility of a flight that would have saved the greater part from the national vengeance.[67]

He then described the military actions finishing with the taking of the peninsula and the surrender of the émigrés:

> Such is, Representatives, the result of this truly astonishing expedition … allegedly so formidable, and which had been spewed onto our shores, by the English government, to undertake the counter-revolution, assassinate the patriots, and ravage the property of those who had remained loyal to the cause of the republic.
>
> I hold in my hand one of the daggers with which all these chevaliers were armed, that they intended to pierce the breast of the patriots, and which they did not make use of for themselves, because they knew the poison that this weapon concealed …
>
> Such are the means employed by this atrocious government to perpetuate amongst us the horrors of the most bloody civil war.
>
> But all Pitt's Machiavellian schemes have foundered before the imperturbable courage of the defenders of the homeland.
>
> 'Representatives,' these brave men said to us, '… Laws against traitors exist, we ask that they are enforced.' We have promised them that justice will be done by the military commission: it is in fact in activity and occupies itself with the application of the law. …
>
> It is for us, dear colleagues, to profit from this victory which ought to hasten the European peace. The armed émigrés are destroyed, but their partisans still count on our divisions, they hope to see the French cut each other's throats.
>
> Let us thwart all their criminal projects by our firmness; let us fight terrorism, whatever its nature, with the same courage as our armies deploy each day to destroy their infamous cohorts.[68]

Meanwhile, when brought before the military commissions, individual émigrés conducted themselves very differently, many refused to recognise the commissions' authority and refused to sign the interrogations while others were more compliant. Some chose to tell elaborate stories to avoid condemnation at all costs while others decided that, as one of them put it, 'It is better to die than live by a lie!'[69] When it was clear any talk of a capitulation was not going to be countenanced they ceased to refer to it.[70] Some successfully described themselves as foreigners, one being Le Grand du Quellenec, *quartier-maître* of the Régiment du Dresnay, who had been born in Mexico. This same line was taken by some not on the basis of their birth but

67 Anon., *Rapport*, pp.1–4.

68 Anon., *Rapport*, pp.8–12. Berthier de Grandry, for one, was outraged by Tallien's 'monstrous villainy' in asserting all the émigrés were armed with poisoned daggers, explaining 'several among us had dirks, it was the officers, who, like all the English officers of this time, suspended this weapon on their shoulder-belt in place of their sword, when they were not on duty.' (Berthier de Grandry, *Récit sommaire*, p.22).

69 Montbron, *Récit*, p.54, quoting an old, unnamed, officer.

70 Closmadeuc, *Quiberon, 1795* p.195.

on the grounds that they were members of the Order of Malta.[71] This was not such an outlandish argument as it may first seem, as the National Assembly had passed a law on 30 July 1791, Article 4 of which stated, 'Any Frenchmen who demand or obtain admission or keep affiliation to an order of chivalry … established in a foreign land, founded on distinctions of birth, lose the quality and the rights of a French citizen'.[72] However, this legal subtlety was not accepted by the commissions.

A common line of defence was that the individual had served in some non-combatant role and thus had not carried arms against the Republic, and another was that the British had tricked or forced them to serve in France. Combinations of several of these stories were also used. A number sought reprieve on the basis that they had emigrated, along with a father or other relative, as a boy. Many of the young, or young looking, officers, cadets and volunteers chose to lie about their age and take this line. This was because Blad directed the commissions to take a lenient interpretation of the law – namely, not to condemn anyone who had emigrated before the age of 16. One explanation why he did so is that his leniency was obtained through the tearful pleading of the mother, or pretty sister, of a young prisoner, *Sous-lieutenant* Claude-Louis-Vincent de Talhouët, an officer in Dresnay and son of the *lieutenant-colonel*. This may well, however, be another apocryphal story about the 'Martyrs of Quiberon'.[73] Nevertheless, the reprieve was short, the Committee of Public Safety declined to confirm Blad's edict and on 9 August it ordered that those who had left France before they were 16 years old and had been taken with arms would be condemned.[74]

Some of the republican officers and men tried to assist émigré prisoners, either for reward or out of sympathy. *Général de brigade* Pierre-Paul Botta, brought to Auray mortally wounded, heard that a former comrade was among the émigré prisoners in the town. Before the Revolution Botta had risen through the ranks in the Régiment de Normandie to be breveted *capitaine*, the same rank as the noble Charles-Gabriel-Germain de Chenu, an NCO in the Damas chasseur company, and before his death on 28 July, Botta asked an official to do what he could for Chenu. However, despite his best efforts all the latter could do was obtain a stay of execution and Chenu, along with many others over the next weeks, was shot on the banks of the river north of the town.

Several émigrés attempted to avoid execution by pretending to be a servant, some meeting their deaths under assumed names, while more had been mixed with the French and foreign soldiers who were prisoners. Louise-Françoise-Claudine de Bennes, a chasseur in Damas, was among them describing herself as a washer woman who worked for the men, only wearing a uniform out of convenience. Conditions were basic, she recalled

71 Villeneuve-Laroche-Barnaud, *Mémoires*, vol.II, p 208.

72 Duvergier, *Collection complète des lois*, Tome III p.199, Decree relative to the suppression of the orders of chivalry.

73 Montbron, *Récit*, p.42. Uncharacteristically Closmadeuc, who made a habit of contradicting such stories with evidence, is silent on this subject.

74 Closmadeuc, *Quiberon 1795*, pp.216–218, 230–232.

that while at Auray the prisoners only received a pound of coarse bread a day and not even straw to lie on.[75]

After three weeks, the soldier prisoners were marched to Vannes where they were soon confined in an expansive walled enclosure, the grounds of a suppressed religious community, le Père-Éternel, with little or no protection from the elements. There, surrounded by men from different units any deserter or émigré, officer or soldier, lived in fear of being denounced. Gesril de Papeu suffered such a fate and was condemned on 27 August. Once it was suspected Bennes was a noble émigrée there were attempts to have her denounced. Firstly, a Damas soldier was promised to be set, 'at liberty that very day, if he would declare who I was. This honest fellow, (who by the bye was a Dutchman) replied, that he could not tell, as he himself had never enquired.'[76] Then, before a commission, three more soldiers were offered bribes to denounce her but they said, '… that they could not tell things they were ignorant of. Yet these good fellows knew everything about me. Their generosity cannot be too much admired.'[77] Informed that she was to be executed anyway she managed to escape, firstly to a safe house and subsequently to the British squadron off shore.

Along with those that escaped other émigrés avoided execution by persuading the commissions that they were simple soldiers who had been captured and then forced to serve against the republic. Tallien, in front of the National Convention, had already made clear soldiers who had faced such cruelty by the enemy, especially the British, should receive sympathy:

> A throng of French prisoners groaned in the prisons of England; each day the harshness towards them redoubled; successively the bread ration which served as their nourishment was reduced; the degree of weakening of their physical strength was calculated: then the émigrés presented themselves, and offered to improve their lot, if they would engage in their corps. Many resisted for a long time; but the horrors of starvation, the contagious diseases, the spectacle of their companions in misfortune perishing by their thousands, determined a great number to take part [but soon deserted once in France] … At the time and after the attack on the fort, a great number of soldiers, also enrolled by force, came to lay down their arms …[78]

Among them were four Hervilly officers who had previously served in that grade in the republican army before joining Royal-Louis at Toulon, that none were seemingly of noble birth may have aided them in their subterfuge. They were *Sous-lieutenant* Xavier (du) Verne, *Lieutenant* François (de) Traissac and *Sous-lieutenants* Pierre-Joseph Cognet and Michel Barret; the last three were acquitted and immediately enlisted as soldiers in the 11e bataillon des volontaires de la formation d'Orléans.[79] Another man who saved his life

75 Bennes, *A narrative*, p.37. She describes her interrogator as General Lemoine, himself.

76 Bennes, *A narrative*, p.39.

77 Bennes, *A narrative*, pp.40–41.

78 Anon., *Rapport*, p.9.

79 Closmadeuc, *Quiberon 1795*, pp.519–527.

by a similar trick was Damas chasseur Bernard de Corbehem and, in his memoirs, he sheds light on how the French soldier prisoners were treated once they had been acquitted by a commission:

> On leaving the presence of the commission, and becoming free again, we were led to the bivouac outside the town, where all the absolved prisoners were collected. … We were three to four hundred in this bivouac; at the end of a few days, the commanders of the different corps stationed in the town, and whose battalions were not complete, came to review us, and to each take a certain number of men. I was chosen with many others for the 42e régiment d'infanterie, formerly the régiment de la Reine [*sic*], and we were transferred to a location encompassed with walls, also situated outside the town, and which the regiment occupied. Some tents had been erected for it; others were for us, at a certain distance. It seemed that we were not worthy of being approached, or that, novice republicans, we would have a trial period to pass before being called to the honour of fraternising with them.[80]

These new recruits carried out fatigue duties under the supervision of two NCOs armed with batons, but after a fortnight or so, when he was included in a party sent to Vannes to collect the regiment's food rations, he slipped away unseen to a safe house he had been told about. Smuggled out from the town, he and five other escapees were taken to Cadoudal. They agreed to serve under the latter's orders and joined a group of about 30 to 40 émigrés who formed a unit of volunteers, without formal structure or assigned duties, that attached themselves to different chouan bands for operations. They were always on the move, were not paid, but had their needs provided by the country folk. They received no news from the outside world and were surrounded by people who only spoke and understood the local Breton tongue.[81]

It appears that it is this polyglot band of officers, volunteers and soldiers from different émigré units that is referred to, by sources, as the company of Loyal Emigrant left in Brittany or its Breton Company, rather than Coquet's detachment. Corbehem served with it for only about three months, others remained with the chouans in Morbihan or moved on to other areas. One of Corbehem's comrades, in Damas and the band, Emmanuel-François-Joseph Le Cointe de Guéfontaine went on to be an officer among the chouans in Maine and was killed at Ballée on 20 October 1799.[82] Another was Félix-Cyrille-Joseph Dujardin who later became a chouan officer in Morbihan. He had deserted from the republican army and joined the Austrian army before enlisting as a soldier in Rohan, then enrolled into the republican army after Quiberon. He deserted at Locminé to join the chouan unit of former soldiers.[83]

---

80 Corbehem, *Dix ans*, pp.215–216.

81 Corbehem, *Dix ans*, pp.224–236.

82 Émile Quernau-Lamerie, 'Les Choauns de la Basse-Mayenne', *Bulletin de la commission historique at archéologique de la Mayenne*, 2e série, Tome 28, 1912, p.373

83 Alfred Comte Boulay de La Meurthe, *Correspondance du Duc d'Enghien (1801–1804) et documents sur son enlévement et sa mort* (Paris: Alphonse Picard et fils, 1904), vol.I, p.484.

The largest group of prisoners were local Bretons, mainly from the countryside, who ranged from committed chouans, those who had been swept up in the enthusiasm after the landing at Carnac or those who had joined from fear of indiscriminate reprisals by the republican soldiery. Their number had been reduced immediately after the capture of the Quiberon peninsula when around 3,000 women, old men and children had been set free at Plouharnel, and others had escaped during the march to Auray. At the town, packed in various ecclesiastical buildings, they suffered from neglect and, as early as 25 July, the Auray authorities were raising concerns about typhus breaking out among them with some already dead and an epidemic looming. These fears were followed by protests to the commissaries and Lemoine that they were not being fed, pointing out that, in their opinion, most of the prisoners were non-combatants who had been forced to work on the defences.[84] On 30 July Blad ordered that their numbers be reduced by transferring them elsewhere principally to Vannes, and by 22 August there were only 300 left at Auray, sick or serving a sentence of imprisonment.[85]

However, typhus was transferred to Vannes along with the Breton prisoners. What is more, their number had grown when on 31 July about 1,200 Bretons who had previously taken refuge on the British ships landed at Vannes from chasse marées, having been refused permission to land at Quiberon the previous day. Blad ordered that the women and children under the age of 14, about half their number, be released to return home.[86] Almost 3,000 prisoners, the majority Breton peasantry, were detained in the grounds of the former Ursuline convent, without cover, in unsanitary conditions and with little food. Typhus was rampant here and soon it broke out in the other places holding such prisoners while they waited for an enquiry and judgement. Around 500 prisoners in all died of sickness or neglect at Auray and Vannes. Finally, on 6 September, with 3,000 prisoners, almost all Bretons, still in custody, it was decided that they would be freed on certain conditions being met. These were that any arms they held should be forfeited and that grain to the value of a third of the prisoner's annual income should be delivered to the republic's stores. Over the next few weeks 2,425 men were released and others followed later, although many sick remained. The 200 young men among the prisoners who were subject to conscription however were not free to go, for them the republican army awaited.[87]

The final tally of all the prisoners' fates vary to some extent between sources, however an official return prepared at the end of the year, gives the following: shot – 713, 'chouans condemned to several months detention' – 184, 'acquitted and incorporated into various battalions of the army and the navy' – 2,848, 'set at liberty by the orders of the representatives of the people' – 2,000, 'deaths in the prisons and hospitals' – 400 and 'old men, women, children set free at the entry of the army to Quiberon' – 3,000; so

84 Closmadeuc, *Quiberon 1795*, pp.105–108.
85 Closmadeuc, *Quiberon 1795*, pp.107, 109, 114, 142–143
86 Closmadeuc, *Quiberon 1795*, p.211.
87 Closmadeuc, *Quiberon 1795*, pp.143–145, 232–233, 244.

in all a total of 9,145.[88] While Closmadeuc, who had republican sympathies and thus could be suspected of playing the down the fatalities, states that the commissions, sitting between 27 July 1795 and 29 March 1796, made almost 5,000 judgements: 751 condemnations to death, 2,918 acquittals of French prisoners, 80 transferred as prisoners of war, and 1,200 chouans acquitted.[89]

Behind the numbers was human loss and this had particular impact when members of the same immediate or extended family served in the expedition. Among the many examples were the Villeneuve-Laroche-Barnaud brothers of whom two, Jean-Louis-Alexis of Damas and François of Rohan, were executed on 2 August at Quiberon, but the other, Louis-Gabriel, escaped and rejoined the British squadron. In London on 6 August Wickham received a letter from the émigré Comte de la Bassetiere who was in the state of 'the most harrowing disquiet' about the fate of four of his sons; two of whom were Loyal Emigrant volunteers, one a *chasseur* in Damas and the other a *lieutenant* in Hervilly, the regiment in which the comte's 'first cousins', father and son, also served.[90] Of his four sons, two had already been executed and the others went on to serve in the Vendée where one was to be killed; of his cousins, the father had been killed in action and the son was to be executed on 26 August.[91]

88 Reproduced by Closmadeuc, *Quiberon 1795*, p.556.

89 Closmadeuc, *Quiberon 1795*, p.244.

90 BL: Add MSS 37860: Bassetiere to Wickham 6 August.

91 Although there is some conflict between names and dates see La Gournerie, *Les Débris*, pp.106, 120, TNA: WO 12/11681: and Anon., 'Un gentilhomme Vendéen sous la Révolution: Constant-Hubert de La Bassetiere' 24 March 2013, <http://shenandoahdavis.canalblog.com/archives/2013/03/24/26730389.html>, accessed 10 August 2021.

10

Response

The Reaction of the British Government

At 7:30 a.m. on Tuesday 28 July the *Anson* came into Plymouth Sound, having passed the ships with Graham's troops and the cadres, who had been gathered so hastily from the Solent and the Channel Islands, in Cawsand Bay.[1] They, along with another convoy bound for the West Indies, were waiting for a change of wind, however, the westerlies which prevented their sailing had brought the *Anson* to port. The next day, 29 July, Captain Durham arrived in London with the reports for the British Government, but no public announcement was made. The news was not only a military defeat but also a political blow. Opponents were all too ready to criticise in any way the administration's conduct of the war and indeed that the war was being conducted at all, in a period of social unease and food shortages. So, for instance, one opposition-leaning newspaper ran a commentary piece on 31 July, entitled '*True cause of the present scarcity*.'

> It is in prosecution of this *just* and *necessary* war, a large body of emigrants have all the year been supported in this country with our bread ... and even now, large contracts are made for wheat and bread, which are every week shipping off for the supply of the emigrant army in France, and of our troops in the West Indies.[2]

That very day the defeat of the émigré force at Quiberon began to be reported. *The Kentish Weekly Post* added a 'Postscript. Friday, July 31. London. Emigrant Expedition.' It opened by quoting *The Morning Herald*:

> The insufficiency of the emigrant expedition to the coast of Brittany to the attainment of any beneficial or desirable purpose, must, from the commencement of it, have been obvious to every one whose wishes do not enslave and incapacitate his judgement; and it is with much pain we relate, that the period is arrived which affords a melancholy testimony to the truth of this observation.

1 TNA: ADM 51/1117: *Anson* log.
2 *The Chester Chronicle*, 31 July 1795.

The substantial article that followed concluded with a, well informed, '*Letter from an Officer in Sir J. B. Warren's fleet, Bay of Quiberon, 25th July*.'

> What I feared has at length happened, and the Emigrants have lost the Peninsula of Quiberon – a place of such strength, that half the men they had might have defended it against any force that could have been brought against it, if treachery had not been employed to sacrifice them. From the extreme want of discipline in many of the corps employed upon the expedition, desertions had been very frequent, and strong suspicions were entertained of secret correspondences kept up between some of the troops, and the Republican army under General Hoche. – These suspicions are at length but too completely verified. ... [An account of the action followed] ... This misfortune has arisen from the jealousies which had taken place in many of the corps; from the ill disposition of many of the privates to the cause they affected to espouse, and to the inability of M. de Puisaye, who was a man ill calculated for this difficult and arduous situation, though certainly very hearty in the enterprise he had undertaken. If the Comte de Hervilly had commanded, this misfortune would not have happened; but want of attention to the conduct of the emigrant troops has proved the ruin of the expedition. The enemy has suffered, from the carelessness of the emigrant commander, to tamper with their troops; and treachery seemed hardly suspected, till it burst forth in an almost general defection of the emigrants.
>
> In spite of the loss of this place, which was certainly of considerable importance, it is impossible not to be sanguine of ultimate success: this part of the country is entirely in favour of the Royalists cause. ... We do not believe, from every thing we have heard and seen, that there is one man in ten of the country people, favourable to the Convention in this part of France; and, with an able Commander, the Royalist Cause may scarcely doubt success.[3]

The government had much to consider, as on the same day that it learnt of the defeat at Quiberon, 29 July, it received the news that Spain had concluded a peace treaty with France the week before. Despite the hopes and wishes of those émigrés who had preferred Spain as an ally to Britain, the country had provided at best half-hearted support for their cause and, more widely, for the Coalition in the war against France. The peace was to have several implications for the continuation of the campaign in Western France. There was the prospect that French republican troops, previously stationed along the Pyrenees could be immediately deployed in the Vendée or even Brittany, while more British troops would need to be sent to the West Indies. Britain was already committed to a costly campaign in Haïti, the western end of Hispaniola, and now, as part of the price for peace, Spain had handed the eastern part of the island to France. Any reinforcement of the forces in Quiberon Bay was immediately suspended, and time would be needed before deciding the next steps. This, however, left Warren, with the survivors of 21 July on his ships, without any official directions so Earl Spencer, First Lord of the Admiralty, knowing that a dispatch boat was about to leave, wrote to him privately on 31 July:

3 *The Kentish Weekly Post*, 31 July 1795.

> Though very much chagrined and mortified at the unfortunate event of the 21st … we are still willing to hope that matters may not be yet quite so desperate as to make it necessary to give up all ideas of further offensive proceedings on the coast of Brittany, &c. The loss, however, of a post so favourable as that of Quiberon, with all its attendant circumstances, was so unexpected as well as so discouraging an event, as might well be supposed capable of causing some little hesitation or at least some deliberation on what was next to be done. I am therefore unable to give you positive assurances on this subject at present …
>
> Lord Bridport is instructed to use his best endeavours for communicating with and protecting you … The Thunderer is making every exertion to sail as soon as possible, and, I hope, may be ready to put to sea by to-morrow. … we have sent you four revenue cutters, who may be of great use in any of the operations for cutting off the communication with Belleisle. They sailed three days ago. We have ordered four of the best remaining gunboats to go out with the Thunderer, if they get round to Portsmouth in time. If not, she is not to wait for them, as Captain Bertie will carry with him everything he can put on board that can be of the most use.
>
> Pitt and Windham are going down to-day to meet Lord Moira in the country, and till the result of their meeting is known no further instructions can be sent to you, but most probably the Thunderer will carry out instructions to you, and I hope she may reach you soon after, if not even before this does.[4]

The conference between Pitt, Windham and Moira took place that day at Hartford Bridge, on the road between London and Southampton, north of Basingstoke. It would have been an interesting meeting as relations between the general and the administration, which were always somewhat strained given his Whig political affiliations, had worsened dramatically. In his letter of 30 July confirming his attendance to Pitt, he went as close as he could to explicitly accusing the Government of briefing against him, using the *Sun* 'a newspaper known to be published under the immediate direction of Government' to do so:

> The object of the paragraph clearly is that the misfortune at Quiberon should be inferred to have proceeded from my delay in affording the necessary support: an insinuation so deeply injurious to my character & at the same time so utterly unfounded that it must not stand uncontradicted … I had rather owe the correction of this misstatement to your equity & liberality of sentiment than to any step of my own.[5]

In fact the preparations for Moira's expedition to sail were almost complete, the loading of the commissary stores at Southampton having finished on 29 July.[6]

4 Corbett (ed.), *Private Papers*, pp.96–97. The *Anson* could not return to Warren immediately as she required a dockyard refit, she was however ready to sail on 10 September.

5 Aspinall, *George III*, pp.365–368, Moira to Pitt 30 July.

6 TNA: WO 1/176: Moira to Huskisson 29 July.

The *Thunderer*, having taken on supplies and equipment at Spithead, only managed to leave on 5 August and then endured a voyage hampered by poor or contrary winds.[7] Warren received Spencer's letter on 8 August.[8] It was just as well he had as the *Thunderer* brought no orders, and it would be quite some time before he received any further direction from London.

The news of the defeat and its repercussions reached the British troops and émigrés waiting in Cawsand Bay, so on 31 July Major Harness, 80th Foot, was able to finish a letter to his wife with, 'Our expedition, my Bessy, is at an end. We have it announced, but we know not whether we are to return to Portsmouth or remain here; in a few days I shall see you. ... This failure will make a considerable noise in Town and blame will attach.'[9] At 11:00 a.m. on 3 August, the frigates *Jason* and *Arethusa* set sail from Cawsand Bay, escorting the 48 transports with the British troops and émigrés back to the Solent. At noon on 5 August the convoy anchored in Cowes Roads and the warships, over the next few days, continued to Spithead, the *Jason* coming to anchor there on 10 August.[10]

The transports, meanwhile, had worked their way into Southampton and on 7 and 8 August most of the troops disembarked. The British troops marched west of Southampton, the 80th Foot to Eling Barracks, near Totton, and the others to a camp established on Nursling Common.[11] On 12 August the British regiments were included in the weekly state for Moira's corps. There was a considerable number of troops committed to the venture, although their readiness for field service had been shown to be at least questionable on the departure of the contingent with Graham and it was be tested again. The force consisted of three cavalry regiment: 4th Dragoon Guards (292 officers and men present); the 12th and 25th Light Dragoons (152 and 240 respectively) and 14 infantry battalions.

The officers and men of the white cockade regiments, including *Lieutenant* d'Asnières's Hector detachment, returned to their depots. The cadre corps also remained in the Solent area, Léon and Trésor were landed and sent to Romsey, while Williamson appears to have been kept on board vessels in the River Itchen, where it was reported there were 'now near 200 transports.'[12] Complaints had already arisen about the conditions on board the vessels from the volunteers, some of them becoming ill, when they had been at Cawsand Bay.[13] They had only expected to be at sea for a short time before active service. Toussaint-Ambroise Talour de la Cartrie, a gentleman in Léon, recalled that before embarking, 'I parted with all my clothes except the coat on my back and two shirts, being sensible that in such a war it were better to have no superfluities to attend to.'[14]

---

7 TNA: ADM 51/1103: *Thunderer* log.

8 Corbett (ed.), *Private Papers*, p.97.

9 Duncan-Jones (ed.), *William Harness*, pp.80–81.

10 TNA: ADM 51/1164: *Jason* log, and *The Times*, Tuesday 4 and Thursday 6 July 1795.

11 Cook, 'St George Diary', p.246. Nursling (or Nutschalling, then) Common was what is now the area built-up with housing between Romsey Road (A3057) and Rownhams Lane.

12 *The Ipswich Journal*, 15 August.

13 BL: Add MS 37860: Harcourt forwarded the complaint on 3 August.

14 Toussaint-Ambroise Talour de la Cartrie, *Memoirs of the Count de Cartrie* (London: John Lane, 1906), p.182.

Table 11: 'Weekly State of the Army under the Command of Lieut. General the Earl of Moira, Southampton 12th Aug. 1795' – infantry battalions.[15]

Regiment	Officers and staff	NCOs and drummers	Rank and file present and fit for duty	Total
12th Foot*	29	63	724	816
14th Foot*	21	58	656	735
19th Foot	21	50	590	661
27th Foot*	21	59	501	581
28th Foot*	27	61	587	675
33rd Foot	25	49	801	875
42nd Foot	17	46	608	671
57th Foot*	23	61	626	710
1/78th Foot	29	71	754	854
80th Foot*	26	74	638	738
1/90th Foot	24	64	819	907
101st Foot	19	53	413	485
103rd Foot	22	62	518	602
109th Foot	27	63	375	465

* denoting those that had landed from Graham's force

On the British Ships in Quiberon Bay

On 21 July almost 1,000 troops, officers and men, had reached the safety of the British ships along with about 2,000 others – chouans, priests, women, children and other men. The situation was chaotic. So, the next day Warren instructed that 'the Officers, Soldiers, Chouans who are at present scatter'd in the Men of War, Transports [and] Chasse Marées' should be re-distributed, in their appropriate units, when an accurate count could be made of their numbers. The infantry were allocated to warships, transports receiving the others.[16]

This was only the initial allocation of troops to the ships and over the next few days there were frequent changes, as ships were required for other missions. So, those on the *Venus* and *Lark*, for example, soon had to shift as on 26 July, Halstead, commanding the former, was ordered to be ready to sail with some empty transports, as well as the hospital ships carrying the wounded, in convoy as soon as the weather permitted.[17] The warships weighed anchor and sailed from the bay in the early afternoon of 29 July, with 33 transports and a Swedish brig, arriving at Spithead on 8 August.[18]

15 TNA: WO 17/239.

16 TNA: ADM 80/136: Eyles to officers commanding ships 22 July.

17 TNA: ADM 1/1913: Halstead to Nepean 8 August, it appears that one of the transports was the *Burton* onto which 'all the wounded' had been sent on 23 July (Wetton, 'Journal', p.69)

18 TNA: ADM 51/1117: *Venus* and ADM 51/1167 *Lark* logs.

Table 12: Distribution of personnel in the ships in Quiberon Bay, with estimated numbers, 22 July 1795[19]

Ships	Units	Officers	'Men'
HMS *Robust*	Hervilly	30	207
HMS *Venus*	Hervilly	7	40
	Dresnay, Salm & Damas	19	76
HMS *Pomone*	Loyal Emigrant	12	97
HMS *Galatea*	Rohan	13	75
HMS *Leda*	Hector, Béon & Périgord	19	74
Disko Bay	Artillery	22	133
Kingston		24	200
John	Chouans with officers and women included	–	268
Leighton		–	248
Aurora (2nd)		–	312
Silver Eel		–	248
Aurora (1st)		–	248
Goodwood	Priests	–	18
In addition prisoners were re-distributed:			
HMS *Anson*	From *William & Robert*		128
HMS *Lark*	From *William & Robert* and the *Atlantic* (12)		64

Among those sailing was *Sous-Lieutenant* de Jarrige de La Morélie, of Hector, who was wounded on 16 July and had only escaped on 21 July through the care and loyalty of one of his company's soldiers who brought him a horse, on which he was able to reach a chasse marée and safety. From Portsmouth, he was transferred to hospital in Southampton where he wrote to his brother, 'Nothing is spared in our care, and I will remain here until in perfect health.'[20] The wounded in the worst condition were only taken as far as the naval hospital at Haslar, on the Gosport side of Portsmouth Harbour, and it is there that *Capitaine* de Kerouartz, another Hector officer, died on 17 August.[21]

In Quiberon Bay, the French Emigrant Artillery was the most complete unit in terms of both numbers and formation, however Rotalier still had problems ascertaining where his men were as he explained in a letter of 18 August, 'Several gunners … reached, by swimming, a gun vessel, which was soon after sent to a station off Belle-Isle; I have with pleasure seen them return, when the vessel had finished the mission.' He was also able to report the escape of Bombardier Alexandre Henriere, with three Rohan soldiers, from Auray; it is certainly this man who recounted the fate of Rotalier's men held there: 'All our unfortunate prisoners of the artillery, officers and soldiers have been shot by the patriots, only for their designation, as for the infantry soldiers the patriots have them undergo a form of examination; they shoot those who did not give patriotic replies; and incorporated in their regiments those in whom they believe to have found republican sentiments.'[22]

19 TNA: ADM 80/136: Eyles to officers commanding ships 22 July.
20 Guibert, *Les Émigrés Limousin*, p.15, letter of 15 August.
21 La Gournerie, *Les Débris*, pp.147, 190.
22 TNA: PRO 30/11/225: Rotalier to Cornwallis 18 August.

Rotalier was one of the most senior officers with a British commission and so had a leading role in bringing order to the units, to do so he remained on board the *Pomone*. On 25 July he certified the submission of a return showing the number of troops remaining with each unit (Table 13).

Table 13: 'Situation state of the French Corps in H. Britannic M.'s service' – certified 25 July 1795.[23]

	Hervilly	Hector	Dresnay	Loyal Emigrant	Artillery
Officers	37	20	6	7	34
Cadets	–	5	–	–	–
NCOs	26	6	4	5	12
Drummers	4*	3	–	6*	1
R&F	242	[45]	25	91	249
TOTAL	309	[56]	35	109	296
Wounded	17	23	6	27	7
	Salm	Rohan	Périgord	Damas	Béon
Officers	3	6	2	–	3
Cadets	–	8	2	–	15
NCOs	2	6	2	2	–
Drummers	–	31	–	–	–
R&F	13**	61	9	12	17
TOTAL	18	84	15	14	35
Wounded	–	9	7	1	3

A later return, of 5 August, shows similar numbers except that there is an additional officer (possibly Lieutenant de Chamillard) in Périgord and the artillery has one NCO and 25 other ranks extra.[24] Another, undated, report comparing the numbers present and those lost showed that three officers and seven other ranks of the Warren Hussars had escaped and of the other categories of people: 'Chouans with some few women & children taken off the 21 [July]' – 1,464, 'Crews & some few Chouans in 43 Chasse Marées' – 429, 'Women & children in the Chasse Marées' – 99, Priests – 21, 'Staff Officers, Administrators, etc.' – 20, Engineer Officers – nine and 'Chouan Officers of distinction' – five.[25]

The condition in which the men reached the ships was of immediate concern. On 29 July Rotalier described the state of his own men and unit:

> Nothing of all that had been landed … was able to be re-embarked, everything fell into the possession of the enemy; generally all the officers have lost their personal effects; the soldiers their packs; having been able to barely reach the boats in person; several even undressed and swam to be able to save themselves absolutely naked.
>
> All the Sergeant Major's and Quarter Master's papers [and] all mine have been lost …[26]

23 TNA: PRO 30/11/225. *Included in these numbers are a fifer in Hervilly, two musicians in Rohan and an unspecified number of musicians in the Loyal Emigrants; **This number includes an armourer. In addition, it is noted that there was a woman with Béon and a woman and a domestic with Damas.

24 TNA: WO 1/388, also WO 12/1197: Périgord pay list.

25 TNA: ADM 80/136.

26 TNA: PRO 30/11/225: Rotalier to Cornwallis 29 July.

All the men who required clothes were supplied with slops, coarse and loose working jackets and trousers issued to sailors, 'to cover their nakedness.'[27] After his escape, Villeneuve-Laroche-Barnaud was provided with the Rohan uniform of his dead brother.[28] Those officers of the Second Division who survived were better off than their comrades of the First, their effects had remained on the ships.[29]

Despite everything, Warren, for one, was not ready to give up. In his letter of 22 July in which he had informed Spencer of the defeat, he wrote, 'I think it will be wrong to give up the business.' In his reasoning he emphasised the renewed activity of the Vendéens, under Charette. Thus, he intended to take full possession of Houat and Hoëdic, as well to continue the blockade of Belle-Île, but he made it clear that '... eatables, canteens, tents, and forage for the horses must be had without a moment's loss of time.'[30]

On 24 July the squadron came into Houat Roads, to the east of the island, and with his anchorage secure, as long as the protection provided by the main fleet blockading Lorient and Brest continued, Warren consolidated his position. He took full possession of both islands, placing a garrison of Emigrant Artillery, commanded by Captain de la Noeseche, in the fort on Houat. A supply of water was available on both Houat and Hoëdic, which had already been supplying the ships' needs. However, when he reported this on 31 July, he was concerned that these sources would prove to be inadequate. He also, again, wrote of the urgent need for supplies, including water, beer and, especially, fresh food to prevent scurvy.[31] This was already emerging as a problem amongst the ships' crews, so as soon as 2 August, the *Robust* sent her launch 'on shore with the scorbutic men to gather herbs.'[32] In the same report, of 31 July, Warren stated that he had, as has been seen above, returned 1,300 old men, women and children to the mainland, so that now only 500 chouans remained.

Warren continued to try to make the best of the situation. Sailors dug wells on Houat and Hoëdic so that, from 5 August, the islands were producing sufficient water for the needs of all the transports. Furthermore, sailors 'enlarged' ovens on Houat so that by 6 August boats were arriving to collect bread, produced by bakers from the infantry and artillery, twice weekly for the troops. The possession of the islands also brought a responsibility towards the islanders and fortunately there was an ample supply of flour from the American merchantmen, so on 6 August the agent on the *Sarah* transport was ordered to provide Houat's mayor with six barrels of it for distribution.[33]

---

27 TNA: ADM 1/103: Warren to Nepean 22 July.

28 Villeneuve-Laroche-Barnaud, *Mémoires*, vol.II, p 294

29 Corbett (ed.), *Private Papers*, p.89, Warren to Spencer 22 July.

30 Corbett (ed.), *Private Papers*, p 89, Warren to Spencer 22 July also TNA: ADM 1/103: Warren to Nepean the same day.

31 Corbett (ed.), *Private Papers*, p.94, Warren to Spencer 31 July.

32 TNA: ADM 51/1130: *Robust* log.

33 TNA: ADM 80/136: Keats to Lieutenant Symonds (given as Simmonds after this entry) 6 August.

Natural building materials were scarce on the islands, Houat possessing only one tree, a mulberry standing in the cemetery.[34] So when the chouans were landed there on 9 August they were provided with planks and canvas sacks, made by the British sailors, to make sand bags for shelter. They were also armed ready to return to Brittany in line with Puisaye's plans.[35] The lack of provisions was becoming critical with Warren reporting, on 14 August, that there was only a month's supply remaining and that scurvy had 'made its appearance in a great degree' on board the *Robust*, his largest warship.[36] Nevertheless he was 'unwilling to abandon these islands and this bay whilst offensive measures continue.'[37]

The *Thundrerer* finally arrived at the anchorage at 2:00 p.m. on 16 August and the provisions she had on board were immediately distributed among the other ships.[38] The tents that she had also brought meant that the more reliable men of the émigré infantry could now land. Their presence on the ships had brought challenges, even for Warren who noted that he had 'twelve French officers in my cabin, and fourteen with my officers below.'[39] Some appear to have already been on shore as, on 15 August, the few remaining soldiers of Damas had an order read out to them that, 'In case of attack by the enemy, the régiment de Damas is to retire into the fort and will occupy the platform which is on the fort.' It was read out to them by the unit's commander, its senior NCO, *Fourrier* Claude-Marie Mercier des Pelle-Saunier.[40]

On 18 August tents, new clothing and equipment were to be landed on Houat for the troops who were to be disembarked. So, on 22 August, when the Salm Regiment landed they were to be provided with 70 infantry tents, the requisite camp equipment, and five days provisions.[41] For some unexplained reason the surviving members of the Warren Hussars were treated differently. On 21 August they were taken on board the *Aimwell*, which appears to have been in a poor condition, to be taken to Hoëdic, where they were landed and then taken on board again each night. This continued for the next week or so until the gun vessel returned to the squadron on 1 September.[42]

Despite Puisaye's presence on Houat, it was Contades and Talleyrand-Périgord who took responsibility for the troops, Warren later writing, 'I have been much indebted, however, to Monsieur De Périgord, … and to Monsieur Contades, who have exerted themselves in keeping things together during the army being encamped at Houat.'[43] This was a necessity as Warren observed, with some understatement, on 28 August that 'The General [Puisaye] and the army are not on good terms' describing, later, that Puisaye had 'been as it

34 Contades, *Coblenz*, pp.225–226 and Villeneuve-Laroche-Barnaud, *Mémoires*, vol.II, p.297.

35 TNA: ADM 80/136: and Corbett (ed.), *Private Papers*, p.98, Warren to Spencer 8 August.

36 TNA: ADM 1/103: Warren to Nepean 14 August.

37 Corbett (ed.), *Private Papers*, p.100, Warren to Spencer 14 August.

38 TNA: ADM 51/1103: *Thunderer*, ADM 51/1130 *Robust* and ADM 51/1149 *Pomone* logs and Contades, *Coblenz*, p.222.

39 Corbett (ed.), *Private Papers*, p.94, Warren to Spencer 31 July.

40 State Archive of the Russian Federation (GARF): 758/2/52: In his early twenties Pelle-Saunier had served as a *cadet-gentilhomme* in the régiment d'Aquitaine.

41 TNA: ADM 80/136: Keats to Simmonds 18 and 22 August.

42 TNA: ADM 51/4406: *Aimwell* log.

43 Corbett (ed.), *Private Papers*, p.104, Warren to Spencer 11 September.

were at war' with the troops.[44] If such relations had been strained before, his conduct on 21 July meant they had now completely broken down.

The speed and disastrous nature of the defeat and the losses incurred had crushed the émigrés' spirits, as Contades wrote, 'all our hopes had vanished.'[45] This provided a challenge for Warren who wrote to Spencer on 8 August:

> I shall endeavour to keep up the spirits of the people now with me as much as *it is possible* so to do; but there are so many of them who think of a return to England before any service that I cannot get them to work with energy or vigour. The arrival of Lord Moira would perhaps oblige them to look about them, and inspire some degree of confidence. … They are what is called disorganised and unarmed, and clothed piecemeal …[46]

By the end of the month, although the troops were better clothed, sickness had emerged to further dampen spirits, on 28 August Warren wrote:

> I have remained in anxious expectation of receiving orders to send back the troops here, who are in a miserable state, … and to return home, or to have seen Lord Moira with the British Army. … There is a fever on those [ships] with the troops, and some have died, and near 115 of them in hospital. The rest are encamped as well as our means and circumstances would admit; but their fidelity, except the remains of three regiments, very little can be said, as I am persuaded they would not stand fire, and many of them join the enemy.[47]

This last prospect was not mere speculation as there was evidence of growing French republican naval strength and activity at Lorient, the Loire estuary, and at Rochefort – threatening the British ships in the bay.[48] Contades was also concerned, hearing the soldiers, when he walked among the tents occupied by the Régiment d'Hervilly, who 'all generally regretted not having passed to the enemy, and avidly promised, if the occasion presented itself, to not make the same error.'[49] The disaffection seems may have even spread to the Béon Regiment, the longest standing unit of the Second Division, as on 22 August orders were made for some of its officers to be placed on the *William & Mary* transport who were not permitted 'on any account to go out of the Ship.'[50] On 11 September, Warren wrote:

> It is certain [the troops], except the artillery and La Châtre [Loyal Emigrants], Rohan, Salm, and Damas, have behaved very ill and are not to be trusted, one half of them Republicans. A great deal may however be placed to discouragement and

44 Corbett (ed.), *Private Papers*, pp.102, 104, Warren to Spencer 28 August and 11 September.
45 Contades, *Coblenz*, p.223.
46 Corbett (ed.), *Private Papers*, pp.97–98.
47 Corbett (ed.), *Private Papers*, p.101, Warren to Spencer.
48 TNA: ADM 1/103: Warren to Nepean 8 August and to Nepean and Bridport 28 August.
49 Contades, *Coblenz*, p.223; he indicates that only the soldiers disembarked were those considered the more reliable.
50 TNA: ADM 80/136, Keats to transport agent.

no regularity of measures taken in the commanding of them since D'Hervilly's being wounded.[51]

Continued Naval Operations

Meanwhile Warren's ships had not been idle as they continued to assert their presence not only in Quiberon Bay but also, despite the increased threat from the republican navy, further afield between Belle-Île and the La Baule-Guérande Peninsula. Generally the line-of-battle ships, and *Pomone*, remained on station, the *Standard* lying, for most of the time, off Belle-Île and the *Robust* off Houat. When the latter, accompanied by the *Pelter*, sailed for England early on 20 August due to the increasing cases of scurvy on both vessels, the *Thunderer* took over her role in the bay.[52] On operations one or two frigates commanded and supported the smaller vessels, while on smaller-scale, inshore, missions gun-vessels took over this role. There was also the fleet of chasse marées which on 4 August comprised 43 vessels, with 429 men and 99 women and children on board, this number included the 14 boats that had been 'detained at Quiberon' on 29 July, when they had tried to land the Bretons there.[53] The fleet was led by Jean Rohu's brother, Vincent, of the *Bonport* and they continued to be supplied with arms and ammunition, Vincent Rohu being supplied with '6 swivels with a quantity of powder, shot, wads & musquet ball cartridges' on 13 August and 'sundry Articles of Gunners Stores' on 26 August.[54] They often actively operated with naval ships (which provided them with victuals), liaised with royalists on the mainland (often bringing back messages, intelligence and even escaped prisoners), and acted as tenders in the squadron.

The revenue cutters Spencer had mentioned also joined Warren, the *Speedwell* and *Dolphin* arrived on 31 July and were apparently soon followed by the *Swan* and *Greyhound* and then the *Falcon*, which arrived on 18 August.[55] Despite the unusual role for them, they proved to be very useful additions to the squadron.

On 14 August Warren, writing to the Admiralty, described his squadron's activities, 'I have continued to annoy the Enemy by stationing small Cruizers round this Bay; as well as Bellisle; and several Skirmishes have taken place between the Launches fitted as Gun Boats; as well as other small Vessels employed on that Service.'[56] Ten operations are recorded in various ships' logs between 1 August and 12 September, six of which were attacks on Fort Penthièvre, or vessels anchored under it, by gun-vessels and ships' boats. On the morning of 29 August the *Galatea*, *Teaser* gun-vessel and *Greyhound*

51 Corbett (ed.), *Private Papers*, p.104, Warren to Spencer 11 September.

52 TNA: ADM 1/103: Warren to Nepean 19 August, and ADM 51/1130: *Robust* log. Two crewmen on the *Robust* died on the voyage home, she arrived at Spithead on 28 August and the sick were immediately transferred to Haslar Hospital.

53 TNA: ADM 80/136: report.

54 TNA: ADM 51/1130: *Robust* and ADM 51/1103: *Thunderer* logs.

55 TNA: ADM 51/1149: *Pomone* log and ADM 1/103: Warren to Nepean 18 August.

56 TNA: ADM 1/103: Warren to Nepean 14 August.

revenue cutter sailed from Houat with six chasse marées laden with chouans and out towards Île Dumet. The *Galatea* remained off the island while the other vessels proceeded towards the coast, where the chouans landed at 1:00 a.m. on 30 August, an operation that took an hour to complete. The location is not given but cannot have been far as the vessels had re-joined the *Galatea* before the chasse marées left for Houat at 4:00 a.m.. The warships and cutter then cruised off Le Croisic, from where they were fired upon, and at 2:00 p.m. they made sail and came into Houat Roads at 9:00 a.m. the following morning.[57] Between 5 and 9 September the *Teaser* protected four consecutive overnight landings, from four chasse marées, again the landing point is not stated but was only about two hours sailing time from Houat.[58] Other operations appear to have simply been cruises to keep the republican defences on their toes. For example, on the afternoon of 11 September the *Teaser* gun-vessel and *Swan* Revenue cutter had 'several shots fired at us from Pt St Jacques which we returned with shot & shells, we knocked down the West End of the Guard House.' The two vessels then continued their cruise to Île Dumet before arriving off Houat at 11:00 p.m. the next evening.[59]

Charette had continued to be in touch with Warren and in early August a messenger arrived, named Le Febvre, who had an intimate knowledge of the coast of the Vendée, requesting that a landing of supplies be made between Saint-Jean-de-Monts and Saint-Gilles-Croix-de-Vie, Charette promising 'that he would come down to the coast with 25,000 bayonettes [*sic*] to protect it.'[60] At 5:00 a.m. on 3 August the frigate HMS *Concorde*, *Pelter* gun-vessel, *Speedwell* revenue cutter, a powder sloop, and two chasse marées set sail. One of the latter was piloted by Le Febvre, she had been captured from the republicans earlier in the campaign, taken into British service, armed and renamed the *Duke of Clarence*. On 8 August the vessels joined HMS *Artois* and *Greyhound* revenue cutter off the Île d'Yeu, then, on the morning of 10 August, after receiving notification that a landing could take place, stores were immediately transferred to the chasse marées.[61]

In order to cover the landing Charette had called on the cooperation of the neighbouring Vendéen leader Charles Sapinaud de La Rairie, to prevent the republican garrison of Challans intervening, while 3,000 or so of his own men protected the landing itself at the Plage des Becs, six kilometres south of Saint-Jean-de-Monts.[62] Captain Hunt, of the *Concorde*, noted the afternoon's events in his log:

> At 2 some of Charette's army appeared on the sand, sent the sloop, Chasse mari & Boats with the arms & ammunition to the army. At 6 saw the Royalist army & Republican army in action, at ¾ past 6 saw the Republican army retreating & the

57 TNA: ADM 51/4042: *Teaser* log.
58 TNA: ADM 51/4042: *Teaser* log.
59 TNA: ADM 51/4042: *Teaser* log.
60 Corbett (ed.), *Private Papers*, p.99, Warren to Spencer 8 August.
61 TNA: ADM 51/1111: *Concorde* log.
62 Alphonse Beauchamp, *Histoire de la Guerre de la Vendée et des Chouans, depuis son origine jusqu'à la Pacification de 1800* (Paris: Giguet et Michaud, 1806), vol.III, p.261.

> Royalist army pursuing them. At 12 rec'd an account that the Republicans lost 300 Men killed.[63]

The republican force, of 400 to 500 men, had marched from Saint-Gilles-Croix-de-Vie but were defeated with the loss of 50 dead and 60 wounded, the royalists also lost men including Le Febvre.[64] The landing of the supplies continued through into the following day. The quantity of what was delivered to Charette was significant: 400 barrels of powder, 1,400 muskets, 250 'suits of cloathing, hats etc.,' 25,000 musket flints, 6,000 loaded musket cartridges, 300 cavalry swords, two 8-pounder field pieces with their equipment, and a 'quantity of paper for making cartridges.'[65] On 12 August Captain Nagle, of the *Artois*, reported that, 'notwithstanding it is a bad Beach for the purpose, I landed the whole without a single article getting wet or damaged and saw the whole Carted and escorted away.'[66]

The *Speedwell* immediately left with news of the landing and the *Greyhound* chased a schooner that had stood off to the north of the beach. Having received the signal that Charette had safely received the supplies, the vessels sailed at 9:00 p.m. for Houat.[67] Despite the success of the mission, it was ominous that Charette's men had not been able to secure the beach before the landing and had to fight to defend it as it took place; it did not bode well for the future. Although not directly relevant to the landing, the fighting in the Vendée took another dark turn when Charette decided to take revenge for the executions at Vannes and elsewhere, having 300 of the republican prisoners he held at Belleville shot in front of his men.[68] On 20 August vessels sailed from Quiberon Bay, loaded with supplies, on a similar mission. However, despite cruising for some days off the Île d'Yeu, the *Concorde*, *Borer* and *Greyhound* to the north and the *Artois* and *Duke of Clarence* to the south of the island, they saw no signal so they returned to anchor off Houat on 26 August.[69] Nevertheless Warren, who still felt that all was not lost in the theatre, remained convinced that Charette offered the best chance of success.

Uncertainty and Concern

Warren was still without official orders from London, but he was nevertheless not completely uninformed of what was happening there. The arrival of the *Thunderer* had meant that he was aware of what had happened in the Solent up to 5 August and he appears to have received a private letter from Lord Moira to tell him more troops were on their way.[70] This, and his disinclination to give up, meant that he wanted to remain as long as practicable, but he

63 TNA: ADM 51/1111: *Concorde* log.
64 Beauchamp, *Histoire*, p.261.
65 TNA: ADM 1/103: list supplied.
66 TNA: ADM 1/103: Nagle to Warren 12 August.
67 TNA: ADM 51/1111: *Concorde* log.
68 Robert, *Expédition*, pp.200–201, and Beauchamp, *Histoire*, pp.258–259.
69 TNA: ADM 51/1111: *Concorde* log.
70 TNA: ADM 1/103: Warren to Nepean 20 August.

had two distinct drivers to leave. The first was that Bridport was anxious to quit his station, off Brest and Lorient neutralising the threat from the French republican navy in those ports, and informed Warren that he would do so on 14 September so, with his position in turn untenable, Warren replied that he would leave Quiberon Bay the same day.[71] Later Warren was to express his frustration by Bridport's conduct writing, 'I have been perplexed beyond measure by the remonstrances and letters of Lord Bridport … [he was] very much displeased at my not coming out of the bay immediately. I, however, certainly wished to remain until the last moment, knowing the importance of our appearance even to the general cause.'[72] However, it is clear that he had already been working on a similar timescale, having informed the Admiralty on 14 August that his ships only had enough provisions for one month.[73]

The other driver was the condition of his crews and the soldiers. As noted above, on 28 August he reported fever had broken out among the troops resulting in some deaths and 115 hospitalised.[74] Houat's limited resources, including the shellfish found on the shore, were exhausted.[75] Fever, probably cholera, had also affected the chouans and among the first to die, on 15 August, was Saint-Morys, Puisaye's commissary-general.[76] The sickness spread to the island's population of whom about a dozen died, including the island's *recteur*, Jean-Marie Lorcy, a non-juror priest, who had only returned in February after being detained for his stance in Port-Louis and then the pontoons off Rochefort.[77]

Preparations were already in hand to leave. On 28 August orders were issued designating transports for the troops 'when the signal is made' to embark, with their camp equipment, stores and baggage with it.

Table 14: Allocation of transport for the troops embarking from Houat, 28 August 1795.[78]

Units	Transports	Officers	Men
Emigrant Artillery	*Silver Eel, Disko Bay*	30	283
Hector, Rohan	*Aurora (2)*	11	132
Hervilly	*Aurora (1), Kingston*	30	247
Loyal Emigrant, Dresnay	*John*	14	125
Salm, Périgord, Béon, Damas, Warren Hussars	*Sarah*	11	79
All sick and surgeons	*Leighton*	–	–
Commissaries	*William and Mary*	–	–

71 TNA: ADM 1/104: Warren to Bridport 3 September.

72 Corbett (ed.), *Private Papers*, p.103, Warren to Spencer 11 September.

73 TNA: ADM 1/103: Warren to Nepean 14 August.

74 Corbett (ed.), *Private Papers*, p.101, Warren to Spencer 28 August.

75 Villeneuve-Laroche-Barnaud, *Mémoires*, vol.II, p.297.

76 *The Caledonian Mercury*, 1 October 1795.

77 Anon., 'Etymologie et Histoire de Houat', *InfoBretagne.com*, (undated) <http://www.infobretagne.com/houat.htm>, accessed 4 September 2021; the site contains photographs (postcards) of Houat from the early 20th Century.

78 TNA: ADM 80/136.

The embarkation was scheduled to be completed by 10 September.[79] Warren was particularly concerned by the forts on Houat and Hoëdic so, on his own initiative, decided that they should be destroyed, 'As the Forts upon the Islands … are very strong, and may annoy any Vessels coming into the Bay in future; and having no Garrison that can be depended upon, to leave in them; I have ordered preparations for their being blown up previous to our Departure.'[80] The task was not easy, for instance, from 3 to 11 September the *Thunderer* sent working parties as well as at least 46 barrels of gunpowder to destroy the fort on Houat.[81]

As this was going on Puisaye departed for the mainland, it is not clear when he left but Warren, who had been advocating it for some time, wrote that he had done so by, or on, 3 September.[82] Puisaye was under pressure following the defeat and he had burnt bridges not only with the émigrés but also the Morbihan chouans, as it had been his chosen men, Tinténiac and then Pontbellanger, who had led the Armée rouge with the élite of the Morbihan chouans, on what had been a wild goose chase. The paid troops regarded him as responsible for what had happened on 21 July, a day in which he had shown reprehensible personal behaviour. Warren wrote that Puisaye had gone with 'the intention of penetrating into the Interior, and putting himself at the head of the Chouans & having no further occasion for the Army'.[83] Puisaye inflicted one last snub to the troops, contravening his earlier instructions he 'carried with him the cash of the chest and refused paying the soldiers here, as he said it was destined for the Chouans.' Warren continued with the following observation, 'I believe he is, if I may be excused speaking freely upon a point in which my country is concerned, a character capable of doing much good or being no inconsiderable enemy and full of intrigue, and, I wish it were possible to say, possessed of equal bravery.'[84] Despite everything Puisaye was unabashed, declaring in a letter to Bouillon of 30 August, 'I leave for Brittany to repair there the harm that treason, presumption and envy have done to us here.'[85]

On the evening of 6 September, the prospects suddenly changed with the return to Quiberon Bay of the *Swan* revenue cutter.[86] The master, Francis Sarmon, was able to inform Warren that on 2 September, off Portland, he had

79 TNA: ADM 1/104: Warren to Nepean undated in September (but would have been in the first three days); Contades, *Coblenz*, p.228, says the troops had embarked on 9 September.

80 TNA: ADM 1/104: Warren to Nepean 1–3 (?) September. Hutt referring to a copy held in the 'Sudbury Hall MSS' gives the date of the letter as 3 September, Hutt, *Chouannerie*, p.343, note 93. Warren had asked specifically for orders about the forts on 28 August but had received none.

81 TNA: ADM 51/1103: *Thunderer* log.

82 TNA: ADM 1/104: Warren to Nepean 1–3 (?) September and Corbett (ed.), *Private Papers*, p.102, Warren to Spencer 28 August. Contades wrote that Puisaye had left to avoid an enquiry that he, supported by Talleyrand-Périgord, had demanded be held when Artois arrived (Contades, *Coblenz*, pp.227–228). However this is put in doubt as, if and when the latter would arrive, was not known at that stage.

83 TNA: ADM 1/104: Warren to Nepean 1–3 [?] September.

84 Corbett (ed.), *Private Papers*, p.104, Warren to Spencer 11 September.

85 TNA: HO 69/22: Puisaye to Bouillon, Houat, 30 August; the letter was to be delivered by Chambray who would be able to explain matters more fully to Bouillon.

86 TNA: ADM 51/1118: *Pomone* log.

passed a fleet with a huge convoy of transports carrying troops heading for the bay, thus vindicating Warren's decision to stay, because a new effort was to be made. The *Swan*, which had been sent with dispatches, also brought some practical relief for Warren's crews as she was loaded, apparently on the master's own initiative, with fresh vegetables which, although only sufficient to supply the ships with what was needed for two days, were in perfect condition so particularly effective in countering scurvy.[87]

Although, the following day, Warren had sent HMS *Lively* with pilots on board to find the fleet and bring it into Quiberon Bay, he was still without any orders from the Admiralty as to how he was to proceed. So on 10 September he informed them that, as a result, he had embarked the troops, destroyed the forts and in four days' time, 'I shall proceed … sending the Troops and Chasse Marées to Guernsey and Jersey, under convoy of the Leda and Lively, the Ordnance and Hay Ships to Portsmouth with the Thunderer and accompany the remainder to Plymouth.'[88] However, that very day he received a message from Captain Charles Stirling of HMS *Jason* that he, having been joined by the *Lively* and in company with the *Arethusa*, was off Belle-Île with a convoy of 123 transports, with the Comte d'Artois and Major General Welbore Ellis Doyle. Warren immediately sent the frigates, *Leda* and *Galatea* and the brig, *La Trompeuse*, with several chasse marées with more pilots 'to conduct them into the Bay.'[89] It was to be the next day that Warren finally received the Admiralty's orders.[90]

The Comte d'Artois and Light Cavalry

The Comte d'Artois, since the death of his nephew on 8 June 1795, had become heir to the throne as his brother, Louis, was childless and so he was distinguished by the further title of Monsieur. On 19 June, six days after Puisaye had sailed for France, Grenville, on behalf of the British Government, informed him the expedition had gone to supply the royalists in Brittany with arms so that they would rise in such strength 'that His Royal Highness can put himself at their head without compromising too much.'[91] His chance to take a lead in the restoration of the monarchy in France was no longer a vague promise. Then, when the news of the successful landing had reached London on 5 July, secret instructions were prepared for Lieutenant General David Dundas, commanding the British forces that remained in Germany.[92] He was informed of the landing, that Bretons had joined the troops, and that

87 TNA: ADM 1/104: Warren to Nepean 8 September. Warren commended Sarmon who had 'conducted himself with great attention upon this occasion' (Warren to Nepean 10 September); he was later to describe him as an 'eccentric character' (Warren to Nepean 17 October).

88 TNA: ADM 1/104: Warren to Nepean 10 September.

89 TNA: ADM 1/104: Warren to Nepean 10 September.

90 TNA: ADM 1/104: Warren to Nepean 11 September.

91 Hutt, *Chouannerie*, p.238, Grenville to Bute 12 June.

92 He was a substantive major general but had the local rank, on the continent, of lieutenant general from 1 December 1794, however this appointment was only shown in the Army List of 1796.

the government wanted 'to take immediate measures for enabling the Count d'Artois to join the [royalist] Army.' He was told it was the King's command,

> to desire that you will communicate to His Royal Highness the pleasing intelligence conveyed to you in this letter, and that you will inform Him that one of His Majesty's Ships of War will forthwith be ordered to proceed to the Elbe, in order to receive His Royal Highness, with His Servants and Baggage, and to convey Him, in the first instance, to Spithead, where, on His arrival, His Royal Highness will be made acquainted with the subsequent intelligence which may reach us from Brittany respecting the state of affairs in that Province, by which His further proceedings must of course be regulated.[93]

Dundas was further advised to suggest that Artois keep his entourage 'to as small a number as his situation and circumstances will admit.' Although it was hoped these proceedings would remain secret it was recognised that should that not happen Artois 'will receive from every quarter pressing applications for permission to follow His fortune'.[94] True to form, the news immediately leaked from the prince's circle and applications flooded in from émigrés who wished to share the prestige of being part of a military expedition with a member of the immediate royal family at its head.

It had been intended that a force of émigré light cavalry would follow the Second Division from Germany and on 23 June Lieutenant General Dundas was informed:

> It being judged necessary that a Detachment from the French Regiments of Light Cavalry, now on the Continent under your command should be embarked in order to join [the Second Division] … I am commanded to signify to you His Majesty's pleasure that a force consisting of not less than 500 Hussars is to be held in readiness for Embarkation as soon as the transports, destined to receive them, shall arrive … I have not specified any particular Corps, though it would certainly be proper, if equally convenient in other respects, to give the preference to the Hussars of Rohan, not only because it will be an advantage that they not be separated from the Regiment of Infantry of the same name, but on account of their strength which, by the returns I have seen, is nearly equal to the number required. – The decision on this point is, however, left to your discretion …[95]

He was warned that it would be at least two weeks before transports would be available. Nevertheless in anticipation that the cavalry would embark at Lehe, now part of Bremerhaven, on the Weser estuary, the strongest of the foreign and émigré cavalry regiments moved to a camp, further up the river. Louis-Joseph-Amour de Bouillé, colonel of the Uhlans Britanniques and son of the general who suppressed the Nancy mutiny, recalled,

93 TNA: WO 1/173: Horse Guards to D. Dundas undated July; Robert, *Expédition*, p.219 quotes a letter with the same information, and using the same phraseology, which he states was from Grenville to Artois dated 7 July.

94 TNA: WO 1/173: Horse Guards to D. Dundas undated July.

95 TNA: WO 6/25: Henry Dundas to David Dundas 23 June.

> … at the end of June, I received the order to go with my regiment to Hoya, to be part of a cavalry camp that was to be formed near this town … this camp, composed of my regiment of uhlans and of those of the Rohan, Choiseul, Hompesch and Salm hussars, was under the orders of Major General Lord Cathcart, who had also under his command several regiments of English cavalry cantoned in the area.[96]

Dundas soon learnt that a further delay, until the end of the month, was anticipated, resulting in the hussars still waiting when Artois learnt that he was also to leave for the same destination.[97] On 15 July he went to the camp at Hoya, accompanied by his eldest son, the Duc d'Angoulême, who described the ceremony that resulted:

> On the 15th, my father arrived at seven o'clock and reviewed twenty-five squadrons which rendered him all honours. Lord Cathcart was at their head, sabre in hand. There were two thousand five hundred horses in all, formed in four squadrons of light horse [British Light Dragoons], four squadrons of Choiseul Hussars, four squadrons of Rohan Hussars, two of the Uhlans Britanniques, four of the Salm Hussars, and three of the Hompesch Hussars. Lord Cathcart formed in close column the three regiments of Choiseul, Rohan and Uhlans Britanniques which were to embark, and then he presented them to my father … [who] addressing the oath, said 'Messieurs, the English general has the grace to assemble you so that I can announce that H.B.M. will allow you to embark with me to follow the path of honour.' At these words, the air was rent with shouts of "Vive le Roi! Vive Monsieur!" The three colonels, the Duc de Choiseul, the Prince de Rohan and the Comte Louis de Bouillé drew their sabres, had their regiments place them in their hands, and said to them: 'Swear that you will be true to God, to the King, and that you will follow Monsieur everywhere' they shouted 'Yes, we swear it!'[98]

Finally, on 26 July, Lieutenant General Dundas reported that not only the cavalry was about to embark but also that Artois had sailed on HMS *Asia* for England.[99] The number of transports that had arrived meant that not only more light cavalry could embark but also men, some accompanied by their families, who belonged to, among others, two further cadre corps. So, on 2 August, Dundas wrote that he had 'ordered nine hundred Horses (of which 180 belong to Officers) Uhlans and Choiseuls to march … They will begin to embark on Tuesday [4 August], and I hope may sail by the End of the Week – Besides these, the Transports will bring three or four hundred People assembled by d'Allonville and Others'.[100] The departures were reports by a French republican agent:

96 TNA: WO 1/173: D. Dundas to H. Dundas 28 June and Louis-Joseph-Amour Marquis de Bouillé, *Souvenirs et fragments pour servir aux mémoires de ma vie et de mon temps* (Paris: Société d'histoire contemporaine, 1908), Vol.II, pp.256–257.

97 TNA: WO 1/173: Dundas to Dundas 6 July.

98 Abel Hugo, *Vie anecdotique de S.M. Charles X* (Paris: J M Maurice, 1824), pp.59–61. Duc d'Angoulême to his younger brother, the Duc de Berry.

99 TNA: WO 1/173: D. Dundas to H. Dundas 26 July.

100 TNA: WO 1/173: D. Dundas to H. Dundas 2 August.

> The night was spent in packing their poor rags and, on the 27th, four to five hundred knights of Saint-Louis and Malta, priests and pastors, women, girls and children were packed in about twenty boats for Bremerlehe, where all are already on the open seas for the counter-revolution in Brittany. This embarkation was in truth the most lamentable spectacle in the world, being accompanied by a frenzy that approached madness.[101]

The men referred to in such unflattering terms were of the cadre corps of Allonville and Quiefdeville (artillery) reported to be 250 and 47 men, respectively, along with a further 50 men of Williamson's corps.[102]

The light cavalry that finally sailed were detachments from the Uhlans Britanniques and the Hussards de Choiseul under the command of Bouillé, the senior hussar officer being *Major* Léonard-Philippe Desvieux. Both units had been formed to supplement the British Army when it was fighting in the Low Countries. The capitulation for the Uhlans Britanniques, which as the name suggests were armed with lances, being dated 2 November 1793 and that for Choiseul 15 March 1794. They saw a good deal of service, particularly during the retreat into Germany during the previous winter. The reason that the Régiment de Rohan did not go, according to Bouillé, was that '... its colonel, the prince de Rohan-Montbazon, ... refused, doubtless, to go over to Brittany, so as not to find himself there under the orders of the chiefs who had already been sent there, particularly M.M. d'Hervilly and Sombreuil, or in concurrence with them.'[103]

Table 15: 'Report of cavalry left camp for embarkation at Bremerlehe, 2 August 1795'.[104]

	Uhlans Britanniques	Hussards de Choiseul	Total
Officers	17	11	28
Staff	2	1	3
NCOs and trumpeters	17	21	38
Rank and file	310	372	682
Servants, women and vivandières	47	38	85
Horses	431	474	905

The detachments embarked on 28 transports on 4 and 5 August 'and the convoy, which was also composed of quite a large number of other ships, steered, on 6 August, for the coast of England.'[105] The remainder of the two regiments as well as other units of émigré light cavalry, including those of the Béon and Damas, remained in Germany, expecting that in time they would also be sent to France. In addition, the two strongest of the white cockade

101 Jean Kaulek and Alexandre Tausserat-Radel (eds), *Papiers de Barthélemy, ambassadeur de France en Suisse, 1792–1797, publiés sous les auspices de la Commission des Archives des Affaires étrangères* (Paris: F Alcan, 1894), vol.V, p.408, report from the agent Sturler dated Bremen, 30 July.

102 *The Times*, 20 August 1795.

103 Bouillé, *Souvenirs*, vol.II, p.264.

104 TNA: WO 1/173: report 2 August.

105 Bouillé, *Souvenirs*, vol.II, p.265.

regiments raised on the Continent, Castries and Mortemart, were brought towards the coast to be ready to embark as well. They would all soon learn of the defeat at Quiberon, news which the troops who had embarked left without knowing.[106]

HMS *Asia* arrived at Spithead where Artois and his suite immediately transferred to HMS *Canada* on 10 August.[107] Monsieur had to remain on board ship as he was at risk, should he land, of being arrested on behalf of his creditors for unpaid debts. Nevertheless his arrival caused a stir among the émigrés in London who 'had readily named [him] their El Cid' and many travelled to gather around him so that when he transferred to HMS *Jason*, on 15 August, he was accompanied by 'a large suite.'[108] In the end he was surrounded by about 40 senior officers, 'of the staff, or of the prince's court to say more accurately.'[109] It was a busy time for the crew of the *Jason*:

> [17 August] Saluted the Marquess of Buckingham [with] 11 guns on his coming on board and shortly after saluted His Royal Highness the Prince of Wales with 21 guns on his coming on board. At noon we hoisted the Royal Standard when the whole fleet saluted. PM at 2 the Prince of Wales left the ship when we hauled down the Standard & saluted him with 21 guns.
>
> [18 August] Saluted Monsieur with 21 guns on his going out of the ship and on his return.
>
> [24 August] His Royal Highness the Duke of Gloucester came on board, hoisted the standard & saluted [with] 21 guns & 21 more on his going.[110]

The Duc d'Angoulême was able to go ashore as described by an émigré at Romsey in a letter dated 13 August:

> We had yesterday the pleasure of seeing the Duke d'Angouleme and Lord Moira; they have reviewed the troops encamped between Southampton and this place, and we expect them this day to review the French troops on cantonments here, consisting of the Gentlemen of Normandy, commanded by M. Du Tressor [sic]; and those of Brittany, under the orders of the Prince de Leon, besides the remains of the regiments of Du Dresnay and d'Hector.[111]

A New Expedition Prepares

The British Government's response to the news of the defeat that had arrived on 29 July had been decided by 11 August when Moira was given his instructions. While he remained in England he was to send an advance force from his corps, under the command of Major General Doyle, who was to

---

106 Bouillé, *Souvenirs*, vol.II, p.265, and Kaulek and Tausserat-Radel (eds), *Papiers de Barthélemy*, vol.V, p.426, Sturler bulletin 13 August.
107 TNA: ADM 1/103: Curtis to Nepean 11 August.
108 Bouillé, *Souvenirs*, vol.II, p.266 and TNA: ADM 51/1164: *Jason* log.
109 Bouillé, *Souvenirs*, vol.II, p.294, also see p.275.
110 TNA: ADM 51/1164: *Jason* log (dates have been converted from 'ships' days).
111 *Saunders's News-Letter*, 21 August.

sail with four battalions of infantry; the 12th, 1/78th, 80th and 1/90th Foot, with an artillery detachment, which were to embark in transports already at Southampton.[112] They were then to sail for Quiberon Bay, accompanied by a squadron commanded by Rear Admiral Sir Henry Harvey who was to relieve Lord Bridport.

On 19 August, the British infantry units embarked, and then sailed to the rendezvous at Spithead the next day.[113] The return shows that the four infantry battalions boarded with just under 3,300 all ranks, as well as 194 women and 110 children.[114] They were to draft further men, in a similar fashion as before, from the 112th, 113th and 127th Foot and this caused delay. Moira explained, 'For we are obliged to investigate all their claims on their old Regiments for fear of Mutiny.'[115] Furthermore, as Colonel Thomas Graham of the 90th, explained, 'We were to have been made up to 1,000 each [battalion], but the fresh drafts sent us were so execrable that more than one-half were rejected'.[116] Other men had been discharged, so the exercise had no effect as shown in the monthly return of 1 September.

Table 16: 'Monthly Return of the Army Commanded by Major General Doyle on Board Transports at Sea' 1 September 1795.[117]

Unit	Officers & staff	NCOs & drummers	Rank & file present & fit for duty	Total	Change since 12 August (infantry only)
12th Foot	35	89	667	791	-25
1/78th Foot	31	72	718	821	-33
80th Foot	29	88	599	716	-22
1/90th Foot	25	79	842	946	+39
Artillery	5	5	93	103	
14th Light Dragoons	1	5	59	65	
Horse Dept.	3	14	417	434	

In addition to the 'Horse Department,' made up of commissary officers, artificers and drivers, there were 12 civilian administrators and artificers, these and the artillery had 609 horses and the 14th Light Dragoons had 115 present.

Some officers from the units of the Second Division were part of the expedition, for example the colonel and at least three officers of Périgord, and Louis-Joseph-Jean-Baptiste de la Boëssière Comte de Chambors, the recently appointed major of the Damas Regiment.[118] Officers and men of the three white cockade regiments of the first expedition also embarked. Records do

112 TNA: WO 1/176: Dundas to Moira, 11 August.
113 Cook, 'St George Diary', p.246.
114 TNA: WO 1/176: 'Embarkation Return of the Corps detached under the Command of Major General Doyle, Southampton, 19th Augt. 1795.'
115 TNA: WO 1/176: Moira to Huskisson (private), 14 August.
116 Alexander Delavoye, *Life of Thomas Graham Lord Lynedoch* (London: Richardson & Co., 1880), p.93, Graham to Cathcart 26 August.
117 TNA: WO 17/234.
118 Villeneuve-Laroche-Barnaud, *Mémoires*, vol.II, p.294, and Hughes de Bazouges and Alistair Nichols, *For God and King A History of the Damas Legion (1793–1798)* (Warwick: Helion and Company, 2021), p.203.

not show the numbers from Dresnay but Montmuran, who had recruited for the regiment at Portchester and was now a *capitaine*, sailed.[119] Those for Hector show that a *capitaine*, nine *lieutenants* and two *sous-lieutenants* embarked on 'the 2nd Expedition' one of the *lieutenants* being Carrey d'Asnières, who stated in a later return of service, 'Mr. Hector united under my orders all the men of his regiment remaining at the depot and those coming from the hospitals. We were employed in the second Expedition of Quiberon, where His Royal Highness Monsieur was ...' suggesting a substantial number of other ranks embarked.[120] *Capitaine* de Saint Paer, two *lieutenants*, six *sous-lieutenants*, an *aide-chirurgien*, and 84 other ranks from Hervilly embarked on 22 August.[121] A difficulty with the Transport Board had delayed their embarkation.[122] It had been intended that the Régiments de Castries and Mortemart would have also sailed with this force but they had still not left Germany.[123] However, the future of the white cockade regiments was in doubt, Dundas informing Moira on 24 August:

> As it does not appear possible that the regiments commanded by Messrs. D'Hervilly, Du Dresnay and Hector should be employed again on their present footing, it will not be necessary to send the officers belonging to them to join their corps at Houat, or that they should accompany the expedition unless they are embarked as volunteers to join the Royalist Army, or with the permission of Monsieur.[124]

Moira declined to follow this order as, 'The officers ... have men embarked under their care, and it might be impracticable, just at the moment of departure, to make any other arrangement for keeping these soldiers in order during the passage.'[125]

On the face of it, the cadre corps were not to be part of this expedition, on 9 August lacking 'clothing, appointments and necessaries of any kind' Williamson and Trésor were to return to the Channel Islands where their stores were, while Léon was to remain at Romsey.[126] Then, rather bizarrely given their condition, the earlier idea of their being used to threaten the French coast was briefly revived on 11 August and then shelved a week later.[127] As late as 21 August the Comte du Trésor had not been told that he and his corps were not, in fact, going to the Channel Islands, although he had suspected it for quite some time. By then the cadres were at Spithead, Trésor had embarked on 18 August and joined Williamson which was already at

---

119 Robert, *Expédition*, pp.342–343, Montmuran to his sister 13 September.
120 TNA: WO 12/11741: Hector contrôles and ANF: MAR/C/7/53: dossier 24 Carrey d'Asnières memorandum 10 July 1826. He was soon promoted *capitaine* in the regiment.
121 TNA: WO 12/11951: and WO 12/11681: Hervilly contrôles.
122 Aspinall, *George III*, vol.II, p.384, Moira to Dundas 19 August.
123 Aspinall, *George III*, vol.II, p.373 Moira to Dundas 13 August.
124 Aspinall, *George III*, vol.II, p.392 Dundas to Moira secret 24 August.
125 Aspinall, *George III*, vol.II, p.392 Moira to Dundas 25 August.
126 Aspinall, *George III*, vol.II, p.369 Moira to Dundas 9 August, Dundas to Moira 10 August and TNA: HO 69/23: Trésor to Bouillon 14 August.
127 TNA: ADM 1/103: Strachan to Nepean 18 and 20 August.

the anchorage while Léon embarked at Southampton at the same time as the British units.[128] The most likely explanation for sending the cadre corps with the expedition is that they were to make up for the lack of émigré infantry to accompany Artois, in the absence of Castries and Mortemart, and that the decision was made at the eleventh hour.

This expedition was again to carry ample supplies for the royalists, there were even 80 waggons on board the ships, most of which were intended for transporting them to Charette, who was also to receive £50,000 in dollars. Artois was also provided with £10,000 for his use and that of his suite, all of whom were also supplied with camp equipment and accessories.[129]

Meanwhile, as the transports with the cavalry and the other émigrés were making slow progress in the North Sea, émigrés of distinction continued to arrive at the North German ports with the intention of joining the expedition. One was the Louis-Henri Duc de Bourbon, only son of the Prince de Condé, who arrived at Bremen, and whom Artois had asked to join him as his 'right hand and companion in arms' and regretting that they could not have sailed together.[130] The republican agent at Bremen reporting, 'The Duc de Bourbon is still here with his fleur de lysed generality. … they await Monsieur's orders from Spithead. The duke and his generality are full of hope that the great expedition will still take place and succeed; the one which failed at Quiberon was only a prelude'.[131] The transports with the cadres from Germany arrived at Spithead on 22 August and those with the cavalry arrived with a second convoy in the morning of 26 August.[132] Harvey had already been given his sailing orders on 25 August so, when he acknowledged receiving them the next day, he reported:

> I am now getting under sail the Squadron under my command and the Convoy that were assembled at Spithead. The Transports having on Board the Foreign Cavalry … arrived this morning from The Downs, but as they have scarce any water or forage remaining on Board, they cannot be ready for sailing for some days. I therefore avail myself of the present favourable wind that no time may be lost …

Thus, Harvey was preparing to leave without the cavalry, leaving instructions that their transports be supplied with water and forage 'with the utmost expedition.'[133] He set sail from Spithead that day but the winds immediately dropped so the squadron and convoy had to anchor off Saint Helens on the other side of the Solent.[134]

128 TNA: HO 69/23: Trésor to Bouillon 14 and 21 August and *The Times* 20 August, report dated 18 August.

129 Aspinall, *George III*, vol.II, pp.374, 385 and 387, 14, 19 and 20 August.

130 TNA: FO 74/10: extract from a letter Artois to Bourbon 20 July.

131 Kaulek and Tausserat-Radel (eds), *Papiers de Barthélemy*, vol.V, pp.426–427, Sturler's bulletin 13 August.

132 TNA: WO 1/392: memo of *Lieutenant-colonel* de Perthuis, officer commanding Quiefdeville, 3 December and *The Oxford Journal*, 29 August. The ships form Germany had been brought from The Downs, off Kent, in different convoys.

133 TNA: ADM 1/103: Harvey to Nepean 26 August.

134 TNA: ADM 1/103: Harvey to Nepean 28 August.

Bouillé was already concerned about the cavalry horses which had been embarked for three weeks and he sought to ameliorate their situation:

> I thought it necessary, in the interest of the service as well as in theirs, to ask the general [Moira] to have them disembark, so that they could recuperate. I made the observation to him that the continuation of their stay on board, where they were very poorly and where they would probably be kept for a long time, by the uncertainty to find a secure disembarkation point, would only diminish their number and render what remained of this cavalry more embarrassing than useful, whereas on landing them they would recover, thus being in a state to render service, on their arrival on the coasts of France, where they could be transported promptly, immediately it was judged to be necessary. Lord Moira agreed with my grounds and told me that after having informed his government of them he would give me the order to disembark the cavalry. Unfortunately for my regiment and that of Choiseul ... The Comte d'Artois was informed of it and, fearing to see his retinue diminished thus, which only was to serve to add to the number of witnesses and victims of his pusillanimity, he immediately sent to London ... one of his aides de camp, to oppose it, in which he succeeded.[135]

Artois backed this intervention up with a letter to Bouillé, on 27 August, in which he pressed him, '... to employ ... all the means that can rest with you, to press and hasten, as much as possible, the embarkation of the objects that are indispensable for the prompt departure of the two regiments.'[136] He could not order him to do so as the two cavalry units and Allonville's cadre had been specifically placed under Doyle's command.[137]

However, Artois got his way as, despite Harvey's efforts, contrary winds had prevented the ships from leaving the Saint Helens anchorage. The delay also gave Artois the opportunity to receive French émigré officers who had returned from Quiberon on the *Robust* as she arrived at Spithead in the morning of 28 August.[138] Vossey went on board the *Jason* where he,

> ... was presented to his august Prince, with M. de Tromelin, capitaine aide-major to the régiment du Dresnay, and several other officers. His Royal Highness said the most flattering things to them, and received from them, with the most profound sorrow and a visible grief, the details that they gave him on the fatal and so unfortunate Quiberon expedition. H.R.H. Monsieur testified, tears in his eyes, how much he regretted the loyal and true Frenchmen who ended up shedding their blood and gloriously sacrificing their life in this disastrous campaign.[139]

It was to be only on the morning of 31 August that the ships finally managed to leave and set sail for Quiberon Bay.[140] The fleet consisted of Harvey's line-

135 Bouillé, *Souvenirs*, vol.II, p.269.

136 Bouillé, *Souvenirs*, vol.II, p.270.

137 Aspinall, *George III*, vol.II, p.383, Moira to Doyle 17 (?) August.

138 Of the crew of the *Robust*, nine men had died on the voyage home and 212 men had to be immediately sent to Haslar Hospital suffering from scurvy – Wetton, 'Journal', p.70.

139 Vossey, 'Récit Fidèle', p.12.

140 TNA: ADM 51/1164: *Jason* log.

of-battle ships, HMS *Prince of Wales* (98 guns), *Queen Charlotte* (100), *Prince* (98), *Russell* (74) and *Orion* (74) and the convoy of the 38-gun frigates HMS *Jason* and *Arethusa*, and the lugger HMS *Experiment* (10), with around 130 transports.[141]

Doyle was originally going to be the only British general with the expedition but on Moira's suggestion Major General The Honourable Francis Needham went as second-in-command, and he also had the French émigré officer, La Rozière, as an advisor.[142] The orders that Moira had been instructed to give Doyle were explicit and detailed, clearly dictating the conduct of the expedition: Doyle was firstly to liaise with Warren to ascertain the respective forces operating in the area. He was then, if 'safe and practicable' to sail, under Warren's protection, to the Île de Noirmoutier with his units and as many of the émigré troops as he thought 'expedient'. There Warren was to arrange for a reconnaissance of the island's defences and, if both commanders agreed that it could be done 'without material loss or risk to the Troops or Squadron', the island was to be taken. However, if either of the officers 'shall judge that the attempt will be attended with material difficulty or hazard, or if, after having possession he shall find, contrary to expectation, that the post cannot afford entire security against any probable attack which may be made upon it, he is in such case to return with the troops under his command' to the south coast of England. In the case of success there were further explicit instructions. As Graham had been instructed previously, the 'White flag of France' was to be hoisted alongside that of Britain and for it to be made publicly clear that the island was held on behalf of the 'Royal and Catholic Army'; its possession was only to facilitate the landing of supplies to the royalist forces.[143]

The royalist leaders were to be told that despite Britain having had the intention to send a larger force of British troops to act alongside the royalists this was no longer the case after the defeat at Quiberon and the Franco-Spanish peace treaty, which necessitated the protection of British interests in the West Indies. Thus 'it will probably not be practicable to take any other Step than that of holding possession of Noirmoutier as a point of communication for the purpose of supplying succours of Arms, Ammunition & Money.' This was to enable the royalist leaders to make an informed decision on their future conduct. The British would quit Noirmoutier if the royalists decided to give up the struggle or it was no longer safe to remain. In conclusion Moira was told to 'strongly inculcate on his [Doyle's] mind the necessity of making no attempt which can expose to any material risk the valuable body of British Troops which will be entrusted to his command.'[144] The following day Moira received additional instructions to impart to Doyle, as information from Warren indicated that the Île d'Yeu could be taken in addition, or as an alternative, to Noirmoutier. All previous instructions and caveats now

141 TNA: ADM 51/1102: *Arethusa* log.

142 Aspinall, *George III*, vol.II, p.375, Dundas to Moira 15 August and p.383, Moira to Doyle 17 (?) August.

143 TNA: WO 1/176: Horse Guards to Moira, 11 August.

144 TNA: WO 1/176: Horse Guards to Moira, 11 August.

applied to the taking and holding of this island as well.[145] Doyle was also given specific instructions by Grenville, the Foreign Secretary, as to how he was to work with the prince,

> ... as soon as you shall have reached the coast of France you are to impart to Monsieur all the intelligence you may receive respecting the state of that kingdom; to inform him of all the plans which you may be led to adopt in consequence; and to concert measures with him in every respect that may not be a departure from these instructions.[146]

Doyle's operational instructions were explicit with the only decision left to his discretion being whether to land, and even in this it was clearly stated that he had to avoid any risk to the British troops. The decision he was to convey to the royalists – that the British would restrict military support to securing the conduit for supplies – had only been made under the changed circumstances appears to have been disingenuous. Moira's letter to Pitt, of 30 July, indicates that it had been considered earlier and at least around the time of Graham's embarkation, when he wrote,

> ... when you, Sir, proposed to me to hold with a small force the Peninsula of Quiberon or some other post for the sole purpose of forwarding stores to the Royalists whilst they should take the active part in the field, I did say that I could not voluntarily accept such a mission tho' I must obey were it enjoined. This reluctance did not rest solely upon the idea that the function was a part so secondary as to be humiliating to the British General, but, from the material consideration that I should thence be to appearance implicated in a plan very generally (tho' I am sure groundlessly) ascribed to Ministers; namely, that the object was only to weaken France by fomenting civil war, without aiming at the completion of our professed purpose. The participation in such a scheme would have been justly degrading, and I thought, Sir, that upon my representation you concurred in the propriety of avoiding any measures of so doubtful an appearance.[147]

The decision had already been made to take a measure 'of so doubtful an appearance.' Doyle was indeed, if practicable, to secure the supply of the royalists, chiefly Charette, to pursue the civil war in France. The continued retention of the rest of Moira's corps in Southern England and their preparations to land in France were a sham designed to hide a change of strategy. These troops were to be sent to the West Indies under another commander and Moira considered his own position untenable. On 14 August he asked, both officially and unofficially, to retire from his post, in the latter case writing, 'For Heaven's sake get me now removed from this Command as soon as possible.'[148] Sir Ralph Abecromby took command of the troops

145 TNA: WO 1/176: Horse Guards to Moira, 12 August.

146 Aspinall, *George III*, vol.II, p.383, Moira to Doyle 17 (?) August.

147 Aspinall, *George III*, vol.II, p.367, Moira to Pitt, 30 July.

148 Aspinall, *George III*, vol.II, p.374, Moira to Pitt, 14 August and TNA: WO 1/176: Moira to William Huskisson, Dundas's undersecretary, 14 August.

destined for the West Indies on 25 August and, although relieved, Moira remained for three or four days longer to ensure a smooth hand over.[149]

Despite the efforts to keep secret the object of the expedition, British newspapers reported that it was heading to Noirmoutier before Doyle had even departed. So, on 20 August, fearing that the French republicans would be prepared, Dundas adjusted his instructions to Doyle. If he had to 'relinquish' all his intended attacks he was to remain in Quiberon Bay, if possible, liaise with Charette and in conjunction with him he could land the British troops at a port or other place, even if it was not be held permanently, to enable the royalists to receive the supplies. As well as avoiding any risk to his troops, the caveat was that he was to have Dundas's approval before he attempted anything outside his original instructions.[150]

British officers sailing with the expedition were sceptical of the prospect of success, Colonel Thomas Graham writing on 26 August:

> What so small a force can accomplish I am at a loss to guess. It is said we are to try to possess ourselves of Noirmoutier, and keep it as a dépôt to supply Charette. If they are in force the odds are against our attempting to land; and, by what I hear, if we had it, of the extensive posts, it will not be easily kept except with the constant assistance of a fleet. At low water it is fordable to the continent; but it is to be supposed, if we are to be of any use, that Charette must keep possession of the opposite coast.[151]

There was frustration amongst Artois's staff. His aide de camp Armand-Sigismund Comte de Sérent had complained about the small number of British infantry being sent on the expedition:

> I cannot forbear mentioning to you the very great sorrow which I experienced this morning, when I was given to understand that, instead of four thousand men bearing arms, which we were taught to expect … there were not on board the transports a greater number than about three Thousand. … if the fact is true, as I am afraid it is, such deficiency … would be indeed the ruin of an Expedition already reduced to its lowest minimum.[152]

The mood could not have been improved on the voyage, if it was uncomfortable for the men it was worse for the horses, as Doyle reported on September, when the ships were off Ushant, 'I fear we shall find a considerable loss of Horses from the bad weather we have had … some ships have lost six, some eight.'[153]

149 Aspinall, *George III*, vol.II, p.374, Moira to Pitt 25 August.

150 Aspinall, *George III*, vol.II, p.386, Dundas to Moira 'most secret' 20 August.

151 Delavoye, *Life of Thomas Graham*, p.93, Graham to Cathcart 26 August.

152 BL: Add MS 37860: Comte de Sérent, on board the *Jason*, Spithead, to Windham, private and confidential, 25 August.

153 TNA: WO 1/176: Doyle to Dundas. Doyle was able to send the letter after encountering HMS *Indefatigable* which was returning to England.

11

Return

Noirmoutier

As the ships came into Quiberon Bay on the morning of 12 September the arrival of so many vessels was impressive, and this was enhanced by the honours made to welcome royalty. At 3:00 p.m., as Artois boarded the *Pomone* to dine with Warren, the ships of the commodore's squadron fired 21 gun salutes while their crews manned the rigging.

Doyle and Warren conferred immediately. The commodore had received a copy of the general's instructions from Harvey so already knew the restricted parameters Doyle had to operate within. He was to express his frustration to Earl Spencer, 'The number of infantry sent out is rather too small as the orders seem to rather tie up the General from anything that is hazardous, and without some risk in a war like this nothing can be done or expected to succeed.'[1] As for the intelligence Warren shared about the opposing forces in the adjacent regions of western France, it was thought that 18,000 to 20,000 troops who had been released from the Pyrenean frontier were now stationed on the Îles de Ré and Oléron. The assessment was however optimistic about the royalists, particularly Charette, who was thought to have up to 30,000 men at Belleville-sur-Vie, north of La Roche-sur-Yon, and was said to have 'destroyed & dispersed near eight thousand' of the republican forces.[2] So Warren and Doyle wrote to the Vendéen leader to co-ordinate action; the *Concorde* and *Trompeuse* sailing with a chasse marée on the morning of 14 September and landing two couriers the following evening.[3] However, what was not known was that Hoche, who now had overall command with his appointment at the head of the Armée de l'Ouest at the end of August, was renewing active operations in the Vendée.[4]

1 Corbett (ed.), *Private Papers*, p.107, Warren to Spencer 3 October.
2 TNA: WO 1/176: Doyle to Dundas, 15 September.
3 TNA: WO 1/176: Doyle to Dundas, 15 September and ADM 51/1111: *Concorde* log.
4 Hutt, *Chouannerie*, p.358. Hoche was nominated on 29 August and was confirmed in the post two days later; he announced his command to the army in an order of the day on 17 September – Ornano, *Hoche*, p.220.

One immediate concern for Doyle was that, yet again, supplies which should have been embarked were missing, '… the Powder promised did not come with us and everything depends on those people being supply'd with Arms, Ammunition, etc. without which the object of this expedition, tho' successful, would be defected.'[5]

Now in French waters, Artois had royal duties to fulfil, including receiving the surviving senior émigré officers as well as those who had managed to escape from captivity.[6] He also attended a service of remembrance on Houat for the fallen, led by Charles-Eutrope de la Laurencie, Bishop of Nantes, whose brother François had been killed on 16 July serving in Hector. The prince received the welcome and homage of the loyal Bretons, both those who had survived as well as others who had travelled from the mainland to see him.

The condition and demeanour of the soldiers of the white cockade regiments continued to be a concern, Doyle writing on 23 September:

> The Commodore has thought it expedient to send home the sick of the French Corps in the Transports that are ordered to return. He agrees with me that it is better to send the remains of the Regts of Hector, Du Dresnay & D'Hervilly who may perhaps be of more service elsewhere but cannot be employed here with the other French Regts without great inconvenience & perhaps danger.[7]

Despite the arrival of Monsieur and the prospect of renewed activity, the morale of the émigrés in general showed no improvement, with Contades noting, 'Confidence is lost from our side; the means of defence augmented on the other.'[8]

With the theatre of operations shifting eastwards, the responsibilities for the Royal Navy ships increased as the threat from the ports of Brest and Lorient continued while that from Rochefort became more significant. Warren's principal concern was operations on the Vendéen coast but, with shallow approaches and exposed to the elements, the retention of the anchorages in Quiberon Bay was essential to provide places of safety in stormy weather as well as a rendezvous. Indeed, within days, he was firstly asking if he should keep ships off Belle-Île and then if Harvey could take responsibility for safeguarding the roads off Houat and Hoëdic.[9] Despite the focus shifting from Quiberon Bay support for the chouans on its shores continued to be provided. Vessels continued to patrol the waters of the bay and maintain contact with the shore, indeed Madame de Bennes, of Damas, after her escape from Vannes picked up by 'a long boat, which took me to the British fleet' and thus she went onboard the *Arethusa*.[10] Supplies were also landed, the boats of the *Standard* landing 17 barrels of

5 TNA: WO 1/176: Doyle to Dundas 15 September.
6 Villeneuve-Laroche-Barnaud, *Mémoires*, vol.II, p.284.
7 TNA: WO 1/176: Doyle to Dundas, 23 September.
8 Contades, *Coblenz*, p.229.
9 TNA: ADM 1/104: Warren to Nepean, 23 and 27 September.
10 Bennes, *A narrative*, p.45.

powder over three mornings, 23 to 25 September, and in the evening of 3 October a party of marines from the *Arethusa* joined the *Falcon* cutter to protect Vincent Rohu's chasse marée, *Bonport*, as it landed supplies, perhaps including two field pieces and ammunition, as well as men and dispatches that night.[11]

The line-of-battle ships were to remain in Quiberon Bay while the frigates escorted the transports with the British battalions to Bourgneuf Bay and Noirmoutier, so on 15 September the *Thunderer* sent its launches, armed with carronades and complete with crews, one to the *Anson* and the other to the *Jason*, and at 3:00 p.m. Artois and his suite transferred to the *Standard*.[12] He was not to go with this first wave but was to follow soon afterwards, so he wrote to Charette, that day, announcing that within 48 hours he would be leaving the bay to approach Noirmoutier.[13] In the evening of 16 September the frigates, *Pomone*, *Anson*, *Jason*, *Galatea* and *Leda*, accompanied by the *Swinger* and *Teaser* gun-vessels, the *Swan* revenue cutter, 42 transports and 13 chasse marées began to work their way out of Quiberon Bay.[14] Meanwhile, 'the horse transports and some Emigrants under convoy of the *Thunderer* Capt. Bertie, and the *Lively* ... sailed for Quiberon in order to draw all the enemy troops to that quarter'.[15] The feint was successful in that it drew republican troops to the coast and raised alarm with urgent demands for reinforcements.[16]

However, weather, particularly wind, not for the first or last time, interfered with the operations and both flotillas made slow progress, so that Warren returned with the troops to the anchorage off Hoëdic during the course of 20 September. A few days later Major Harness, 80th Foot, described what had happened and the state they were in on board the transport:

> ... the wind setting against us, we were obliged to return hither after four days struggle in which we did not advance more than ten miles. Several of the Ships are in want of water and most of those with Horses on board are not only without it, but in total want of forage. ... We are very fortunately remarkably well, not having a sick man on board. I fancy we are considerably warmer than Hampshire, and having so many men on board for so long a time, to prevent the crowd of them below, I have prevailed upon the Captain to spread awnings over the Decks, under which two thirds of our people sleep while at anchor.[17]

Contact had been made with Charette, and on 17 September two of his officers came aboard the *Concorde* and then, the following morning, joined Warren and Doyle. As a result, on 21 September the *Concorde*, *Trompeuse* and a chasse marée left with arms and ammunition for Charette, which were

11 TNA: ADM 51/1127: *Standard* and ADM 51/1102: *Arethusa* logs.
12 TNA: ADM 51/1103: *Thunderer* and ADM 51/1127: *Standard* logs.
13 Hutt, *Chouannerie*, p.348.
14 TNA: ADM 51/4042: *Teaser* log, among others.
15 Cook, 'St George Diary', p.247.
16 Robert, *Expédition*, p.232.
17 Duncan-Jones (ed.), *William Harness*, pp.81–82, to his wife 23 September.

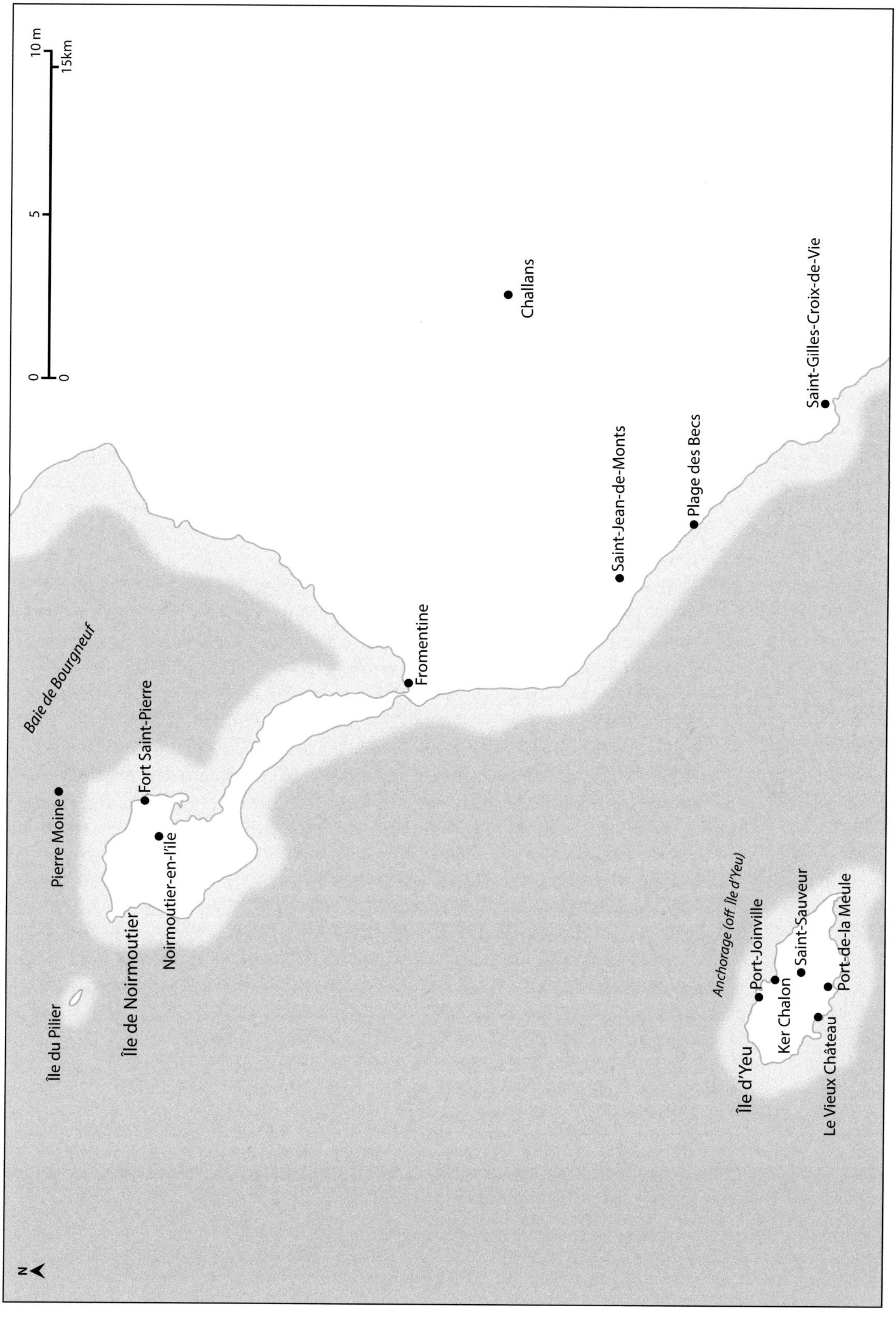

Noirmoutier and the Île d'Yeu.

delivered to the shore by the chasse marée, along with the Vendéen officers, overnight 22 to 23 September.[18]

In preparation for another attempt to approach Noirmoutier on 21 September Warren sent Captain Richard Keats in HMS *Galatea* to Bourgneuf Bay to reconnoitre Noirmoutier with La Roziere, the émigré staff officer, Lieutenant Colonel William Stewart, Doyle's adjutant general, and two other French officers. His tasks included,

> … taking the Soundings & endeavouring to find a place in which a Body of Troops may be disembarked, where they cannot be annoy'd by the Batteries: and you will also mark upon the Chart the position of the Enemy's Cannon. You will likewise procure all the Information possible of the Enemy's Force upon this Island, by seizing some Fishing Boat, or Soldier; or by any other mode in your power …[19]

Warren's flotilla then set sail in the afternoon of 23 September and, as the wind had changed, they arrived off the Pierre Moine rock, north of Noirmoutier, from noon the next day. This time Artois and his staff sailed on the *Jason*, her log entry for that morning illustrates the hazards of sailing along this coast. After passing close to the Île d'Yeu the ship continued towards Noirmoutier which was soon spotted, 'at 9 bore up and ran along the back [south] of the Island for Pilier … at about 2 miles from the land which was a great deal too near as it ought not to be approached within 4 or 5 miles at low water.'[20]

Keats was now given the tasks of preventing communication between the 'south', or more precisely the southwestern, side of Noirmoutier and the mainland and also to neutralise the threat from 'the French Corvette, Luggers and Gun Boats, within the above Island' – small vessels which could interfere with a landing as the frigates could not get close enough to the shore.[21] Keats immediately sent the *Penelope* cutter, accompanied by Captain Lieutenant Julien-Marie de Missy of the French Engineers, to reconnoitre the south side of the island and the next day the *Trompeuse* moved to cover the passage between the island and Fromentine, on the mainland, to prevent any of the enemy's light vessels escaping through and any communication across that passage.[22] Keats then turned his attention to the republican vessels on the other side of Noirmoutier. In the afternoon of 25 September the *Teaser* and *Swinger* set out with some boats to attack two gun-vessels 'placed to command the passage between the Island and the Main.'[23] Progress was slow, the *Teaser* grounding several times before sticking fast until pulled off by Keats with four launches. Once underway again she was under fire from a gun-vessel

18 TNA: ADM 51/1111: *Concorde* log.

19 TNA: ADM 80/136: orders from Warren to Keats, the officers are listed as 'Gen. Roziere, Monr. Voujeron, Massy, Col. Stuart' – the spelling of the last name indicates that little care was taken over French or British names. The second officer has not been identified but the third would have been Missy, mentioned below.

20 TNA: ADM 51/1164: *Jason* log.

21 TNA: ADM 80/136: Warren to Keats 24 September.

22 TNA: ADM 80/136: Keats to Lieutenant Birdwood (*Penelope*) 24 September and Commander Lucius Dawson (*Trompeuse*) 25 September.

23 TNA: ADM 51/1164: *Jason* log.

and two shore batteries that soon found their target and the *Teaser* was hit several times resulting in three men being wounded and her cutter being 'shot to pieces.' She returned fire with her 24-pounders and carronades and at 1:00 a.m. the republican gun-vessel, the 12-gun *Le Rude*, ceased fire and the launches were sent towards her. The republican crew had abandoned her but attempts by the British to warp her off shore failed due to the continuing fire from the island, so they set fire to her and at 4:00 a.m. she blew up.[24]

In the meantime, boats from the frigates attempted to cut out the republican corvette under the cover of the guns of Fort Saint-Pierre, the fort's guns prevented them but the corvette was driven ashore.[25] Another unsuccessful attempt was made to cut the corvette out late on 29 September while other boats fired on the republican camp on the island. Although small scale actions, their intensity can be measured by the boats from the *Jason* expending ninety 18-pound shot as well as 35 grape and 28 'tin shot' (canister) from the carronade.[26]

At 11:30 a.m. on 26 September Colonel Thomas Murray, Doyle's quartermaster general, went with a flag of truce to summon the republican commander, *Général de brigade* Alexis-Aimé-Pierre Cambray, to surrender the island 'to His Royal Highness and His Allies.' Cambray, apparently buying time for reinforcements to arrive from the mainland, accompanied Murray when he returned to the *Pomone*, and asked for a truce for 24 hours which was refused, 'but the Weather being such as to render the attack impossible, no further notice was taken of it [the summons].'[27] No attempt to land was made and the troops, the British contingent, including the survivors of the Loyal Emigrant artillery detachment serving with that of the Royal Artillery, remained onboard the transports in Bourgneuf Bay.[28] There were also detachments drawn from the cadres, 100 from Trésor and 150 from both Léon and Williamson that formed three ad hoc companies, each officered by a *capitaine*, *lieutenant* and *sous-lieutenant* from the respective cadre.[29] The men, the most able to undertake service, had been brought together as a personal guard for Artois, and this was commanded by *Maréchal de camp* Jean-Frédéric de La Tour du Pin Vicomte de La Charce, Gentleman to the Prince.[30] Although as part of the expedition they came under Doyle's command, this ad hoc royal guard came under the immediate direction of Artois's staff.

---

24 TNA: ADM 51/4042: *Teaser* log. One of the men was so seriously wounded that he had to be transferred to the *Pomone* (ADM 51/1118: *Pomone* log). The identification of *Le Rude* is from Winfield, *British Warships in the Age of Sail*, p.132.

25 TNA: ADM 51/1118: *Pomone* log.

26 TNA: ADM 51/1164: *Jason* log.

27 TNA: ADM 51/1118: *Pomone* log, Cook, 'St George Diary', p.247, and TNA: ADM 1/104: Warren to Nepean 28 September.

28 Some historians with republican sympathies have stated otherwise, for instance Amédée de Cesena, *Notice Biographique sur M. Jean-Jacques Duboys* (Angers: Cosnier et Lachèse, 1846), p.25, who described the defence of Noirmoutier as a 'brilliant feat of arms.'

29 TNA: HO 69/23: Trésor to Bouillon 14 and 24 September and HO 69/24: Comte de Pontbellanger to Bouillon 8 October.

30 Grouvel, *Les corps de troupes*, vol.I, p.169.

A decision now had to be made on what the next step was to be. Warren warned Doyle on 27 September, 'that from the appearance of the Weather, Gales of Wind may be expected: in which case it will be perhaps impossible for some days to carry on any Naval Operations' and nothing could be done to stop Noirmoutier being reinforced. He was also concerned that the rest of the transports remained in Quiberon Bay with only two line-of-battle ships to protect them.[31] This was because, after some delay, those with the remnants of Hervilly, Hector and Dresnay, as well as many of the officers of other émigré regiments, and the *Leighton* hospital ship had left the bay on 26 September under convoy of the *Lively* and *Leda*.[32] A council of war was held on 27 September attended by Doyle and Warren with the participation of the officers commanding the four British infantry battalions and artillery detachment as well as Needham, Murray and Stewart. The decision was straightforward, between 'an immediate attack on Noirmoutier, or of taking possession of Isle Dieu [*sic*]' and the key factor was Charette's ability to hold the adjacent mainland, to ensure its security and the distribution of supplies that would be landed there. Charette had already given his response:

> By his Letter to Monsieur it is evident that he thinks it an attempt of great risk and uncertainty to force all the Posts opposite Noirmoutier, should he fail, he points out in strong terms the impossibility of afterwards establishing the communication; without which the Object of Government is frustrated and the possession of the Island become of little value.[33]

The unanimous advice was to secure the Île d'Yeu and Doyle was fully in agreement with the advice, 'it is perfectly my opinion that without co-operation with Charette even a successful attack on Noirmoutier would not answer the intent of the expedition.'[34] Bouillé agreed with the decision contending that it would have been impossible to hold the island at low tide which would have compromised the British and been 'a catastrophe like that of Quiberon' for the émigré troops who accompanied them.[35] In his letter of 28 September to Dundas, informing him of the decision, Doyle gave the Vendéen's message as a reason not to attack Noirmoutier, he also pointed out that 'the weather has been so bad since that even if Charette had approached it would have been impossible to proceed.' He also referred to the means he had at his disposal:

> You know Sir that the number of [British] Troops fall very short of what was thought right to send on the expedition and the French Troops found at Quiberon are equally deficient in Number to what I was taken to believe. The British are

31 TNA: ADM 1/104: Warren to Doyle, 27 September.

32 TNA: ADM 1/104: Warren to Nepean, 23 September and ADM 1/4406: *Aimwell* log.

33 TNA: ADM 1/104: statement of the council's advice, 27 September

34 TNA: ADM 1/104: Warren to Doyle, 27 September.

35 Bouillé, *Souvenirs*, vol.II, pp.287–288.

> only 2870 including sick etc. and the remains of the French Regts to about 200 soldiers. The Cadres are about 280 effective.[36]

What Doyle was not to know was that Charette had suffered a costly defeat at Saint-Cyr-en-Talmondais, between Luçon and Sables-d'Olonne, on 25 September, subsequently described as a 'disastrous day [that] cast discouragement in the [Vendéen] army and provoked divisions among the officers'.[37] Then in the night of 28 September the British commanders received a letter from Charette, probably written before his defeat, as Warren explained:

> [He] it seems is in motion, but wishes us to take possession of Sables d'Olone [*sic*] as the Point of communication. The General and myself however consider the necessity of first taking the Isle Dieu if practicable as a Place of Refreshment for the Troops and Cavalry, who must other ways suffer extremely from being so long onboard.[38]

Île d'Yeu

The decision had already been made to take the Île d'Yeu as at 6:30 p.m. that afternoon, 28 September, the *Galatea*, *Anson*, *Trompeuse*, *Swinger*, *Penelope*, *Teaser* and *Duke of Clarence* sailed with 13 transports carrying the 12th and 80th Foot for the island, under the command of Captain Keats and Major General Needham, and arrived in its anchorage almost 24 hours later, where they joined the *Concorde*. The *Teaser* was immediately sent to patrol off the west side of the island for the next five days.[39] Two officers immediately went ashore under a flag of truce to summon the island's defenders to surrender, Needham described what happened,

> By half past seven O'clock, an Officer of the National Guards, and two principal Inhabitants came aboard the Galatea with their Answer, signifying they were willing to give up the Island with certain exceptions, but would on no account accede to its surrender to Louis the eighteenth as the Lawful King, nor would they allow his having a right to claim any authority over it.
>
> They were therefore sent back and the Island taken possession of about ten O'clock in the name of the King of Great Britain & Louis the eighteenth to which the Mayor assented, saying, we were the strongest, and it rested with us. The British and French flag was hoisted, since which everything has been perfectly quiet.[40]

---

36 TNA: WO 1/176: Doyle to Dundas, 28 September.

37 Beauchamp, *Histoire*, p.281.

38 TNA: ADM 1/104: Warren to Nepean, 28 September.

39 TNA: ADM 80/137: Warren to Keats, 28 September also ADM 51/1117 *Anson*, ADM 51/4042 *Teaser* and ADM 51/1111 *Concorde* logs.

40 TNA: WO 1/176: Needham to Doyle, 30 September.

About 400 British soldiers initially landed and took the island without opposition although one report states that some British picquets were fired upon during the night so the troops 'lay on their arms all that night and patrols were sent over the island to take up all stragglers and all soldiers belonging to the enemy.'[41] Needham reported that the republican forces consisted of four officers and 140 men as well as an armed cutter, armed lugger and some small craft. Conscious that his dispatch may well be published he added that 'the Inhabitants have manifested the most favourable and friendly disposition towards the British Troops who have entered amongst them as friends'.[42] Major Harness, 80th Foot, did not contradict him but portrayed a less glorious picture, '... we found about a hundred Republican troops without any means of defence. ... The Inhabitants of it are said in peace to amount to nearly two thousand men, but the men have been forced to serve in their Navy, and we find scarcely anything but women and children.'[43]

The rest of the troops, baggage and supplies were brought ashore over the next two days, which was just as well as strong gales and heavy rain set in from the morning of 1 October.[44] So the problems with the island's anchorage were immediately tested, 'The bottom all over this anchorage very hard & bad and perfectly open to NW & SE winds nor can it be safe in a gale from any quarter' in foul weather the ships had to return to take shelter in Quiberon Bay.[45] The island did have two ports but Port-de-la Meule, on the south coast, was found to be fit only for chasse marées and although it could hold many of them it was difficult to access in southerly or westerly winds. On the north side the main port, now known as Port-Joinville, was,

> ... capable of receiving at Spring tides about 30 Vessels from 7 to 11 feet draft of water, but at Neep Tides not more than 7 or 8 feet at farthest can be carried into it: And even these Vessels with the Winds from the North and Eastward must be liable to receive injury, the Piers and Rocks on each side not being sufficient to protect them from a Swell at High Water.[46]

Immediately it was recognised that that the island had no resources and that the troops who were camped there would require everything to be delivered for their use; Harness observed:

> A little corn is grown, and I am told there are about eighty head of horned cattle on the Island and about four time that number of sheep, but very small, ... we hear the fish is excellent, but for almost everything else I find they send to the Continent. An Inhabitant ... informed me they were supplyed [*sic*] from

41 *The Hull Advertiser*, 17 October correspondence dated 3 October and Cook, 'St George Diary', p.247.

42 TNA: WO 1/176: Needham to Doyle, 30 September.

43 Duncan-Jones (ed.), *William Harness*, pp.82–83, to his wife 3 October.

44 TNA: ADM 51/1117: *Anson* log.

45 TNA: ADM 51/1164: *Jason* log.

46 TNA: ADM 1/104: Keats to Warren, 30 September.

> thence with every article down to a Match to light their Candles. ... There are an abundance of Hares and Partridges but shooting is forbidden.[47]

The need to ensure the island was supplied, given the constraints imposed by the weather and the island's geography, was to strain the resources of the navy and transports as well as the nerves of the commanders. The taking of the Île d'Yeu did however ease some immediate concerns and at 5:00 p.m. on 1 October Warren arrived in the roadstead with the *Pomone, Jason* and the transports with the troops. The following morning Artois came ashore, with his suite, receiving royal honours, and took up residence in the maison Cadou. His staff occupied other houses in Port-Joinville, while the British and émigré troops camped 500 metres away on a plain beside the sea, between the port and Ker Châlon.[48] A return of the British troops on the island, dated 1 October, shows little change had taken place amongst the men but 19 horses of the 14th Light Dragoons detachment had died over the month. For the first time the Loyal Emigrant artillery detachment, or 'company', was included, having a 1st lieutenant, a 2nd lieutenant, two sergeants, two corporals and 24 gunners present.[49]

By 4 October the troops, supplies and provisions had been landed on the island as well as some equipment from the warships, the *Jason* supplying six carronades with equipment and ammunition to the troops.[50] Warren informed the Admiralty that, 'I am now waiting the Transports and Men of War to join me from Quiberon Bay, when the Cavalry will be immediately landed.'[51] Once empty all these transports would sail to Quiberon Bay and then England, under convoy of the *Jason* and *Arethusa*. Only the shallow-draught vessels and chasse marées that could come into Port-Joinville were to be kept. He continued by explaining how the expedition's aims were to be achieved:

> I shall also give instructions to Lieutenant Smith of the Teazer Gun Boat, ... to convoy every favourable opportunity, any supplies of Ammunition and Stores, that may be sent in my absence to the Coast of La Vendée; ... I shall endeavour to execute the remaining part of my Orders, in conveying to the Continent His Royal Highness Monsieur; the Emigrant Troops; Stores and Ammunition; with all convenient speed ...[52]

In a private letter to Spencer he described the vessels he would be leaving with Lieutenant Smith, who he described as 'an officer of merit and enterprise,' in addition to the *Teaser*, he would have:

47 Duncan-Jones (ed.), *William Harness*, pp.83–84, to his wife 3 October.

48 Paul Comte du Breil de Pontbriand, *Le Comte d'Artois et L'Expédition de l'île d'Yeu* (Paris: Honoré Champion, 1910), p.76.

49 TNA: WO 17/234: return 'Isle d'Yeu' 1 October; the cadres and other émigrés are not shown as they were administered by the prince's staff.

50 TNA: ADM 51/1164: *Jason* log 3 October.

51 TNA: ADM 1/104: Warren to Nepean 4 October.

52 TNA: ADM 1/104: Warren to Nepean 4 October.

> [A] schooner (a large flat vessel taken at Noirmoutier, and fitted to carry a long 24-pounder and two carronades of 18 lbs.) with four launches of my plan, each with an 18-pounder [carronade], and a small hired cutter, to act as a naval establishment for the island … I am also selecting all the light brigs to go into the harbour for the troops in case of necessity …[53]

This arrangement was in place on 12 October when the *Teaser* came into the harbour.[54]

In the late morning of 5 October the *Robust* arrived in the island's anchorage with seven victualler vessels from England. On board was the Duc de Bourbon, with 43 émigré officers. He had travelled to London before going on to Portsmouth to join the ship early on 27 September as she was about to sail; the duke and his suite landed on the Île d'Yeu the morning after their arrival. Warren assigned the *Robust* to Harvey's command and she left for Quiberon Bay on 7 October, after distributing lime juice to the warships at anchor on the roadstead.[55]

There had been no communication from Charette, despite a messenger having been put ashore on 30 September, in marked contrast to the ready exchange that had taken place until this date. Artois and the British commanders were non-plussed, only republican activity could be seen on the shore.[56] On 5 October Artois wrote again to Charette urging him to reply as the opportunity to effectively assist him was closing due to the season. Arms, ammunition, clothing and artillery were ready on suitable boats. Artois asked him to:

> Now indicate a place on the coast where we can carry out the landing of all these objects. General Doyle will have this operation supported and protected by a corps of six hundred English with two hundred French, and we will immediately go to the location that you will have positively indicated, with the means that General Doyle can employ in this operation.
>
> If you find too many difficulties for the prompt execution of this project, or if the circumstances did not allow you to support it with a sufficient part of your army, *I ask you, I order you even*, to designate for me some point on the coast, from Bourgneuf to the Pointe de l'Aiguillon [opposite Île de Ré], where you can bring, on a nominated date, a corps of several hundred horse. *I will be there without fail.* I will join your intrepid army there, and we will then agree on the place where we can join hands with the English and establish a constant and firm communication with them.[57]

Although Charette received the letter he was unable to get any reply to Artois. On 30 September, a republican column had reached his base at Belleville-sur-Vie to find he had gone and from then on he was perpetually on the

53 Corbett (ed.), *Private Papers*, pp.106–107, Warren to Spencer 3 October.
54 TNA: ADM 51/4042: *Teaser* log.
55 TNA: ADM 51/1130: *Robust* log and Wetton, 'Journal', p.70.
56 Breil de Pontbriand, *Comte d'Artois*, p.78.
57 Breil de Pontbriand, *Comte d'Artois*, pp.78–80.

move.[58] His army was spent as an effective force, in conventional terms and on 9 November Hoche informed his government 'What can Charette do? The troops that he commands do not extend beyond a thousand foot-soldiers and three hundred bad cavalrymen.'[59]

On the Île d'Yeu morale among the émigrés, especially the cadres, was low and a letter written on 7 October, although a little obstruse in style, also indicates that their relations with the inhabitants were not particularly positive:

> We are here, since several days, established in one of the villages of the island, after having remained for six weeks at sea. … The inhabitants of the place did not expect our visit: also, their appearance is a little glum. They were careful to hide the few provisions they had. We are obliged to deal out a punch to procure us some food, paying twelve and eighteen sous a pound for bread; but we make sure of avoiding being ripped off. … Judge the rest. Everything is a great secret; but one can see, on certain faces, how weary they are of all this. … There reigns discontent among the cadres: they are obliged to camp, and to serve as soldiers; this does not suit them: also, they are outraged against their chiefs. One takes care of having them pass by individually; this proves how much one is unsure of the result. … I believe the expedition failed, the season being unfavourable, and the ardour very slackened. … October spent, we will occupy ourselves with the means to return.[60]

Many of the younger, and so the fittest, members of the cadres had little or no formal military experience and objected to doing service as soldiers. The lack of clarity about the corps' destination may well have contributed to a lack of preparedness and their deployment, in improvised companies, could not have helped discipline. There may also have been some antipathy towards them from Monsieur's staff, as Trésor had observed, 'to the cadres and their chiefs, those surrounding Monsieur are not our supporters'.[61]

It was just as well that provisions had been landed when they had as more gales arrived on 7 October, and continued for the next six days. Warren informing the Admiralty that he considered 'it almost impossible for the Troops, and Stores to be removed, with the least safety, until Spring.'[62] Once the weather had relented somewhat on 13 October Doyle made it clear to Dundas the precarious situation the troops found themselves in:

> I … must repeat that the existence of this Army depends on an immediate supply. As to the Horses, I fear the supply will come too late, all I have on shore are turned

58 The letter was later found among Charette's possessions (Breil de Pontbriand, *Comte d'Artois*, p.82) and Ornano, *Hoche*, p.225.

59 Breil de Pontbriand, *Comte d'Artois*, p.143.

60 Anon.(ed.), *Olivier d'Argens*, pp.445–446, letter written on 7 October to 'M. Simany de Brantière et Siszhag, negociant of Southampton by Olevry, officer of Artois's army.' The writer has not been identified, the name may, of course, be false to hide his identity which was just as well as the letter fell into republican hands. It is also quoted by Robert, *Expédition*, pp.240–241, but redacted, giving it a different tenor.

61 TNA: HO 69/23: Trésor to Bouillon 14 September.

62 TNA: ADM 1/104: Warren to Nepean 7 October.

> out to take their chance except Thirty belonging to the Dragoons, Artillery and those of the Staff, allowing them a little Indian Corn in addition to what grass they may pick up in this late season and on this barren soil. I have received the very worst accounts of the Cavalry and other Horses not yet disembarked, supposed to be at Quiberon, having twice attempted to come here; when they arrive, they must be all turned loose and I fear a few days will put an end to the existence of the greater number unless a supply arrives. … we have … only Twelve days meat, and when the other Ships arrive they won't make Thirty. I beg leave to remark that all provisions have been taken out of the Transports so that there is no reserve either to reimbark [*sic*] or remain …
>
> The weather continues very bad, and I am sorry to say the Soldiers fall sick very fast, and I fear fatal consequences if we cannot get them under cover, which the defence of the Island will not permit me to do in the straggling Villages; Lumber therefore becomes necessary with meat and the other essential supplys [*sic*]. … Artificers, Lumber, Tools, nails etc. will be wanting should it be thought right to stay.[63]

In his letter of the same day, to the Admiralty, Warren seconded Doyle's plea for material '… to make Huts, or moveable Barracks.' As for the absence of the cavalry, he did not hide his frustration, '… I have been much disappointed, and delayed by the Convoy with the Horse and Provisions, under Captain Bertie in the Thunderer; with the Standard, who had got down as far as Bourgneuf; instead of coming forward, having put back to Quiberon Bay.'[64] The *Thunderer* and *Standard* had sailed from Quiberon Bay, with their charges, in the afternoon of 3 October, arrived in Bourgneuf Bay the next day and then attempted to make progress on 6 October, but after a few hours returned to anchor again, leaving the next day for the anchorage off Hoëdic to arrive that evening.[65] On 13 October Keats, with the *Galatea*, returned to Quiberon Bay to take command there, replacing Bertie.[66] The *Thunderer* sailed for the Île d'Yeu that same afternoon, arriving in the morning of 16 October; the *Standard* followed on 18 October and anchored off the island the following evening, the period of comparative calm allowed the provisions they brought to be landed.[67]

It was now that the Duc de Bourbon requested that Warren arrange passage for him as 'he was obliged to return immediately home; so as to proceed to Germany, in order to join the Army before the end of the Campaign'.[68] The *Anson* took him and his suite to Quiberon Bay on 13 October where, the next day, they transferred to the *Jason* which sailed, after repairing rigging damaged in a gale the day before, on 17 October coming into Plymouth Sound, after a very speedy voyage, two days later when Bourbon went ashore immediately.[69] The real reason for the brevity of Bourbon's stay is not clearly

63 TNA: WO 1/176: Doyle to Dundas 13 October.

64 TNA: ADM 1/104: Warren to Dundas 13 October.

65 TNA: ADM 51/1127: *Standard* and ADM 51/1103: *Thunderer* logs.

66 TNA: ADM 51/1164: *Jason* log and ADM 80/137: Keats' correspondence.

67 TNA: ADM 51/1127: *Standard* and ADM 51/1103: *Thunderer* logs.

68 TNA: ADM 1/104: Warren to Nepean 17 October.

69 TNA: ADM51/1117: *Anson* and ADM 51/1164: *Jason* logs.

stated, after all Louis XVIII had wished to see him beside Artois at the head of the royalists in western France. Bouillé put it down to the duke 'not wishing to associate himself with incapacity that he could thwart neither by his counsel nor his example'.[70] Bourbon, himself, was to claim that Artois had prevented him landing in the Vendée.[71] Perhaps this was from personal animosity, the two had quarrelled at a masked ball resulting in a mutually face-saving duel in 1787, or fear of competition from other branches of the royal family, Bourbon was not only a member of the Condé branch but also linked to that of Orléans by an, albeit unhappy, marriage.

The commanders on the ground, and at sea, were, once again, operating without official instructions from England, on 14 October Major Harness wrote to his wife:

> Days and weeks roll on, my beloved Bessy, without giving us one word from England. General Doyle has not had the scratch of a pen since he left it. When will the joy be given me of hearing from you. We are living in so regular a way on this little Island, one day seems so much like another that a sheet of paper would give the whole history of us since our landing on it. We are all in good health. We look out with anxiety for provisions from England. This small encompassed spot is nearly exhausted. The Emigrants brought nothing from England. Monsieur and Eighteen of his Suite dine every day with General Doyle. He is extremely gay, and has spirits that no trick of fortune can effect. … The wind here is very squally, particularly they say at this season. We have such gusts of wind and violent showers that we can scarcely get our marquees to stand, the poor fellows' tents are constantly blown up.[72]

The men and horses still onboard ships in Quiberon Bay were suffering and on 16 October, in a private letter to Earl Spencer, Warren wrote:

> The cadres are anxious to return home again, and the cavalry owing to their retrograde motion [back to Quiberon Bay] have not been able to disembark, if they were in a state for that purpose which is not the case, as the men are half ill of the flux [dysentery] and horses dying in numbers, that the General [Doyle] from seeing their inability and a want of forage has requested I will return them home again, which I shall do by the first convoy. … I have a hard task to go through in combating the despondency and want of enterprise of the French and the impatience of our own side.[73]

Antoine-Michel d'Amphernet Comte de Pontbellanger, *capitaine* in Léon and the vicomte's elder brother, put the dissatisfaction among the cadres in the bay to being embarked for 'three months onboard transports, reduced to a single ration is a very severe diet for individuals who are not at all

70 Bouillé, *Souvenirs*, vol.II, p.296.
71 Breil de Pontbriand, *Comte d'Artois*, pp.122–129.
72 Duncan-Jones (ed.), *William Harness*, p.84.
73 Corbett (ed.), *Private Papers*, p.110, Warren to Spencer 16 October.

accustomed to this regime of life.'[74] The sickness amongst the cavalrymen affected the Choiseul Hussars in particular, with a hundred men sick on 6 October.[75] Doyle told Warren he only wanted '50 of the best Cavalry' from each of the émigré regiments, on the Île d'Yeu along with the all the British cavalry as well as 100 draught horses with 200 drivers and 20 waggons with their harnesses.[76] It is not clear when these troops and horses arrived on the island.

Suddenly, just after midday on 15 October, an opportunity for more active and profitable service for the warships off the island arose. Early that morning two frigates of Harvey's squadron, HMS *Melampus* and *Latona*, spotted three French republican ships, the frigates *Tortue* and *Néréïde* and the brig-corvette *Eveillé*, off Lorient. They were part of a small squadron returning from a two month cruise. The British frigates immediately gave chase and were soon joined by HMS *Orion* and *Thalia* as the French vessels ran for their home port of Rochefort. Warren was notified at 11:00 a.m. and left the anchorage off the Île d'Yeu with the *Pomone* and *Concorde* to join the chase. Nevertheless, the two French frigates managed to evade their pursuers and eventually reached the safety of the anchorage off the Île d'Aix. The *Eveillé* was not so fortunate as it found itself trapped between the *Pomone* and *Thunderer*, that had been on its passage to the Île d'Yeu, and after receiving broadsides from both warships struck her colours at 6:00 p.m., unable to return fire having jettisoned her 16 or 18 guns while trying to get away. Taken as a prize of the *Pomone* she was brought into the anchorage the next morning.[77] From the prisoners, Warren learnt that the French squadron had captured 12 West Indiamen on their cruise and finally, on 14 October, the *Swan* revenue cutter, carrying his dispatches to England. She had been taken into Lorient by the French squadron's other frigate, the *Forte*. Reporting the capture of the *Swan* to the Admiralty, Warren wrote, 'I lament the situation of Colonel Clive and several French Officers, who were going to England passengers on board her [the *Swan*].'[78]

There is no indication of why Lord Edward Clive, the son of Robert Clive 'of India,' colonel of the Shropshire Militia and a wealthy and well-connected peer, was with the expedition or, otherwise, returning from France.[79] He had been placed onboard the *Forte* and very soon exchanged, his arrival in London being reported in early December.[80] The six other prisoners were on the *Tortue* and so arrived at Rochefort where five identified themselves as Frenchmen and valets to the Comte d'Artois and one claimed to be a British

74 TNA: HO 69/24: Pontbellanger to Bouillon 8 October.

75 Bouillé, *Souvenirs*, vol.II, pp.290–291.

76 TNA: ADM 1/104: Doyle to Warren 17 October.

77 TNA: ADM 1/104: Warren to Nepean 17 October; ADM 51/1111: *Concorde*, ADM 51/1118: *Pomone* and ADM 51/1103: *Thunderer* logs and James, *Naval History*, vol.I, pp.296–298.

78 TNA: ADM 1/104: Warren to Nepean 17 October.

79 There was no other colonel of that surname in the army (The Army List 1795) and a French report named him as 'Lord Clives' (Breil de Pontbriand, *Comte d'Artois*, footnote p.141).

80 As 'Colonel Clive', *The Chester Chronicle*, 4 December 1795. The crew of the *Swan* appear to have been exchanged as Sarmon was killed in 1796 in an action with a privateer off the Isle of Wight (*The Hampshire Chronicle*, 31 December 1796).

officer named Ferdinand Christin. The republican authorities questioned the real identities of all of them especially Christin, to whom his companions were remarkably deferential. He was placed under house arrest while the five others were imprisoned. There was speculation that he may indeed be Artois himself and his escape on 5 November, probably by means of bribery, only added to the speculation.[81] It was decided to send the five remaining prisoners to Versailles, their last place of abode in France, to confirm their identities and on 25 December four set off under guard, one being left behind, gravely ill. However, they were intercepted by an armed gang, assumed to be chouans, who managed to free three of them, so only one, Pierre-Valentin Faiseau, his identity apparently confirmed, was finally judged on 25 September 1796.[82]

Two of the West Indiamen captured by the French squadron had already been retaken, one by the *Orion*, and the other, the *Kent of London*, by the *Pomone* on 9 October, but not by any great exploit of daring British seamanship; 'it blowing very hard, night coming on, and supposing this Squadron to be French, she anchored [in the Île d'Yeu roadstead].' A boat was sent to retake her.[83]

Not a Word from England

The concerns about the troops, and horses, both on the Île d'Yeu and in Quiberon Bay and the crews and ships of all kinds continued unabated as the frequency of bad weather only increased. Although no convoy had been so far appointed, on 18 October Keats requested directions about sending the men of the cadre corps and the Emigrant Artillery who were in the bay to England, to which the general replied:

> With respect to the Cadres I wish them to return to England, Guernsey or Jersey, having with me all those supposed fit to serve, they came with the Expedition contrary to Orders, and the sooner they return the better. The French Artillery that remain with their Commanders, being reported to me as unfit for service should return home. If an Officer or two could be sent of that Corps to this Place it would be advisable.[84]

Two days later Keats informed Warren that 'complaints of the Cadres & other Corps multiplying makes me the more anxiously desirous of receiving your ultimate Commands respecting them …' adding that '… unless some measures be immediately taken the total Destruction of the Horses appears inevitable.'[85] Even more pressing was the notice from Harvey, who had

---

81 Some later historians have supported this, despite the weight of evidence that Artois never left the Île d'Yeu during this time.

82 Breil de Pontbriand, *Comte d'Artois*, pp.131–142.

83 TNA: ADM 1/104: Warren to Nepean 13 October.

84 TNA: ADM 1/104: Keats to Warren 18 October with Doyle's comments added.

85 TNA: ADM 80/137: Keats to Warren 20 October. He addressed the complaints in his letters to *Lieutenant-colonel* de Perthuis, officer commanding Quiefdeville, of 19 October and to Captain Robinson, 20 October (also TNA: ADM 80/137).

sheltered with his squadron in the bay since 9 October and was leaving on 21 October, that he was taking his warships further out to sea due to the seasonal weather and so could not guarantee the safety of the transports held in the bay.[86] Warren immediately, on 20 October, ordered that the transports with the émigré units return to England. However four days later Keats reported that 'the Continuance of the bad Weather & Westerly Winds has prevented them from sailing.'[87] Despite Doyle having already agreed to the measure, in reply to Keats letter of 18 October, there was resistance from the commanders of the two cavalry units to the destruction of the horses in the worst health, so the healthier would have sufficient to eat, as Keats explained, '... although they acquiesce in the propriety & necessity of the Plan they do not consider themselves to be authorized to do so. The Cte de Bouillé I understand mentioned it to the General ... but it is opposed I believe by some customary Army Arrangements.'[88]

In his memoires Bouillé describes sailing to the Île d'Yeu on the *Thunderer*, arriving on the morning of 16 October, and having an interview with Doyle at which he made a number of representations about the émigré cavalry, and his unit in particular, but he does not mention discussing the destruction of any horses. This meeting finished with Doyle agreeing with Bouillé that the units should be sent back to England as soon as possible and issuing an order to that effect.[89] Unfortunately there are number of inconsistencies in Bouillé's account, some of which can be explained by him writing his memoires much later in life and in poor health, but others cannot. He does appear to have sailed on the *Thunderer* and arrived on 16 October, as he includes the capture of the *Eveillé* in his account, however he states he returned to Quiberon Bay in the *Galatea*. More significantly, he describes the detachment of uhlans on the island, when Doyle had asked for it on 17 October, and dates the interview and Doyle's order for his unit to return to England, which he reproduces in full, to that day when Warren's letter to Spencer, of 16 October, shows that that decision had already been taken.

Some of the troops in Quiberon Bay, however, were not to go to England. On 17 September instructions had been issued by the War Office in London that the white cockade regiments of Hervilly, Hector and Dresnay, as well as the black cockade units of Béon, Damas, Salm, Périgord and Rohan were to be disbanded. This was to take place with immediate effect, although the official date for this was 24 September for the black cockade units and 24 October for the three others. The instructions stated that 'The Whole of the Non Commissioned Officers & Privates ... are to be transferred to the Regt. of Loyal Emigrants.'[90] However it was quickly recognised that the capitulation, for raising the white cockade regiments, dictated that their men could only be drafted into another such regiment, it was only the men of the black cockade units who could be transferred to the Loyal Emigrants as it

86 TNA: ADM 80/137: Keats to Warren 20 October.

87 TNA: ADM 80/137: Keats to Warren 24 October.

88 TNA: ADM 80/137: Keats to Warren 24 October.

89 Bouillé, *Souvenirs*, vol.II, pp.298–303.

90 TNA: WO 4/735: Windham to Woodford 17 September.

was of 'a similar formation.'[91] The order for this appears to have arrived by 8 October as the five units were mustered that day. Present were: Béon – two officers, two staff and 35 other ranks (including eight cadets); Périgod – 12 other ranks; Rohan, with its artillery detachment (of 11) – five officers, four staff and 83 other ranks (including six cadets) and Salm – two officers and 17 other ranks; unfortunately, the list for the Damas Regiment no longer exists.[92] On 23 October Keats ordered that these soldiers be taken from transports due to leave for England, 'in which they are at present & to be put onboard the vessels remaining in Quib[eron] Bay in order to their being sent to their proper Regt. at Isle Dieu.'[93]

These new additions to the Loyal Emigrants soon sailed to join the regiment on the Île d'Yeu, the return of 1 November shows that 112 men had joined it since 1 October and five more joined in the following month.[94] All of them did not go, as the officers and wounded returned to England, while others, the volunteers and cadets, joined the cadres. One of these latter was *Fourrier* Mercier des Pelle-Saunier, the last commander of Damas, who joined Léon. By the time the new Loyal Emigrant soldiers arrived the troops on the island were, since 24 October, no longer under canvas, the weather being 'too cold and damp.'[95] Rising sickness rates had forced Doyle's hand and on 1 November the four British battalions had 495 rank and file sick, in comparison to 169 the previous month, with four men dying in the intervening period, in addition, there were 15 fewer officers present than on 1 October, for whatever reason.[96] The next day, 25 October, Harness wrote to his wife:

> We have not had a word from England. We yesterday marched from camp into cantonments. The wind and rain have rendered it quite necessary, but the difficulty was to find houses. We are in two miserable villages. The Houses are but of one room with two doors, which are opposite to each other, one serving for a window or a door as the wind blows. I have fortunately a window in mine. The wretched Inhabitants are put pell mell into a few houses that are allotted them, and the soldiers take possession of the rest. The distress of these poor people, carrying their beds about, is painful to witness. They are civility itself but this in no way diminishes the sufferings they undergo from a brutal Soldiery, who take advantage of their consternation to plunder them; but I am happy to see every precautionary means taken to prevent as well as the strongest measures to punish these disorders.[97]

---

91 TNA: WO 4/377: Windham to Brownrigg 23 January 1796.

92 TNA: WO 12/11732: musters customarily took place on the 25th day of the month. There is a note written on the outer sleeve of all the lists, apparently by an archivist, that the Damas list was found to be missing on 3 September 1912.

93 TNA: ADM 80/137: Keats to the Agents of Transports.

94 TNA: WO 17/234: monthly return Île d'Yeu 1 November. This is the first time the regiment is returned as part of Doyle's command with its colonel, a lieutenant colonel, three captains, 14 subalterns, three staff, 30 sergeants, eight drummers and, of the rank and file, 167 were present and fit for duty, 46 were sick and 38 were otherwise employed 'on command.'

95 Cook, 'St George Diary', p.284.

96 TNA: WO 17/234: monthly returns.

97 Duncan-Jones (ed.), *William Harness*, p.85.

Montmuran, who had landed on the island in anticipation of joining the Vendéens, also wrote to England at this time and like Harness he described his personal situation in a comparatively positive light, but also did not hide that of the cadres and their worsening morale and discipline:

> I write to my brother by the Prince de Léon who left yesterday with a party of his cadres all very tired and weary. These Gentlemen have been quite mistreated; one made them do very arduous duty, and the most part of them are hardly clothed; it has been atrocious weather for three weeks. MONSIEUR desired to have the cadres for his guard, then they would have been less worn; but the English, who answered for his person on their head, did not want him guarded by any but themselves. Meanwhile I find that these Gentlemen who had a right to make fair complaints, have gone too far; many have taken resolutions of the greatest indecency and made the authorities disgusted with employing the French. This remains between us. …
>
> The sort of life that I lead here is not arduous, as I have nothing to do, but very boring. … I get up at ten o'clock in the morning and go to bed at eight in the evening; I had been 60 days without getting into a bed: you see that I am making it up to myself. I am lodged by billet in the home of a poor fisherman where I have a chair and a bed, while the poor cadres are on straw. I have the ration of an English captain and with that I am doing wonderfully … All the troops are cantoned.[98]

In fact the cadres had gone into cantonments 12 days before the British, on 12 October, when they took up quarters in the south of the island, with posts at La Meule and the Vieux Château. This meant that although they were no longer in tents they were now not in a position to form a guard for Artois. Nevertheless the complaints continued, one of their number writing that they were, 'badly fed, exhausted, having no other beds than bundles of straw, clothes and linen in rags, covered with vermin.'[99] As Montmuran alluded to, there were acts of insubordination and neglect of duty and on 13 November, by Monsieur's order, five volunteers from Williamson were placed under arrest until further orders having, 'refused the duty for which they were commanded and abandoned the guard with which they had left the cantonment, saying the worst and most indecent things for French gentlemen.'[100] Thomas-Gabriel-François Vicomte de Williamson, the unit's *aide-major* and the *colonel*'s brother, later summed up the underlying issue for his corps, common to them all, '… we are an assembly of French royalist officers, imperceptibly one wishes to make us ordinary soldiers, under fire we will be grenadiers but never will we be soldiers for guard duty, or interior discipline, we know to respect military discipline but we will not suffer to be treated as soldiers.'[101]

Rumours and conjecture ran rife with Harness writing, 'We are amused with a thousand extravagancies as is ever the case with people who are cut

98 Robert, *Expédition*, pp.343–344, Montmuran to his sister 27 October.
99 Grouvel, *Les corps de troupes*, vol.I, p.169, quotation not referenced but in the Léon section.
100 Grouvel, *Les corps de troupes*, vol.I, p.172.
101 TNA: HO 69/23: Vicomte de Williamson to Bouillon 6 June 1796.

off from information.'[102] It was reported, falsely, that peace negotiations were progressing in London and also, correctly, that fighting was taking place in Paris. This had occurred on 5 October (13 vendémiaire), in the last days of the Convention before it was replaced by the Directory, when an uprising in the city was bloodily suppressed by the republican army. Whether this really was an attempted coup by royalists, an all too convenient set of culprits, or a last attempt by the Parisians, who were angry at two-thirds of the Convention simply transferring their seats to those in the Directory, to control the course of the Revolution is questionable. The event, however, provided Napoleon Bonaparte, who directed the artillery, another step up in his rise to power. Other conjecture was more mundane, and immediate, 'Some believe that we will soon evacuate this island, others that we will spend the winter here; what is certain is that batteries are being constructed.'[103] On 1 November two 24-pounders, along with shot, were taken from the *Teaser* 'to mount on a Near Battery in defence of the Port.'[104]

Although letters had arrived from England, no orders had come, and on 27 October Warren warned the Admiralty that unless some arrived he would have to return with the *Pomone* and *Standard* 'as they are destitute of every article of Rigging, as well as Coals, Wood, Candles, etc. and have great numbers of their Crews sick of the Flux & Fever.' He informed them that he was waiting for some provisions to arrive and, after landing them, he would leave for Quiberon Bay.[105] Soon severe storms forced Warren to withdraw all his ships from the Île d'Yeu anchorage to that off Hoëdic on 31 October. When he reported this to the Admiralty on 3 November he pointed out that the troops on the island would need to be supplied very soon with everything they needed for winter and, in the meantime, as soon as the weather improved he would land further supplies as they only had 20 days' supply left. In addition, he informed them that the transports that should have left in September had still not done so, 'the Winds being contrary, and the Weather very tempestuous the whole of last month.' To this letter he enclosed a list of these vessels, 110 in all, including the prizes, *Eveillé* and the 600-ton West Indiaman *Kent of London*, the rest being transports and victuallers of various descriptions ranging from the *Ocean* ship, 482 tons and with a crew of 18 to the *Habe* sloop, 52 tons and a crew of four.[106]

Finally, this huge fleet of transports managed to get away under convoy of the frigates HMS *Arethusa* and *Concorde*, *Aimwell* gun vessel and *Expedition* cutter, leaving the bay during 4 November. It was a trying voyage and although the frigates and many of the transports put into St. Mary's Sound in the Isles of Scilly on 10 November, the convoy continued to disperse as it entered the Channel.[107] The *Concorde* managed to put into Portland Road late on 13 November, where Captain Hunt and various British and émigré officers

102 Duncan-Jones (ed.), *William Harness*, p.85 to his wife 25 October.
103 Robert, *Expédition*, p.344, Montmuran to his sister 27 October.
104 TNA: ADM 51/4042: *Teaser* log.
105 TNA: ADM 1/104: Warren to Nepean 27 October.
106 TNA: ADM 1/104: Warren to Nepean 3 November.
107 TNA: ADM 51/1102: *Arethusa* and ADM 51/1111 *Concorde* logs. Bouillé left the *Arethusa* in the Scillies to take a fishing boat to Penzance (Bouillé, *Souvenirs*, vol.II, pp.306–307).

went ashore to go to London, before returning to Plymouth Sound the next day. The *Aimwell*, which was in a particularly poor state already, took shelter in Falmouth Harbour on 14 November and only got into Plymouth Sound three days later.[108] Some of the transports made fast progress; the *Disko Bay*, with Lieutenant Colonel Rotalier's artillery and, perhaps, Quiefdeville's cadre arrived at Spithead off Portsmouth on 11 November before going into Southampton on 20 November.[109] Finally the *Arethusa*, after having put into Plymouth Sound, arrived in the Solent with many of the convoy, including those carrying the émigré cavalry, on 30 November.[110] The delays had meant further suffering for the men and horses on the transports. As an illustration of the number of horses that died during the expedition, Bouillé stated that the officers of his regiment had embarked 89 horses in Germany in August and only eight returned to England alive.[111] The convoy had encountered particularly severe conditions but had not shared the fate of that commanded by Rear Admiral Hugh Cloberry Christian, belatedly taking Abercromby's troops to the West Indies. Struck by the same storms on 18 November it was dispersed and seven vessels were driven ashore to be wrecked on Chesil Beach, north-west of the Isle of Portland, with the loss of more than 450 people, the bodies of over 100 of whom were never recovered.[112]

While the British ships in Quiberon Bay and the troops on the Île d'Yeu were battered by the autumnal storms, the British Government had already decided that the expedition, as far as they were concerned, was to be abandoned. Having read Doyle's dispatches on 11 October Dundas forwarded them to the King with a note, 'Mr. Dundas feels himself under the necessity of submitting to your Majesty's confidential servants without delay, that he conceives the appropriation of so great a proportion of your Majesty's naval and military force to such an object so altogether unwarrantable.' King George, the next day, replied that he was in agreement with Dundas and approved him placing the opinion before Cabinet.[113] On 14 October the decision was taken that Doyle and his troops were to return to England, but orders could not be immediately issued to this effect as diplomatic protocol and regard for Artois's status required that he be communicated with first. So, the same day, Grenville wrote two letters to Artois telling of the planned withdrawal of the British troops from the Île d'Yeu and the three choices which were open to him: to remain on the island, although the British fleet would withdraw over winter; to land to try to join Charette, with only the help of navy and not Doyle's troops; or to return.[114]

108 TNA: ADM 51/4406: *Aimwell* log.

109 TNA: WO 1/392: Perthuis to Grymes 3 December and PRO 30/11/225: Rotalier 20 November.

110 *The Times*, 2 December and Bouillé, *Souvenirs*, vol.II, p.307.

111 Bouillé, *Souvenirs*, vol.II, p.308.

112 Terence Grocott, *Shipwrecks of the Revolutionary & Napoleonic Eras* (London: Caxton Editions, 2002), pp.20–23; this was the first of the so-called Christian Storms, the second attempt was made on 9 December in which storms again dispersed vessels and drove them back to port by 29 January 1796, but without such a loss of life. Christian finally managed to bring Abercromby's expedition to Barbados on 21 April.

113 Aspinall, *George III*, vol.II, p.411.

114 Hutt, *Chouannerie*, p.359.

As the winter approached and nothing was heard of from Charette, the position became increasingly uncomfortable for Artois and his suite. Harness had seen and conversed with the prince at Doyle's table and, on 14 October, remarked on his demeanour, 'He is extremely gay, and has spirits that no trick of fortune can effect.'[115] Harness had regular contact with the 27-year old Anne-Henri-Réné de Montmorency-Luxembourg Duc de Châtillon, *capitaine* commanding the Léon detachment on the island and considered as *colonel* among the émigrés, and commented on his 'low spirits' contrasting them with those Artois displayed, saying:

> I was surprised at those of Monsieur who I met yesterday at General Doyle's. His are unchanged but he [Châtillon] tells me he sometimes sees him in private when he is in real depression, but that the moment a person enters to whom he is not intimately known, he puts on the shew of his natural character.[116]

The decision he now would have to take would certainly not lighten his mood. Although the prince's answer had not been received, the orders were issued on 22 October and Spencer accompanied them with a private letter to Warren to explain the situation, as well as to explain why he had not replied to an earlier letter from him:

> I delayed answering the former till my answer could be accompanied by some decisive orders for your further proceedings, and those have hitherto been delayed from the extreme difficulty which you may easily be aware existed in explaining everything to the personage whom you have with you. By the conveyance which carries this out to you, you will receive these orders, and I wish you may find it possible to execute them speedily and in a manner which may secure the only object which now seems to remain from the state of things in the quarter where you are, namely, that of withdrawing, with as little loss as possible, the force both British and French which is with you. I say both British and French because, though we thought it right to leave an option to the latter to remain on the island, or even attempt a landing on the mainland if they think fit, yet I feel very little doubt that they will take the wiser determination to return if possible.[117]

Weeks passed before the orders finally arrived for the commanders but the news leaked out to the British public much sooner. *The Times*, of Monday 26 October, reporting, 'The Count d'ARTOIS is about to return, and the troops are recalled home. The stores are also about to be re-shipped.'[118] On the island Harness wrote to his wife on 2 November, 'We begin to be in serious want of provisions' but he reassured her that there was a reserve of 'ships rations.'[119] Some relief came with a convoy, under HMS *Galatea*, of seven victuallers with provisions, a sloop loaded with 'babbins' (bundles of brushwood to be

115 Duncan-Jones (ed.), *William Harness*, p.84 to his wife 14 October.

116 Duncan-Jones (ed.), *William Harness*, p.85 to his wife 6 November.

117 Corbett (ed.), *Private Papers*, pp.111–113, Spencer to Warren (private) 22 October.

118 *The Times* 26 October 1795.

119 Duncan-Jones (ed.), *William Harness*, p.86, to his wife 2 November.

used as fuel) and four transports, one with commissary waggons, one with horses of the 14th Light Dragoons and the other two with horses for the Comte d'Artois.[120] The sea was still very rough and the brig *Friends*, 'which had Monsieur's horses trying to come into harbour struck upon a rock. The horses and everything in her were saved.' The other vessels remained in the roadstead as a result.[121] HMS *Anson* soon brought another convoy of three victuallers, three vessels with ordnance stores, and four transports with horses and, the sea having abated, the cargoes from all the vessels were landed.[122] To improve access, the crew of the *Teaser* made and fixed buoys at the entrance to the harbour to enable vessels to be warped into it and by 14 November there were sufficient provisions on Île d'Yeu for 60 days.[123]

The *Pomone*, with Warren on board, was bringing further supplies from Quiberon Bay when, too close to the shore, she struck a sand bar off the mouth of the Loire in the early hours of 9 November and began to take on 'one foot of Water per Hour.'[124] She came into Yeu Roads and, Warren transferring his pennant to the *Galatea*, she then sailed for England the next day. Despite water levels continuing to rise, even with constant pumping and bailing, she managed to get safely into Plymouth Sound on 13 November.[125]

Hesitation and Indecision

All the available resources were to be used for the evacuation the Île d'Yeu, so Harvey, as the senior officer, was to be in charge and he received his orders on 9 November. He then forwarded them to Warren and Doyle with a request for their advice on how the operation could be carried out. However, Harvey made it clear he was unhappy for his own ships to be used for carrying troops, due to the lack of transports, as they had been at sea for 10 weeks and so were low on provisions and water.[126] There was further delay as it was only on 14 November that the two officers acknowledged receiving his communication and gave their recommendations. Doyle, for his part, explained that there were 5,300 people, of all categories, to be evacuated from the island, along with 400 horses, and there was a need to maintain sufficient defences until the very last moment. Nevertheless he immediately began to embark some provisions and heavy guns. He also sought to address Harvey's concerns by stating that he would ensure the troops came on board the ships with water and provisions. He wanted the 'French Gentlemen & Cadres' to leave on any ship that could be allocated to them and, 'Monsieur I wish to send off as

120 TNA: ADM 80/137: list of transports 3 November.

121 Cook, 'St George Diary', p.248.

122 TNA: ADM 80/137: list of transports 5 November and Cook, 'St George Diary', p.248, two transports carried horses of the 14th Light Dragoons, those of the other two are not specified.

123 TNA: ADM 51/4042: *Teaser* log, 10–12 November and ADM 1/104: Doyle to Harvey 14 November.

124 TNA: ADM 1/104: Warren to Nepean 9 November, the commodore made it clear he blamed 'the Ignorance of a Pilot' for the accident.

125 TNA: ADM 51/1118: *Pomone* log.

126 TNA: ADM 1/104: Harvey to Warren 9 November.

soon as he will consent to go, which will not be I am certain until he has seen the embarkation begun, as he expressed a wish not to embark until every Frenchman has been put on board.'[127]

It is not clear exactly when the British Government's letters to Artois arrived, but it was certainly by 14 November, at the latest, when the orders of 22 October, written a week later, had arrived. Whatever the case, it did not give him and his staff much time to consider the options, although it was clear that anything but leaving would have been, at the very least, foolhardy. Charette's position was so precarious that he could not answer messages let alone provide security to the heir to the French throne during an insurrection; indeed it seems he was already coming to this conclusion a month before.[128] On 17 November Artois sent messages to the commanders of the royalists of the west, informing them of his departure, encouraging them to action and assuring them of his future wish 'to fight at their head, with the certainty, or at least with the well-founded hope, that my presence, without any help from foreign troops, will be decisive for the success of the cause of God and the King.'[129]

On 16 November the line-of-battle ships, *Orion* and *Thunderer*, and frigates, *Anson*, *Galatea*, *Jason* and *Artois* were off the island and Warren issued instructions to their captains for the embarkation. The next day he was joined by the *Robust* and the frigates *Thalia*, *Melampus* and *Latona*, Harvey having sent them to ensure the operation went ahead as fast as possible. Keats was placed on shore with two officers, six mates, six midshipmen and 112 sailors to assist with the operation and a 17-strong naval working party was sent to repair the flat boats and launches in the harbour; all these seamen being housed on the *Teaser*.[130]

In the meantime Harvey was becoming increasingly worried about the embarkation and started to wobble about his decision to press on with it, admitting to Nepean at the Admiralty, 'The whole of this business is extremely difficult and hazardous; and as you may conceive, I feel the utmost anxiety on the occasion.'[131] Again the concern he raised was the lack of drinking water on his warships, the water obtained from Houat and Hoëdic now being very poor in quality. The next day, 17 November, he informed the Admiralty that he had sent his ships to assist the operation, but then lost any confidence he had as, in three separate letters, he insisted Warren 'desist from embarking them [the troops] until a proper number of Vessels may be sent from England for that purpose'.[132] Furthermore he ordered Warren to return his ships, so preventing the operation from being concluded.

127 TNA: ADM 1/104: Warren and Doyle to Harvey 14 and 15 November.

128 Hutt, *Chouannerie*, p.360, citing a letter from Artois to Harcourt of 13 October.

129 Anon.(ed.), *Olivier d'Argens*, p.120, 'Instructions ... handed to M.M. the Chevaliers d'Autichamp and La Beraudière, for Generals Stofflet and Scepaux' 17 November 1795. Robert, *Expédition*, p.254, dismisses the account of Charette's bitter outburst after receiving the news, along with a presentational sword, which is told by those critical of the prince.

130 TNA: ADM 80/137: Warren's General Orders 16 to 18 November.

131 TNA: ADM 1/104: Harvey to Nepean 16 November also see two to Warren 14 November.

132 TNA: ADM 1/104: Harvey to Nepean and to Warren 17 November.

Warren was far from impressed so, on 18 November, when he received Harvey's instructions he enclosed a copy with a brief letter to the Admiralty, in which he wrote that he would, 'do all in my power for the Army; and having fulfilled the Instructions I have received I shall proceed to England in the Galatea; leaving the Men of War that arrived the latest to protect the Isle Dieu.' Then, perhaps with passions cooling, he added that this determination was subject to a number of caveats including the receipt of further orders.[133] In the time remaining to him, Warren took the cadres and other Frenchmen, 280 in all, on board the *Thunderer* in the evening of 19 November and assigned the *Jason* to return to Spithead with the Comte d'Artois.[134] The following morning Artois boarded her, receiving a 21 gun salute as he did so. Harness witnessed his departure:

> A more affecting public scene I never experienced. ... His manners are extremely elegant. His leave on the beach, I know not why, drew tears from many *English*, who have been lately in the habit of meeting him at table. The adieu he gave to every Body was so varied and so feeling, at the time he seemed to feel so little for his individual state, that it will be very long remembered by all.[135]

The *Thunderer* and *Jason* immediately sailed for England and arrived at Spithead on 26 November. Artois was to remain on board the latter until, after some negotiation, he landed at Leith in January 1796 to take up residence at the Palace of Holyroodhouse, Edinburgh, where Scottish law gave him some respite from his creditors.[136]

Meanwhile Warren returned to Quiberon Bay with his ships on 21 November but then two days later Harvey ordered him '... to proceed without a moments loss of time ... [with 10 allocated vessels] to Isle Dieu, and use your best endeavours to Embark His Majesty's Forces on that Island with all the Expedition possible' and bring them to the bay where they would be dispersed among the ships of both squadrons.[137] Then, the very next day, Harvey rescinded the order, informing Warren that the troops could not possibly be taken onto the ships of his own squadron, again because of low water supplies.[138]

Writing to the Admiralty, on 27 November, Harvey justified his second change of mind, obliquely shifting some blame onto Warren, 'I cannot help observing how unfortunate it was that every Transport fit to receive Troops should have been order'd home instead of being placed in a situation and kept compleat in Provisions and Water ready for the immediate reception of

133 TNA: ADM 1/104: Warren to Nepean 18 November.

134 TNA: ADM 1/104: Warren to Nepean 20 November and ADM 51/1103: *Thunderer* log.

135 Duncan-Jones (ed.), *William Harness*, p.86, to his wife not dated.

136 Lord Mackenzie-Stuart, 'French Émigrés in Edinburgh', in Kirsty Carpenter and Philip Mansell (eds), *The French Émigrés in Europe and the Struggle against the Revolution, 1789–1814* (Basingstoke: Macmillan Press Ltd., 1999), p.110.

137 TNA: ADM 1/104: Harvey to Warren 23 November.

138 TNA: ADM 1/104: Harvey to Warren 24 November, followed up with an order of 26 November.

the Troops whenever their removal might be found necessary.'[139] He ignored the fact that his notification to Warren that he would no longer be able to safeguard the ships in Quiberon Bay had led to the decision to return them to England. He concluded his letter by explaining that Warren, now off Houat, was 'supplying the Royalists and affording them such assistance as he may find practicable.'[140] For his part, Warren later mentioned the assistance he had provided to the chouans of Morbihan writing that he had given, 'succours of arms, clothing and cash to the Chouans, who have been down once in force and with whom I have constant communication'.[141]

On 4 December, when the Lords of the Admiralty received Harvey's letter, they directed that he should be informed, as etiquette required, that the reasons for 'bringing away the Troops from L'Isle Dieu still exist & that … he is to attempt it.' Instructions were also to be issued to ensure he was supplied with water and provisions.[142] The letter was duly drawn up and sent on 5 December with Harvey receiving it 12 days later.[143] However Earl Spencer had already written him a private letter which he received in the night of 28 November that stung him into action.

The next morning he wrote to the Admiralty to tell them that, being informed water was coming from Plymouth, he had ordered Warren, with the *Robust, Theseus, Russell, Melampus, Thalia, Anson, Artois, Galatea* and *Porcupine*, to re-embark the troops 'with the utmost dispatch possible' and bring them to Quiberon Bay. Harvey would then sail with them for Spithead. Nevertheless he was still concerned, this time about the anchorage off the Île d'Yeu, 'I cannot therefore but feel exceedingly anxious for the ships ordered on this service; and nothing but the most pressing Orders … could justify me in sending ships there at this season.'[144] Warren and the ships arrived off the island on 2 December; he was aware of the reason for Harvey's newly found decisiveness, as is seen in his private letter to Spencer:

> … I must say our destiny has been changed frequently, as the admiral has been so much alarmed at the idea of the road, so plagued about water by those with him that I have been recalled twice; but at last in consequence of your lordship's letter, I am now here with orders to effect the evacuation if it is practicable … you may be assured no endeavour of mine shall be wanting to obtain this object.[145]

In the intervening time, with the very real prospect of spending the winter on the island, the troops had not been idle. An anonymous officer wrote '… we are ordered to quit this island, at the very moment of the completion of our plan of defence, (the most perfect that was ever contrived) … we had a citadel, and a park of field artillery in the centre, and batteries on all the

139 TNA: ADM 1/104: Harvey to Nepean 27 November.
140 TNA: ADM 1/104: Harvey to Nepean 27 November.
141 Corbett (ed.), *Private Papers*, p.117, Warren to Spencer (private) 3 December.
142 TNA: ADM 1/104: note dated 4 December written on Harvey to Nepean 27 November
143 TNA: ADM 1/104: Harvey to Nepean 17 December.
144 TNA: ADM 1/104: Harvey to Nepean 29 November.
145 Corbett (ed.), *Private Papers*, pp.116–117, Warren to Spencer (private) 3 December.

essential points of the coast.'[146] The crew of the *Teaser* had played their part in this effort by the 'mounting and landing of Guns at the Grand Battery' on 24 and 26 November.[147] The threat of attack from the mainland, although it did not materialise, was real. In November Hoche had proposed such an operation in conjunction with Villaret-Joyeuse but the admiral was not enthusiastic. Preparations were then made for troops to attack Île d'Yeu from Fromentine, Saint-Gilles-Croix-de-Vie and Les Sables-d'Olonne under the protection of ships from Nantes. On 10 December, with only 3,000 men available, Hoche described the plan as 'bold but it will immortalise whoever will successfully lead it.' He was addressing *Général de division* Amédée Willot, recently arrived from Spain who was to command the enterprise. The news of the evacuation, however soon arrived.[148]

The conditions on the island had been far from comfortable during this period of vacillation. The sickness rate among the troops, although stabilised since they no longer camped, was still very high with 517 rank and file men sick in the British infantry battalions on 1 December, an increase of 22 from the previous month and with 19 deaths in that period. The situation in the other units was similar: the Loyal Emigrants had 41 sick and the 14th Light Dragoons and Royal Artillery each had 10 men sink in the ranks, however no men from these units died in this time.[149]

Warren commenced the evacuation almost straight away. On 4 December the 12th Foot embarked on the *Anson* and *Robust* and by the 9 December all the troops were on board except for the rear guard, provided by the 78th and 90th Foot and Royal Artillery. On 16 December the last of the troops had left the island, along with Warren and Doyle, and came into Quiberon Bay on the *Galatea* that evening. The scale of this final operation is illustrated by the returns.

Furthermore provisions, regimental baggage, ordnance, waggons, horses and the hospital, along with the sick, were brought away in 14 more brigs, 12 sloops, three ships, two chasse marées and a schooner.[150]

It must be said that the above embarkation list varies somewhat with an army return for the same period. This, for the first time, includes the 'French Corps' which had come within the responsibility of Artois's staff, until the latter's departure. The 'Corps' consisted of: the Emigrant Artillery – a field officer, Major Jacques-Henri Vicomte de Beaujeu, seven company officers and 132 other ranks (so apparently one company with a field officer); Uhlans Britanniques – a *capitaine*, 50 other ranks, four women and a child (with 26 horses); Choiseul Hussars – a subaltern and 48 other ranks (with 28 horses)

146 *The Hampshire Chronicle*, 26 December 1795.

147 TNA: ADM 51/4042: *Teaser* log, presumably these were the guns that had recently been embarked.

148 Robert, *Expédition*, pp.247–248, Willot was victim of a political purge in 1798 and exiled to Guiana, having escaped he joined, through inclination or circumstances, the royalist party (Jonathan D. Devlin, 'A Problem of Royalism: General Amédée Willot and the French Directory', *Renaissance and Modern Studies*, vol.XXXIII (1989), pp.125–143).

149 TNA: WO 17/234: monthly return.

150 TNA: ADM 80/137: list of transports with stores etc. 3 to 15 December.

and Warren's Hussars – a *major*, a *capitaine*, a subaltern, 13 NCOs and nine rank and file (with three horses).[151]

Table 17: Embarkation of the troops from the Île d'Yeu between 3 and 15 November.[152]

Ship	Unit	Officers	Rank & File	Women & Children	Total
HMS *Galatea*	Staff	16	28***	–	
	78th Foot	5	210	4	
	Royal Artillery	1	26	2	292
HMS *Artois*	14th Light Dragoons	2	26	13	
	90th Foot	9	266	5	321
HMS *Robust*	12th Foot	19	483	97	599
HMS *Anson*	12th Foot	14	215	43	272
HMS *Porcupine*	Emigrant Artillery	6	104	1	
	Uhlans Britanniques	–	17	–	
	Warren Hussars	8	23	–	
	Choiseul Hussars	–	22	–	181
HMS *Artois*	80th Foot	10	190	27	227
HMS *Theseus*	80th Foot	16	477	93	586
HMS *Thalia*	Royal Artillery	2	80	10	
	78th Foot	5	133	67	297
HMS *Melampus*	Loyal Emigrant	22	243	2	
	Emigrant Artillery	2	19	–	
	14th Light Dragoons	1	24	–	
	Uhlans Britanniques	–	7	–	320
HMS *Russell*	90th Foot	?	(361)	69	
	78th Foot	2	164	–	
	French Engineers	4	–	–	600
HMS *Teaser*	90th Foot	3	40	3	46
*Emerzon**	78th Foot	4	40	–	
	Commissary or servants	–	10	–	54
*Small Bridge**	78th Foot	2	40	–	
	Commissary or servants	–	10	–	52
*David**	78th Foot	3	40	–	
	Commissary or servants	–	10	–	53
*Union**	90th Foot	1	20	–	
	Royal Artillery	–	9	–	30
*Aurora**	90th Foot	1	40	–	
	Commissary Bakers etc.	–	15	–	56
*Branchly**	90th Foot	1	20	–	
	Waggoners etc.	–	26	–	47
*Industry**	Commissary Waggoners etc	–	70	–	70
*Ste Anne***	90th Foot	1	24	–	
	78th Foot	1	36	–	62
*St Jacques (1)***	78th Foot	1	24	–	25
*St Jacques (2)***	(78th Foot)	–	20	–	20

* Brigs; ** Chasse Marées; *** Servants; the numbers of the 90th Foot on the *Russell* are not shown but the total is and the unit on the *St Jacques (2)* is missing but from the numbers appear to be from the 78th Foot.

151 TNA: WO 1/176: return for 3 to 16 December.
152 TNA: ADM 80/137.

The activity of the crew of the *Teaser*, while unique given its station at Port-Joinville, illustrates the complexity of the operation. As well as housing, from 3 December, 150 seamen who were landed from the warships to assist in embarking stores, the crew assisted in this work as well. On 5 December, when the island's defences were dismantled, they were dismounting guns at the 'Grand Battery' and over the next few days receiving them on board. However, there were difficulties in getting the gun-vessel out of the harbour so not only did the guns and ballast have to be removed but the crew also had to dig under the hull. Finally on 12 December she was afloat and the crew were able to assist in getting the *Garland* brig, carrying the sick from the hospital, off the rocks she had run onto in a gale the day before. The next two days were then spent in loading the ballast and getting the guns back onboard as well as assisting other vessels out of the harbour. It was the evening of 15 December that she worked out of the harbour to sail the next day.[153]

As the troops arrived in Quiberon Bay some were distributed among Harvey's ships while those of Warren's squadron began to return home. The *Teaser*, in need of repair, sailed on 17 December with some transports and entered Portsmouth Harbour five days later, where preparations commenced immediately to receive her in the dockyard.[154] The *Galatea*, with Warren, Doyle and the army staff, left Quiberon Bay on 26 December, having 'thrown in such supplys [*sic*] for the Royalists that the season would admit of,' and arrived in Cawsand Bay two days later.[155] Chasse marées flying French Royal colours were among the vessels that came into Plymouth Sound with the *Galatea*.[156] Harvey had already announced that they would be arriving in a letter of 17 December:

> Major General Doyle and the Commodore have jointly requested that all the Chasse Marees whose owners and crew have embraced the Royalist Party with the first and second expedition to their Coast and behaved with the utmost fidelity and cannot return to their Houses with safety, may be allowed to repair to England ...[157]

On 10 December Harness had been transferred to Harvey's flagship, the *Prince of Wales*, with nine other officers and 344 men, women and children of the 80th Foot, where the admiral's 'civilities are very flattering, he has done me the Honor to give me the half of his Cabin and his Table.'[158] It was to be some time before he would be on his way home, enabling Harness to

153 TNA: ADM 51/4042: *Teaser* log.

154 TNA: ADM 51/4042: *Teaser* log.

155 TNA: ADM 1/104: Warren to Nepean 28 December; the date of departure is given in Duncan-Jones (ed.), *William Harness*, p.87 to his wife 26 December, his letter being taken by the *Galatea*. Sir James Saumarez, in HMS *Orion*, had been charged with supplying the Vendéens with arms and ammunition while Warren was busy with the evacuation, but was unable to do so due to 'bad weather and other disappointments,' ADM 1/104: Harvey to Nepean 18 December.

156 *The Times*, 1 January 1796.

157 TNA: ADM 1/104: Harvey to Nepean 17 December.

158 Duncan-Jones (ed.), *William Harness*, p.87, to his wife 17 December and TNA WO 1/176, final distribution of troops.

get something of the measure of his host, writing on 26 December 'we are detained in this Bay by contrary winds. The Admiral is very careful of his Convoy, and with so great a charge cannot sail but with moderate weather. … We every hour expect the change of this horrid Wind.'[159]

The wind in fact changed that day and Harvey's ships and the convoy began to slowly work their way out of Quiberon Bay. Part then sailed under the *Orion*, arriving at Spithead on 29 December, while the rest arrived there on 2 January 1796. On 4 and 5 January the troops were transferred to transports and taken to Southampton where they were disembarked. The 12th Foot, for example, disembarked there on the 6 January and marched to Eling Barracks.[160]

Upon reflection Graham, colonel of the 90th Foot, observed dryly, 'In this manner two months were spent at L'Isle Dieu without anything material being effected towards the completion of the object of the expedition.'[161] Fortescue, historian of the British Army, and no admirer of the way the administration, and particularly Dundas, conducted the war, observed:

> After close study of a great number of English expeditions I incline to the opinion that this to Isle d'Yeu was the most disgraceful, in point of negligence and recklessness, that was ever thrust by a British Minister upon a British General. … A more wanton and wicked waste of lives, resources and money was never perpetrated …[162]

159 Duncan-Jones (ed.), *William Harness*, pp.87–88, to his wife.

160 Cook, 'St George Diary', pp.248–249; TNA: ADM 51/1130: *Robust* log; and *The Times*, 13 January 1796.

161 Delavoye, *Life of Thomas Graham*, p.96.

162 Fortescue, *British Army*, vol.IV, pp.422–423.

12

Conclusion

Echoes

The expeditions ended in failure but the impact of this on the insurrections in western France is hard to quantify as it came at a time when their fortunes were already on the wane. In the Vendée Stofflet and Charette were captured and executed; the latter, who was shot on 29 March 1796, had been taken with only 32 remaining followers. In Brittany Puisaye, on his return from Houat, was initially greeted without rancour by the Morbihan chiefs, however relationships soon soured and had broken down by the time Mercier, as Cadoudal's representative, and Vauban, very much Puisaye's man, had visited Artois, separately, on the Île d'Yeu in November. By the next month Puisaye, perhaps having let his mask slip, was referring to the Morbihan chiefs as 'vile intriguers, without education, without principals, and who wish at any cost to get rid of the nobility'.[1]

The chouannerie endured like a heath fire, when damped down at one time or place it was to suddenly flare up in others, indeed from 1796 it spread further into Normandy, particularly under the leadership of Louis de Frotté. Some of the émigré officers who had served at Quiberon returned in 1796 to fight alongside the chouans or Vendéens, one was Montmuran who was, however, betrayed and shot before the year was out. Another was Hippolyte-Marie-Guillaume de Rosnyvinen Comte de Piré, lieutenant in Rohan, who had been wounded on 21 July but had reached safety by swimming. Hoche however, having largely pacified the Vendée, was able to deploy his forces in Brittany and in June of 1796 most of the chiefs had agreed to a peace. Renewed restrictions and persecutions saw another widespread insurrection in Brittany in 1799 which, despite early successes, was quickly controlled. This was followed by a general pacification after another coup d'état in Paris that ushered in the Consulate and so cemented Napoleon's rise to power. He sought to neutralise the royalist movement through compromise and continued this policy after the Peace of Amiens in 1802 drawing the majority of the émigrés back to France. Most retired into private life until the

1 Hutt, *Chouannerie*, p.363 quoting Puisaye to Louvart de Pontigny, 21 December 1795.

Restoration but some took roles under the Empire. Piré, for example, who had volunteered for the French cavalry under the Consulate in 1800, rose to become *Baron de l'Empire* and *Général de division*, even rallying to Napoleon during the Hundred Days, when the Vendée again took up arms in support of the King. Some joined the forces of other nations, such as Russia, Portugal or the German states, following the military and political fortunes of these states during the Napoleonic Wars. A few others entered British service, not returning to France until the monarchy was restored. One of these last, and present at Quiberon, was César-Augustin Champeaux who, not quite 21-years-old, had served as *quartier maître* in the Régiment Royal-Louis and then *sous-lieutenant* in Hervilly. Placed on half pay after the regiment was disbanded, he resumed his career in 1807 as lieutenant in the Watteville Regiment, serving in the Mediterranean, Spain and Canada in that rank, until 1816 when he returned to France and eventually received the pension of a *lieutenant-colonel*.[2]

British support for the royalists had continued. In the spring of 1796 Captain Sir Edward Pellew, with five frigates, returned to Quiberon Bay. However communication with any royalists who were still active in the region was very difficult and so all were sent money via an intermediary except for Cadoudal who received, in addition, arms, ammunition and clothing.[3] Pellew's mission was largely unsuccessful although the day after leaving the Vendéen coast one of his squadron captured *La Unité*, a 38-gun frigate, with ease, 'The cause of so faint a resistance from the enemy was occasioned by the ship's company refusing to fight. Many of them were Royalists, and driven on board only a few days before.' From all he had seen and heard Pellew was not optimistic about the royalists, 'I fear … that all hopes of their affairs being retrieved will be ill-founded.'[4] Nevertheless, on 2 June 1800 he found himself commanding a strong squadron acting in Quiberon Bay with a British force, commanded by the Honourable Thomas Maitland, with local rank of major general, which was intended to capture Belle-Île in order that, purportedly, it could be used to supply and support the royalists. However, with little prospect of success and the need for troops elsewhere, the main body of six battalions – the 2nd, 1/20th, 2/20th, 36th, 82nd and 92nd Foot, with two companies of artillery – sailed on 23 June from Houat, where they had landed, for the Mediterranean.[5] The *Correspondance* also continued to operate, passing men, messages and arms to and from France and the Channel Islands throughout the wars. Indeed, Georges Cadoudal landed in Normandy from a British vessel in the run up to a plot to kidnap or kill Napoleon for which he was arrested and then executed on 25 June 1804.

Hardly a year had passed after the defeat at Quiberon before the French Republic, in turn, sought to exploit insurrection for its own war aims in Ireland. The Society of United Irishmen promised a numerous and

2 SHD: 2 YE 747; and Alistair Nichols, *Wellington's Switzers: The Watteville Regiment in Egypt, the Mediterranean, Spain and Canada* (Godmanchester: Ken Trotman, 2015), p.231.

3 Corbett (ed.), *Private Papers*, pp.124–125, Pellew to Spencer 9 April 1796.

4 Corbett (ed.), *Private Papers*, pp.126–127, Pellew to Spencer 20 April 1796.

5 Fortescue, *British Army*, Vol.IV, pp.777–779, and James, *Naval History*, vol.III, pp.7–8.

widespread rising when a French force landed, the command of which was given to Hoche. Among the troops gathered for this expedition was the 2e Légion des Francs which was formed from prisoners of all descriptions, including a few prisoners of war from the British Army, particularly Irishmen. In early September eight of the latter escaped and arrived in Jersey led by James O'Byrne, a sergeant of the 87th Foot who had been captured in the Netherlands, and, according to his testament, had been forced to join the unit due to having meagre rations and being 'treated harshly' as a prisoner, receiving a commission as *capitaine* for his decision.[6] The unit became known as the Légion Noire as it was clothed in the red coats supplied by Britain at Quiberon which had been dyed black, with varying degrees of success. As a secondary operation, the legion was landed overnight 22 to 23 February 1797 on the Welsh coast near Fishguard with a mission, in essence, to cause mayhem but it ended in surrender after only 24 hours ashore. As if only to add to the echoes of Quiberon, the legion's second in command, who used the name Le Brun, was found to be Jean-Philippe de Rochemure. In 1791 he had been a *capitaine en second* in the Régiment d'Orléans infanterie when Vauban was its *colonel* and had served in the final expedition, as a NCO in Chambray's company of Williamson's cadre corps.[7] On the other hand, 48 of the prisoners taken in Wales and held at Portchester depot made 'repeated applications' to enlist in the Loyal Emigrants. Upon investigation it was found 'that they have all served either amongst the Chouans or Vendeans [*sic*],' four having served in the regiments at Quiberon, two in Hector and one each in the Loyal Emigrants and Damas so their enlistment was approved.[8]

As for Hoche, due to bad weather his force did not land in Ireland and he went on to serve in Germany where he died of tuberculosis on 19 September 1797, his reputation in retrospect largely untarnished, dying as he did before he could be a rival to Napoleon. It was to be Humbert who finally landed in Ireland in support of the Irish Rebellion in 1798 but, after early victories, he and his small force had been taken prisoner within weeks.

The events of 1795 became part of Brittany's distinctive historical and cultural memory, particularly in the Morbihan region where the fighting had taken place and the population had suffered its repercussions both during the operations and in the aftermath. In addition, from the Association bretonne to the chouannerie itself the province's nobility had been widely involved in the counter-revolution. They not only contributed a high proportion of the officers in the units at Quiberon, notably Dresnay, Rohan and Hector, in the latter case due to the close links between the Royal marine and Brittany, but also those who served with the chouans. Thus, the Breton nobility paid a disproportionately heavy price for the defeat when compared with their class from France as a whole.

After the monarchy was restored to France the elevation of those who died during the expeditions, particularly the émigré prisoners who were

6 TNA: WO 1/921: declaration made on Jersey 8 September 1796.

7 Harold Felix Baker Wheeler and Alexander Meyrick Broadley, *Napoleon and the Invasion of England* (London: John Lane, 1908), vol.I, p.61 and TNA: WO 12/12034: contrôles.

8 TNA: WO 1/900: John Ramsay to Huskisson 12 November 1798.

Mausoleum at the Chartreuse d'Auray. (Author's collection)

executed, to the status of martyrs grew apace. This was a powerful statement of the price the émigrés had paid for their loyalty and the wrongs, as they saw it, committed against them in the name of the republic. Indeed, service at Quiberon gained such kudos that some former émigrés, when, for instance, later applying for distinctions or pensions, often stated they had been present even though their part had only been to remain at sea or on the Île d'Yeu.

The focus of this movement was a patch of land at Brec'h, north of Auray, that came to be called the Champ des Martyrs because it was where the condemned prisoners from the town had been brought to be shot and immediately buried, the soil being easily turned as it lay on the very edge of the tidal reaches of the river. On 15 May 1814, within a fortnight of Louis XVIII's return to Paris, their remains were disinterred from the unsanctified ground and brought to the Chartreuse d'Auray, originally a Carthusian monastery, which stood nearby above the river. Soon this became a place of remembrance and later the same year, the Duc d'Angoulême visited to pay his respects. His wife, Marie-Thérèse, who, also being his cousin, was the only surviving member of Louis XVI and Marie-Antoinette's immediate family, was to take a particular interest in the raising of a memorial to the martyrs, wherever they fell. As a result, a commission was formed for the Monument of Quiberon on which several of those connected with the expeditions served, the president of its central committee being Etienne-Charles, now Duc, de Damas formerly colonel of the regiment of his name. Its work led to the construction of a mausoleum at the Chartreuse, inscribed with the names of the 'victims' and below which the recovered bones were placed, and an expiatory chapel on the Champ des Martyrs, which was embanked to secure it from flooding. Both were inaugurated, accompanied by military pomp, on 15 October 1829, those who had served at Quiberon and their families taking a prominent part. In the morning La Villegourio and Vossey, now *contre-amiral*, were among the survivors who attended the service at the mausoleum and in the afternoon, at the Champ des Martyrs, the mass was led by the Bishop of Quimper, Jean-Marie-Dominique de Poulpiquet de Brescanvel, who as *aumônier* of the Régiment d'Hector had swum to a boat and safety on 21 July 1795. The dignity of the 70-year-old prelate drew the sympathy of the thousands who had come to watch:

> The idea of the dangers he had run, his grey hair, his step that the weight of the years rendered heavy and painful, the sorrowful duty that he had put upon himself in coming to this ceremony, … on earth soaked with the blood of his former friends … at the moment marked to honour these heroes, an irrefutable witness to their virtues … in … the same spot where they had received the crown of the martyr …[9]

9 Anon., *Inauguration des Monuments de Quiberon, le quinze octobre 1829* (Vannes: J.M. Galles, 1829), p.19.

Blame

The search to apportion blame, especially if it can be lain at the feet of others, will begin after any defeat, especially one which had been preceded by such hope and expectation, however misplaced it may have been. As US President J. F. Kennedy said on 21 April 1961 after the failure of the Bay of Pigs landing in Cuba, an operation to which Quiberon is sometimes compared, 'victory has a hundred fathers and defeat is an orphan'.[10]

The Comte d'Hervilly had returned to England in the *Anson*, landing at Plymouth, but needed some time before he was strong enough to travel on to London, arriving there on 27 September. He found that some already blamed him, to a greater or lesser extent, for the failure of the expedition and so he began to gather evidence to refute these allegations, even if this shifted the blame to others. However, according to the Comte de Moustier, a high ranking diplomat who was close to the future King Louis XVIII, '... when he could no longer doubt the impossibility of living, he formed the generous resolution to renounce an enterprise which could only give rise to great sorrow to the survivors, and he said to me a few hours before his death that he had not wanted the living to have to suffer information that could only concern a man who was going to descend into the tomb'.[11] Hervilly died on 14 November, the shot that had wounded him still in his body.

Puisaye, who arrived in London on 6 March 1797, took a very different resolution.[12] After being involved in a failed attempt to establish an émigré colony in Canada he returned to the British capital and, in 1803, began to write his memoirs in order to not only absolve himself from any blame for what had happened but also to portray himself as the victim of intriguers. He stated that in fact Hervilly had collected the evidence with the aim of proving his, Puisaye's, innocence from any fault but death had prevented him from doing so, nevertheless he had cleared his conscious to La Jaille before his demise. Puisaye then produced a version entitled, 'Declaration made by M. le Comte d'Hervilly on his deathbed ...' in which the latter is said to have acknowledged '... that if there had been faults committed, it was to him that they should be attributed.'[13] Hervilly was then to have declared '... that I was capable of fulfilling the functions of assistant quartermaster general, but that I had not the necessary knowledge to command an army.'[14] However the document that Puisaye relies on is not a contemporary record but one written by La Jaille almost two years later, and certified by the Vicomte de

10 Gerhard Peters and John T. Woolley, 'John F. Kennedy. The President's News Conference' *The American Presidency Project*, <https://www.presidency.ucsb.edu/documents/the-presidents-news-conference-213>, accessed 9 November 2021. The origin of the saying appears to be Tacitus (Agricola 27:1) '...*prospera omnes sibi indicant, aduersa uni imputantur*' or, roughly translated, '... victory is claimed by all, failure is imputed to one alone.'

11 Curzon, *Comte d'Hervilly*, p.25 quoting Moustier with reference of AN: O3 604.

12 Hutt, *Chouannerie*, p.523.

13 Puisaye, *Mémoires*, vol.VI, p.605.

14 Puisaye, *Mémoires*, vol.VI, pp.606–607.

Balleroy, on 14 October 1797.[15] Even if, after the passing of time, the record was accurate it can be seen that although Hervilly was honestly recognising his faults on 14 July it was far from a *mea culpa* absolving Puisaye, who, having estranged himself from most of the émigré community, never returned to France after the Restoration and continued to defend his reputation until his death in England in 1827.

In time, as mentioned in the preface, blame began to be placed on the British and particularly Pitt's Government – rallying Frenchmen, republican and royalists, against the traditional enemy, perfidious Albion. Indeed in 1799, the Count Semyon Romanovich Vorontsov, Russian ambassador in London from 1784 to 1806, was asked by an émigré about British bad faith in the expedition, in his reply he said:

> This expedition was thus made on the pressing and very persistent demands of the royalists and on the plan that they presented ... There was not a single Englishman who was part of this expedition because the royalists did not want them. The squadron that protected the landing and the re-embarkation was English and exposed itself in the last situation, to the point of risking running aground. This squadron saved M. d'Hervilly and the Duc de Léri [*sic*], both dangerously wounded, and many others, and would have saved Sombreuil and his troops if he had kept his head and not been hasty to make a capitulation as unnecessary as unsure, as the events have proved. I know that a short time after this event, some constitutional and ignorant émigrés, through malice, endeavoured to spread the rumour, as absurd as damaging to the British government, that it had only made this expedition to destroy the French navy by sending on it a corps of officers from the former Royal Navy. ... 40 to 50 lieutenants perished on it. Now, is it probable that such a great power, and the most formidable on the sea due to the most numerous and finest fleet in the Universe, would have spent more than a million pounds, would have compromised its honour and reputation, to arrange the sending of an expedition in order that it failed only to kill off 40 to 50 lieutenants of the French navy ...[16]

Nevertheless, the invective against Britain has persisted and filtered down through the ages, one author writing in the 1980s 'The first expedition had cost England twenty-seven million pounds sterling, the second nine million. But not a single English soldier had been killed, nor even wounded.'[17]

At the opening of Parliament on 29 October 1795 the Opposition immediately attacked Pitt's administration for their conduct of the war as a whole and in particular the ongoing expeditions to western France. Despite being portrayed otherwise, for example by Robert who called the Opposition Members that day 'Forty-nine honest Englishmen,' the main thrusts of their

15 For a discussion of the veracity of this evidence see Hutt, *Chouannerie*, pp.585–586. Jean-François-Paul-Henri de La Cour Vicomte de Balleroy (1724–1802), a former naval officer and the senior *capitaine* in Hervilly, was the paternal uncle of Hervilly's wife and the Marquis de Balleroy, Puisaye's aide.

16 Marc Bouloiseau, 'L'expédition de Quiberon (1795) jugé par l'ambassadeur du tsar à Londres', *Annales historiques de la Révolution française*, no.295, 1994, pp.100–102.

17 Lambert, *Pour Dieu*, p.329.

criticism were the Government's support for the royalist cause and not having made peace with the French Republic.[18] Richard Brinsley Butler Sheridan spoke of:

> These disastrous expeditions where the wretched emigrants were left to the vengeance of their incensed countrymen, however, seemed to awaken no sentiments of English pride or resentment. It was not, indeed, British blood which had flowed, but it was British honour which had bled at every pore, and the murderous enterprises must one day, 'sit heavy on the souls' of the authors of them. … could any league be more destructive to this country than one with the house of Bourbon, who had been the uniform and inveterate enemies of Great Britain? No association with the Republic, could be so destructive to our interests; for never were there worse neighbours on earth than the French during the monarchy.[19]

Soon Charles James Fox stood to deliver a long and wide-ranging speech in which he upheld Sheridan's sentiments but with more subtlety:

> He knew not by whom that expedition [to Quiberon] was planned; he knew not in whose desperate bosom the idea of the horrid expedition was engendered, but it was a scene over which the heart of every manly Briton shed tears of blood; … Good God! To think that so many brave and honourable men, among whom there were gentlemen of the purest feelings and of the most honourable principles, should be led to massacre in the way in which they were! … It was impossible to animadvert upon the conduct of ministers in these expeditions without being astonished at the insanity with which they were planned.[20]

Then, as he gradually brought his speech to a conclusion, Fox criticised the Government for its support for the royalist cause, and the émigrés in particular, because it stood in the way of peace with the French Republic, '… it was neither politic with respect to ourselves, nor kind and considerate with regard to them: that if we employed them on any such expedition, we identified their cause with ours, and made it impossible for us to retract with honour, whatever might be the events of the war.'[21] In response, Pitt refused to be drawn to every point raised, restricting himself to a speech of less than a third the length of Fox's in which he simply said, 'The expedition to Quiberon bay, and the hard fate of the unfortunate emigrants who were fighting for their lawful monarch, must be considered by us as a calamity, independent of its effects. Every man's personal feelings were interested in that event.'[22]

While it is, of course, true that the Bretons and émigrés paid by far the heaviest price, such statements as 'British blood [had not] flowed' ignored

18 Robert, *Expédition*, p.204.
19 Cobbett (ed.), *Parliamentary History*, vol.XXXII, pp.160–162.
20 Cobbett (ed.), *Parliamentary History*, vol.XXXII, pp.170–171.
21 Cobbett (ed.), *Parliamentary History*, vol.XXXII, p.178.
22 Cobbett (ed.), *Parliamentary History*, vol.XXXII, p.185.

the wounds of the British sailors received in action and the deaths of the soldiers and sailors from scurvy and dysentery, at sea or on the Île d'Yeu, but there was no political capital to be made from these.

Several of the survivors, as has already been seen, sought to counter some of the most 'absurd' accusations against the British. Le Charron addressed the issues of alleged British bad faith, the causes of failure and why accusations persisted against the British:

> I affirm with all the candour of my character, that this is a calumny ... I never saw, in all that passed before my eyes, the least thing that could be perceived as an ulterior motive in them, nor any disposition to wish for the failure of the expedition. ... Doubtless there could have been some indiscreet and ill-founded remarks, by some English subaltern officers: some Frenchmen upset by their misfortune and the agony of their friends that they had left on land, could have been annoyed by these remarks; but without recriminating on the mistakes that were made, it can be said that the commanders of both nations had much too much confidence in the position of Fort Penthièvre which had been very wrongly compared to a little Gibraltar. ... The hatred of Bonaparte for the English Government and the august Bourbon family, has contributed since by having these calumnious accusations repeated in several directed or altered works; for example, in that of M. the Comte de V[auban] ...[23]

Vauban's memoirs were mentioned in particular as Le Charron, among many others, considered they had been altered and then published as the price of the former's freedom from prison at the hands of Napoleon's police. Vauban was indeed released and some of his property was restored, however he was never forgiven by the French monarchy.

The émigrés, especially the commanders, were considered to be at fault by one of their own,

> ... the inexperience, the presumption and the rivalry of several chiefs, the indocility of the subordinates, the absence of a single, able, leader, already recommended by success, who, invested with general confidence, would have silenced the petty pretensions, and would have known how to be obeyed, that is the real cause of the disaster of Quiberon.[24]

The choice of commanders, although driven by circumstances, was that of the British Government. As has been seen, although he was regarded as active and able, Hervilly's selection had evolved more by chance, along with his ready availability, than any considered selection. As for Puisaye, even if they had been unaware of his performance in Normandy, he had amply illustrated his lack of military acumen alongside his rampant ambition, a dangerous combination, during the planning process. However, he had come to the

23 Le Charron, *Expédition de Quiberon*, pp.125–127.

24 Henry-Alexandre-Léopold Comte de Castres de Vaux, *Relation d'un voyage sur le bord septentrional de la Mer d'Azof et en Crimée dans la vue d'y établir une colonie d'émigrés* (Paris: A. J. Kilian, 1826), p.xvi.

British Government as the leader of an active and numerous insurrection which they intended to support, so he could not be excluded. He was clearly unwilling to play a secondary role and so the appointment of a commander above his head was impractical. Nevertheless, they sought to rein him in, at least at the beginning, by giving the decision to land to Hervilly and the limited the number of disciplined troops in the first wave, while sufficient to hold a landing point or port, as the mission required, they were too few to fulfil his ambitions until more, be they with Artois or Moira, arrived.

The strategic plan came to nothing as Austria did not budge from the eastern bank of the Rhine, meaning that the Armée de Condé could not move either. British diplomats, who through their agents had strived to build support for a co-ordinated insurrection in Franche Comté and the region east of Lyon, tried to get the Austrians to take advantage of this but, after an interview with their influential minister, Johann Amadeus von Thugut, the ambassador at Vienna wrote, 'M. Thugut said, that their object was to proceed by regular military progress. That their misfortunes in Alsace [in 1793] experienced by an unwise reliance on the assurances of the Emigrants rendered this precaution more than necessary.' Two bridgeheads over the Rhine would have to be secured, otherwise 'in case of failure the Army would be driven headlong into the Rhine' by French republican reinforcements.[25] Meanwhile pre-emptive action by the republican authorities suppressed the royalists in Lyon and Piedmont prevaricated, stating that they intended to invade Dauphiné rather than Provence as originally thought but then did neither.

Blame for particular aspects of what happened can be laid at the feet of individuals, in particular Puisaye and Hervilly, but that for the expedition as a whole falls squarely on the shoulders of the British Government, especially the triumvirate of Pitt, Dundas and Grenville. They were ultimately responsible for the inadequacies of the preparation, resourcing and logistics of the expedition, errors which they simply repeated, although fortunately without the same consequences, in 1800.[26] Their chief responsibility was to have accepted the concept of it in the first place. The royalists continually inflated their strength and successes to attract support. Puisaye, driven by his personal ambition, was an extreme example of it but he was not alone as Major Harness observed of Cadoudal's communication with Warren in October 1795, 'He gives him his wishes, I believe, for realities.'[27]

The British Government built the expedition on the sand of Puisaye's ambition and wishful thinking. Pitt, Dundas and Grenville did not embark upon a Machiavellian plot but, indeed, failed to heed that Florentine's warning:

25 TNA: FO 74/11: Sir Morton Eden to William Wickham 'Most secret and confidential' 22 August.

26 Fortescue, *British Army*, Vol.IV, pp.777–779 and Walter Frewen Lord, *Sir Thomas Maitland The Mastery of the Mediterranean* (London: T. Fisher Unwin, 1897), pp.60–67.

27 Duncan-Jones (ed.), *William Harness*, p.65, Harness to his wife 25 October.

The expiatory chapel at the Champ des Martyrs. (Author's collection)

> The danger of trusting those who are in exile from their own country, being one to which the rulers of States are often exposed, may, I think, be fitly considered … It behoves us, therefore, to remember how empty are the promises, and how doubtful the faith, of men in banishment from their native land. … as for the empty promises and delusive hopes which they set before you, so extreme is their desire to return home that they naturally believe many things that are untrue, and designedly misrepresent many others; so that between their beliefs and what they say they believe, they fill you with false impressions, on which if you build, your labour is in vain, and you are led to engage in enterprises from which nothing but ruin can result.[28]

They would not be the last to fail to heed the warning.

28 Niccolò Machiavelli, *Discourses on the First Decade of Titus Livius* (London: Kegan Paul, Trench & Co., 1883), pp.317–318, 'the danger of trusting banished men.'

Appendix I

Distribution of troops, boats and sailors to row them for embarkation on 26 and landing on 27 June 1795[1]

Ship	No. of men onboard	Boats appointed for them	Nos	Ship supplying crew for boat
Loyal Emigrant				
Under command of a lieutenant from HMS *Robust*				
Flora	135	*Flora*'s Flat Boat	40	*Flora*
		Flora's Long Boat	30	HMS *Galatea*
		Matthew & Thomas's Flat Boat	40	*Matthew & Thomas*
		William & Mary's Long Boat	25	HMS *Galatea*
Burton	100	*Burton*'s Flat Boat	40	*Burton*
		Wirk's Flat Boat	40	*Wirk*
		Burton's Long Boat	20	HMS *Concorde*
Under command of a lieutenant from HMS *Pomone*				
Hardy	66	*Hardy*'s Flat Boat	40	*Hardy*
		Hardy's Long Boat	26	HMS *Concorde*
King George	100	*King George*'s Flat Boat	40	*King George*
		King George's Long Boat	20	HMS *Pomone*
		William & Mary's Flat Boat	40	*William & Mary*
Hervilly, 1st Battalion				
Under command of a lieutenant from HMS *Artois*				
Atlantic	180	*Atlantic*'s Flat Boat	40	*Atlantic*
		Bonitta's Flat Boat	40	*Bonitta*
		Sarah's Flat Boat	40	*Sarah*
		Matthew & Thomas's Long Boat	30	HMS *Anson*

1 TNA: ADM 80/136.

Ship	No. of men onboard	Boats appointed for them	Nos	Ship supplying crew for boat
		Atlantic's Long Boat	30	HMS *Anson*
Sarah	82	*Jane*'s Flat Boat	46	*Jane*
		Wirk's Long Boat	36	HMS *Artois*
Under command of a Lieutenant from HMS *Galatea*				
Catherine	45	*Middleton*'s Flat Boat	45	*Middleton*
William & Robert	75	*William & Robert*'s Flat Boat	40	*William & Robert*
		William & Robert's Long Boat	35	HMS *Artois*
Patty	135	*Patty*'s Long Boat	35	*Patty*
		Aid's Flat Boat	40	*Aid*
		Penelope's Flat Boat	40	*Penelope*
		Aid's Long Boat	20	HMS *Pomone*
Hervilly, 2nd Battalion				
Under command of a Lieutenant from HMS *Anson*				
Jane	130	*Mary (1st)*'s Flat Boat	40	*Mary (1st)*
		Mary (1st)'s Long Boat	35	HMS *Robust*
		Middleton's Long Boat	35	HMS *Robust*
		Penelope's Long Boat	30	HMS *Robust*
Mary (2nd)	144 [*sic*]	*Mary (2nd)*'s Flat Boat	40	*Mary (2nd)*
		Mary (2nd)'s Long Boat	35	HMS *Thunderer*
		Jane's Long Boat	35	HMS *Thunderer*
		Fowler's Long Boat	33	HMS *Thunderer*
Under command of a lieutenant from HMS *Concorde*				
Fowler	138	*Fowler*'s Flat Boat	40	*Fowler*
		Ariel's Flat Boat	40	*Ariel*
		Ajax's Flat Boat	40	*Ajax*
		Eagle's Long Boat	18	*Eagle*
Thomas	178 [*sic*]	*Thomas*'s Flat Boat	40	*Thomas*
		HMS *Pomone*'s Launch	25	HMS *Pomone*
		HMS *Anson*'s Launch	25	HMS *Anson*
		HMS *Artois*'s Launch	25	HMS *Artois*
		HMS *Galatea*'s Launch	25	HMS *Galatea*
		HMS *Concorde*'s Launch	25	HMS *Concorde*

Artillery – under command of a lieutenant from HMS *Thunderer*
HMS *Robust*'s Launch – to take three field pieces with their carriages etc. from the *Penelope*
HMS *Thunderer*'s Launch – to take three field pieces with their carriages etc. from the *Aid*
Medea's Long Boat (crewed by sailors from HMS *Robust*) – to take 15 men of the artillery from the *Aid* and to accompany HMS *Robust*'s Launch
Elizabeth's Long Boat (crewed by sailors from HMS *Thunderer*) – to take 15 men of the artillery from the *Aid* and to accompany HMS *Thunderer*'s Launch
Hope's Insecure Arms's Long Boat – to proceed to the *Aid* and *Penelope* to assist in [embarking and] landing the artillery, field pieces etc.

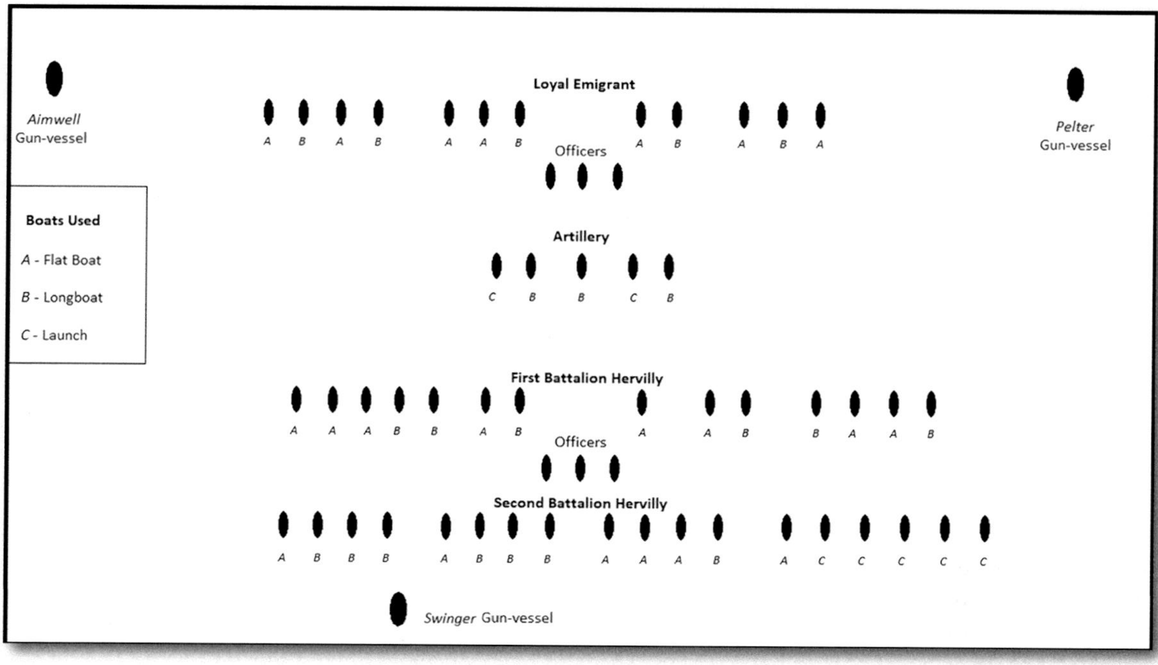

'Station of the Boats' 27 June 1795.

Appendix II

The French Republican Forces

No source has been found to show the strength and composition of the French republican forces in northwest France in the summer of 1795. The best evidence of the units that were present in Brittany at this time is provided by the 'Tableau Général de la situation des troupes de la grande division de l'Ouest de l'Armée des Côtes de l'Océan' (General table of the situation of the troops of the Western grand division of the Army of the Ocean's Coasts) for 15 January 1796.[1] The information it contains is the closest there is to an order of battle for the summer of 1795. Additional information can be gleaned from the incomplete state for the Armée des Côtes de Brest of 26 September 1794 as it includes the 3e Division, which had its headquarters at Vannes, as well as an estimate for supplies to the armies in the region, dated 23 September 1795.[2]

Table 19: 1er Subdivision, Grande Division de l'Ouest de l'Armée des Côtes de l'Océan, grand division and subdivision commanded by *Général de division* Gabriel-Venance Rey, 15 January 1796.

Unit	Station	POWs	Men present under arms	Effectives including officers
Infanterie				
1 Bn 184 D-Bde	Lamballe		720	837
2 Bn "	Quintin	401	596	1,228
3 Bn "	Lanvollon	28	636	832
2 Bn 151 D-Bde	Saint-Brieuc		403	728
1 Bn 144 D-Bde	Guingamp		272	516
1 Bn 32 Regt	Dinan	4	525	851
2 Bn 63 D-Bde	Dinan		623	768
2 Bn de Seine et Oise	Dol-de-Bretagne	7	586	891
2 Bn de l'Ain	Broons	7	443	710
1 Bn Grenadiers de Rhône et Loire	Saint-Servan		437	532
2 Bn 15 Regt	Saint-Malo		162	238
Vétérans nationaux	Saint-Brieuc		16	16
Inf. légère				
1 Bn 19 D-Bde	Rostrenen			
2 Bn "	Cancale			

1 SHD: *Les Archives de la Vendée* B 5/133–2, <http://recherche-archives.vendee.fr/archives/archives/fonds/FRAD085_SHD_B/inventaire/view:8193?RECH_S=Quiberon&rech_mode=and&RECH_eadid=FRAD085_SHD_B&type=inventaire>, accessed 28 October 2021.

2 SHD: *Les Archives de la Vendée* B 5/125–19 and B 5/1124–18.

Unit	Station	POWs	Men present under arms	Effectives including officers
Artillerie				
Various	various	2	1,300	1,684
Additional units				
Det 12 Bn Sapeurs	Cancale		43	78
Dets 8 Regt Artillerie	Saint-Malo & Saint-Brieuc		206	237
Det 24 Regt Cavalerie	Saint-Malo & Guingcamp		96	100
Det 14 Chasseurs à Cheval	Saint-Malo & Guingcamp	4	339	574

Table 20: 2e Subdivision, Grande Division de l'Ouest de l'Armée des Côtes de l'Océan, commanded by *Général de brigade* Jacques-Nicolas Moynat d'Auxon, 15 January 1796.

Unit	Station	PoWs	Men present under arms	Effectives including officers
Infanterie				
1 Bn 1 Regt Inf Marine	Brest	112	203	971
2 Bn 1 Regt Inf Marine	"	137	171	1,043
1 Bn 2 Regt Inf Marine	"	114	220	875
2 Bn 2 Regt Inf Marine	"	104	234	1007
2 Bn 92 Regt	"		439	724
2 Bn de la formation d'Orléans	Saint-Renan		422	564
1 Bn 67 D-Bde	Quimperlé		325	466
3 Bn 67 D-Bde	"		435	576
2 Bn 106 Regt	"		277	299
1 Bn 141 D-Bde	Morlaix	22	573	683
2 Bn 141 D-Bde	Brest	6	567	651
3 Bn 141 D-Bde	"	27	628	734
2 Bn 111 Regt	Roscoff	73	456	777
1 Bn 197 D-Bde	Carhaix-Plouguer	33	561	854
2 Bn 197 D-Bde	Lesneven	51	471	849
3 Bn 197 D-Bde	Quimperlé		428	845
1 Bn provisiore des Côtes de Brest	Landerneau		279	319
Artillerie				
Various	various	265	1,843	3,413
Other divisional troops				
12 Bn de Sapeurs	Brest		258	1,010
Cie d'ouvriers	"		57	60
Cie du Génie	"		109	125
Additional units				
Det 8 Regt d'Art	Brest, Pouldu		48	75
Det 3 Bn de la formation d'Orléans	Colonne mobile		158	170
Det Gren 2 Bn 67 D-Bde	Quimperlé		23	24
Det Gren 2 Bn de Seine et Oise	"		71	72
Det escoaude de mineurs	Brest		12	14
Det 3 esc. 14 Chasseurs à Cheval	Landerneau		27	27

Table 21: 3e Subdivision, Grande Division de l'Ouest de l'Armée des Côtes de l'Océan, commanded by *Général de brigade* Louis Lemoine, 15 January 1796.

Unit	Station	POWs	Men present under arms	Effectives including officers
Infanterie				
10 Bn du Var	Vannes		566	725
5 Bn du Bas-Rhin	Vannes		481	629
1 Bn Loire Inferieur	Vannes		215	466
7 Bn du Jura	Hennebont	2	415	940
12 Bn de la formation de l'Orléans	Port-Louis		250	370
11 Bn de Paris	Île de Groix	7	523	864
6 Bn de la Côte d'Or	Quiberon		515	764
1 Bn 60 Regt	Locmariaquer	2	379	607
1 Bn 72 Regt	Auray		639	756
11 Bn de la formation de l'Orléans	Rochefort-en-Terre		386	463
4 Bn des Ardennes	La Roche-Bernard	1	295	916
3 Bn d'Ille-et-Vilaine	Ploemel	11	510	614
13 Bn Seine et Oise	Sarzeau		235	255
1 Bn 41 Regt	Pontivy		642	809
5 Bn du Calvados	Lorient		437	813
Vétérans nationaux	Vannes		14	14
Artillerie				
Various	various	2	671	970
Cavalerie				
10e Hussards	Pontivy		317	318
Additional units				
Grenadiers 2 Bn d'Orléans	'Saouen' [?]		85	93
Gren & det 67 D-Bde	'Saouen', Auray		239	328
Gren 111 Regt	Port-Louis		72	73
Gren des Côtes du Nord	Locmariaquer		31	46
Gren 6 Regt	Pénestin		45	70
Gren 9 Bn de Paris	Rohan	2	89	104
Gren 184 D-Bde	Muzillac		82	92
Gren 106 Regt	Pénestin		66	66
Gren 76 D-Bde	Penerf		68	68
Gren & det 3 Bn de l'Ain	Josselin etc.	2	163	199
Det 144 D-Bde	Sarzeau		95	165
Cie franche des Antilles	Muzillac	8	101	153
Det 2 Bn de la Rébublique	Langoëlan		45	69
Det 12 Bn de Sapeurs	Vannes etc.		252	257
Det 2 Bn de Sapeurs	Elven		96	96

Table 22: Belle-Île Garrison, Grande Division de l'Ouest de l'Armée des Côtes de l'Océan, commanded by *Général de brigade provisoire* Balthazar Romand, 15 January 1796.

Unit	Station	POWs	Men present under arms	Effectives including officers
Infanterie				
4 Bn de la Gironde	Le Palais		435	623
3 Bn du Loir et Cher	Citadelle	18	549	727
1 Bn 4 Regt	Sauzon		570	754
1 Bn de Seine et Oise	Locmaria		696	743
Artillerie				
Various	Forts & batteries		450	473
Additional units				
Det 8 Regt d'Art	"		107	109
Det 10 Hussards	-		16	17
Det 12 Bn de Sapeurs	"		34	39

Table 23: 4e Subdivision, Grande Division de l'Ouest de l'Armée des Côtes de l'Océan, commanded by *Général de division* Louis-François-Jean Chabot, 15 January 1796.

Unit	Station	PoWs	Men present under arms	Effectives including officers
Infanterie				
8 Bn de Seine et Oise	Nantes		421	623
2 Bn 67 Regt	Ancenis		412	543
4 Bn de l'Orne	Ancenis, Varades		319	333
3 Bn d'Arras	Nort-sur-Erdre		241	442
1 Bn 67 Regt	Blain		421	556
2 Bn de la Réunion	Nozay		176	257
8 Bn du Bas Rhin	Châteaubriant		226	647
8 Bn de la Somme	"		108	176
2 Bn 67 D-Bde	Derval		342	676
8 Bn de la Seine Inférieure	Guérande		309	397
4 Bn des Ardennes	Blain, Montoir-en-Bretagne		281	299
6 Bn de la Charente Inférieure	Savenay		230	486
Inf. légère				
2 Bn de Tirailleurs Belges	Nantes		411	622
Artillerie				
Various	various		337	450
Other divisional troops				
2 Bn de Sapeurs	Nantes, Ancenis etc.		252	597
Gendarmerie Nationale	Nantes, Ancenis		53	53
Additional units				
Det 2 Bn 92 Regt	Nort-sur-Erdre		150	197
Det 4 Bn d'Indre et Loire	Varades		117	117
Det 1 Bn de la Loire Inférieure	Coueron		43	43
Det 2 Bn du Morbihan	Nort-sur-Erdre		25	25
Det 4 Bn Maine et Loire	Ancenis		68	68
Det 4 Bn des Côtes du Nord	"		34	34
Det 4 Bn du Calvados	Varades		41	41
Det 2 Bn de la République	"		26	26
Det 2 Bn 67 D-Bde	Nozay		211	211

Unit	Station	PoWs	Men present under arms	Effectives including officers
Det 2 Bn de la Loire Inférieure	"		53	53
Det 12 Bn de Seine et Oise	Châteaubriant		64	72
Gren 8 Bn Haut Rhin	Nozay		57	77
Colonnes mobiles	Various		164	164
Det 2 Bn de Chasseurs réunis	Sautzon		94	94
Det 23 Regt Inf Légère	Ancenis		65	65
Det 5 Regt d'Art	Nantes		160	202
Det 8 Regt d'Art	Le Croisic		30	55
Det 10 Hussards	Nantes		63	63
Det 14 Chasseurs à Cheval	Blain		8	8

Table 24: 5e Subdivision, Grande Division de l'Ouest de l'Armée des Côtes de l'Océan, commanded by *Général de Brigade* Philippe-Joseph Malbrancq, 15 January 1796.

Unit	Station	POWs	Men present under arms	Effectives including officers
Infanterie				
1 Bn 8 Regt	Rennes, Pont-Réan etc.	5	596	820
28 D-Bde	Rennes, La Prevalaye etc.		2,191	2,876
1 Bn 82 Regt	Rennes, Cesson-Sévigné etc.		472	605
1 Bn de la Seine Inférieure	Mordelles, Plélan-le-Grand etc.	2	462	604
8 Bn de la formation d'Orléans	Montfort-sur-Meu, Bédée etc.		534	586
3 Bn de Rouen	Redon, La Gacilly etc.	1	398	700
9 Bn de Paris	La Guerche-de-Bretagne, Retiers		376	382
3 Bn des Fédérés	La Guerche-de-Bretagne, Vitré		447	460
Inf. légère				
3 Bn 19 D-Bde L	Vitré, Châteaubourg etc.	10	610	1,027
Bn de Chasseurs du Mont des Chats*	Bain-de-Bretagne, Fougères etc.	5	438	544
Artillerie				
8 Regt d'Art	Rennes		252	1,063
Additional units				
Det 14 Chasseurs à Cheval	Rennes, Vitré		31	31
Det 10 Hussards	Rennes	6	77	140
Gren 1 Bn 144 D-Bde	"		80	97
Gren 3 Bn des Ardennes	"		83	110
Gren 2 Bn des Vosges	Fougères		89	107
Gren 2 Bn 44 Regt	"		60	60
Gren 1 Bn 179 D-Bde	Le Loroux		25	25
Gren 2 Bn 179 D-Bde	Saint-Marc-le-Blanc		82	82
Gren 3 Bn 61 D-Bde	Saint-Aubin-du-Cormier		74	74
Gren 9 Regt	Saint-Jean-sur-Couesnon		72	72
Det Vétérans nationaux	Rennes		47	48
Det 7 Bn de Paris	Pont-Péan		32	32
Det 3 Bn de la Nièvre	Lohéac		80	89
Det 2 Bn 60 Regt	Vitré		208	210
Det Carabiniers 2 Bn 19 D-Bde Légère	Fougères		70	70
Det 3 Bn 17 D-Bde	"		79	79
Det 2 Bn 61 D-Bde	", Saint-Georges-de-Reintembault		330	330
Det 2 Bn 37 Regt	Louvigné-du-Désert		103	103
Det 1 Bn 37 Regt	Le Loroux		54	54

Unit	Station	POWs	Men present under arms	Effectives including officers
Det 2 Bn de Sapeurs	Rennes, Cice		171	243
Dépôt 6 Regt	Châteaugiron		40	40
* The Bataillon des Chasseurs (or Chasseurs tirailleurs) du Mont des Chats was raised around Godewarsvelde, west of Lille on the border with Belgium, on 17 February 1793; it went to form the 24e Demi-brigade légère on the second formation, 6 October 1796. It was in the Netherlands in January 1795, it is sometimes confused with the Bataillon du Mont-Cassel (place nearby).				

Table 25: Résumé of the strength of the Grande Division de l'Ouest de l'Armée des Côtes de l'Océan 15 January 1796.

	Men present under arms	Effectives including officers
1er Subdivision	7,922	11,754
2e Subdivision	8,956	16,845
3e Subdivision	7,491	11,637
Belle-Isle	2,700	3,320
4e Subdivision	4,539	7,157
5e Subdivision	6,776	9,667
Total of Grande Division	38,384	60,380
Dépôts & Détachements	5,904	7,122
TOTAL	44,449	67,502

Table 26: 'Grande Division du Sud de l'Armée des Côtes de l'Océan' (Southern grand division in the Vendée) 15 January 1796.

	HQ location	Men present under arms	Effectives including officers
1er Subdivision	Machecoul	6,932	10,716
2e Subdivision	Cholet	6,276	12,639
3e Subdivision	La Châtaigneraie	8,061	18,041
4e Subdivision	Les Sables-d'Olonne	9,697	14,913
5e Subdivision	Île de Noirmoutier	556	1,595
6e Subdivision	La Rochelle	5,801	10,163
7e Subdivision	Poitiers	179	179
8e Subdivision	Tours	309	312
Garrison of 2e S'div	Saumur	359	823
Garrison of 3e S'div	Fontenay-le-Comte	3,321	7,296
TOTAL		31,552	57,902

Table 27: 'Grande Division de l'Est de l'Armée des Côtes de l'Océan' (Eastern grand division in Normandy) 15 January 1796.

	Département	Men present under arms	Effectives including officers
1er Subdivision	Calvados	2,399	3,427
2e Subdivision	L'Orne	3,349	4,781
3e Subdivision	Mayenne	8,034	11,068
4e Subdivision	Sarthe	4,426	7,550
5e Subdivision	Maine et Loire	5,307	7,145
6e Subdivision	La Manche	6,523	8,332
TOTAL		30,038	42,303

Table 28: 3e Division Armée des Côtes de Brest, commanded by *Général* Simon Canuel, 26 September 1794.

Unit	Station	POWs	Men present under arms	Effectives including officers
Infanterie				
1 Bn des Amis de la République	Lorient		506	617
3 Bn de Loir et Cher	"	7	552	799
2 Bn de la République	"		470	592
2 Cie des Côtes du Nord	Annexed to the battalion		62	95
2 Bn 92 Regt	Port-Louis		809	824
1 Bn 1 Regt de Marine	Auray		147	1,200
2 Bn 1 Regt de Marine	Auray		44	1,182
5 Bn d'Orléans	Vannes		626	688
4 Bn du Calvados	Muzillac		487	579
2 Bn 67 Regt	Pontivy		761	845
2 Bn 32 Regt	Redon	8	736	825
7 Bn du Jura	Josselin	5	493	856
5 Cie Vétérans nationaux	Vannes		15	17
Dépôt 72 Regt	Vannes		14	16
Dépôt 3 Bn Seine et Oise	Vannes		6	7
1 Bn 41 Regt	Quiberon		446	836
Artillerie				
Various	various		431	431
Cavalerie				
Det 24 Cavalerie	Vannes		131	139
15 Chasseurs à Cheval	Pontivy		224	243
Dets 16 Dragons	Vannes, Lorient		116	122
Det 7 Chasseurs à Cheval	Vannes		52	55
'Dragons nationaux de l'Orient'*	Lorient		17	19

* Otherwise known as the 'Garde à cheval de la ville de L'Orient' – it was attached to the town's national guard and appears to have been much larger earlier on in the revolutionary period. The troopers were clothed and equipped as dragoons, with red coats and black facings, leading to their nickname of 'les diables rouges' (the red devils).

Table 29: Estimates of the strength of the republican armies in Western France, 23 September 1795.

Armée des Côtes de Cherbourg	44,500
Armée des Côtes de Brest	41,300
Armée de l'Ouest	90,200
Total	176,000

Appendix III

Some Notes on Uniforms

Royalist Forces

The plates in the colour section are from a collection of contemporary or near-contemporary depictions of uniforms from various countries known as the Berlin Album, now held by the Anne S.K. Brown Military Collection, Brown University Library, USA. In addition comprehensive coverage of the uniforms worn by the white and black cockade regiments, including the cadre corps, is provided by Robert Grouvel in *Les corps de troupes de l'émigration française*, Volume I. The following is additional information from primary sources.

White Cockade Units

The regulations gave the facing colours for the first eight regiments, those for Dresnay being 'vert foncé' (dark green) and 'ventre de biche' (doe's belly – ochre/light tan); Hector's being iron grey.[1]

An officer of one of the regiments raised in Germany, Vioménil, gives some details of its uniforms and there is no reason to suspect those raised in Britain were different. The soldiers' dress was as illustrated however the lining of the coat and tails would have been white and not in the facing colour.[2] In summer the black gaiters were replaced by grey ones, and the soldiers had grey greatcoats. The officers wore three cornered hats with white plumes and gold cockade strap and stiffeners. Their full-dress coats were as the soldiers, buttoned to the waist but with long tails, silver epaulettes (French pattern) and buttons (stamped with a fleur-de-lys), white waistcoat and breeches, American (jockey) style boots, white sword belt, gilt belt plate and sword knot; in undress they wore a heavy frock coat in blue with a red collar and a grey greatcoat with white buttons. The sash that they wore was black.[3] The

1 TNA: WO 24/1112: Article 22, Règlements, also Grouvel, *Les corps de troupes*, vol.I, pp.103, 137.

2 TNA: WO 24/1112: Article 22, Règlements. Furthermore Grouvel, *Les corps de troupes*, vol.I, p.137, states the volunteers of Hector were distinguished by iron grey lacing on the edges of their tails (this would not be a distinction if the tails were already in the facing colour – iron grey).

3 Marquise de Perry de Nieüil, *Mémoires du Marquis de Toustain 1790–1823* (Paris; Plon, 1933), p.53.

black sashes and 'cravats to their Colours' were in memory of the late King Louis XVI.[4] Evidence that they were worn by regiments formed in England is provided by Gouzillon de Bélizal, of Hector, who was given a black sash with silver fringes by an English well-wisher before he left to join his regiment.[5]

The illustrations, from the Berlin Album show the soldiers with white crossed belts, with no plate, and a sabre briquet. This is contrary to the list of arms and equipment to be supplied, at government expense, in the regulations. All ranks were, indeed, to have crossed belts, one of which carried the cartridge pouch, but with a plate. An example is held by the musée de l'Armée, Paris, which is oval and made of brass, a fleur-de-lys embossed in the centre with HERVILLY above and 8 below – indicating it was made before Hector (and Broglie) were authorised.[6] All had muskets, in addition *sergents* were to have a sword only, *caporaux* a sword and bayonet while all the soldiers just a bayonet, carried on the other belt. Furthermore, *caporaux* were to have epaulettes and the *grenadiers*, epaulettes and bonnets (these last may not have been supplied as insufficient funds were allocated for them).

Later it was decided that the *sergents* of the regiments should have coats with long tails, like the officers, as many were former officers themselves, it is likely that the volunteers of Hector were similarly distinguished.

The regulations specified 'white flags with three fleurs-de-lys in gold.'[7]

In 2010 a drum of the Boissieux's company of the Régiment d'Hervilly was sold at auction. Its shell was very dark blue (the facing colour of the Royal-Louis) with black rims, above and below which were other, narrower, rims apparently in the 'ventre de biche' facing colour. The shell bore the words, in white, 'REGIMENT ROYAL D'HERVILLY' above and 'COMPAGNIE DE BOISSIEUX' below – 'D'HERVILLY' and 'DE BOISSIEUX' appearing on the 'front' between three golden yellow fleurs-de-lys, two above and one below.[8]

Hussards de Warren

The uniform is described as a red dolman with blue collars, cuffs and cords along with blue breeches and a black conical shako with a white cockade and plume to the front.[9] However it would appear that red bonnets de police or similar were customarily worn as Janillion remembered seeing, in this period, hussars dressed in red with, on their heads, 'small toques of the same colour' operating on the isthmus between the opposing positions.[10]

---

4 BL: Add MS 37850: Woodford to Windham 7 October 1794.

5 Vicomte de Gouzillon de Bélizal, 'Journal et Lettres d'un Émigré', *Revue de Bretagne*, vol. XXVII January–February 1902, pp.99–100.

6 'Plaque de baudrier du régiment d'Hervilly' <https://art.rmngp.fr/fr/library/artworks/plaque-de-baudrier-du-regiment-d-hervilly_laiton_1795>, accessed 14 November 2021.

7 TNA: WO 24/1112.

8 'Resultats – Tambour d'infanterie du Régiment Royal d'Hervilly Lot 531', *Binoche et Giquello* <https://www.binocheetgiquello.com/lot/7078/1377648?npp=100&>, accessed 14 November 2021.

9 C.T. Atkinson, 'Foreign regiments in the British Army, 1793–1802: Part VI – Notes on each corps or regiment', *Journal of the Society for Army Historical Research*, vol.22, No. 92 (Winter 1944), p.318, with plate by C.C.P. Lawson.

10 Janillion, *Versailles et Quiberon*, p.54. Toques were small, low, caps or hats with no, or a very narrow, brim – modern examples are low chefs' hats or bobble, or beanie, hats.

Cadres

Most sources state, following Grouvel, that the cadre corps were dressed in grey or green. Specifically, that Léon had green coats and breeches (although Grouvel describes a portrait of a volunteer wearing a red coat with dark blue facings edged with gold lace); Trésor apparently the same; Williamson with, at least waistcoats that were reversible – grey and green – and Allonville in grey. However, there is some evidence to show that Trésor and Williamson, at least wore red coats.[11]

In an undated memo, apparently from late spring or early summer 1795, Trésor wrote that the government appeared 'indifferent' about the colour to be worn but he had chosen red to ensure it was supplied quickly – with each company distinguished by the facing colour on the lapels only (1st), lapels and cuffs (2nd) and lapels and collar (3rd) – unfortunately the facing colour or the cut of the jackets is not stated.[12]

After an inspection of Williamson on 25 April 1796 it was noted that the unit's clothing had been 'in use since March 1795' but 'Thirty-two Volunteers were not clothed in Red.'

Finally, a newspaper reported on the cadres on 25 July 1795, 'A corps of Breton Emigrants landed at Plymouth on Saturday, brought from Jersey and Guernsey. They have red uniform with white facing, made in the French stile [*sic*], and black cockades.'[13]

The confusion may stem from correspondence from 1796 when on 4 October an order was made for 521 greatcoats to be issued to the volunteers of the cadre corps with the attached list in the margin: 'Léon 122, Green – Allonville 160, Grey – Williamson 119, Green – Trésor 120, Grey – 521 Total.' Then when on 12 October an order was made for 521 'complete Suits of Clothing' for the same men, the same list was placed in the margin.[14]

Chouans

Some sources seem to suggest that the issue of red uniforms to the Bretons was some sort of aberration or an attempt pass them off as British soldiers.[15] This ignores that fact that red had been used in the uniforms of the national units of the French royal army, in the line cavalry until the mid-eighteenth century and later in that of the Royal Household. Indeed, it was even used by the garde à cheval de la ville de Lorient (part of the town's National Guard) who, clothed and equipped as dragoons, wore red coats with black facings.

A republican source describes the Armée rouge, with Tinténiac, thus, '… chouans of the Morbihan, armed with English muskets, dressed in red with white linings ['soubastement'].'[16]

11 Grouvel, *Les corps de troupes*, vol.I, p.173.
12 TNA: HO 69/23.
13 *The Oxford Journal*, 25 July 1795.
14 TNA: WO 4/353: Woodford to Lukin 4 and 12 October 1796.
15 For example, Chasle de La Touche, *Relation* p52.
16 Paul Peyron, *La Chouannerie: Documents pour servir à son histoire dans le Finistère* (Quimper: L'Évèché, 1912), p.85, quoting a declaration made by Louis-René-Claude de Couedic to the Directoire du district de Quimperlé, 13 September 1795.

The use of white as a facing colour, for the coats supplied to the chouans and cadres, may have been chosen as it could be readily dyed when the regiments had been formed by combining these two elements, as was originally envisaged.

Bataillon d'Auray

Evidence heard by the military commissions indicate that, after being issued arms and uniforms at Carnac, this battalion wore red coats with 'greenish' facings and hats with white cockades.[17]

Moira's Staff

The émigré officers on Moira's staff, serving in the summer of 1794, were mentioned in a newspaper of the time: 'The number of French emigrants, who have solicited permission to accompany Lord Moira, into Brittany, amounts to 500; principally the Noblesse of that province and Normandy; their uniform is red faced with green; their buttons have a cross in the centre, with this motto, "Pour le loi et le Roi."'[18]

Republican Forces

By 1795 the familiar blue coats with white lapels piped red, with collars and cuffs in the same colours, were worn by the line infantry, national volunteers and national guards.

2e bataillon des tirailleurs belges

An illustration of a carabinier of the battalion is shown wearing a black bicorne with a red carrot-shaped ornament; green long-tailed coat and breeches; red epaulettes; red collar, pointed lapels, cuffs and turn-backs pointed white; green cuff-flaps piped white; white waistcoat; white metal buttons; black short gaiters with Hessian style tops with red edging and tassels.[19]

Garde territoriale

Chasle de La Touche wrote 'Several élite corps had been paid and maintained by the republic under the title of garde territorial; they had grey uniforms with black collars, manoeuvred regularly, and, seasoned by their first combat, could henceforth fight in line.'[20]

---

17 Closmadeuc, *Quiberon 1795*, p.446, 447 and 453.

18 *The Madras Courier*, 6 June 1794 (certainly quoting a British newspaper).

19 Laurent Brayard and Didier Davin, '2e bataillon de tirailleurs (belges)', *Les troupes étrangères au service de la France 1792–1803 SEHRI*, <https://revolutionsehrietranger.wordpress.com/2e-bataillon-de-tirailleurs-belges/>, accessed 5 November 2021.

20 Chasle de La Touche, *Relation*, p.25.

Bibliography

Archives

Jersey Archive
L/F/08/A Series of military documents c.1670 & 1747–1837

Archives Nationales, Paris (ANF)
MAR/C/7 Dossiers individuels de la marine

Service historique de la Défense, Vincennes (SHD)
GR 2 YE Classement alphabétique officiers (1791–1847)
GR 14 Yc Registres matricules de l'Ancien Régime (1682–1793)

Archives départementales de l'Eure, Evreux (ADE)
I J 240: Mémoires de Jacques de Chambray

National Archief, The Hague (NA)
2.21.008.01 Archief van de familie De Constant Rebecque

State Archive of the Russian Federation, Moscow (GARF)
758/2/52 Service britannique, Damas, notices

British Library (BL)
Add MS 7972–8090 Puisaye Papers
Add MS 37842–37935 Windham Papers
Add MS 40633–40635 Stewart Papers
Add MS 46702–46711 Don Papers
Add MS 49086–49172 Napier Papers

The National Archives, Kew (TNA)
ADM 1 Admiralty, and Ministry of Defence, Navy Department: Correspondence and Papers
ADM 51 Admiralty: Captains' Logs
ADM 80 Admiralty: Royal Greenwich Hospital: Miscellaneous Records
FO 74 Foreign Office and predecessor: Political and Other Departments: General Correspondence before 1906, Switzerland,
FO 95 Foreign Office and predecessors: Political and Other Departments: Miscellanea
HO 42 Home Office: Domestic Correspondence, George III
HO 69 Home Office: Bouillon Papers
HO 98 Home Office: Channel Islands, Isle of Man and Isles of Scilly: Correspondence and Papers
MPI 1 Public Record Office: Maps and plans extracted to flat storage from various series of records of departments not assigned an individual map extract prefix
PRO 30/8 Original records acquired as gifts or on deposit: William Pitt, 1st Earl of Chatham: Papers
PRO 30/11 Original records acquired as gifts or on deposit: Charles Cornwallis: Papers

WO 1 War Office and predecessors: Secretary-at-War, Secretary of State for War, and Commander-in-Chief, In-letters and Miscellaneous Papers
WO 4 War Office: Secretary-at-War, Out-letters
WO 6 War Department and successors: Secretary of State for War and Secretary of State for War and the Colonies, Out-letters
WO 10 Commissary General of Musters Office and successors: Artillery Muster Books and Pay Lists
WO 12 Commissary General of Musters Office and successors: General Muster Books and Pay Lists
WO 17 Office of the Commander in Chief: Monthly Returns to the Adjutant General
WO 24 War Office: Papers concerning Establishments
WO 25 War Office and predecessors: Secretary-at-War, Secretary of State for War, and Related Bodies, Registers
WO 54 Ordnance Office and War Office: Entry Books and Registers

Contemporary Newspapers and Journals

Gazette Nationale ou Le Moniteur Universel
Le Conservateur
Saunders's News-Letter
The Caledonian Mercury
The Chester Chronicle
The Chester Courant
The Kentish Gazette
The Kentish Weekly Post
The Hampshire Chronicle
The Hull Advertiser
The Ipswich Journal
The London Gazette
The Naval Chronicle
The Norfolk Chronicle
The Northampton Mercury
The Oxford Journal
The Staffordshire Advertiser
The Times

Contemporary Registers

Britain – *A List of the Officers of the Army and Marines, with an Index, a Succession of Colonels; A List of the Officers of the Army and Marines on Half-Pay, also with an Index* (The Army List) (annual editions)
France – *Etat Militaire de France* (annual editions 1753–1793)
United Provinces – *Naamregister der Heeren militaire Officieren, den Capitein generaal, de Generaals, Lieutenant-Generaals, Generaals-Major, Colonels, Lieutenant-Colonels, Majors, Capiteins, Lieutenants en Vaandrigs…Vermeerded mit eene Lyste der Chefs van alle de Regimenten, zo Cavallery, als Infantery, zedert den Jaare 1713. Mart 1794* (The Hague: 1794)

Published Works

Anon., *Correspondance Secrète de Charrette, Stofflet, Puisaye, et Autres* (Paris: F Buisson, Paris, An VII – 1797/1798)
Anon., *De l'expédition de Quiberon. Par un officier François, à bord de la Pomone* (London: T Baylis, 1795)
Anon., *Inauguration des Monuments de Quiberon, le quinze octobre 1829* (Vannes: J.M. Galles, 1829)

Anon. (ed.), *Mémoires d'Olivier d'Argens et Correspondances des Généraux* (Paris: Baudouin Frères, 1826)

Anon., *Rapport fait à la Convention Nationale, par Tallien, dans la séance du 9 thermidor, An 3, sur la défaite des Émigrés à Quiberon* (Besançon: Chez Métoyer, 1795)

Antrechaus, Jean-Joseph de Geoffroy Baron d', *Relation de M. Le Baron d'Antrechaus, capitaine de vaisseau honoraire, député en 1820, échappé aux massacres de Quiberon* (Paris: L G Michaud, 1824)

Aspinall, Arthur (ed.), *The later correspondence of George III, 1793–1810* (Cambridge: Cambridge University Press, 1962–1970)

Atkinson, C. T., 'Foreign regiments in the British Army, 1793–1802: Part VI – Notes on each corps or regiment' *Journal of the Society for Army Historical Research*, vol. 22, No. 92 (Winter 1944), pp.313–324

Barrow, John, *The Life and Correspondence of Admiral Sir William Sidney Smith, GCB* (London: Richard Bentley, 1848)

Barruel, *Abbé* Auguste de, *Mémoires pour servir à l'Histoire du Jacobinisme* (London: Boussonier, 1798)

Bazin, Christian, *Le Marquis de La Rouerie: Le colonel Armand: De la guerre américaine à la conjuration bretonne* (Paris: Perrin, 1990)

Bazouges, Hughes de, and Nichols, Alistair, *For God and King A History of the Damas Legion (1793–1798)* (Warwick: Helion & Company, 2021)

Beauchamp, Alphonse, *Histoire de la Guerre de la Vendée et des Chouans, depuis son origine jusqu'à la Pacification de 1800* (Paris: Giguet et Michaud, 1806)

Bennes, Louise-Françoise de Houssay de, *A narrative of the sufferings of Louise Françoise de Houssay, de Bennes, who served in the army as a volunteer, from 1792 to July 21, 1795, when she was made a prisoner at Quiberon* (London: privately published, 1796)

Berthier de Grandry, Chevalier Claude, *Récit sommaire de la déplorable affaire de Quiberon* (Nantes: Vincent Forest, 1861)

Bittard des Portes, René, *Les émigrés à la cocarde noire, en Angleterre, dans les provinces belges, en Hollande et à Quiberon* (Paris: E. Paul, 1908)

Bonnechose, Émile de, *Lazare Hoche Général en Chef des armées de la Moselle, d'Italie, des côtes de Cherbourg, de Brest et de l'Océan, de Sambre-et-Meuse et du Rhin sous la Convention et le Directoire 1793–1797* (London: Librairie Hachette et Cie., 1878)

Bouillé, Louis-Joseph-Amour Marquis de, *Souvenirs et fragments pour servir aux mémoires de ma vie et de mon temps* (Paris: Société d'histoire contemporaine, 1908)

Boulay de La Meurthe, Alfred, *Correspondance du Duc d'Enghien (1801–1804) et documents sur son enlévement et sa mort* (Paris: Alphonse Picard et fils, 1904)

Bouloiseau, Marc, 'L'expédition de Quiberon (1795) jugé par l'ambassadeur du tsar à Londres', *Annales historiques de la Révolution française*, no.295, 1994, pp.100–102

Brons, Jean-Antoine de, *Journal d'émigration* (Saint-Quentin-de-Baron: Chez Entre-deux-mers, 2014)

Cadoudal, Louis-Georges de, *Georges Cadoudal et la chouannerie* (Paris: Plon, 1887)

Callan, Comte Charles La Lande de, 'Les énigmes de Quiberon et les partis politiques pendant la Révolution', *Revue des Sciences Politiques*, Jan–Mar 1931, (47e année), pp.204–228

Carpenter, Kirsty, and Mansell, Philip, *The French Émigrés in Europe and the Struggle against the Revolution, 1789–1814* (Basingstoke: Macmillan Press Ltd., 1999)

Castres de Vaux, Henry-Alexandre-Léopold Comte de, *Relation d'un voyage sur le bord septentrional de la Mer d'Azof et en Crimée dans la vue d'y établir une colonie d'émigrés* (Paris: A. J. Kilian, 1826)

Cazotte, Jacques-Scévole, *Témoignage d'un royaliste* (Paris: Adrien Le Clere et cie., 1839)

Cesena, Amédée de, *Notice Biographique sur M. Jean-Jacques Duboys* (Angers: Cosnier et Lachèse, 1846)

Champagnac, Jacques-Philippe, *Quiberon La répression et la vengeance* (Paris: Perrin, 1989)

Chasle de La Touche, Théodore-Gaston-Joseph, *Relation du désastre de Quiberon en 1795, et réfutation des souvenirs historiques de M. Rouget de L'Isle sur ce désastre* (Paris: Delloye, 1838)

Chassin, Charles-Louis, *Le Général Hoche à Quiberon* (Paris: Paul Dupont, 1897)

Chaumereix, Jean-Hughes Duroy de, *Narrative of M. De Chaumereix, who escaped from the Massacres of Aurai and Vannes, after the Expedition of Quiberon* (London: T. Baylis, 1795)

Clair, Somerset de (ed.), *Napoleon's Memoirs* (London: Faber and Faber Ltd., 1948)

Clarke, Stephen, *The French Revolution & What Went Wrong* (London: Arrow Books, 2019)

Closmadeuc, G. Thomas de, *Quiberon 1795 Émigrés et Chouans Commissions Militaires: Interrogatoires et Jugements* (Paris: Société d'éditions littéraires, 1899)

Cobbett, William (ed.), *The Parliamentary History of England, from the earliest period to the year 1803.* (London: Hansard, 1817/1818)

Contades, Gérard de, *Coblenz et Quiberon Souvenirs du Comte de Contades* (Paris: E. Dentu, 1885)

Contades, Gérard de, *Notice sur la Commune de Lonlay-le-Tesson* (Paris: Champion, 1881)

Cook, H. C. B., 'The St George Diary: A Junior Regimental Officer in the Low Countries, 1794–95', *Journal of the Society for Army Historical Research*, vol. 47, No. 192 (Winter 1969), pp.233–250

Corbehem, Bernard de, *Dix ans de ma vie ou Histoire de mon émigration* (Paris: A Phian Delaforest, 1827)

Corbett, Julian S. (ed.), *Private Papers of George, Second Earl Spencer, First Lord of the Admiralty 1794–1801* (London: Naval Records Society, 1913)

Curzon, Alfred de, *Le Comte d'Hervilly 1755–1795* (unknown: 1958)

Delavoye, Alexander, *Life of Thomas Graham Lord Lynedoch* (London: Richardson & Co., 1880)

Demet, Paul, *'We Are Accustomed to do Our Duty': German Auxiliaries with the British Army 1793–95* (Warwick: Helion & Company, 2018)

Devlin, Jonathan D., 'A Problem of Royalism: General Amédée Willot and the French Directory', *Renaissance and Modern Studies*, Vol.XXXIII, (1989), pp.125–143

Doyle, William, *The Oxford History of the French Revolution* (Oxford: Oxford University Press, 1989)

Du Breil de Pontbriand, Paul Comte, *Le Comte d'Artois et L'Expédition de l'île d'Yeu* (Paris: Honoré Champion, 1910)

Duncan-Jones, Caroline M. (ed.), *Trusty and Well Beloved: The letters home of William Harness, an officer of George III* (London: SPCK, 1957)

Duvergier, Jean Baptiste, *Collection complète des lois, décrets, ordonnances, réglemens, et avis du conseil-d 'état* Tome III, V & VII (Paris: Chez A. Guyot et scribe, 1824 & 1825)

E.M.C., *Deux Victimes de Quiberon* (Vannes: La Foyle, 1895)

Floquet, Charles, *Quiberon presqu'île au cours des siècles* (Maulévrier: Hérault-Éditions, 1984)

Forneron, Henri, *Histoire Générale des Émigrés pendant la Révolution Française* (Paris: Librairie Plon, 1884)

Fortescue, John W., *A History of the British Army* (London: Macmillan & Co. 1906)

Glover, Gareth, *The Forgotten War Against Napoleon: Conflict in the Mediterranean 1793–1815* (Barnsley: Pen and Sword Military, 2017)

Gouzillon de Bélizal, Vicomte de, 'Journal et Lettres d'un Émigré', *Revue de Bretagne*, Vol.XXVII, January–February 1902, pp.92–113

Grazebrook, R. M., 'The Campaign in Flanders of 1793–1795: Journal of Lieutenant Charles Stewart, 28th Foot', *Journal of the Society for Army Historical Research*, vol. 29, No. 117, (Spring 1951), pp.2–17

Gregory, Desmond, *The Ungovernable Rock A History of the Anglo-Corsican Kingdom and its role in Britain's Mediterranean Strategy during the Revolutionary War (1793–1797)* (London and Toronto: Associated University Presses, 1985)

Grocott, Terence, *Shipwrecks of the Revolutionary & Napoleonic Eras* (London: Caxton Editions, 2002)

Grouvel, François, *Loyal Émigrant une unite d'émigrés exceptionelle 1793–1802* (Coudoux: F. G. C., 1999)

Grouvel, Vicomte Robert, *Les corps de troupes de l'émigration française* (Paris: Les Éditions de La Sabretache, 1957–1964)

Guibert, Louis, *Les Émigrés Limousin à Quiberon* (Limoges: Ducourtieux, 1886)

Guillot, Jean, *Révolution et Chouannerie en Morbihan* (Gourin: Éditions des Montagnes Noires, 2014)

Harper, Rob, *Fighting the French Revolution: The Great Vendée Rising of 1793* (Barnsley: Pen & Sword, 2019)

Harrington, Peter (ed.), *With the Guards in Flanders; The Diary of Captain Roger Morris 1793–1795* (Warwick: Helion & Company, 2018)

Hewison, W. S., *Not Born to be Drowned: An Orkney Soldier in the Napoleonic Wars* (Kirkwall: Bellavista Publications, 2001)

Huchet, Patrick, *1795 – Quiberon ou le destin de la France* (Rennes: Éditions Ouest-France, 1995)

Hugo, Abel, *Vie anecdotique de S.M. Charles X* (Paris: J. M. Maurice, 1824)

Hutt, Maurice, *Chouannerie and Counter-Revolution: Puisaye, the Princes and the British Government in the 1790s* (Cambridge: Cambridge University Press, 1983)

Hutt, Maurice, 'The British Government's Responsibility for the 'Divided Command' of the Expedition to Quiberon, 1795', *The English Historical Review*, vol.76, No. 300, (July 1961) pp.479–489
Hutt, Maurice, 'Quiberon : l'attaque du 16 juillet 1795', *Annales historiques de la Révolution française*, No. 211 (1973), pp.21–49
Countess of Ilchester, Countess of, and Stavordale, Lord (ed.), *The Life and Letters of Lady Sarah Lennox 1745–1826* (London: John Murray, 1901)
James, William, *The Naval History of Great Britain, from the Declaration of War by France in 1793, to the Accession of King George IV* (London: Richard Bentley, 1847)
Janillion, François-Louis, *Versailles et Quiberon* (Paris: Locard et Davi, Delaunay, 1816)
Kaulek, Jean and Tausserat-Radel, Alexandre, *Papiers de Barthélemy, ambassadeur de France en Suisse, 1792–1797, publiés sous les auspices de la Commission des Archives des Affaires étrangères* (Paris: F. Alcan, 1894)
Knight, Roger, *Britain Against Napoleon: The Organization of Victory 1793–1815* (London: Allen Lane, 2013)
La Chanonie, Charles de (ed.), *Mémoires politiques et militaires du général Tercier, (1770–1816)* (Paris: Plon, 1891)
La Gournerie, Eugène de, *Les Débris de Quiberon: Souvenirs du Désastre de 1795* (Nantes: Catholique Libaros, 1875)
Lambert, Henri, *Pour Dieu et Le Roi ou l'inutile sacrifice Quiberon, juin–juillet 1795* (Lons-le-Saunier: Éditions Marque-Maillard, 1987)
Lanne, Adolphe, *La Mystère de Quiberon 1794–1795* (Paris: Dujarrie et cie, 1904)
La Rochejaquelein, Marie-Louise-Victoire de Donnissan, Marquise de, *Mémoires de Mme la marquise de La Rochejaquelein* (Paris: Baudouin Frères, 1823)
La Villegourio, Louis-Marie de, *Ma Sortie de Quiberon* (Saint-Brieuc: Prud'homme, 1815)
La Villegourio, Louis-Marie de, *Cinq Lettres sur la catastrophe Quiberon* (Paris: Delaforest, 1826)
Le Cam, Louis-Marie, *Quiberon à travers les âges* (Quiberon: Robert, 1936)
Le Charron, André-Louis-Lambert Baron, *Expédition de Quiberon, suivie de L'Évasion des Prisons de Vannes* (Paris: Ambroise Dupont et Roret, 1826)
Le Falher, Jules, *Le Siège de Josselin Juillet 1795: Épisode de l'histoire de l'Armée rouge d'après des documents inédits* (Vannes: Lafolye frères, 1909)
Le Garrec, Eugène, *Quiberon* (Vannes: Lafolye, 1895)
Le Garrec, Eugène, *Les Vrais Martyrs de Quiberon (1795)* (Vannes: Lafolye & J. de Lamarzelle, 1935)
Le Garrec, Eugène, *Les Héroïnes de Quiberon (1795)* (Vannes: Imprimerie Galles, 1936)
Lord, Walter Frewen, *Sir Thomas Maitland, The Mastery of the Mediterranean* (London: T. Fisher Unwin, 1897)
Machiavelli, Niccolò, *Discourses on the First Decade of Titus Livius* (London: Kegan Paul, Trench & Co., 1883)
Mackenzie-Stuart, Lord, 'French Émigrés in Edinburgh', in Kirsty Carpenter and Philip Mansell (eds), *The French Émigrés in Europe and the Struggle against the Revolution, 1789–1814* (Basingstoke: Macmillan Press Ltd., 1999), pp.108–123
Michel, Didier, *Du Héros de Rennes en 1788 à la Contre-Révolution Blondel de Nouainville L'itinéraire d'un noble normand (1753–1793)* (Cherbourg: Éditions Isoète, 2012)
Montbron, Joseph de, *Récit de l'Evasion d'un Officier pris à Quiberon* (Paris: Adrien Egron, 1815)
Moreau de Jonnès, Alexandre, *Aventures de Guerre au temps de la République et du Consulat* (Paris: Pagnerre, 1858)
Nichols, Alistair, *Wellington's Switzers: The Watteville Regiment in Egypt, the Mediterranean, Spain and Canada* (Godmanchester: Ken Trotman, 2015)
Ornano, Ernest Cuneo d', *Hoche Sa vie et sa correspondance* (Paris: Librairie militaire J. Dumaine, L Baudoin et Cie., 1892)
Peyron, Paul, *La Chouannerie: Documents pour servir à son histoire dans le Finistère* (Quimper: L'Évèché, 1912)
Phipps, Ramsay Weston, *The Armies of the First French Republic and the Rise of the Marshals of Napoleon I: The Armée du Nord* (London: Oxford University Press, 1926)
Phipps, Ramsay Weston, *The Armies of the First French Republic and the Rise of the Marshals of Napoleon I: The Armies in the West 1793 to 1797, and the Armies in the South 1792 to March 1796* (London: Oxford University Press, 1931)
Puisaye, Joseph de, *Mémoires du Comte de Puisaye qui pourront servir l'histoire du parti royaliste français durant la dernière révolution* (London: Cox, Fils et Baylis, 1803–1808)

Quernau-Lamerie, Émile, 'Les Choauns de la Basse-Mayenne', *Bulletin de la commission historique at archéologique de la Mayenne*, 2e série, Tome 28, 1912, pp.70–90, 182–195, 265–285 and 367–392

Robert, Charles, *1795 Expédition des Emigrés à Quiberon Le Comte d'Artois à l'isle d'Yeu* (Paris: Lamulle & Poisson, 1899)

Rohu, Jean, 'Mémoires autographes de Jean Rohu', *Revue de Bretagne et de Vendée*, Tome II (December 1857) pp.595–613, III (January 1858) pp.28–42 and (May 1858) pp.406–418

Ross, Charles (ed.), *Correspondence of Charles, First Marquis Cornwallis* (London: John Murray, 1859)

Rouget de Lisle, Claude-Joseph, 'Historique et Souvenirs de Quiberon' in Anon. (ed.) *Mémoires de Tous. Collection de Souvenirs contemporains* Tome II (Paris: Alphonse Levasseur, 1834) pp.3–130

Roussel, Claude-Youenn, and Bergevin, Benoît de, *Un Survivant de Quiberon Louis-Ignace-Jean-Joseph Le Grand du Quellenec (1753–1830)* (Paris: Guénégaud, 2008)

Rousselin (de Corbeau Saint-Albin), Alexandre, *Vie de Lazare Hoche* (Paris: Buisson, 1798)

Schama, Simon, *Patriots and Liberators: Revolution in the Netherlands (1780–1813)* (London: Harper Collins, 1977)

Secher, Reynald, *A French Genocide: The Vendée* (Notre Dame: University of Notre Dame, 2003)

Sibenaler, Jean, *Quiberon pour le Roi et l'Autel* (Coudray-Macouard: Cheminements Éditions, 2007)

Talour de la Cartrie, Toussaint-Ambroise, *Memoirs of the Count de Cartrie* (London: John Lane, 1906)

Vauban, Jacques-Anne-Joseph Le Prestre de, *Quiberon Mémoires pour servir à l'histoire de la guerre de la Vendée* (Paris: Aux armes de France, 1941)

Veuillot, Eugène, *Les Guerres de La Vendée et de La Bretagne (1790–1832)* (Paris: Ambroise Bray, 1868)

Vidalenc, Jean, 'L'affaire de Quiberon' in Anon. (ed.) *Actes du 87e Congrès National des Sociétés Savantes Poitiers 1962* (Paris: Imprimerie Nationale, 1963), pp.299–333

Villeneuve-Laroche-Barnaud, Louis-Gabriel de, *Mémoires sur l'expédition de Quiberon, précédés d'une notice sur l'émigration de 1791 et sur les trois campagnes de 1792, 1793 et 1794* (Paris: Le Normant, 1814 & 1822)

Vossey, Guy-Toussaint-François de, 'Récit Fidèle et Impartial de l'Expédition de Quiberon', *Société d'Émulation des Côtes-du-Nord Bulletins et Mémoires*, vol.XXXVI (1898), pp.1–18

Winfield, Rif, *British Warships in the Age of Sail 1793–1817: Design, Construction, Careers and Fates* (Barnsley: Seaforth Publishing, 2005)

Wetton, Thomas, 'Manuscript Journal, Remarks on board HMS Robust (transcribed by Louis Roeder)', *The Trafalgar Chronicle*, (1995) pp.58–76

Wheeler, Harold Felix Baker, and Broadley, Alexander Meyrick, *Napoleon and the Invasion of England* (London: John Lane, 1908)

Wickham, William (ed.), *The Correspondence of the Right Honourable William Wickham from the year 1794* (London: Richard Bentley, 1870)

Unpublished Works

Condon, Mary Ellen, *The Administration of the Transport Service during the War against Revolutionary France, 1793–1802* (unpublished thesis, University of London, 1968)

Online Sources

Anon., 'Antoine-Henri d'Amphernet de Pontbellanger', <http://maison.omahony.free.fr/ascendants/fiche_amphernet_AntoineHenri.html>, accessed 12 May 2021

'Archives militaires de la guerre de Vendée conservées au Service historique de la Défense (Vincennes)' *Les Archives de la Vendée*, <http://recherche-archives.vendee.fr/archives/archives/fonds/FRAD085_SHD_B/inventaire/view:8193>, accessed 28 October 2021

Anon., 'Etymologie et Histoire de Houat', <http://www.infobretagne.com/houat.htm>, accessed 4 September 2021

Anon., 'Fichier de la garde constitutionnelle de Louis XVI (1791–1792)', Archives nationales 2016, <https://francearchives.fr/findingaid/fe3c62602114da74bf7575d392895499917388fe>, accessed 21 September 2020

Anon., 'Le Fort de Penthièvre', Le Ministère des Armées 13 December 2013, <http://www.defense.gouv.fr/actualites/memoire-et-culture/le-fort-de-penthievre>, accessed 29 September 2015

Anon., 'Manoir de Kerdavid. Plus ancienne demeure de la presqu'île de Quiberon', *Le Télégramme*, 6 April 2018, <https://www.letelegramme.fr/soir/manoir-de-kerdavid-le-plus-ancien-de-la-presqu-ile-06-04-2018-11916640.php>, accessed 14 November 2021

Anon., 'Un gentilhomme Vendéen sous la Révolution: Constant-Hubert de La Bassetiere' 24 March 2013, <http://shenandoahdavis.canalblog.com/archives/2013/03/24/26730389.html>, accessed 10 August 2021

Brayard, Laurent, and Didier Davin, Didier, '2e bataillon de tirailleurs (belges)', *Les troupes étrangères au service de la France 1792–1803 SEHRI*, <https://revolutionsehrietranger.wordpress.com/2e-bataillon-de-tirailleurs-belges/>, accessed 5 November 2021

Peters, Gerhard, and Woolley, John T., 'John F. Kennedy. The President's News Conference' *The American Presidency Project*, <https://www.presidency.ucsb.edu/documents/the-presidents-news-conference-213>, accessed 9 November 2021

Thorne, R. G., 'Nepean, Evan (1752–1822), *The History of Parliament*, <https://www.historyofparliamentonline.org/volume/1790-1820/member/nepean-evan-1752-1822>, accessed 13 October 2021

'Plaque de baudrier du régiment d'Hervilly', <https://art.rmngp.fr/fr/library/artworks/plaque-de-baudrier-du-regiment-d-hervilly_laiton_1795>, accessed 14 November 2021

'Resultats – Tambour d'infanterie du Régiment Royal d'Hervilly Lot 531', *Binoche et Giquello*, <https://www.binocheetgiquello.com/lot/7078/1377648?npp=100&>, accessed 14 November 2021